THE ROMAN LAW

OF

DAMAGE TO PROPERTY

BEING

A COMMENTARY

ON THE TITLE OF THE DIGEST

AD LEGEM AQUILIAM (IX. 2)

WITH

AN INTRODUCTION TO THE STUDY OF

THE CORPUS IURIS CIVILIS

BY

ERWIN GRUEBER, DR. JUR.

M.A. AND READER IN ROMAN LAW IN THE UNIVERSITY OF OXFORD

THE LAWBOOK EXCHANGE, LTD.
Clark, New Jersey

ISBN 978-1-58477-447-1

Lawbook Exchange edition 2004, 2020

The quality of this reprint is equivalent to the quality of the original work.

THE LAWBOOK EXCHANGE, LTD.
33 Terminal Avenue
Clark, New Jersey 07066-1321

Please see our website for a selection of our other publications and fine facsimile reprints of classic works of legal history:
www.lawbookexchange.com

Library of Congress Cataloging-in-Publication Data

Grueber, B. Erwin (Bernhard Erwin), 1846-1933.
The Roman law of damage to propert : being a commentary on the title of the digest Ad legem aquiliam (IX.2) : with an introduction to the study of the Corpus juris civilis / by Erwin Grueber.
p. cm.
Originally published : Oxford : Clarendon Press, 1886.
Includes bibliographical references.
ISBN 1-58477-447-9 (cloth: acid-free paper)
1. Damages (Roman law) 2. Malicious mischief (Roman law) I. Title.

KJA2627.G78 2004
340.5'4--dc22

2004043220

Printed in the United States of America on acid-free paper

THE ROMAN LAW

OF

DAMAGE TO PROPERTY

BEING

A COMMENTARY

ON THE TITLE OF THE DIGEST

AD LEGEM AQUILIAM (IX. 2)

WITH

AN INTRODUCTION TO THE STUDY OF

THE CORPUS IURIS CIVILIS

BY

ERWIN GRUEBER, Dr. Jur.

M.A. AND READER IN ROMAN LAW IN THE UNIVERSITY OF OXFORD

Oxford

AT THE CLARENDON PRESS

MDCCCLXXXVI

London
HENRY FROWDE

Oxford University Press Warehouse
Amen Corner, E.C.

TO

HIS FRIENDS AND COLLEAGUES

THOMAS ERSKINE HOLLAND, D.C.L.

AND

WILLIAM MARKBY, D.C.L.

AS A TOKEN OF

GRATITUDE AND RESPECT.

PREFACE.

THE Board of the Faculty of Law in the University of Oxford, being convinced that a more thorough knowledge of Roman law would be the best means of advancing a scientific understanding and culture of English law, has recently encouraged candidates in the Final School of Jurisprudence to exhibit a knowledge of some portion of the Digest, and has selected for that purpose the title 'Ad legem Aquiliam,' considering that it contains, perhaps more fully than any other title in the Digest, the chief materials referring to one particular topic, viz. the Roman law of damage to property.

Intending to furnish the student with the necessary help in attaining this knowledge, I had to take into account that my book is to be a text-book for students who only know the elements of Roman law, as they are explained in lectures on the Institutes, whilst I had to explain a particular topic in full detail, and in the various relations in which it is dealt with in the Digest. It is due to these circumstances that I have taken great pains to bring out my points very fully, and it even may be that I have gone too far in doing so, but I thought it best to err, if anywhere, on the side of over-fulness.

Another point which was to be considered is the peculiar method in which topics of Roman law are dealt with in this country. Usually they are explained in the form of a commentary on the Roman texts, although it is at the same time recognised that a systematic exposition, which deals exhaustively with a whole topic under certain distinct headings, is preferable. I thought it therefore desirable not only to give an exact interpretation of the passages of the title, but also to explain systematically the Roman law on the topic of damage to property. But if I intended to accomplish this double task, it also seemed necessary to give information as to the principles to be followed in so explaining the sources of Roman law.

It was with this view that the contents of the present book and their arrangement were determined. The Introduction is intended to inform the reader shortly as to the use of the Corpus Iuris Civilis in general, keeping however in view the special topic with which we have to deal. Part I. contains an interpretation of all passages of the title 'Ad legem Aquiliam,' in the order in which they follow each other in the Digest. Part II. is devoted to a systematic exposition of the Roman law of damage to property. Thus the two chief portions of the book form distinct and severally self-sufficing treatises. But as the passages of the title refer chiefly to the law of damage to property, it must be admitted that Part II. contains a considerable amount of repetition. This, however, could not be avoided, if the educational object which I had in view, namely, to show in a practical instance, how out of the single decisions and enactments a system is to be developed, was to be attained. I venture, however, to cherish the hope that the student who has gone carefully through the Commentary will not be disappointed, but rather feel satisfaction, if he becomes aware that he fully understands the matter under consideration. Having thus a test for the knowledge he has acquired, he will also find this knowledge increased by discussions of a more general character and explanations of such passages as do not fall within the province of the title commented upon. The references, which have no pretension to completeness, are chiefly intended to facilitate the access of the reader to the literature on the single questions, partly also to bring a particular point into due connection with the reader's institutional knowledge on the topic. But as the usual text-books on the Institutes are commentaries, references of the second kind are implied in all cases where a passage of the Institutes of Gaius or Justinian is quoted.

The reader who merely wants to know what is the Roman law on the topic of damage to property may refer to the Second Part only, and he who objects to expositions of a more antiquarian and historical character, may, instead of reading §§ 1–4 of that part, satisfy himself by reading the short abstract of these sections in the Summary at the end of the book.

This Summary is intended not only to give a short and precise survey of the whole topic, and the connection of its single parts with one another, but proposes also to enable the reader to find quickly each particular point he wants to be informed on, and the chief passages referring to it.

Whether or no the book will contribute to the great object which I have had constantly in view, is a question which time alone can decide. I can only say that I am desirous to do my best in adapting its contents more and more to the practical purposes which it has to serve, and that I shall gratefully receive advice from anyone who takes an interest in the important subject of legal education in this country.

At the same time I feel deep satisfaction in availing myself of the present opportunity in order to express my warmest thanks for the constant support which I have received in my endeavours during the whole time I have been teaching in this University. I shall always gratefully remember the kindness which I have here received: a kindness which in particular is intimately connected with the origin and the progress of the present book.

ERWIN GRUEBER.

OXFORD: *February* 7, 1886.

CORRIGENDA AND ADDENDA.

P. 42 sq.: cf. with reference to the note to fr. 11. § 10 the contents of p. 148, n. 1.

P. 45 sq.: cf. with reference to the view stated in these pages the exposition on p. 246 sqq.

P. 91, line 32, cf. here p. 251, n. 1.

P. 137, line 5, *for* § 11 and § 2 *read* fr. 9. § 2.

P. 196, line 5, *for* D. 44. 7. 32 *read* D. 44. 7. 56.

P. 214, line 8, *for* 45 *read* 45 pr.

CONTENTS.

LIST OF BOOKS FREQUENTLY QUOTED.

PERNICE, *Zur Lehre von den Sachbeschädigungen nach römischem Rechte.* Weimar, 1867.

HASSE, *Die Culpa des Römischen Rechtes.* Second edition, by Bethmann-Hollweg. Bonn, 1838.

ARNDTS, *Lehrbuch der Pandekten.* Eleventh edition, by Pfaff and Hofmann. Stuttgart, 1883 [§ 324[1]].

BRINZ, *Lehrbuch der Pandekten.* Second edition, hitherto 2 vols. Erlangen, 1873–1882 [§ 340[1]].

VANGEROW, *Lehrbuch der Pandekten.* Seventh edition, 3 vols. Marburg and Leipzig, 1863–1869 [§ 681[1]].

WINDSCHEID, *Lehrbuch des Pandektenrechts.* Fifth edition, 3 vols. Stuttgart, 1879 [§ 455[1]].

C. G. v. WÄCHTER, *Pandekten.* Edited by O. v. Wächter. Leipzig, 1880 and 1881.

SAVIGNY, *System des heutigen Römischen Rechts.* 8 vols. Berlin, 1840–1849.

UNGER, *System des österreichischen allgemeinen Privatrechts.* Vols. I and II (general part), fourth edition. Leipzig, 1876.

MOMMSEN (Friedrich), *Beiträge zum Obligationenrecht.* Braunschweig, 1853–1855.

HOLMES, *The Common Law.* London, 1882.

MOYLE, *Imperatoris Iustiniani Institutionum libri quattuor.* 2 vols. Oxford, 1883.

PUCHTA, *Cursus der Institutionen.* Ninth edition, by Krüger, 2 vols. Leipzig, 1881.

RUDORFF, *Römische Rechtsgeschichte.* 2 vols. Leipzig, 1857 and 1859.

KELLER, *Der Römische Civilprocess und die Actionen.* Sixth edition, by Wäch. Leipzig, 1863.

LENEL, *Das Edictum perpetuum.* Leipzig, 1883.

VOIGT, *Die XII Tafeln.* Leipzig, 1883.

[1] This section deals with the law of damage to property and is subsequently referred to if not expressly quoted.

INTRODUCTION.

We are told by Justinian in his Institutes (I. 2. 3), that leges, senatus consulta, principum placita, magistratuum edicta, and responsa prudentium are the sources of written law. This statement is doubtless true so far as the contents of these laws are concerned; they were still in force in the time of Justinian, so far as they had not been abrogated by later laws, but the statement is not literally true with reference to the laws as such. Since the fourth century A. D. the leges, senatusconsults, and edicts of the magistrates, had never been quoted in the courts, but the commentaries of the jurists on them had alone been referred to; and the same must be said of the earlier constitutions of the emperors. The writings of the jurists formed, therefore, the only source from which the knowledge of the early law, the 'ius vetus,' was derived. The only source of new law, the 'ius novum,' was the legislation of the emperors, which had taken the place of the original legislation by the people. It is on this account that the imperial constitutions are described as 'leges,' in the same way as the resolutions of the popular assemblies were formerly described, and in opposition to that term the law laid down in the writings of the jurists is simply called 'ius.' Thus ius and leges in the new sense of these terms now formed the only sources of written law[1].

The mass of the juristical writings was very considerable, and the number of single imperial constitutions was immense. It was, therefore, but natural that steps should be taken with a view to regulating[2] and facilitating the use of these two great masses of law. It is to these endeavours that the different legal collections, especially those

[1] Rudorff, Römische Rechtsgeschichte, vol. i. § 6 and § 79.

[2] E. g. The Law of Citation, 426 A. D.

of the imperial constitutions [1], were due. These efforts were brought to a conclusion by the Emperor Justinian, who undertook not only to collect and sift the whole law of the imperial constitutions, but also the law laid down in the writings of the jurists. It is well known that the codification of the 'ius,' the so-called Digesta or Pandektae, was published on December the 16th, 533, as the only and exclusive source of law contained in the juristical writings, whilst eleven months afterwards, on November the 16th, 534, the Codex (repetitae praelectionis) was issued as the only and exclusive source of law made in the form of constitutions up to that date. In addition to these two collections, in the year 533, by order of Justinian, a short elementary book, Institutiones, was compiled, which was to serve as an introduction to the course of legal study, but had at the same time the force of law. Lastly, after the publication of the Codex a great many new constitutions, Novellae Constitutiones or Novels, were issued by Justinian in the years 535–565, and were also collected, although not by the Emperor himself [2].

These four collections—Institutes, Digest, Codex, and Novels—form together what is called with us the Corpus Iuris Civilis. It is true, that after the death of Justinian, legislation in the Byzantine empire did not cease to adapt the condition of the existing law more and more to practical purposes, and that even new and comprehensive compilations, especially the Basiliks, were made; nevertheless, it is through the codification of Justinian that Roman law has exercised its immense influence on the whole of the civilised world: an influence which is very considerable even in those countries where, as for instance in England, Roman law has not been actually received. For it is perfectly true, as Sir Henry Maine asserts in speaking of the law of England, 'that texts of Roman law have been worked at all points into the foundations of our own jurisprudence [3].'

The legal collections of Justinian are thus the subject-matter of juris-

[1] Codex Gregorianus, Hermogenianus, Theodosianus.

[2] See, with regard to the legislation of Justinian, Professor Bryce's article on Justinian in the Encyclopaedia Britannica, and with regard to the history of Roman legislation in general Mr. Moyle's Introduction to his Commentary on the Institutes of Justinian. Much useful information is also given by Mr. Roby's Introduction to the Study of Justinian's Digest, Cambridge, 1884, especially with reference to the jurists quoted in the Digest.

[3] Village Communities, 3rd edition, p. 332.

tical investigation. Out of the numerous enactments of the Corpus Iuris, which refer to a great extent to particular cases thereby decided, a system of the Roman law has to be developed. But for the accomplishment of this task two things are necessary—first, to understand exactly the single passages in their significance and importance; and secondly, to connect their contents, by way of co-ordination and subordination, into a uniform whole. We have accordingly to deal, I. with the interpretation of single passages, and II. with interpretation, undertaken with the view of establishing a system [1].

I.

Before interpreting a law there must be a text of the law [2]. This question raises no difficulty with regard to laws which are accessible to us in the form in which they have been published by the lawgiver. It is otherwise with the Corpus Iuris Civilis, for though there are numerous manuscripts of the collections of Justinian, yet no authentic manuscript published by the Emperor himself has come down to us. A special inquiry will therefore be necessary, in order to ascertain the true words which were used by the lawgiver; this is the so-called textual criticism. Its object is on one side to examine the different manuscripts and to classify them according to their value (diplomatic criticism), and, secondly, to settle the reading of every single passage [3]. In order to do so the critic may choose between the different readings confirmed by the manuscripts; but he may even, in exceptional cases, alter the text without being supported by any reading of the existing manuscripts (conjectural criticism), for it is possible that all copyists have made the same mistake, e.g. have misunderstood in the same way a certain abbreviation of their original [4].

[1] Arndts, § 5 sqq.

[2] See for the following: Arndts, § 9; Brinz, §§ 3–6; Vangerow, § 23; Unger, § 12; Savigny, vol. i. §§ 38 and 39.

[3] The best critical edition of the Corpus Iuris Civilis, which is made use of in the present book, is that by P. Krüger, Th. Mommsen and R. Schoell (Corpus Iuris Civilis. Editio stereotypa. Berolini 1868 sqq.), of which hitherto only volumen prius (containing the Institutiones by Krüger and the Digesta by Mommsen) and volumen secundum (containing the Codex Iustinianus) have been published, whilst the third volume (containing the Novels by Schoell) is still in progress. Arndts, § 2. n. 5.

[4] In D. h. t. 13. § 3, 25. § 1, 27. § 28, 27. § 34, the text of the manuscripts must be altered. See the notes to these passages in Part I.

A chief help in reconstructing the text of the codifications of Justinian is the comparison, on one side, with those sources from which the passages in the Corpus Iuris are taken, and on the other with enactments which more or less literally reproduce the contents of these passages in later times. It is for this reason that the relics of the ante-Justinian law, as well as the ius Graeco-Romanum, are invaluable for the textual criticism of the different parts of the Corpus Iuris [1].

When the text of a law is settled, we may proceed to interpret [2] its contents, i. e. to find out the idea which the lawgiver intended to express in the tenour of the law. The question is, what was the intention of the lawgiver in the words he used?

In order to decide this question it will be, first of all, necessary to settle the sense of the passage to be interpreted, according to the rules of grammar and the usage of language, so that the words are to be understood in the sense attached to them at the time of the issue of the statute and in their whole connection with one another. Terms which are also used in a technical legal sense are to be taken in that sense; general terms are to be taken in the full generality of their meaning, and so forth.

Whether the result arrived at by means of this so-called grammatical interpretation really expresses the intention of the lawgiver or not, is necessarily uncertain, for it is always possible that the lawgiver had not chosen the right expression. Probably in most of the cases the words convey exactly the idea he intended to express, but it is equally conceivable that they are an inadequate expression of his opinion, either because he intended to say something else, or because the words or their connection do not express any definite sense, being either ambiguous or wholly unintelligible.

The interpreter, therefore, must go beyond the mere words of the statute, and must by other means attempt to ascertain the real intention of the lawgiver. Interpretation in this direction is the so-called 'logical interpretation.' The means which we may make use of for this kind of interpretation are very different.

1. Laws commonly will be issued to meet certain circumstances of life.

[1] Arndts, § 15.

[2] For the following see: Arndts, §§ 6–8; Vangerow, § 24; Windscheid, §§ 20–22; Unger, §§ 13 and 14; Wächter § 26.

Strength is to be given to the existing relations of life, or a different state of things is to be brought about by the operation of the enactment. It is therefore of the highest importance to ascertain the object the lawgiver had in view in issuing his statute, the so-called 'ratio legis.' Particular laws, however, are frequently only the consequent expression of a general principle, and in so far the knowledge of the principle, the so-called 'ratio iuris [1],' may be of value in determining the intention of the lawgiver. Even the external event which has occasioned the making of the law, the so-called 'occasio legis,' may sometimes throw light on the intention of the lawgiver [2].

2. Another point which is to be observed is the connection of a law with other enactments which are equally applicable. It therefore often happens that the contents of one enactment throw light on the sense in which another is to be understood and applied in actual life (systematical element of interpretation).

3. Not only the connection of a law with those laws which are at the same time in force, but also their relation to the earlier and the later laws, may be of use in settling the sense of a statute. In interpreting passages of the law of Justinian it will therefore be very useful to understand at the same time the development of the legal institutions in the earlier and in the later law [3] (historical element of interpretation). On this account the fragments of the juristical writings and the remnants of the old codes of constitutions, as well as those of the Byzantine law, are of great use in interpreting the law of Justinian.

The result of the logical interpretation may be that the lawgiver had exactly expressed what he intended to say; words and intention cover one another; therefore no further question can be raised, and the will of the lawgiver is to be carried into execution. If it is however settled that the lawgiver intended to express something else: either more—because he had used too narrow a term; or less—because his expres-

[1] Sometimes also 'ratio legis.'

[2] In case of the S. C. Macedonianum the 'occasio legis' was the parricide of Macedo; the 'ratio legis' was the desire of the lawgiver to prevent usurious transactions being entered upon with filiifamilias (Moyle, p. 560), whilst its contents were at variance with the fundamental principle underlying the Roman contractus re, 'contra rationem iuris introductum.'

[3] The nature of the actio ex edicto aedilium in quadruplum in D. h. t. 27. § 28 is explained by the contents of the later law on the same topic; and in D. h. t. 27. § 11 the intention of Justinian with reference to the employer's liability is apparent from a comparison with the remnants of the earlier law.

sion was too wide; or something which is different in its meaning from the sense of the words, the question arises whether the result arrived at by the logical interpretation is to be preferred to the sense which the words bear according to the rules of grammar and the usage of language. There is no doubt that the merely restrictive interpretation is unconditionally admissible [1], for the lawgiver has actually expressed what he intended to say, although he has used too wide a term; but whether the results of the extensive interpretation and that which alters are equally to be accepted seems to be doubtful, for law is only what has been actually published by the lawgiver; it is therefore necessary that the incongruity of expression and intention should be apparent from the enactment itself or other enactments of the same legal system. An extensive or an altering interpretation, however, would not be justified by using helps which lie outside the law itself, e. g. by reference to discussions which took place during the progress of a bill through a legislative assembly [2].

A similar difficulty does not arise in case the sense of a law is indefinite, being either ambiguous or obscure. It is obvious that here a definite result cannot be attained by the mere grammatical interpretation; for thus it can merely be stated that the text admits of various senses. It follows, therefore, that the logical interpretation is but very little prejudiced by the words of the statute, and therefore its result must be accepted, provided only that the sense thus ascertained is not at variance with one of the senses which possibly might attach to the tenour of the law. But if it is impossible to ascertain any definite sense, and thus certainty cannot be arrived at, the interpreter must satisfy himself with probability. The more probable sense is to be preferred to the less probable [3]. Accordingly, first of all, the object of the law is to be taken into account, and that sense is to be accepted which serves best to the realization of that object [4].

[1] See e. g. D. h. t. 33. § 1, and the notes to this passage.

[2] It is commonly said to be an instance of an extensive interpretation when the Roman jurists declared the word 'rumpere' in the third chapter of the Aquilian statute to be equal to 'corrumpere' (D. 9. 2. 27. §§ 5 and 13). This is true if the word was used in that sense by the lawgiver. Otherwise what is called interpretation of the statute would have been in reality an extension by way of analogy. An instance of an (admissible) interpretation which alters may be taken from D. h. t. 33 pr. Here the words of Paulus seem to exclude the assessment of consequential damages in the Aquilian action, but it is quite clear from other passages that this was not the intention of that jurist.

[3] D. h. t. 50. 17. 114.

[4] D. 50. 17. 67.

Besides, the sense which attaches significance and importance is to be preferred to that which expresses nothing but what is to be understood by itself[1]. Further, it is a general principle that, in case of doubt, the interpreter must decide in favour of that which forms the smallest deviation from the existing or the regular laws; accordingly, corrective statutes and those which contain a 'ius singulare' are to be taken strictly, and are to be interpreted in the narrower sense[2]. And lastly, if these rules cannot be applied, preference is to be given to the more humane opinion[3].

Although all the helps which we have hitherto considered must be used in interpreting a law, the interpreter must always be guided by the idea that the lawgiver has deliberately chosen the expression of his intention, and that nothing has been said by him without having its significance. If, therefore, the sense of the words of a statute is perfectly clear, that is to be taken to be the contents of the law[4], unless another sense can be proved with absolute certainty[5]. Hence it follows, that if a law has made a provision for certain cases, its application is to be restricted to those cases; and that the contrary is true of all other cases[6]; in other words, the so-called argumentum a contrario is admissible with reference to laws. Nevertheless, great care must be taken in applying this argument, especially with regard to the provisions of Roman law, for a very considerable portion of the Corpus Iuris—the responsa in the Digest, the rescripta in the Codex—does not consist of leges or statutes properly so called, but of decisions of single cases, and so it has often happened, that amongst the facts of the case a circumstance is reported, the existence of which is by no means necessary for the decision of the case. It would be entirely wrong if in such cases a rule was formulated with a restriction corresponding to the circumstance which has been stated in the report of the facts and if, accordingly, the contrary was said to be applicable to

[1] D. 1. 3. 19, and see in illustration of the principle D. h. t. 45. § 5.

[2] C. 3. 28. 35 pr.

[3] D. 50. 17. 56, 168 pr., 192. § 1. Therefore in case of an ambiguous penal law, the milder punishment is to be applied; D. 48. 19. 42.

[4] 'Cum in verbis nulla ambiguitas est, non debet admitti voluntatis quaestio.' D. 32. 25. § 1.

[5] D. 27. 1. 13. § 2: '. . etsi maxime uerba legis hanc significationem habent, tamen sententia legis latoris aliud flagitat.' Cf. I. 1. 26. § 16.

[6] D. 28. 1. 20. §§ 5. 6, D. 22. 5. 18, D. 1. 3. 22. A consequence of the above principle is expressed in the sentence: 'Exceptio firmat regulam in casibus non exceptis,' i. e. if an exception is made by a law for certain cases, the contrary, as a rule, holds good of all other cases.

all other cases [1]. It is, therefore, with regard to enactments of such a kind that the proverb has been formulated: 'Unius positio non est alterius exclusio.'

There is yet another point to be observed in dealing with passages of the Corpus Iuris. The passages which are embodied in the compilation of Justinian were for the most part written at a far earlier date, when the whole legal system differed considerably from that of the time of Justinian. In order to bring them into harmony with the law prevailing at the time of the compilation, the fragments embodied in the codification have been altered (these alterations are the so-called emblemata and interpolationes Triboniani), but even in cases where no alteration has been made, a passage was sometimes written by its original author (Paulus, Ulpianus, etc.), in a sense differing from that in which it is understood in the compilation of Justinian. If this is the case and the interpreter attempts to ascertain the sense which a passage had in its original conception as well as a part of the law of Justinian, then we speak of an 'interpretatio duplex [2].'

An interpretation made by a jurist in accordance with the principles which we have laid down is a scientific interpretation (interpretatio doctrinalis). Such interpretation is to be accepted by the judge only if it really expresses the true sense of the statute interpreted. It is otherwise if the contents of a law are interpreted by a later law (interpretatio legalis). This is so if either the lawgiver has himself declared how a certain statute is to be understood (authentical interpretation), or if a custom has been developed according to which a certain enactment is to be taken in a certain sense (interpretation by usage). In both these cases there is not only an interpretation of a law, but law itself, and therefore this interpretation is absolutely binding on the judge, whether it puts a right or a wrong meaning on the law which it professes to interpret.

[1] An instance may be taken from the law of servitudes. According to a rescript of Antoninus Caracalla it seems to be necessary in order to acquire a servitus by usucapion (longi temporis quasi possessio) that it has been exercised as right with the knowledge of the owner of the praedium seruiens; cf. C. 3. 34. 2: 'Si aquam per possessionem Martialis *eo sciente* duxisti, seruitutem exemplo rerum immobilium quaesiisti.' But with reference to this passage the argumentum a contrario is not admissible, for the emperor merely repeats what has been asserted by the party applying to him, and it is clear from several other passages that in order to acquire a servitude—personal or real—nothing is required, but that it has been exercised as a right during ten or twenty years, 'nec ui nec clam nec precario,' without any distinction whether the owner of the res serviens knew of this fact or not. See Arndts, § 189, n. 1.

[2] See the notes to D. h. t. 11. § 7, p. 39 below.

II.

If all the single enactments are understood in their significance and importance, we may proceed to establish a system out of these materials. This is to be done in the way of coordination and subordination according to certain leading principles. But what is the mark or distinction in virtue of which the whole field of law is to be divided? It is obvious that all law deals with certain relations of life: relations which, in so far as they are dealt with by law, are made *legal relations*. Thus a sale taking place between two persons is, no doubt, an actual relation between the parties who agree on that transaction, but it is at the same time a legal relation, because the law recognises transactions of such kind, and secures their fulfilment. If accordingly law merely determines certain relations of life, the contents of the law are necessarily dependent on their nature and variety. It is therefore on the difference of the legal relations themselves that the leading classifications of a legal system are to be based[1].

Applying these views to the sphere of private law, we see that there are two kinds of essentially different relations which are regulated by its provisions:—1. All men requiring the satisfaction of their natural necessities are necessarily in certain relations with regard to the objects of the external world; and 2. there are certain permanent relations between individuals uniting them with one another, e.g. the union of male and female and the relations of parents and children. In accordance with these distinctions the field of private law is naturally divided into two great departments: first, the law of property regulating the competition of individuals with reference to the objects of the external world; and secondly, family law containing the rules which determine the family relations.

The relations, however, which form the subject-matter of the law of property are twofold again, for there are either direct relations recognised over the objects of the external world—as if I am

[1] Legal authors, however, have often based their system on the nature and difference of the rights created by the law. But see Unger, Österreiches Privatrecht, vol. i. p. 2; Beseler, System des Gemeinen Deutschen Privatrechts (3rd edition, 1873), vol. i. §§ 5–7; E. Grueber, in the Kritische Vierteljahresschrift für Gesetzgebung and Rechtswissenschaft, N. F. vol. vii. p. 200.

in possession of a horse and the law declares me to be its owner —or only relations through the medium of other persons—as if a person is under the necessity to deliver a horse to me, and the law accordingly has imposed a duty on him. The relations of the first kind are the object of the 'law of property' in the narrower sense (Sachenrecht), those of the latter kind are determined by the 'law of obligations.' The law of obligations, again in accordance with the difference of the legal relations concerned, is chiefly subdivided into the 'law of contract' and the 'law of tort,' or 'delicts,' of which the law of damage to property, the special topic of the subsequent investigation, is a special branch.

We may carry the sub-division still further in considering the law of damage to property. If we look at the different enactments which refer to this subject, we find that there are rules relating, first, to the nature of the act of damage; it must be a 'commission' done 'iniuria' and 'culpa,' and resulting in a 'damnum;' secondly, to the person who is entitled to sue by an Aquilian action; it may be the owner, persons with a ius in re aliena, the colonus, or a free person who has been wounded; thirdly, to the person to be sued, the delinquent, his employer (?), or the owner of a delinquent slave; fourthly, to the evidence in the action; fifthly, to the object of the judgment, originally the highest value of the thing during the last year or month, afterwards the 'interesse' of the plaintiff; and sixthly, to certain peculiarities of the action, that it is penal in its nature, although compensation is attained thereby.

So far it is made clear that by means of subordinating the contents of the single enactments to higher principles, and by means of coordinating the contents of those provisions which are connected with one another, a system of the whole (private) law, or of one of its branches, will be gained. A system of law, however, must necessarily answer two requirements: first, it must be uniform, i. e. must not contain any contradictions; and secondly, it must be complete, i. e. must cover all cases which possibly may come within its sphere [1]. If therefore, within the orbit of the sources which form the materials of the system to be established, the contents of the passage are in conflict with another, these contradictions are to be removed [2]; and further, if

[1] Savigny, vol. i, p. 262.

[2] Arndts, §§ 10–14; Windscheid, § 23; Savigny, vol. i. §§ 42–45

there are questions or cases to be decided, for which there is no provision in the existing system of law, although they fall within its province, such gaps are to be filled up.

The chief help for removing contradictions of legal enactments is expressed in the proverb 'Lex posterior derogat priori.' Accordingly a later enactment repeals an enactment of an earlier date, if they both determine the same question in a different way. But a later law of a general character does not necessarily supersede an earlier law of a special character, although referring to the same topic. For the contents of such laws are not necessarily incompatible with one another; it might even have been the intention of the lawgiver that the lex specialis should remain in force. Therefore the rule has been formulated: 'Lex posterior generalis non derogat priori speciali[1]:' a rule which of course will be applicable only as long as it is not proved in a single case that the contents of the lex specialis are in conflict with those of the lex generalis.

In accordance with the principle of the repealing effect of the later law, the contents of the Novels of Justinian are to be preferred to those of the three collections, the Institutes, the Digest, and the Codex, and it is equally certain that each of the later Novels is to be preferred to a Novel of an earlier date; but, generally speaking, the rule does not apply to the relation of the Institutes, Digest, and Codex to one another, although they were not published quite simultaneously, for these collections were intended by Justinian to form one whole in which no contradictions were to be found.

It is, however, possible that several passages, none of which deserves preference on account of the date, contradict one another. In this case it will be necessary to inquire whether their contents may not be combined with one another. This can possibly be done, in a systematical way, by showing that one passage only determines or restricts the application of the other[2]. Or, by reference to the historical

[1] It is in accordance with this principle that the actio de aedibus incensis of the XII Tables was not superseded by the publication of the lex Aquilia (chapter iii). See p. 193, n. 1, below.

[2] According to D. 41. 3. 27 a so-called titulus putativus, i.e. the mere opinion of a person that there is a iustus titulus in his favour, is not sufficient to enable him to acquire by usucapion. In opposition to this in D. 41. 8. 9 a titulus putativus is recognised under certain circumstances. These restrictions suggest the way of uniting the two passages. As a rule, no doubt, a titulus verus is required, but in exceptional cases where there is a justifiable cause for assuming the existence of a title, a titulus putativus is sufficient; D. 41. 4. 11.

development of law, namely, if we prove that only one passage expresses the intention of the lawgiver, whilst the other is merely of historical value [1], perhaps intended to contrast the earlier law with that which prevails at the present time.

It is, of course, also possible that two passages contradict one another so clearly as not to admit of any union. Then there is a real antinomy; the contradictory decisions mutually cancel one another, and that decision is to be accepted which follows from the recognised principles of the existing system of law.

In this way we have stated at the same time the principle to be adopted wherever there is a gap in the system of law [2]. Questions and cases which are not provided for by the existing law, are to be decided on the analogy of that law. It is not seldom that new relations come into existence, and that therefore cases are to be decided which were entirely unknown to the existing law. It then becomes necessary to examine carefully the nature of the case and the peculiarities of the relation concerned, and to decide it in accordance with the principles underlying the existing system of law. If here the analogy is founded on the principles of the whole positive law, in other and more common cases the analogy is based merely on a single enactment. This is so if a similar case has been decided by the law and the principle underlying its decision (the ratio iuris) is equally applicable in the case not provided for by its contents. Then the latter case will be decided on the analogy of that statute, in the sense of its provision. It is clear that this kind of analogy differs in its nature from extensive interpretation, with which it has sometimes been confounded; for by the extensive interpretation a statute may be extended only to cases, which, although they were not comprehended in its tenour, were yet intended to be comprehended by it, whereas in the way of analogy a statute is extended to cases which were not intended to be included in the lawgiver's disposition. Thus the principal difference of interpretation and analogy in general is indicated: it is the object of interpretation to ascertain the real intention of the lawgiver; it is the object of analogy to find out the intention

[1] This must be admitted of the view stated in D. 43. 24. 7. § 4, which is in conflict with the decision in D. h. t. 49. § 1. Cf. pp. 162 and 219 sq. below.

[2] Arndts, § 14; Unger, § 10; Vangerow, § 25; Windscheid, §§ 22 and 23; Wächter, § 25.

which the lawgiver would have had, if he had known the particular case to be decided. But although these two notions are clearly to be separated from one another, it must nevertheless be observed that the word interpretation is often used in a wider sense, in which it signifies not only the scientific exposition, but also the scientific extension of the positive law, and it is in this sense that the word has been used by Roman jurists. It is well known that, under the name of interpretation, Roman law was developed to a very considerable extent in the way of analogy, and perhaps the most remarkable instance of this development is just the topic we have to deal with, the law of damage to property[1].

[1] Every case in which an actio in factum or actio utilis was given, is an instance of the extension of the Aquilian statute in the way of analogy. And even if the jurists declared the word 'rumpere' in the third chapter to be equal to 'corrumpere,' this was not interpretation, but extension by analogy, provided we are right in assuming that the word of the statute had not been used by the lawgiver in that wide sense. See p. xviii, n. 2, above.

PART I.

COMMENTARY

ON THE

TITLE OF THE DIGEST

'AD LEGEM AQUILIAM'

(IX. 2).

AD LEGEM AQUILIAM.

1 *pr.*—Ulpianus libro XVIII ad edictum. Lex Aquilia omnibus legibus quae ante se de damno iniuria locutae sunt derogauit, siue duodecim tabulis, siue alia quae fuit: quas leges nunc referre non est necesse.

According to this passage the lex Aquilia repealed (derogauit) all laws which had previously dealt with damage to property (damnum iniuria datum): the laws of the XII Tables, as well as any other laws published afterwards, and it was therefore not necessary to reproduce in the title the contents of these laws.

'Derogare' is the term properly used to denote that a law is partially repealed as opposed to 'abrogare,' which is used to denote that a law is totally repealed by a later one. 'Derogatus legi quum pars detrahitur, abrogatur quum prorsus tollitur,' says Modestinus in D. 50. 17. 102 (cf. Ulp. fr. pr. § 3). The expression 'derogare' as here used should, therefore, mean that all the former law on the same topic was abolished only so far as it is inconsistent with the provisions of the lex Aquilia. But this interpretation must be rejected, for then the passage would simply express what is understood by itself, that later law displaces the former: 'lex posterior derogat priori.' Besides, in this case, it would not be superfluous to know the previous laws on the topic, but, on the contrary, it would be absolutely necessary to know their contents in order to determine how far they were still in force. It is clear that, in the opinion of Ulpian, the lex Aquilia had superseded all the former law on the same topic without any distinction. The use of the expression 'derogare' is explained by the fact that the former law was for the most part contained in a code, the XII Tables, which were of course only partially repealed, i. e. in those enactments, which determined the topic of damnum iniuria datum. In spite, however, of the certainty that this was Ulpian's meaning, it does not seem to be correct, for there are actions as to damage to property given by the XII Tables, which were still in force a long time after the issue of the lex Aquilia. These actions are—

1. The 'actio de aedibus incensis' (D. II. 14. 7. § 13), which was given in case a person set on fire a house or a stack of corn near a residence, and which made the delinquent liable 'noxiam sarcire,' i.e. to make good in natura the damage done (D. 47. 9. 9). But it is quite natural, that in course of time this was superseded by the 'actio legis Aquiliae,' which undoubtedly was applicable in such cases; for the restoration in natura was not only unknown to later times, but the valuation which took place in case of an 'actio legis Aquiliae' was more favourable to the plaintiff, who received in virtue of it the highest value which the thing damaged had attained during the last month.

2. The 'actio de pastu pecoris' (D. 19. 5. 14. § 3), given in case a person let his cattle graze on another's soil; but this is also practically superseded by the lex Aquilia, for although the third chapter did not comprehend such cases, they were brought by the interpretation of the jurists (who considered the word rumpere to be equal to corrumpere) within the operation of the lex, C. h. t. 3. 35. 6.

3. The 'actio de arboribus succisis,' given in case trees of another person were unlawfully felled (Gaius IV. 11, D. 47. 7. 3. § 3, D. 12. 2, 28. § 6, D. 43. 24. 19). This action has also disappeared from the later law, and the lex Aquilia is applicable to such cases (D. h. t. 27. § 6). It is true that there is still an action of a similar kind which is recognised by the modern Roman law, the 'actio arborum furtim caesarum.' This action, which was introduced by the praetorian edict, although leaning on the enactment of the XII Tables, has the special requirement that the trees must have been felled furtim, secretly, and it was necessary to have such cases punished, independently of whether damage was done in this way or not.

It is thus untrue that by the Aquilian law every other law relating to the topic of damnum iniuria datum was repealed. It seems, therefore, that the derogating effect was restricted to those cases which were expressly provided for by the lex. Thus, by the first chapter the 'actio de servo quadrupedeue occiso,' and by the third chapter the action given in case of damage done by rumpere, 'actio de rupitiis,' recognised in the XII Tables were abolished. But gradually, as explained above, all the different cases of damage done to property were brought within the operation of the lex Aquilia, and considering this state of things, from which there was no real exception[1], Ulpian was entitled to say that the Aquilian law has repealed all the previous law concerning its topic. The mistake made by Ulpian is only that he attributed to the lex itself an effect which actually resulted from its gradual extension.

See Part II. § 2.

1. § 1.—Quae lex Aquilia plebiscitum est, cum eam Aquilius tribunus plebis a plebe rogauerit.

This lex Aquilia was a plebiscitum, for it was asked for by Aquilius a tribune of the plebs.

Being a plebiscite the lex Aquilia was passed in the comitia tributa, in which ascendancy was given to number, and therefore to the plebs, in opposition to the comitia centuriata, where ascendancy was given to wealth, and thus to the patricians. In early times, the latter alone were entitled to make real leges or populiscita (originally in a certain connection with the ancient comitia curiata), but gradually the force of law was granted to the decisions of the comitia tributa, which undoubtedly take the place of leges, since the issue of the lex Hortensia 467 A. U. C. Very likely it was this very year in which the lex Aquilia was passed, for we gather from the principium of our passage that it was made a good time after the XII Tables (302–304), since there were some laws passed after this and before the lex Aquilia—and on the other hand, we know that this lex was in the beginning of the seventh century A. U. C. the subject of a rather detailed interpretation on the part of the jurists [cf. D. h. t. 27. § 22] and therefore it must then have been some time in existence. To these circumstances which direct the investigator to the middle of the fifth century A. U. C. is to be added that Theophilus in his paraphrasis on the Institutes of Justinian [ad IV. 3. § 15] expressly declares that it was made 'tempore discordiae,' in a time of quarrel between patricians and plebeians, a statement which clearly

[1] Such an exception is not to be found in D. 9. 4. 2. § 1, and D. 44. 7. 32.

alludes to one of three secessions of the plebs, and this could have been only the third and last one, 'in montem Janiculum,' 467 A. U. C[1].

While the fragment of Ulpian is thus a help in settling the date of the lex Aquilia, it reminds us also of the manner in which laws were made in the popular assemblies in Rome. Usually a bill was drawn by the magistrate, who afterwards presided over the comitia which had to decide by their votes, whether it should or should not be accepted as law binding on the whole people. After certain preparatory measures, especially the promulgation of the bill, it was brought before the comitia, which were asked by the magistrate who had drawn it, whether they would accept his proposal. This so-called Rogatio was either accepted, in the form 'Uti rogas,' or it was rejected, in the form 'Antiquo,' by the members of the assembly. From the moment it was carried, the bill became a statute, either a lex (in the narrower sense) or a plebiscitum (which frequently in the later times is also called lex). In a statute three portions are to be distinguished: (1) the beginning, always containing the name of the magistrate or tribune who had put the Rogatio to the assembly (populus or plebs); (2) the Rogatio itself, i. e. the whole contents of the enactment; and (3) the Sanctio, i. e. provisions made for the case of disobedience to its precepts[2]. As our fragment says, it was the tribune Aquilius who had put the Rogation to the people, and his name undoubtedly stood in the beginning of the lex [very likely in the form: 'Aquilius tribunus plebis plebem rogauit, plebsque ita sciuit']. It is only in accordance with a custom which was followed nearly without exception that the lex also has derived its name from its author.

Pernice, p. 15 sqq.; Windscheid, § 455. n. 1.

2 *pr.*—Gaius libro VII ad edictum prouinciale. Lege Aquilia capite primo cauetur: 'Ut qui seruum seruamue alienum alienamue quadrupedem uel pecudem iniuria occiderit, quanti id in eo anno plurimi fuit, tantum aes dare domino damnas esto.'

The principium of lex 2 reproduces—apparently in its original

[1] For further information on this question cf. Part II. § 1.

[2] For further information cf. Rudorff, Römische Rechtsgeschichte, vol. i. p. 17 sqq.

form—the contents of the first chapter of the lex Aquilia, whilst the words of the third chapter are delivered in 27. § 5. If a man, so says our passage, has unlawfully killed a slave or four-footed cattle belonging to another person, then he shall be obliged to pay to their owner whatever was their highest value in that year, i. e. the year previous to the injury by which the death of the slave or cattle was caused.

Although the passage is on the whole a literal reproduction of the terms of the lex, several minor variations are clearly indicated; especially we must read (1) instead of 'ut qui' in the beginning (which is not in accordance with the imperative mood: 'damnas esto') 'si quis,' a reading which amongst other circumstances is confirmed by the Greek translation of the fragment in the Basiliks; (2) instead of 'uel,' 'ue,' for the two words quadrupedem and pecudem must be read together, and are intended to describe such four-footed animals as belong to pecudes, i. e. are usually kept in flocks or herds; and (3) instead of 'domino,' 'ero,' according to 11. § 7, where this latter expression is commented upon as the term in the lex Aquilia.

We may abstain from a more detailed interpretation of this fragment as its single terms are subject matter of closer investigation in the following fragments (fr. 2. §§ 2–23, § 7). Thus the word 'quadrupes' is explained in 2. § 2, 'iniuria' in 3–7 pr., 'occiderit' in 7. §§ 1–11, § 5, 'ero' in 11. §§ 6–20, and the expression, 'quantiis homo in eo anno plurimi fuisset' in 21–23. § 7.

Pernice, p. 11 sqq.; O. Lenel, Das Edictum perpetuum, Leipzig, 1883, p. 157. n. 1; Windscheid, § 455. n. 2, 14 and 20; Vangerow, vol. III. p. 577; Savigny, System, vol. VI. p. 205.

2. § 1.—Et infra deinde cauetur, ut aduersus infitiantem in duplum actio esset.

In addition to the quotation of the fundamental precept, it is said that it is provided in a following part of the law, that the defendant who denies his liability may be sued for double damages, for the actio legis Aquiliae belongs to those cases in which it is said, 'lis infitiando crescit in duplum' (Windscheid, § 263. n. 2; Arndts, § 252. n. 2). Accordingly if the defendant admitted his liability the object of the action was only compensation for the loss sustained, which was to be fixed in the peculiar way provided by the Aquilian law; but if he denied that he had done the damage and thus compelled the plaintiff to prove his claim, the double of the sum due in case of admission was to be paid. The words of the passage (infra—cauetur) admit of a doubt whether this peculiar consequence was limited to the case in which an action was brought on the basis of the first chapter, but according to other passages it is quite certain that it was a precept which was applicable to the whole Aquilian law (cf. G. III. 216; Paulus Sent. Rec. I. 19. § 1; Inst. IV. 6. §§ 19. 23. 26; C. h. t. 4). But the consequence takes place only if the plaintiff becomes thus compelled to prove his claim in another way than by oath (ius iurandum) D. 12. 2. 30 pr. If this was unnecessary, i. e. if either the plaintiff had sworn that he had the claim asserted by him, or if the defendant had refused to swear the oath tendered to him, then the defendant was to be condemned in simplum only, because the plaintiff was not obliged to produce further evidence (by witnesses, records, etc.).

Windscheid, § 263. n. 3; Vangerow, vol. III. p. 579.

2. § 2.—Ut igitur apparet, seruis nostris exaequat quadrupedes, quae pecudum numero sunt et gregatim habentur, ueluti oues, caprae, boues, equi, muli, asini. sed an sues pecudum appellatione continentur, quaeritur: et recte Labeoni placet contineri. sed canis inter pecudes non est. longe magis bestiae in eo numero non sunt, ueluti ursi leones pantherae. elefanti autem et cameli quasi mixti sunt (nam et iumentorum operam praestant et natura eorum fera est) et ideo primo capite contineri eas oportet.

This section attempts to determine the notion of quadrupeds, which —without any doubt—from their importance in ancient Rome (where agriculture was the chief occupation of the citizens) are placed by the lex Aquilia on the same level as slaves. But only such quadrupeds as belong to cattle (quae pecudum numero sunt) and usually are kept in flocks or herds, fall under the law; for instance, sheep, goats, oxen, horses, mules, and asses. There were doubts whether pigs were included, but considering the fact that they graze not uncommonly in herds, the question was answered in the affirmative (cf. Inst. h. t. § 3). It is otherwise with dogs, which certainly do not belong to the pecudes. Still more the wild animals do not belong to their number, as bears, lions, panthers, and the like. Doubts have been raised as to tamed elephants and camels, as their nature is wild; but as they do the work of draught-cattle (iumentorum operam), i. e. of a special class of pecudes, they were considered to be included in the first chapter.

Windscheid, § 455. n. 2.

3.—Ulpianus libro XVIII ad edictum. Si seruus seruaue iniuria occisus occisaue fuerit, lex Aquilia locum habet. iniuria occisum esse merito adicitur: non enim sufficit occisum, sed oportet iniuria id esse factum.

With this passage the explanation of the word *iniuria* begins. It is true, so says Ulpian, if a slave was slain, the lex Aquilia is applicable; but it must have been done *iniuria*, unlawfully, for the mere fact of having slain a slave does not bring the Aquilian law into operation.

The necessity of iniuria is clearly stated in these words, but what is meant by iniuria is by no means defined by the jurist. From the cases which are subsequently dealt with, we learn that it is used in a double sense: (1) A person is said to have slain a slave iniuria who had done so without having a right to do such an act; but if he had done so, whilst attacked by a slave who intended to rob him, in exercising his right of self-defence, there is no iniuria on his part and therefore no liability according to the lex Aquilia, D. h. t. 4. 5 pr. (2) The act by which the injury was done (the slave slain) must be attributable to the will of the person acting, because he had either intended the result—was acting dolo—or was not sufficiently careful to avoid it, thus being guilty of negligence, culpa, D. h. t. 5. §§ 1 and 2[1].

4 *pr.*—Gaius libro VII ad edictum prouinciale. Itaque si seruum tuum latronem insidiantem mihi occidero, securus ero: nam aduersus periculum naturalis ratio permittit se defendere.

[1] For further information cf. Part II. §§ 6 and 7.

This passage gives at once an illustration of the principle expressed in fr. 3. In case I should have killed your slave who was waylaying me, I should be safe, for common sense permits me to repel violence by violence. Acts therefore which were committed in self-defence do not create any liability, although damage was done in this way, for every man has a right to do such acts as are necessary for his own defence. This is clearly expressed in D. 1. 1. 3, where the maxim that it is permitted to repel violence by violence is declared to be a rule of the ius gentium, with the addition, 'nam iure hoc euenit ut quod quisque ob tutelam corporis sui fecerit, iure fecisse existimetur.' No doubt, the ius gentium in this passage means the same as the naturalis ratio in our fragment, for it is apparently used in the sense of the law, 'quod naturalis ratio inter omnes homines constituit,' and which therefore is observed by all nations in the same way (J. I. 2. § 1, D. 1. 1. 9, Gaius I. 1). Cf. D. h. t. 45. § 4: 'uim—ui defendere omnes leges omniaque iura permittunt;' and D. 43. 16. 1. § 27: 'uim ui repellere licere Cassius scribit idque ius natura comparatur.'

Pernice, p. 36; Windscheid, n. 11; Lenel, Das Edictum perpetuum, p. 157.

4. § 1.—Lex duodecim tabularum furem noctu deprehensum occidere permittit, ut tamen id ipsum cum clamore testificetur: interdiu autem deprehensum ita permittit occidere si is se telo defendat, ut tamen aeque cum clamore testificetur.

This section is evidently closely connected with the principium of the fragment. Not only a robber, but also a thief, may be killed with impunity, that is the connecting idea between the two sections. The XII Tables permit a person to kill a thief whom he had seized by night, provided he calls attention to the act by crying out, but if the thief was taken during the daytime, they permit killing only if he defends himself with a weapon, and the killer in this case also testifies the commission of the act by his cries.

The reason for this enactment seems to be clear. In case of a theft by night there would be naturally the danger that the thief would take away the things he had stolen, and thus they would be irrevocably lost for their owner. Therefore the latter is allowed to kill the thief. It was different, if a furtum was committed in the daytime; here the person whose things were stolen could recognise the thief and afterwards sue him for the theft. Therefore in this case, the right of killing is restricted to the case where the thief defends himself with a weapon, whilst the owner attempts to seize him in order to take back the things which belong to him, which he undoubtedly was entitled to do; cf. 52. § 1.

It seems to be certain that in the enactment of the XII Tables we are discussing, a principle was established which was a material element in the law of self-defence as recognised in the later times of the Roman Empire. Whilst in the earlier law killing is permitted in certain cases (as theft) and under certain circumstances, in order to protect one's person and property, it is a general principle of the modern law, that self-defence is permitted wherever an unlawful attack is made upon a person or his property; but, again, this right is limited by the nature of the attack itself. The defence may go only as far as it is necessary to repel the attack, otherwise there would be a transgression of the right of self-defence, which, if not excused by special circumstances, would make the transgressor liable. It is quite clear that this principle is not in accordance with the sentence of the XII Tables which we have explained. But there can be no doubt that the quotation of the latter is merely intended as a historical notice, for according to Ulpian in D. 48. 8. 9, a person who kills a fur nocturnus will be free from liability only if he could not spare him without bringing himself into danger (furem nocturnum si quis occiderit, ita demum impune feret, si parcere ei sine periculo suo non potuit).

Pernice, p. 37.

5 *pr.*—Ulpianus libro XVIII ad edictum. Sed et si quemcumque alium ferro se petentem quis occiderit, non uidebitur iniuria occidisse: et si metu quis mortis furem occiderit, non dubitabitur quin lege Aquilia non teneatur. sin autem cum posset adprehendere, maluit occidere, magis est ut iniuria fecisse uideatur: ergo et Cornelia tenebitur.

By this passage the principle of self-defence as stated in the notes to fr. 4 is clearly recognised. Not only in case a person has killed a robber (4 pr. cf. Coll. VII. 3. 4.) (so says Ulpian), but also if he kills a person who is going to attack him with a drawn sword, he is not considered to have killed iniuria (and therefore he is not liable according to the lex Aquilia). The same is the case, if some one being in fear of his life (metu mortis) has killed a thief (without any distinction whether he was going to steal by night or in the daytime). But if he had chosen to kill the thief when he might have seized him (and thus have recovered his property), then, according to the prevalent opinion, he is considered to have killed iniuria (and thus he is liable to an actio legis Aquiliae). But he is also liable to an accusation on the basis of the 'lex Cornelia de sicariis et ueneficis,' by which, among other things, killing and poisoning people was made a special crime (Rudorff, Römische Rechtsgeschichte, vol. I. § 35).

From this fragment we learn, that in order to exercise one's right of self-defence, it is not necessary that an attack should be actually made; it is sufficient if the attack was imminent: therefore I am permitted to kill a person who has drawn his sword in a threatening attitude against me, although he had not yet touched me. In a similar way, I am entitled to kill a thief provided I was acting under the impression of fear of death, which, as a rule, will happen only if the thief was going to attack me (before or whilst I was going to seize him). It is true, I may kill the thief because in my anxiety I suppose that he is going to kill me, even although this supposition is untrue; in such a case there is a transgression of the right of self-defence, which in itself would make a person liable, but which may be excused by the peculiar circumstances of the case, in so far as I was acting under the impression of a reasonable fear (iustus metus), which may move even a man of firmness, as if a person should see a thief in his cellar, armed with pistols, and suppose the thief would kill him at once, if he did not prevent him from doing so. But if there are no such circumstances, the person who kills a thief will be liable according to the lex Aquilia, and if the deed was done intentionally he can be prosecuted also in virtue of the lex Cornelia, which enactment required 'dolus' (D. 48. 87), whilst the Aquilian law was also applicable if the damage was done by mere negligence (culpa). And this double liability takes place whether the furtum was committed by night or by day, and whether the thief defended himself with a weapon or not. That the later law superseded thus the rule of the XII Tables, quoted in fr. 4. § 1, is clearly implied by our passage. An express proof for this supersession is given by the passage in the Coll. VII. 3. §§ 2–4, where the fragment of Ulpian is quoted without the abbreviations made by the compilers of the Digest. There the question is discussed whether a person who kills a thief is liable according to the lex Aquilia, with reference to the XII Tables which permit killing a thief under the circumstances mentioned. And relying on the authority of Pomponius, who does not think that the rule of the XII Tables is still in use, Ulpianus asserts that only in case the act was done under the impression of fear of death, the Aquilian law should not be held applicable.

Pernice, p. 103; Windscheid, n. 11 and 12.

5. § 1.—Iniuriam autem hic accipere nos oportet non quemadmodum circa iniuriarum actionem contumeliam quandam, sed quod non iure factum est, hoc est contra ius, id est si culpa quis occiderit: et ideo interdum utraque actio concurrit et legis Aquiliae et iniuriarum, sed duae erunt aestimationes, alia damni, alia contumeliae. igitur iniuriam hic damnum accipiemus culpa datum etiam ab eo qui nocere noluit.

Accordingly the term 'iniuria' here (i.e. in the first chapter) is not to be taken in the sense of insult, as in the case of the 'actio iniuriarum,' but of what is done *unlawfully*, that is against the law, i. e. if some one has killed by his fault, 'culpa' (in the wider sense of the word, i. e. either intentionally or negligently): and therefore sometimes both the actions are available: the 'actio legis Aquiliae' as well as the 'actio iniuriarum,' but each has its own measure of damages: in the former the loss, in the latter the insult is estimated. We must therefore apply the term 'iniuria' in the sense of 'culpa' in 'damnum *culpa* datum,' i. e. damage done by someone's fault, although possibly by a person who did not intend to do damage.

This passage introduces a second signification of the term 'iniuria.' It is explained in fr. 4 and 5 pr. that there is no iniuria on the part of a person who is acting *in virtue of his right of self-defence*, but if he kills a slave otherwise than when exercising this right, then (so says 5 pr.) he is considered to have killed 'iniuria.' Killing a slave without having a right to do so apparently is killing 'iniuria.' Consequently the notion of iniuria is not only used to designate the absence of a right to do the act of damage, but also in some other sense, for even if a person was killed by another who had no right to do so, the question still remains whether there is iniuria on the part of the person acting. What is to be understood by iniuria was entirely left to the interpretation of the jurists, who determined that *there is iniuria* on the part of a person if *the damage is due to his culpa*, i. e. if it can be attributed to his will, either because he intended the injurious effect (dolus—malicious intention) or was not careful enough in avoiding it (culpa in the narrower sense, equal to negligence).

In accordance with this interpretation, in a particular case of damage, the 'actio legis Aquiliae,' as well as the 'actio iniuriarum,' may be applicable, i. e. whenever the culpa of the doer is combined with the special intention to insult the person damaged, the so-called 'animus iniurandi,' as required by the 'actio iniuriarum;' for instance, where a person had killed or wounded a slave in order to show his contempt for the slave's master. In such cases the person injured will be entitled to the 'actio legis Aquiliae,' as well as to the 'actio iniuriarum.' But the object of the two actions will be different; in the former the plaintiff will receive compensation for the damage done to him according to the peculiar provisions of the Aquilian statute, in the latter a penalty for the insult which he had suffered (duae erunt aestimationes, alia damni alia contumeliae)[1].

Another inference from the interpretation of jurists is drawn in the last sentence. As the term 'iniuria' is to be understood of 'damnum *culpa* datum,' and the word culpa covers negligence as well as malicious intention, that damage also which was not intended by the doer will come within the operation of the Aquilian statute. Instances

[1] In strict accordance with this view is D. 47. 10. 15. § 46 (from Ulpian also); cf. Savigny System, vol. v, p. 244. C. 9. 35. 8. seems to be in opposition in so far as it is said that in case an actio iniuriarum is brought by a person because his slave was beaten, account is to be taken of the damage done. But these words are easily explained by recollecting that the penalty for the insult in question naturally must be heavier, if the injury is considerable; cf. Glossa ad hanc legem: Habetur ratio damni sed non ut damni: sed ut contumeliae.

of such damage done, 'ab eo qui nocere noluit,' may be found in numerous passages of the Corpus Iuris Ciuilis, cf. e. g. D. h. t. 27. §§ 8 and 9, 45. §§ 2 and 4, 52. § 2. Pernice, pp. 27, 32, and 37.

5. § 2.—Et ideo quaerimus, si furiosus damnum dederit, an legis Aquiliae actio sit? et Pegasus negauit: quae enim in eo culpa sit, cum suae mentis non sit? et hoc est uerissimum. cessabit igitur Aquiliae actio, quemadmodum, si quadrupes damnum dederit, Aquilia cessat, aut si tegula ceciderit. sed et si infans damnum dederit, idem erit dicendum. quodsi inpubes id fecerit, Labeo ait, quia furti tenetur teneri et Aquilia eum; et hoc puto uerum, si sit iam iniuriae capax.

It is, therefore, a question whether an Aquilian action would lie if a lunatic has done damage. Pegasus has answered the question in the negative, for what fault (culpa) can there be in a person who is not sound in his mind? and this is quite true. Therefore the Aquilian action will not lie just as it does not lie if a quadruped had done damage or a tile had fallen down. But also in case a little child (infans) had done damage, the same is to be said. In the case, however, of a person under age ('impubes'), Labeo says, he will be liable to an Aquilian action, because he is also liable for theft, and this is right in the opinion of Ulpian, if he is already capable of doing an unlawful act.

The connecting link between this and the previous section is quite clear. As damage can be done even by a person who does not intend to do harm, the question may be asked whether it may not be done by a person without a will: a lunatic. This question is, however, answered in the negative, for there is nothing which can be attributed to a person lacking the necessary capacity of action. If therefore damage is actually caused by the corporeal movements of a lunatic, an Aquilian action is as little applicable as in other cases of a mere accident, e. g. if a tile had fallen down or a quadruped had done damage. It is hardly necessary to say that such events would lose the nature of mere accidents if their happening were due to the culpa of any determinate person, and it is also understood that damage done by quadrupedes under certain conditions may give rise to an 'actio de pauperie.' (Cf. D. 9. 1 and I. IV. 9.)

The rule stated with reference to lunatics is also applicable to infantes, i.e. children below the age of seven years, who up to that age are considered by law to be absolutely incapable of doing an act. Accordingly they are no more than lunatics subject to an actio ex delicto, nor can they become bound or entitled under a contract or any other juristic act performed by them.

The condition of an impubes, i.e. a person above seven but below fourteen, is different. He is subject to an actio ex delicto if he is already capable of committing the injury, 'iniuriae capax,' or as other passages say, 'doli' or 'culpae capax' (cf. D. 44. 4. 4. § 26, and D. 47. 2. 23). Accordingly if damage is done by an impubes, the decision depends on an inquiry whether he had the mental capacity (judgment and will) in virtue of which the delict is to be attributed to him. But in case he is pubertati proximus, the capacity of doing the injury is presumed by law. It is worth while to notice that whilst the impubes may thus be liable ex delicto, he cannot become bound under any other obligation, nor can he alienate any part of his property without the authority of his guardian (tutor).

In opposition to infantes and impuberes, the civis pubes is absolutely capable—provided he is sound in his mind—of being sued in an actio ex delicto, and—if he is not a declared prodigal—in an actio ex contractu and quasi ex contractu.

Savigny, System, vol. III. p. 42 f.; also vol. III. p. 84; Pernice, p. 52; Arndts, §§ 36 and 59.

5. § 3.—Si magister in disciplina uulnerauerit seruum uel occiderit, an Aquilia teneatur, quasi damnum iniuria dederit? et Iulianus scribit Aquilia teneri eum qui eluscauerat discipulum in disciplina: multo magis igitur in occiso idem erit dicendum. proponitur autem apud eum species talis: sutor, inquit, puero discenti ingenuo filio familias, parum bene facienti quod demonstrauerit, forma calcei ceruicem percussit, ut oculus puero perfunderetur. dicit igitur Iulianus iniuriarum quidem actionem non competere, quia non faciendae iniuriae causa percusserit, sed monendi et docendi causa: an ex locato, dubitat, quia leuis dumtaxat castigatio concessa est docenti: sed lege Aquilia posse agi non dubito:

6.—Paulus libro XXII ad edictum. praeceptoris enim nimia saeuitia culpae adsignatur.

If a master, in the course of instruction, has wounded or killed a slave (who was his apprentice), the question arises whether he is liable under the Aquilian law as having done unlawful damage (viz. to the dominus of the slave). And Julianus says, that a master who has put out an eye of his pupil, in the course of instruction, will be liable under the lex Aquilia; this must, therefore, be held all the more to be the case if he had killed him. There was, however, the following case discussed before that jurist: A shoemaker had beaten his apprentice, who was a free-born filius familias, and who had not done what he was directed to do, with a shoe-last about the head, and so knocked out one of his eyes. Julian accordingly declares that the actio iniuriarum does not lie in this case, for the master had not beaten the boy with the intention to insult anyone, but in order to admonish and teach the boy. The same jurist entertains doubts whether an actio ex locato would be applicable because at least a slight castigation is allowed to the master, but I (so adds Ulpian) have no doubt that an action 'ex lege Aquilia' may be brought, for too great harshness in a teacher is considered to be culpa.

The question discussed in § 2, was whether a person under legal incapacity could not be made liable for damage done. The question raised in the section we are now going to consider, is whether a person who has a right to do the act from which damage had resulted might not become liable. As a general principle this question must be answered in the negative. Therefore, it may be asked, whether in case a master had, in the course of instruction, wounded or killed his apprentice, being the slave of another person, he will be liable to be sued in an Aquilian action by the boy's owner. This question is answered by Julianus in the affirmative, in case the master was evidently acting in excess of his right of castigation, as, if he had dashed out an eye of his pupil or had killed him.

Far more complicated is the second case discussed in the passage. A shoemaker who has knocked out an eye of his apprentice, who was filius familias of another, might possibly be subject to three actions: (1) to the actio iniuriarum, which, however, is not applicable in the given case, as there is clearly no intention to insult on the part of a master who was teaching his apprentice; (2) an actio ex locato, for there was, without any doubt, a contract of hiring and letting made between the master and the father of the apprentice, and the severe injury done to the latter might be considered to be a violation of the duties arising from this contract. But Julianus is a little doubtful as to whether such liability is to be recognised, although he seems to be inclined to assume that the action ex contractu would lie, as the act complained can hardly be thought to be a leuis castigatio; but, according to Ulpian, there is no question whatever that the master is liable (3) to an action under the Aquilian statute; the reason is the same as in the first case, for he was evidently acting in excess of his powers, and, so we must add, acts done in excess of a person's right are exactly the same as acts done without any right at all.

The contents of the passage are for several reasons very remarkable:—

1. It is, as shown above, an instance that a person may become liable under the Aquilian statute, although he was exercising a right of his own (cf. the notes on fr. 4 and 5 pr., and Part II. § 6).

2. It shows clearly that in case the applicability of an actio ex lege Aquilia, as well as an actio ex contractu on account of a certain act was in question, the jurists examined separately whether the requirements of each action were present (cf. the words: 'an ex locato, dubitat, quia . . . sed lege Aquilia posse agi non dubito'). The passage is, therefore, a strong argument against the opinion of those writers who assert that, in such cases of concurrence, the liability under the Aquilian law was lessened, if according to the contract in question a smaller degree of diligence was required from the person who was acting (cf. Part II. § 7).

3. The passage contains a very peculiar extension of the Aquilian law. Not only if slaves were killed or wounded, but also if free filii familias were wounded, an action ex lege Aquilia is applicable. Filii familias, however, are not subject to ownership like slaves and other things. On this account, in such cases, an actio directly under the terms of the statute, actio legis Aquiliae (directa) was not applicable, for it was given only to *the owner* (dominus, fr. 2 pr.), and therefore an extended actio, 'actio utilis,' was necessary for the cases in question. This is clearly stated in 13 pr., and must be understood

with regard to the passage under consideration also, although the final words point rather to the direct action 'sed lege Aquilia posse agi non dubito;' the meaning of the jurist is, however, only to declare that an action founded on the Aquilian statute would lie without thinking whether it is given directly or merely by analogy.

4. The passage raises the question whether an 'utilis' action would lie in case a 'filius familias' had been *killed* unlawfully. This was apparently not the case in Roman law. There is some evidence to the contrary in the passage itself; for whereas the jurist declares the liability of a master in a case of wounding, and also of killing the slave-apprentice, only the case of wounding a free person is taken into account, and only for this case the legal consequences are determined. In a similar way, in 13 pr., only the case where a 'pater familias' is injured is mentioned, the case of his being killed is not mentioned. In exact accordance with these passages are D. 9. 1. 3 and D. 9. 3. 7. In the former passage the 'actio de pauperie' is given only in the case 'si patrem aut filium familias vulneraverit quadrupes,' but no action is provided in case the quadruped has killed such persons, and in the latter fragment the 'actio de effusis et deiectis' is applicable in precisely the same cases. In both these passages the compensation to be paid is fixed in the same way as in the passage under consideration, and in both the passages deformity caused by the injury is not to be taken into account, 'quia liberum corpus nullam recipit aestimationem.' Similarly, D. 9. 3. 1. § 5 asserts that in case a person had been killed by an 'effusio' or 'deiectio,' no estimation of the damage ('in duplum') takes place 'quia in homine libero nulla corporis aestimatio fieri potest.' From all this it clearly follows that the Romans did not impose any liability for compensation in case a freeman was killed, although in such cases heavy loss might have resulted from his death to other persons (his wife and children). Roman jurists were apparently labouring under the idea that as a free person is not subject to ownership he has no money value of his own—'liberum corpus aestimationem non recipit'—and, therefore, there was no possibility of assessing damages.

Pernice, p. 90 sq. 147; Windscheid, n. 6, 11, 12, 19; Vangerow, vol. III. p. 592.

7. *pr.*—Ulpianus libro XVIII ad edictum: Qua actione patrem consecuturum ait, quod minus ex operis filii sui propter uitiatum oculum sit habiturus, et impendia, quae pro eius curatione fecerit.

By this action the father will recover the loss arising from the diminished value of his son's labour on account of the loss of the eye, and the outlay which he had incurred for the son's cure.

This sentence is clearly at variance with the terms of the lex Aquilia, according to which the highest value of the thing during the last year or month is to be given to the plaintiff. But as gradually, by means of the interpretation of the jurists, the value of the thing ('quanti res est') was replaced by the so-called 'interesse' ('quanti *interest* actoris,' cf. 21. § 2), i. e. the actual loss sustained by the plaintiff in his property, there was of course no difficulty in extending the action to cases in which damage done to a corporeal thing of the plaintiff was not concerned.

The only question was therefore in case a 'filius familias' was wounded, how to determine the damage sustained by the father. It was declared to consist in the expense incurred by him for the cure together with the loss of the son's labour, for the father acquired ownership in the earnings of his son, and though this is altered by the law of Justinian, the father has still a usufruct in the son's property. But the 'pater familias' is not entitled to claim compensation for the disfigurement of his son (arg. D. 9. 1. 3, and D. 9. 3. 7), although a master might claim compensation in case his slave had been disfigured by a wound inflicted on him, the value of the slave being diminished.

Cf. Pernice, p. 245; Windscheid, nos. 6 and 9; Vangerow, vol. III. p. 583.

7. § 1.—Occisum autem accipere debemus, siue gladio siue etiam fuste uel alio telo uel manibus (si forte strangulauit eum) uel calce petiit uel capite, uel qualiter qualiter.

We must, however, accept (a slave) as having been slain 'occisum' (in the sense of the statute), whether death was caused by a sword or a cudgel or any other weapon, or by one's own hands—if the delinquent, for instance, had strangled the slave, or had killed him by striking him with his heel or his head, or in any other way.

In the previous passages (3–7 pr.), the notion of 'iniuria' was expounded; with this passage the explanation of the term '*occidere*' as used in the first chapter opens and it is carried on down to 11. § 5.

As we learn from the fragment under consideration, the word 'occidere' in the lex is—in accordance with its derivation from 'caedere' and 'caedes' (see 51 pr.)—understood in the strictly literal sense of the immediate act of slaying or killing with one's hand or cudgel or any other weapon. Gradually, however—as will be shown by the following passages—an 'occidere' was assumed in cases which were not comprehended within the original notion of that word.

Lenel, Das Edictum perpetuum, p. 157.

7. § 2.—Sed si quis plus iusto oneratus deiecerit onus et seruum occiderit, Aquilia locum habet: fuit enim in ipsius arbitrio ita se non onerare. nam et si lapsus aliquis seruum alienum onere presserit, Pegasus ait lege Aquilia eum teneri ita demum, si uel plus iusto se onerauerit uel neglegentius per lubricum transierit.

Also in case a person whilst carrying too heavy a burden has thrown it off and killed a slave, the Aquilian action is applicable, for it was left to his own judgment not to burden himself in such way. For also in case a person whilst falling has crushed a slave belonging to another with his burden, Pegasus says he will be bound under the lex Aquilia, if he had either burdened himself too heavily, or was walking carelessly over a slippery place.

In the case of a person who lets fall his burden on account of its weight, and who thus kills a slave passing by, there is strictly speaking not an 'occidere' in the sense of the previous section. But still the act in question has caused the death of a slave, and therefore liability of the doer under the first chapter is recognised, provided there is culpa on his part. It is obvious that a person who lets fall something which he cannot sustain is so far not in culpa, but it is clearly his fault that he had burdened himself in such way, and on that account the death of the slave is to be attributed to his negligence.

Without culpa, however, there is no liability. Therefore a person who by falling down crushes with his burden a slave of another, will only be liable if this fact is due to his negligence, e. g. if he had over-burdened himself or went carelessly over a slippery place. But if his fall were due to mere accident, for instance a sudden blast of wind, he would not be liable.

Pernice, p. 148 sq.; Windscheid, n. 12.

7. § 3.—Proinde si quis alterius inpulsu damnum dederit, Proculus scribit neque eum qui impulit teneri, quia non occidit, neque eum qui impulsus est, quia damnum iniuria non dedit: secundum quod in factum actio erit danda in eum qui impulit.

In the same way Proculus writes that in case a person having been pushed by another has done damage to property, neither the person who has pushed the other will be liable, because he has not killed, nor the person who was pushed, because he has not committed unlawful damage; accordingly an 'actio in factum' is to be given against him who had pushed the other.

The case dealt with in this passage is the following: A negligently pushes B, a passer by, who consequently stumbles over the slave, who falls and is killed. The question arises whether an action under the first chapter lies in the case; certainly not against A ('qui impulit'), for an act of 'occidere,' as required by the law, was not performed on his part. But there is also no action applicable against B ('qui impulsus est'), because he has not done unlawful damage; it is true by his bodily movement the damage was caused, but as it is not due to his culpa, the damage is not unlawful, 'damnum iniuria non dedit' (cf. 5. § 1 above). It is, however, quite clear that A is guilty of the damage done, for although he has not caused it by an immediate action upon the thing damaged, he has yet mediately damaged the thing of another; it is true there is no 'damnum corpore corpori datum,' as required by the Aquilian statute, but there is still a 'damnum corpori,' which is due to his action. Thus, though the action given by the lex Aquilia itself is not applicable, yet an action on the caes, so-called actio in factum, was given to the injured person, i. e. in our case to the master of the killed slave.

Pernice, p. 33; Windscheid, n. 5.

7. § 4.—Si quis in colluctatione uel in pancratio, uel pugiles dum inter se exercentur alius alium occiderit, si quidem in publico certamine alius alium occiderit, cessat Aquilia, quia gloriae causa et uirtutis, non iniuriae gratia uidetur damnum datum. hoc autem in seruo non procedit, quoniam ingenui solent certare: in filio familias uulnerato procedit. plane si cedentem uulnerauerit, erit Aquiliae locus, aut si non in certamine seruum occidit, nisi si domino committente hoc factum sit: tunc enim Aquilia cessat.

If in a public contest or wrestling match, or pugilistic combat, one has slain the other, the Aquilian action will not be applicable, for here the damage seems to have been committed for the sake of glory and bravery, and not unlawfully. This rule, however, does not apply to a slave, because freeborn persons are accustomed to fight with one another, but it does apply to a wounded 'filius familias.' But the Aquilian action will lie if some one has wounded a fellow-player who has given way, or if without a combat a person has killed a slave, unless it was done by permission of his master, in which case the Aquilian action is not applicable.

According to this passage the Aquilian action does not come into operation if several persons have joined in a wrestling match, or have joined together in a similar exercise, and one of the players has been injured. Although such injury, as a rule, will be due to the culpa of one of the players, he is not liable—provided it was not done intentionally, cf. fr. 9. § 4,—for it is within the nature of such exercises that every fellow-player must do his utmost to become the victor; otherwise their object to develop strength and activity as far as possible cannot be attained.

But according to custom slaves ought not to take a share in such exercises, and therefore a person who has killed or injured a slave in such game will be liable. This consequence must, however, be taken as subject to the restriction that if the slave behaved himself as a freeman, and was taken as such by the fellow-players, they would not become liable on account of an injury done to him.

Whilst thus the rule under consideration does not apply to slaves, it does apply to 'filii familias' if they were wounded: 'in filio familias *vulnerato*[1] procedit,' but it refers only to the actual condition of wrestling or fighting; therefore an injury done to one of the players who had already given way would entail liability under the statute. Accordingly also a person who without a combat had killed or wounded a slave will be liable unless he had done so by permission of his master. For in virtue of the permission he has a right to do the act, and on that account the damage is not done 'iniuria;' cf. fr. 4. § 1, and 5. § 3. Pernice, pp. 41 and 54; Windscheid, n. 12.

7. § 5.—Sed si quis seruum aegrotum leuiter percusserit et is obierit, recte Labeo dicit lege Aquilia eum teneri, quia aliud alii mortiferum esse solet.

But if a person has inflicted a slight blow on a sick slave, who has died in consequence, Labeo says rightly that he will be bound under the Aquilian statute, because one thing kills one person and another thing another.

In this section a new question is decided. The act by which a slave is killed may be such that under ordinary circumstances death would not result from it; the act in itself would, in so far, not fall under the notion of 'occidere.' It is, however, decided that nevertheless there is a liability, i. e. under the first chapter; therefore a person who has killed 'iniuria' a sick slave merely by slightly beating him will be liable to pay the highest value of the slave during the last year. The reason given by the jurist is that the deadly effect of a certain act depends always on the individuality of the person injured thereby. Therefore if an act has the effect of killing a person, the doer will be liable on account of this effect.

7. § 6.—Celsus autem multum interesse dicit, occiderit an mortis causam praestiterit, ut qui mortis causam praestitit, non Aquilia, sed in factum actione teneatur. unde adfert eum qui uenenum

[1] The express addition of this word is strong evidence in favour of the view that the Aquilian action is not applicable in case a freeman was killed, for if this would be the case the use of the word would be not only superfluous but also inaccurate.

pro medicamento dedit et ait causam mortis praestitisse, quemadmodum eum qui furenti gladium porrexit: nam nec hunc lege Aquilia teneri, sed in factum.

Celsus, however, says that there is a great difference between the case of a person who has killed, and the case of him who originated the cause from which death resulted; hence a person who had only produced the cause of the death is not liable under the lex Aquilia, but subject to an 'actio in factum,' in the same way as a person who had given a sword to a madman; for he also will not be sued under the Aquilian statute, but by an 'actio in factum.'

Although the term 'occidere' was by way of interpretation extended to cases (see §§ 2. 5 above, and compare also § 7 below) which did not fall under the original meaning assigned to that notion in § 1 above, it was still required in all the extensions, that there should be a physical act upon the body of a slave or animal by which its death was caused. It was, however, different if a person by his conduct furnished merely a condition, 'causa,' from which damage resulted. As there is then no 'occidere,' no liability could arise under the terms of the lex Aquilia, chapter I, therefore no 'actio legis Aquiliae' (viz. 'directa'), but an analogous action, a so-called 'actio in factum,' was granted. (Compare the following passages of Ulpian, in which the same distinction between 'occidere' and 'mortis causam praestare' recurs: 9 pr. 11. § 1 and 49 pr. further below.) Thus a mere 'causa damni' is furnished by a person who had either intentionally or negligently put near a sick slave, instead of medicine, poison, which afterwards was taken by the patient. The same is to be said of the case where some one has given a sword to a mad slave who killed himself with it. In both these cases the person who has caused the death of the slave will be liable to an 'actio in factum.'

Pernice, p. 148; Windscheid, n. 5.

7. § 7.—Sed si quis de ponte aliquem praecipitauit, Celsus ait, siue ipso ictu perierit aut continuo submersus est aut lassatus ui fluminis uictus perierit, lege Aquilia teneri, quemadmodum si quis puerum saxo inlisisset.

But if a person has pushed a slave from a bridge, Celsus says that he will be liable under the lex Aquilia, without any distinction whether the slave was killed by the blow itself, or had been at once submerged, or had perished from having been overpowered by the force of the stream; in the same way as if some one had thrown a boy against a rock.

If a slave had been pushed from a bridge, and thus was drowned, the doubt may be raised, as he was not killed by the act of pushing itself, whether there is not a 'causam mortis praestare' in such case. But it is answered by Celsus that here the delinquent will be liable under the Aquilian statute, and therefore subject to an 'actio legis Aquiliae directa,' whether the death was caused at once by the blow or happened afterwards in the water. This decision clearly implies a new extension of the notion of 'occidere,' for in the cases contemplated, where a slave, pushed from a bridge, was drowned, or where a boy had been thrown against a rock, death has resulted only mediately, i.e. through the medium of the water or rock, from the act complained of, and the act itself was not the cause of the damage in question. The cases under consideration, however, resemble those directly falling under the terms of the statute, as they also suppose a physical act upon a certain thing (a push or blow) in consequence of which it is destroyed, and this is evidently the reason why they are treated alike by the jurists.

Pernice, p. 149.

7. § 8.—Proculus ait, si medicus seruum imperite secuerit, uel ex locato uel ex lege Aquilia competere actionem.

Proculus says that if a surgeon has been wanting in skill in operating upon a slave, either an action under the contract of hiring and letting, or one under the Aquilian statute, will be applicable.

The case is clearly the following: A master had asked for the services of a surgeon to have his sick slave operated upon, and had accordingly, expressly or tacitly, promised a reward for the services rendered, and thus a 'locatio conductio' was entered upon between master and surgeon. The latter, however, lacking the necessary skill for his profession, had performed the operation badly, and thus caused the death of the slave. According to Proculus the surgeon will be liable under the contract, as well as under the lex Aquilia. His liability under the contract is doubtless based on the fact that he had not rendered properly the services which he had promised. But he also will be subject to an 'actio legis Aquiliae,' for by his operation damage was caused to the master of the slave. Nevertheless, this decision is remarkable, not for the fact that an act which is intended for the benefit of another may entail liability, but rather for the reason that the act does not seem to be attributable to his negligence, as he actually is unable to render better services. It is, however, a principle of Roman law that the want of the qualifications for some kind of work is put on the same level as negligence: 'Imperitia culpae adnumeratur,' says Gaius in D. 50. 17. 132. This view is justified by the reason that a person who does certain work without possessing the necessary qualification either knows, or should have known, if he had taken care, that what he did might become dangerous for others. (Compare 8. § 1 below.)

It is obvious that the surgeon might have rendered his services without being asked to do so, as a so-called negotiorum gestor; for instance, if he had found the slave wounded, lying in a street. This fact, however, would not substantially affect the decision in the text. The liability ex contractu would only be replaced by a liability quasi ex contractu, the surgeon being, in virtue of the negotiorum gestio, in the same way liable as under the contract of locatio conductio.

Windscheid, n. 12; Vangerow, vol. III. p. 588.

8 *pr.*—Gaius libro VII ad edictum prouinciale: Idem iuris est, si medicamento perperam usus fuerit, sed et qui bene secuerit et dereliquit curationem, securus non erit, sed culpae reus intellegitur.

The law is the same, if a medical man has wrongly used a bad medicine: also he who has operated successfully and afterwards neglected to attend to the cure will not be free from liability, but is considered to be guilty of culpa.

The first of the two cases in question is very simple: A physician has wrongly applied a medicine; he will be liable for the same reasons as stated in the last passage, 'ex contractu' (or 'quasi ex contractu'), and under the Aquilian statute. The only peculiarity of the case is, that the fact of giving a medicine, in consequence of which the death of the patient was caused, is also considered to be an 'occidere,' although it is not the act of giving, but that of taking the medicine to which death was due.

Greater difficulties are attached to the second case of the fragment. It may seem at first sight that if a surgeon is declared to be liable, who has neglected to attend a patient after having performed a successful operation, he is made liable not on behalf of a positive act, but on account of an omission. This would be at variance with the provisions of the Aquilian statute, because the term 'occidere' clearly refers to positive acts. It is however, strictly speaking, not an omission which raises the liability in the case under consideration, though it is sometimes so assumed. The death of the patient is not caused by an omission, but, on the contrary, by the positive act of incision, which is clearly in itself—without the subsequent dressing of the wound—a dangerous act, and is to be attributed to the culpa of the surgeon, who evidently has not performed the operation on the slave as he ought to have done. Accordingly, the fragment is not opposed to the general rule expressed in D. 7. 1. 13. § 2, that it is always a commission by which liability is entailed under the Aquilian statute; nor are there other passages which would affect this principle, as is asserted by some scholars. Compare Part II. § 5, and Hasse, Culpa, p. 22; Windscheid, n. 9.

8. § 1.—Mulionem quoque si per imperitiam impetum mularum retinere non potuerit, si eae alienum hominem obtriuerint, uolgo dicitur culpae nomine teneri. idem dicitur et si propter infirmitatem sustinere mularum impetum non potuerit: nec uidetur iniquum, si infirmitas culpae adnumeretur, cum affectare quisque non debeat in quo uel intellegit uel intellegere debet infirmitatem suam alii periculosam futuram. idem iuris est in persona eius qui impetum equi, quo uehebatur, propter imperitiam uel infirmitatem retinere non poterit.

Also a mule driver who, for want of experience, could not restrain his mules, is commonly declared to be liable on account of culpa, if they have run over the slave of another person. The same must be said, if he could not restrain the mules on account of infirmity. And it does not seem to be unfair if infirmity is put on the same level as culpa, for a person should not pretend to do a thing when he either knows, or should know, that his infirmity might make it dangerous to another person. The same law applies to a person who could not master the impetuosity of a horse on which he was riding, lacking either the necessary experience or strength.

According to this passage, a person who has caused by his want of experience or strength the death of a slave, or, more generally speaking, damage to the property of another, will be liable under the Aquilian statute: the reason clearly being that infirmity and imperitia, or, to use a comprehensive term, the absence of the qualifications necessary for the performance of certain work, is considered to amount to culpa.

Cf. 7. § 8, and notes on this passage; Fr. Mommsen, Beiträge zum Obligationenrecht, vol. III. p. 366 (Braunschweig, 1855).

9 *pr.*—Ulpianus libro XVIII ad edictum: Item si obstetrix medicamentum dederit et inde mulier perierit, Labeo distinguit, ut, si quidem suis manibus supposuit, uideatur occidisse: sin uero dedit, ut sibi mulier offerret, in factum actionem dandam, quae sententia uera est: magis enim causam mortis praestitit quam occidit.

In case a midwife had given a medicine to a woman who died in consequence, Labeo makes this distinction—that if the midwife had administered the medicine with her own hands, she is considered to have killed the woman, but if she had only offered it, so that the woman might take it herself, she has rather brought into existence a state of things from which the woman's death has resulted, than killed her.

We learn from the passage that already Labeo, living in the days of Augustus, considered poisoning to be 'occidere,' but only if effected by an immediate act of the poisoner, in which case he is liable to an actio legis Aquiliae directa. But if a person had merely put near a patient a noxious medicine or poison, and it was taken by him, he merely furnished the means of death, and, therefore, he is subject to an actio in factum.

Pernice, p. 149 sq.; Windscheid, n. 5.

9. § 1.—Si quis per uim uel suasum medicamentum alicui infundit uel ore uel clystere uel si eum unxit malo ueneno, lege Aquilia eum teneri, quemadmodum obstetrix supponens tenetur.

If, by force or persuasion, one person has administered medicine to another, either into his mouth or by giving him a clyster, or if he has anointed the other with a poisonous substance, he will be liable under the Aquilian statute, just as the midwife is liable who herself has administered the medicine.

The passage does not need any explanation. It contains merely several applications of the principle, recognised in 8 pr. and 9 pr., that poisoning is an 'occidere' in the eye of the law, provided the poison was administered by an immediate act of the delinquent.

Windscheid, n. 5.

9. § 2.—Si quis hominem fame necauerit, in factum actione teneri Neratius ait.

If a person has killed a slave by starvation, according to Neratius he will be liable to an actio in factum.

The case underlying the decision of the jurist is doubtless the following: a slave was imprisoned unlawfully and lacking the necessary food was starved in consequence.

Here the master will have no direct action under the statute, because there is no physical act on the part of the delinquent through which the slave has been killed; but the master will be entitled to an actio in factum, for the delinquent, by shutting up the slave, has caused a state of things from which his death has resulted.

This is perfectly clear. It must, however, be remarked that in the same case according to Gaius, III. 219 and Inst. IV. 3. § 16, an actio utilis is applicable. But this does not imply any substantial difference between the passages in question. For the term actio utilis is used in the Roman sources in a sense which comprehends every action the formula of which is framed by some alteration of the formula of a previously existing action, whether this alteration is made by adding or deducting words, by changing the usual terms of the formula, by inserting a fiction into it, or even by *replacing the 'intentio'* of the formula *by a statement of fact.* (Cf. D. 19. 5. 21 and D. 24. 3. 64. § 9; Keller, Der Römische Civilprocess, § 89. II; Rudorff, Römische Rechtsgeschichte, vol. II. § 51.) Accordingly, in this sense, the term 'actio utilis' comprehends the 'actio in factum' and so the passages which, in cases of extensions of the Aquilian statute, declare an actio in factum, and those which declare an actio utilis to be applicable, do not contradict one another. The expression 'actio utilis,' however, does not exclude the possibility that an analogous action was given which was not 'actio in factum,' but 'actio in ius concepta,' especially such an action with 'formula ficticia.'

It is, however, probable that—as a rule—formulae in ius conceptae were not given, for, if there was a case which did not fall under the terms of the statute, i.e. if there was not an 'occidere iniuria,' according to the first chapter, an 'urere, frangere, rumpere rem,' according to the third chapter, but damage done in some other way, 'alio modo,' the 'intentio in ius concepta' was not applicable, and, therefore, the 'condemnatio' in the formula was to be made dependent on the truth of a 'factum.' Only in one case—if an Aquilian action was given to and against an alien—we are expressly told that a 'formula ficticia'—accordingly an 'actio in ius concepta'—was applicable (Gaius, IV. 37), but this is not a case, in which damage was done 'alio modo,' than that stated by the terms of the statute, and, therefore, its decision does not contradict the numerous passages which declare an 'actio in factum' applicable in cases wherever damage was done in another way than determined by the Aquilian law. See D. 9. 2. 33. §. 1; D. 19. 5. 11; D. 9. 1. 1. § 7; cf. also D. h. t. 7. § 6. 9 pr., 11. § 1, and 49 pr.

It may be added that the difference between actio directa legis Aquiliae and actio utilis and in factum, does not affect the substantive law. The whole question whether one action or the other was applicable refers only to procedure. In the time of the formulary system it had of course to be decided whether a case was covered by the terms of the law, for only in this case could an actio directa be brought, otherwise an action on analogy ('utilis' or 'in factum') was to be given; but whether in the particular case a formula in factum or ficticia was granted, was probably a matter of the praetor's convenience.

Cf. Part II. § 3, see also Savigny, System, vol. V. p. 96, Lenel, Das Edictum perpetuum, p. 160. n. 1.

9. § 3.—Si seruum meum equitantem concitato equo effeceris in flumen praecipitari atque ideo homo perierit, in factum esse dandam actionem Ofilius scribit: quemadmodum si seruus meus ab alio in insidias deductus, ab alio esset occisus.

If, by irritating the horse on which my slave was riding, you have caused the slave to be thrown into the river, and consequently to perish, you will be subject to an actio in factum, just as if my slave had been enticed into an ambush by one person and had been killed there by another.

It is obvious that a person who merely irritates a horse on which a slave is riding cannot be said to have killed the latter—there is no physical operation on the slave himself—but he has furnished a 'causa mortis,' and therefore an actio in factum can be brought against him. In the same way the person who has enticed a slave into an ambush is liable to an actio in factum, whilst the person who has killed him is subject to the actio legis Aquiliae directa. We learn from the last sentence that the person who has aided and abetted the commission of the act by another is liable in the same way as the principal delinquent, for the difference between actio directa and in factum is a mere matter of form. This follows necessarily from the principle of the Aquilian statute, according to which every culpa is sufficient to make a person liable. The distinctions drawn by the criminal law between several persons who in the same way have joined to commit a delict, or persons one of whom has instigated by his counsel, command, etc. another, or has aided and abetted another in the commission of a delict, are entirely irrelevant with regard to liability on the ground of the Aquilian statute. See also 11. § 1.

Pernice, p. 216.

9. § 4.—Sed si per lusum iaculantibus seruus fuerit occisus, Aquiliae

locus est: sed si cum alii in campo iacularentur, seruus per eum locum transierit, Aquilia cessat, quia non debuit per campum iaculatorium iter intempestiue facere qui tamen data opera in eum iaculatus est, utique Aquilia tenebitur.

10 *pr.*—Paulus libro XXII ad edictum. nam lusus quoque noxius in culpa est.

If a slave were killed by persons who were throwing javelins for amusement, the Aquilian action was applicable. But if, whilst others were throwing javelins in the place devoted to such exercises, a slave crossed that ground, the action would not lie, because the slave should not have walked over the training field at an unseasonable time. A person, however, who had thrown a missile at him intentionally would be liable under the Aquilian statute, for a mischievous jest is equivalent to a fault.

People who kill a slave by throwing javelins to amuse themselves will be liable to an Aquilian action, as the damage is certainly due to their culpa. It is different if they are practising on the proper place—campus iaculatorius—and a slave crosses it whilst the game is going on. Although in such case also negligence on the part of the injurer cannot be denied, the damage would have been avoided if the injured person had taken due care. Thus he has contributed by his own culpa to the injury complained of (contributory negligence), and on that account a so-called culpa-compensation takes place, i. e. the culpa of the injurer is set off against the culpa of the injured person. The reason for admitting culpa-compensation is that the injurer has to attribute, at least to some extent, the damage to his own fault, and 'Quod quis ex culpa sua damnum sentit, non intellegitur sentire,' says Pomponius in D. 50. 17. 203. Further instances of culpa-compensation are to be found in 11 pr. and 28 below, and in Paulus, Sent. Rec. I. 15. § 3; see also 31 h. t. (Cf. Part II. § 7.)

It is assumed in the passage that the slave is not one of the players, otherwise there would be, according to 52. § 4, no liability under the Aquilian statute. Moreover, it must be remarked that culpa-compensation does not come into operation when there is 'dolus' on the part of the injurer. Therefore, if one of the players has purposely thrown at the slave, perhaps only to show his dexterity in not hitting him, he will be liable to an Aquilian action, for, as Paulus says, such a mischievous jest must be considered to be culpa.

The decision given by Ulpian does not seem to express the view of Justinian on the topic. For in the Inst. 4. 3. § 4 (a passage which in its present form is doubtlessly derived from the compilers) in exactly the same case (when people were throwing javelins and a slave passing by was wounded), it is said to constitute a difference, whether a soldier had done the damage whilst practising in the place set aside for such purposes or not. Only in the former case the injurer will be held not to be liable, in all other cases the person who has caused the damage will be liable. The rule stated by Ulpian, therefore, must be taken with the restriction made in the Institutes.

Pernice, pp. 55, 61 sq., 72, and 73; Windscheid, § 455. n. 12, and § 258. n. 17 and 18.

11 *pr.*—Ulpianus libro XVIII ad edictum: Item Mela scribit, si, cum pila quidam luderent, uehementius quis pila percussa in tonsoris manus eam deiecerit et sic serui, quem tonsor habebat, gula sit praecisa adiecto cultello: in quocumque eorum culpa sit, cum lege Aquilia teneri. Proculus in tonsore esse culpam: et sane si tibi tondebat ubi ex consuetudine ludebatur uel ubi transitus frequens erat, est quod ei imputetur: quamuis nec illud male dicatur, si in loco periculoso sellam habenti tonsori se quis commiserit, ipsum de se queri debere.

Similarly Mela writes, if whilst people were playing at ball, one of them had struck his ball too vehemently, and so thrown it into the hands of a barber, whereby the throat of a slave whom the barber was shaving has been cut, the razor being just in contact with it, he of the persons concerned who is in culpa will be liable under the Aquilian statute. Proculus says that the culpa is on the part of the barber. And certainly (so adds Ulpian) there is some blame to be imputed to the barber, if he was shaving in a place where it was usual to play, or where many people were passing, although it may also be said with truth that a person who entrusts himself to a barber who has his stand in a dangerous place has only himself to complain of.

The case under discussion is the following: In the course of a game one of the players threw his ball, striking it too violently, against the hand of a barber who was just shaving a slave, and thus the throat of the latter was cut. An action under the Aquilian law seems to be applicable, but who is to be sued? The answer is: the person by whose culpa the damage was caused. The decision of this question depends on further particulars, which, however, are not given. According to the facts which are stated, one would think that the person who has thrown the ball is liable. Proculus, however, says that the barber will be liable. In this Ulpian agrees, if it was usual to play in the place, or if the place was a frequented one, for on such an assumption there would be culpa on his part. But the circumstances of the case might have been of such a character that there was also culpa on the part of the person injured, and this is the case if he allowed himself to be shaved in a place which he knew[1] to be a dangerous one. This fact, of course, would not affect the existence of culpa on the part of the injurer, but it would cause the principle of culpa-compensation to come into operation, and therefore the Aquilian action would be excluded. Cf. the Notes to 9. § 4 above. Pernice, pp. 60, 73; Windscheid, n. 12.

11. § 1.—Si alius tenuit, alius interemit, is qui tenuit, quasi causam mortis praebuit, in factum actione tenetur.

If one person has held a slave whilst another has killed him, the former, as having furnished the cause of his death, will be liable to an actio in factum.

This passage is quite clear. It is understood that he who has killed a slave is liable to an actio directa under the first chapter of the statute. In addition to this, the passage further illustrates the principle explained in the notes on 9. § 3, that the manner in which several persons participate in the commission of damage is absolutely irrelevant as regards their liability under the principles of the Aquilian law. It is hardly necessary to say that the case mentioned in the last words

[1] It is obvious that culpa cannot be imputed to a person who has not such knowledge; for instance, a blind man or a stranger to the place.

of 9. § 3, 'si servus meus ab alio in insidias deductus, ab alio esset occisus,' in its legal aspect, is identical with the case under consideration.

Pernice, p. 216; Windscheid, n. 5.

11. § 2.—Sed si plures seruum percusserint, utrum omnes quasi occiderint teneantur, uideamus. et si quidem apparet cuius ictu perierit, ille quasi occiderit tenetur: quod si non apparet, omnes quasi occiderint teneri Iulianus ait, et si cum uno agatur, ceteri non liberantur: nam ex lege Aquilia quod alius praestitit, alium non releuat, cum sit poena.

But if several persons have beaten a slave, we may consider whether they will all be liable as having killed him. And if it appears by whose blow he was killed, that man will be liable for having killed him. But if it does not appear, Julian says that all will be liable as having killed the slave, and if the action had been brought against one of them the others will not be released, for what one person has paid under the lex Aquilia does not release the others, because it is a penalty.

Several persons have together beaten a slave, who has died in consequence. The question arises whether they are any of them liable on account of killing the slave, i. e. to an action under the first chapter of the lex. If it can be proved that the death was due to the act of a certain person, he will be liable under the first chapter, but it is understood that the others are subject to an action arising from chapter III; arg. 11. § 3. If, however, it cannot be proved by whose act the death was caused, all who have taken part in the struggle will be liable under the first chapter, for, as far as appears, they have all caused the death of the slave; nothing else is in evidence. In other words: there were simultaneous blows inflicted on the slave by several persons, which blows had the effect which might have been expected, according to common experience, and therefore that effect is attributed to the culpa of these persons. The passage of Julian to which Ulpian refers is contained in 51. § 1, where Julian quotes the authority of the veteres, i. e. the jurists before the time of Augustus, in favour of this rule.

The several persons concerned are liable each for the whole amount which can be claimed under the statute—in solidum,—but if one has paid it the others are not released, because it is a penalty 'ex lege Aquilia quod alius praestitit alium non relevat cum sit poena.' These words clearly show that though the object of the action was, as a matter of fact, compensation for the plaintiff, it was considered as a penalty inflicted on the defendant, and therefore it might be claimed from the several accomplices, in the same way as an actio furti might be brought against the different persons who had participated in the commission of the furtum (C. 4. 8. 1, see also D. 47. 7. 6. *pr.*, where the same is mentioned of the actio arborum furtim caesarum). It is true that in other actions ex delicto which have compensation for their object, as e. g. the condictio furtiva and the actio quod metus causa (C. 4. 8. 1, D. 4. 2. 14. § 15), compensation can be received only once; but this is probably explained by the fact that the origin of these actions is due to the praetorian edict, whilst the Aquilian action was introduced by the ancient civil law. It may be mentioned that the Glossa accounts for the difference we are considering by asserting that the word 'poena' in the passage is understood only of the surplus of the highest value of the thing destroyed over the actual loss sustained by the plaintiff, and that it is this surplus which can be claimed as a penalty from every accomplice, whilst the real compensation could be claimed only once. That this interpretation is in no way indicated in the passage is obvious, and that it is inconsistent with the whole spirit of the law is shown in Part II. § 14, which may be compared for further particulars.

Pernice, pp. 121, 130, 232; Windscheid, n. 22 and 26; Brinz, § 340. n. 39; Vangerow, vol. III. p. 585.

11. § 3.—Celsus scribit, si alius mortifero uulnere percusserit, alius postea exanimauerit, priorem quidem non teneri quasi occiderit, sed quasi uulneraverit, quia ex alio uulnere periit, posteriorem teneri, quia occidit. quod et Marcello uidetur et est probabilius.

Celsus writes, that if one person has inflicted on a slave a deadly wound, and another has afterwards actually put him to death, the former will not be liable for having killed, but only for having wounded the slave, who has perished from another wound, but the latter will be liable for having killed the slave.

Whilst in the previous section the case where death was the consequence of several wounds simultaneously inflicted on a slave is discussed, in this passage the case is discussed where several persons have wounded at different times a slave who died in consequence. The facts of the case are apparently the following: A wounds the slave of another person mortally, but before the slave dies B comes and kills him, e. g. by cutting off his head. It naturally follows that B is liable under the first chapter, whereas A is liable only under the third chapter for wounding the slave; for though from the nature of the wound death must necessarily have resulted, yet in this case the death of the slave was caused by the subsequent act of decapitation. This view which, as we learn from the passage, is concurred in by Celsus, Marcellus, and Ulpian, underlies also the decision in 15. § 1, where Ulpian, in harmony with Julian, states that a person who had mortally wounded a slave, who was afterwards killed by the fall of a house or by shipwreck, will be liable under the third and not the first chapter of the lex. There is, however, another passage of Julian, 51. § 1, which at first sight seems to express a different view, and which has induced several writers to assert that it really contradicts the fragment we are considering. There also a case is supposed, in which a slave who was mortally wounded by one person was afterwards wounded by another, and died in consequence; but here both the persons are declared to be liable under the first chapter. A careful examination of this passage, however, shows that the second wound is not in itself absolutely deadly—like a decapitation,—but that it has only caused, in concurrence with the wound already inflicted on the slave, that his death followed earlier ('ut maturius interficeretur') than was expected from the first wound. Accordingly both the wounds were necessary to effect the death just at the time when it happened, and therefore both the delinquents are liable for having killed the slave.

Pernice, p. 179 sqq.; Vangerow, p. 585 sq.

11. § 4.—Si plures trabem deiecerint et hominem oppresserint, aeque ueteribus placet omnes lege Aquilia teneri.

In case several persons had thrown down a beam, and thus crushed a slave, all of them were, according to the opinion of the ancient jurists, liable under the lex Aquilia.

This passage is noticeable for two reasons: first, it is a fresh example of the interpretation of the term 'occidere' (cf. 7. §§ 2, 5, 7), and secondly, it is a new illustration of the rule that several persons who commit together damage to property are equally liable, without any distinction whether any single individual is more or less in 'culpa.' In the case under consideration all the persons carrying the beam are therefore subject to an actio (directa) under the first chapter, as they have together caused by their unlawful act the death of the slave. Cf. the notes to 9. § 3, and 11. § 1 above.

Pernice, p. 149.

11. § 5.—Item cum eo qui canem irritauerat et effecerat ut aliquem morderet, quamuis eum non tenuit, Proculus respondit Aquiliae actionem esse: sed Iulianus eum demum Aquilia teneri ait qui tenuit et effecit ut aliquem morderet: ceterum si non tenuit, in factum agendum.

Similarly, according to Proculus, an actio legis Aquiliae will lie against a person who has irritated a dog, and so caused it to bite some one, although he has not hold of the dog. But Julian says that only the person who has hold of the dog and caused it to bite will be liable, but if the delinquent has hold of the dog an actio in factum must be brought against him.

The connection between this and the previous passage is, that, according to the opinion of Proculus, in the case cited a direct action is also applicable. But it must be noticed that this passage has, strictly speaking, no reference to the contents of the chapter which the jurist is engaged in interpreting. For this passage does not speak of killing but merely of wounding. It is not, therefore, the first but the third chapter which is applicable.

It is well known that in case damage was done by an animal a so-called actio de pauperie might be brought against the owner of the animal. This action, however, is not applicable if the animal has been irritated by some one else (D. 9. 1. 1. § 6), and so the question arises as to the liability under the Aquilian statute. Proculus thought a direct Aquilian action to be applicable, apparently taking the dog merely as an instrument like a sword or beam by which damage was inflicted. Julian, however, restricted the applicability of a direct action to cases where a person has hold of the dog whilst causing it to bite another. The reason is evidently because Julian thought that only in this case there was what is called a damnum corpore corpori datum, whilst in a case where a person had instigated the dog without holding it, there was merely a damnum corpori datum, and therefore an actio in factum was applicable.

11. § 6.—Legis autem Aquiliae actio ero competit, hoc est domino.

The actio legis Aquiliae is given to the erus, i.e. the owner.

Hitherto the terms of quadrupes, iniuria, and occidere had been explained; with the passage we are about to consider commence the comments on the term *dominus*, and they are continued down to 20. Considering that Ulpian uses the archaic word erus, whilst expressly commenting on the terms of the lex Aquilia, we may safely assume that this word, the use of which is fully in accordance with the antiquity of the Aquilian statute, stood originally in the lex itself, instead of the synonymous expression dominus, which is commonly employed in later times. It is hardly necessary to call attention to the fact that the Aquilian statute only mentions the owner as being entitled to bring actions arising upon it, therefore he alone can bring a so-called actio directa, whilst other persons, to whom it was considered to be fair to extend the advantages of the lex, had to use either an actio in factum, or an actio utilis.

Pernice, p. 183; Windscheid, n. 14; Brinz, § 340. n. 21; Lenel, Das Edictum perpetuum, p. 157. n. 1.

11. § 7.—Si in eo homine quem tibi redhibiturus essem damnum iniuria datum esset, Iulianus ait legis Aquiliae actionem mihi competere, meque, cum coepero redhibere, tibi restitutum.

If damage was done unlawfully to a slave whom I, the purchaser, intended to restore to you, the seller, Julian says that the Aquilian action belongs to me, and that I shall transfer it to you, when I am going to avail myself of the right of restoring the slave bought.

The case supposed by the jurist is of the following kind: Titius has sold and delivered his slave to Seius without telling him certain defects of the slave. Seius is therefore, according to the edict of the

Aediles, D. 21. 1. 14. § 10; Arndts, § 304, entitled to claim either proportional diminution of the price agreed on by a so-called actio quanti minoris, or to recede, in virtue of his actio redhibitoria, altogether from the contract by returning the thing bought and recovering the price which he had paid. Seius having become aware of the defect of the slave, chooses the latter alternative, and intends to restore the slave to Titius. But before carrying out his intention the slave is unlawfully damaged by Sempronius.

It is obvious that in this case the seller, who was about to receive back the thing he had sold, is the person who actually suffers the loss. The actio legis Aquiliae, however, was not given to him, but to the purchaser, who, in consequence of the traditio ex causa emtionis, had become the owner of the slave; but as he was about to avail himself of the right given by the edict of the Aediles, that is, to recede from the sale agreed on, he was also bound to give up the advantages which he had acquired under that contract, and was therefore declared to be bound to transfer the Aquilian action to the seller.

We have assumed above that the slave was sold and delivered to the purchaser by traditio, and this assumption is undoubtedly right as regards the law of Justinian, of which the fragment forms a portion. The case, however, as supposed by the author of this passage, was that the slave sold was transferred by mancipatio (possibly also by in iure cessio). For slaves belonged to res mancipi, which, in the time of the classical jurists, were transferred either by mancipatio or in iure cessio, though the use of the latter form had already in the second century A.C. become very exceptional. Gaius, II. 22–25, I. 119–122; Ulpian, frag. I. 19. § 1–6. Accordingly the passage furnishes an instance of what is called 'duplex interpretatio.'

11. § 8.—Sed si seruus bona fide alicui seruiat, an ei competit Aquiliae actio? et magis in factum actio erit danda.

But if a slave serves another person in good faith, we may ask whether the latter has the Aquilian action. It seems, however, better to give him an actio in factum.

A slave (as supposed in the passage) has taken another person as his master, and has rendered services to him supposing that his new master had acquired the slave by some title (usually emtio venditio) which would have transferred the ownership to him, if the alienor (usually the seller) had been the owner; but as this was not the case, the successor (usually the purchaser) became merely a bonae fidei possessor. The question arises whether the possessor will be entitled to an Aquilian action, if the slave in his possession is killed or wounded by a third person. The answer given by the jurist is that he will not have the direct action, but an actio in factum. This decision is quite clear, but it seems to be doubtful to what extent the action is given to the bonae fidei possessor. If we consider that a possessor in good faith has practically the position of an owner, inasmuch as he thinks himself to be the owner, and is practically taken as such, we should hold that in case of damage to the property in his possession the action is to be given to him in the same way as to the owner. This is supported by a very strong analogy. It is well known that the bonae fidei possessor is protected in the enjoyment of his peculiar right by the actio publiciana, which, being a utilis rei vindicatio (under the fiction of ownership on the part of the plaintiff), has the full effect of rei vindicatio against every possessor who has not a better claim to the possession than the plaintiff himself.

It is true that the bonae fidei possessor may always be sued by the owner, and he is then bound to hand over the thing in his possession with all its accessories, and is restricted to claiming compensation for certain expenses incurred on account of the thing, the so-called 'impensae necessariae' and 'utiles,' by means of an 'exceptio doli' opposed to the 'rei vindicatio,' Arndts, § 168. n. 1. So far it may be said that the absolute value of the usufruct consists only in the value of these recoverable expenses, and thus several authors have been led to the assertion that the action given to the bonae fidei possessor under the Aquilian statute must be restricted to claiming such outlay of the plaintiff. This view, however, would have the very unsatisfactory result that in all cases in which the plaintiff, although the owner of the thing damaged, did not succeed in proving his ownership[1], the

[1] To prove ownership in a thing is, as a rule, a very difficult task (see Part II. § 12). Owners frequently are not in the condition to afford such evidence, but can only prove that they have acquired bona fide and iusto titulo (i. e. acquisition of bonae fidei possessio).

delict would remain without its legal consequences. Besides, it is strongly opposed to D. 5. 3. 55, according to which passage the bonae fidei possessor is bound to restore to the vindicant everything which he had received by the Aquilian action. But if he had received merely compensation for his outlay there would be nothing to be restored to the plaintiff. Thus we are driven to share the opinion that the bonae fidei possessor simply brought the action in the place of the owner; but as his right was dependent on that of the owner, exception must be made in case a collision between them should occur. Such collision takes place (1) if the bonae fidei possessor and owner sue the injurer at the same time under the Aquilian statute; and (2) if the owner himself is sued by the bonae fidei possessor on account of damage done to him unlawfully, see Fr. 17. In both the cases the object of the action will be restricted to compensation for the impensae utiles and necessariae.

Compare for further particulars Part II. § 9.

11. § 9.—Eum, cui uestimenta commodata sunt, non posse, si scissa fuerint, lege Aquilia agere Iulianus ait, sed domino eam competere.

Julian says he to whom garments were lent cannot sue under the lex Aquilia if they were torn by another, that the owner, however, is entitled to the action.

Whilst a bonae fidei possessor is, as a rule, entitled to exercise the right which the owner has under the lex Aquilia, the right to sue for damage done is denied in the above passage to the commodatarius and is reserved to the owner who has lent him the thing damaged (the commodans). Although the fragment refers only to the case of commodatum, the decision of the jurist seems to be merely an application of a general rule, viz. that a person who has only a right in personam in regard to a thing cannot sue on account of damage done to it. For there are several other cases the decision of which is in exact accordance with that given in the passage we are considering; thus, if a person has promised to give to another his slave and the slave was slain afterwards, not the stipulator, who could claim the slave, but the promissor, who was still the owner, is entitled to the action ex lege Aquilia; D. h. t. 54, and D. 4. 3. 18. § 5.

Similarly, in case a thing sold had been unlawfully damaged before it was delivered to the purchaser, and had thus passed into his ownership, the actio legis Aquiliae belongs to the seller, who, however, is bound to transfer it to the purchaser, D. 19. 1. 13. § 12, and I. III. 23. § 3. i. f.

The principle of the Roman law thus established is, however, subject to one exception, viz. that a person who is in virtue of a right in personam entitled to take the fruits of a thing instead of its owner (e.g. the colonus) is also permitted (in 27. § 14) to sue on account of damage done to them.

Pernice, p. 208; Windscheid, n. 17; Brinz, § 340. n. 27.

11. § 10.—An fructuarius uel usuarius legis Aquiliae actionem haberet, Iulianus tractat: et ego puto melius utile iudicium ex hac causa dandum.

Julian deals with the question whether a usufructuary and usuary may have the actio legis Aquiliae; I think it, however, better to give an actio utilis on that account.

Here we are told that Julian has discussed the question whether or no the usufructuary should have the Aquilian action. These words are ambiguous. They might mean that Julian had entertained doubts as to the applicability of an actio damni iniuria in general (without distinguishing between actio directa, utilis, and in factum) or that he was in doubt as to the applicability of the actio legis Aquiliae, properly so called, i. e. the actio directa. But we may assume that his doubt was confined to the latter alternative, for Ulpian adds that he thinks it *better* to give in such cases an actio utilis. The difference thus indicated in the opinion of the two jurists is explained by the assumption that Julian thought a direct action might be applicable in the cases we are discussing. This idea of Julian is explained by the fact that the usufructuary is in a condition similar to that of the owner, in so far as he is entitled to the enjoyment of all the advantages conferred by the property which is the subject of his right just like an owner, wherefore we should also expect that he would have his right of action. Ulpian, however, taking into account that the formula of the direct action had to be modified in some way or other, in order to be applicable to the cases under consideration, thought it more correct to give an actio utilis (cf. also D. h. t. 12; D. 7. 1. 17. § 3; D. 4. 3. 7. § 4, and 18. § 2; D. 43. 24. 13 pr.). Similarly, an actio utilis is given to a person entitled to an aqueduct in 27. § 32 below, and, under certain conditions, an actio in factum to the creditor pignoris in fr. 17, and 30. § 1. These provisions lead to the assumption that an action for damage was considered to be applicable in all cases in which a person had a ius in re aliena, and that it is a mere accident that there are no cases in the Corpus Iuris in which the action is given to the superficiarius and the emphyteuta.

But though all authorities agree on this point, it is not yet decided to what extent the action is given to persons who have a 'ius in re.' According to the above remarks it seems to be probable that the usufructuary—and the same applies to the usuary (Arndts, § 182)—had the Aquilian action in the place of the owner, and this supposition will be confirmed by a special inquiry into the topic (see the notes to 12 below). Persons, however, who have one of the other 'iura in re aliena' can claim compensation only for the injury to their own right, whilst the owner has an action for injury to his remaining right of ownership. Such a division of the action under the Aquilian statute is expressly recognised in case a 'pignus' had been damaged in 30. § 1 below.

Pernice, p. 199; Savigny, System, vol. V. p. 95; Windscheid, n. 15; Brinz, § 340. n. 25 and 26.

12.—Paulus libro X ad Sabinum: Sed et si proprietatis dominus uulnerauerit seruum uel occiderit, in quo usus fructus meus est, danda est mihi ad exemplum legis Aquiliae actio in eum pro portione usus fructus, ut etiam ea pars anni in aestimationem ueniat, qua nondum usus fructus meus fuit.

But if the owner himself has wounded or killed a slave in whom I have a 'usufruct,' I shall have an action against him by analogy to the Aquilian statute for his portion of the usufruct, so that also that part of the last year is to be taken into account in assessing the damages in which the usufruct did not belong to me.

I have a usufruct in a thing which was damaged by the owner himself, who, being restricted to the nuda proprietas in it, is called the 'dominus proprietatis' in the passage. I am declared by Paulus to be entitled to an actio ad exemplum legis Aquiliae or an actio utilis (see also D. 4. 3. 7. § 4, and 18. § 2), the reason clearly being that as far as the thing is subject to my ius in re it does not belong to the owner, and is withdrawn from his control; accordingly my right may be violated by him. The same view applies also to other iura in re aliena, and is especially recognised with regard to a person who has a ius pignoris and a bonae fidei possessor in 17 below. We are therefore safe in saying that every person to whom the Aquilian action was extended in the course of time may bring this action also against the owner himself, if he has committed the damage complained of.

It is, however, a more difficult question to ascertain what the object of the action was in the case we have to consider. The usufructuary is said to have the 'actio pro portione ususfructus.' This may signify that the action lies to recover damages in the proportion which the value of the usufruct bears to the value of the full ownership; an explanation with which the Glossa to the passage is in accordance. But it may also denote that the usufructuary brings his action merely for his portion, because the right of usufruct is divided between several persons, and this view is supported by the paraphrasis in the Basiliks (Schol. Bas. 60. 3. 12; edition of Heimbach, vol. V. p. 276).

It is obvious that, according to the first of these two views, it is the value of the usufruct which would form the object of the action; according to the second view, however, nothing is determined as to what is that object, we know only that each of the usufructuaries may bring his action for his portion; but whether he sues for compensation of his right of usufruct, or brings the action instead of the owner, is not declared. Although the division of the usufruct between several persons is in no way indicated in the beginning of the passage which states the facts of the case, the second view seems to deserve preference, for thus the words 'pro portione ususfructus' find a very simple explanation (without requiring such supposition as the first view stated above), and this view is confirmed by the Scholiast in the Basiliks.

Under such circumstances, the question as to the object of the action of the usufructuary is yet to be answered.

Three ways of assessing damages are conceivable:—

1. An annual income may be given to the usufructuary equal in value to the annual use and proceeds of the usufruct.

2. The object of the action may be the value of the usufruct itself, to be assessed by calculation, taking into account on one side the value of the annual use and profits, and on the other the probable duration of the lifetime of the usufructuary. Here the owner could still bring the Aquilian action to be compensated for the loss of his nuda proprietas.

3. The usufructuary may simply exercise the action of the owner claiming full compensation for the damage done, and accordingly excluding the action of the owner.

It is obvious that the terms of the passage have not in view the first alternative; but whether the second or the third is preferable is very difficult to ascertain. There are, however, several objections to the second way of assessing damages; for the usufructuary who had a right for his life may complain that he may live much longer than is expected according to the rule of probabilities; and the owner who was burdened by the usufruct for the lifetime of the usufructuary may complain that the latter may live for a much shorter time than that assumed in the calculation.

The only satisfactory solution seems to be furnished by the third of the above possibilities. It is true that in this case the usufructuary will receive the full compensation which, strictly speaking, is due to the owner. But the possession of the sum of money thus received will be subject to the same conditions as the enjoyment of the individual thing which had been subject to the usufructus; only the usufructus of the thing will be replaced by a quasi ususfructus in the money. Although the (former) usufructuary will become owner of the money, he will be bound to restore the same amount on the occurrence of an event which would have terminated his usufruct, and this obligation is secured in the same way as the obligation of the usufructuary to restore the individual thing, i. e. by the 'cautio usufructuaria,' which certainly extends to the quasi ususfructus also. This view, which fully meets the necessities of the case, is at the same time supported by what is said in 11. § 10 above, for the doubt of Julian, whether an actio legis Aquiliae was to be given to the usufructuary and usuary, is explained only by the assumption that they exercised a right of action really belonging to the owner. But if the usufructuary brought the action in place of the owner, either alone, or if the right of usufruct was divided between several persons, 'pro portione,' in either case the highest value which the slave who was killed had during any one period of the preceding year will furnish the measure of damages, although the slave was not then subject to the right of the plaintiff, 'ut etiam ea pars anni in aestimationem veniat, qua nondum usufructus meus fuit.'

Pernice, pp. 163 and 198 sq.; Windscheid, n. 15 and 18; Glück, vol. X. p. 372. n. 12 and 13.

13 *pr.*—Ulpianus libro XVIII ad edictum: Liber homo suo nomine utilem Aquiliae habet actionem: directam enim non habet, quoniam dominus membrorum suorum nemo uidetur. fugitiui autem nomine dominus habet.

A wounded freeman has an actio utilis on his own account, but not an actio directa, because no one is considered to be the owner of his limbs. But if a fugitive slave has been wounded, his master has the direct action.

The fragment is in strict accordance with the contents of 5 § 3 ad fin. 6 and 7. *pr.* The only difference is that there a case of wounding a filius familias is dealt with, and therefore the action is given to his father, whilst here a pater familias himself (i. e. a persona sui iuris) is injured, who accordingly can sue on his own account. But in both the cases the actio is utilis, for just as a son is not considered to be subject to his father's ownership, so the pater familias himself is not considered to be owner of his limbs; an idea which seems to be only another expression of the principle 'liberum corpus aestimationem non recipit' (D. 9. 1. 3 and D. 9. 3. 1. § 5.) Further, the object of the action is the same in both cases, namely, compensation for the expenses incurred for the cure and for the value of the labour which had been lost, and will be lost in the future, in consequence of the injury.

In addition to this it must be noticed that no liability is recognised either in case a filius familias, or in case a pater familias had been killed (cf. for particulars Notes to 5. § 3 ad fin. and 6.) The case of the fugitive slave is added because he actually is at the moment in the condition of a freeman (D. 21. 1. 17. § 10), but nevertheless an actio directa is given to his master, if he is wounded or killed, for in the eye of the law he is still subject to his master's ownership.

Windscheid, n. 7, 14, and 19; Vangerow, vol. III. p. 583.

13. § 1.—Iulianus scribit, si homo liber bona fide mihi seruiat, ipsum lege Aquilia mihi teneri.

Julian writes that if a freeman renders to me the services of a slave in good faith, he himself will be bound to me under the Aquilian law.

It is certain that a slave cannot be under an obligation to his own master. The question was therefore raised whether this principle should not apply to the case of a person who was, as a matter of fact, in the condition of a slave to another, and had negligently damaged his property. Considering, however, the fact that the person was in reality a freeman, and accordingly capable of legal duties, Julian declared that he should be subject to an Aquilian action, although the peculiar condition which compelled him to be constantly handling the plaintiff's property, was to be taken into account, and therefore he was declared (by Modestinus in D. 41. 1. 54. § 2) to be answerable for culpa lata only.

Vangerow, vol. III. p. 590.

13. § 2.—Si seruus hereditarius occidatur, quaeritur, quis Aquilia agat, cum dominus nullus sit huius serui. et ait Celsus legem domino damna salua esse uoluisse: dominus ergo hereditas habebitur quare adita hereditate heres poterit experiri.

If a slave belonging to an inheritance (not yet entered upon) is killed, the question arises as to the person who can bring the action, as there is actually no owner of the slave. Celsus, however, says that it is intended by the law that the owner should be indemnified for damage; therefore the inheritance itself shall be taken as the owner, and accordingly the heir will be enabled to bring the action when he has entered on the inheritance.

Here the case is supposed of a slave who is killed whilst he belongs to an inheritance not yet entered upon. Strictly speaking, there is no owner of the slave, and consequently no one to whom the right of suing under the Aquilian statute would accrue. The Roman jurists, therefore, provided for cases of this kind by a fiction; namely, that the hereditas iacens was itself a person. The fiction was necessary, because in some cases the heir did not acquire the inheritance for a long time after the death of the deceased, and during this period the inheritance had to be kept together, and treated as an aggregate of rights and duties, just as if the deceased were alive. The Roman jurists, therefore, by a fiction, considered all the rights and duties and burdens of the deceased person to be attached to the inheritance which represented the person of the deceased. Compare especially Gaius in D. 28. 5. 31. § 1: 'Creditum est hereditatem dominam esse, defuncti locum obtinere;' see also D. 41. 1. 34; D. 30. 116. § 3; I. II. 14. 2, and Arndts, § 465. n. 1. In this way it was rendered possible that new rights would be acquired by, and new duties imposed on, the inheritance, which rights and duties were, as a portion of the inheritance itself, transferred to the heir as soon as he had entered it.

The same views underlie the arguments here used by the jurist. As there was in truth no owner of the slave, the object of the lex Aquilia that the owner should be indemnified for damage, 'domino damna salva esse,' could not be carried into execution, as Celsus remarks. In order to meet this difficulty the inheritance is conceived as the owner of the slave ('dominus ergo hereditas habebitur'), and thus the right of action is acquired in its favour and will accordingly be transferred to the heir at the moment of the 'aditio hereditatis,' and he may then sue the delinquent under the first chapter of the lex.

13. § 3.—Si seruus legatus post aditam hereditatem sit occisus, competere legis Aquiliae actionem legatario, si *non*[1] post mortem serui agnouit legatum: quod si repudiauit consequens esse ait Iulianus dicere, heredi competere.

If a slave, bequeathed by a legacy, is killed after the heir has entered on the inheritance, the Aquilian action belongs to the legatee,

[1] Th. Mommsen proposes to read *vel* instead of *non*, which is attested by the manuscripts: this conjecture, for the reasons stated in the notes, is accepted in the following paraphrase.

even in case he had declared his intention to take the legacy after the death of the slave, but if he has refused the legacy, it is, according to Julian's opinion, a consequence of this, that the action belongs to the heir.

The slave Stichus of the testator—such is, in its essence, the case supposed by the jurist—was bequeathed by him to his friend Titius by means of a legatum vindicationis (Titio hominem Stichum do lego, Gaius, II. 193). The effect of such a legacy, according to the opinion of the Sabinians (Gaius, II. 195), which is recognised by Justinian in the Corpus Iuris (see D. 28. 1. 16. § 1; D. 31. 77. § 3; D. 44. 7. 24 pr.; Arndts, § 555, N.; Windscheid, § 643), is to transfer ownership in the thing bequeathed to the legatee as soon as the heir has entered on the inheritance. A declaration of the intention of the legatee to take the bequest, which formerly was considered to be necessary according to the view of the Proculians (see Gaius, II. 195), is not required, for the legatee acquires without his will, although not against his will, since he can refuse (repudiare) the legatum. But if he did refuse, he was considered as never having acquired the res legata, which therefore was taken to have been subject to the ownership of the heir from the moment of the aditio hereditatis. Therefore, if the seruus legatus was killed after that period, the Aquilian action will belong to the legatarius as the owner of the slave, unless he has repudiated the legatum, in which case the heir is considered to be the owner, and accordingly entitled to sue under the Aquilian law. It seems, however, strange that the assertion of the jurist that the legatee is entitled to the Aquilian action is made dependent on the condition 'si non post mortem servi agnovit legatum,' i.e. if he had not declared his wish to take the legatum after the death of the slave, at a time accordingly when ownership of the slave could not any longer be acquired. It is not impossible that this restriction is to be explained by the assumption that Ulpian adhered to the opinion of the Proculians, although he lays the chief stress on the aditio hereditatis (see also 15 pr.), but at any rate this opinion is at variance with the law of Justinian, and hence it seems necessary to accept the conjecture proposed by Th. Mommsen to substitute the words 'si vel' for the 'si non' in the manuscripts, so that the passage would express the opinion that the legatee could bring the Aquilian action even in case he had accepted the legacy after the death of the slave, as acceptance in the opinion of the jurist is an entirely irrelevant act.

Pernice, pp. 187 sq.; Brinz, § 340. n. 21.

14.—Paulus libro XXII ad edictum. Sed si ipse heres eum occiderit, dictum est dandam in eum legatario actionem.

But also if the heir himself had slain the slave, it is said that the Aquilian action is to be given to the legatee.

The fragment is merely a continuation of the previous passage, and presupposes therefore the same case, namely, that the seruus legatus has been killed after the aditio hereditatis. The legatarius was accordingly his owner, and therefore entitled to the Aquilian action whoever might have been the delinquent, even the heir, who had absolutely no right in the slave bequeathed. It would be otherwise if the heir had killed the slave before he had entered on the inheritance, for in this case the legatee would be restricted to a personal action ex testamento in order to claim compensation from the heir, D. 4. 3. 7. § 5.

15 *pr.*—Ulpianus libro XVIII ad edictum. Huic scripturae consequens est dicere, ut, si ante aditam hereditatem occidatur legatus seruus, apud heredem remaneat Aquiliae actio per hereditatem adquisita. quod si uulneratus sit ante aditam hereditatem, in hereditate quidem actio remansit, sed cedere ea legatario heredem oportet.

It follows from this that if the bequeathed slave is killed before the heir has entered on the inheritance, the Aquilian action will remain with the heir, having been acquired through the inheritance. If, however, the slave has been wounded, the action, it is true, remains with the inheritance, but the heir must transfer it to the legatee.

Before the heir has entered on the inheritance, the hereditas itself, as a juristic person (see 13. § 2 above), will acquire the right of action arising from damage done to hereditary property, and this right passes over to the heir as a portion of the inheritance as soon as he has entered on it.

With regard to the possible claims of the legatee however, we have, according to the fragment under discussion, to distinguish between two cases—whether the res legata has been destroyed, or merely damaged. In the first case, if, as supposed in the passage, the bequeathed slave has been killed, there is nothing left in which the legatee could receive ownership at the moment of the aditio hereditatis, and therefore the whole legatum becomes void. In the second case, if the seruus legatus has been wounded, ownership in the thing passes over to the legatee at the period mentioned, and as there is now no reason why the right of action on account of the injury done should belong to the heir, as a portion of the inheritance, he is declared to be bound to transfer it to the legatee as the present owner of the slave.

The result thus arrived at is strange: if the res legata is wholly destroyed, the legatee does not receive anything, whilst the heir gets compensation in his place; if it is only partly destroyed, the legatee receives the thing, as well as compensation for the damage done. This anomaly is explained by the peculiar nature of the early law of legacies. If a thing was bequeathed by a legatum per vindicationem, the only remedy given to the legatee was the rei vindicatio, by which he could claim the thing from every possessor, but he had no personal action against the heir to secure fulfilment of the disposition of the testator.

Under the law of Justinian, however, a legatee to whom property of the testator was left, not only acquired an actio in rem (rei vindicatio), but had besides an actio in personam against the heir or other person who was burdened with the bequest (Windscheid, §§ 646 and 647; Arndts, §§ 558 and 560). Being thus a creditor, the legatee could, like every other creditor, in case of its having become impossible to give the thing due to him, claim cession of those actions which were created by the event (i. e. furtum, damnum iniuria datum) from which the impossibility arose (arg. D. 18. 1. 35. § 4; D. 19. 1. 13. § 12; D. 43. 24. §§ 8–10; D. 47. 2. 14 pr.; Arndts, § 253, n. e.). Hence it follows that, if the res legata had been destroyed, hereditate iacente, as supposed in the passage above, the actio legis Aquiliae, which had passed over as a portion of the inheritance to the heir, had to be transferred to the legatee, in lieu of the thing destroyed.

Pernice, p. 187; Brinz, § 340. n. 21.

15. § 1.—Si seruus uulneratus mortifere postea ruina uel naufragio uel alio ictu maturius perierit, de occiso agi non posse, sed quasi de uulnerato, sed si manumissus uel alienatus ex uulnere periit, quasi de occiso agi posse Iulianus ait. haec ita tam uarie quia uerum est eum a te occisum tunc cum uulnerabas, quod mortuo eo demum apparuit: at in superiore non est passa ruina apparere an sit occisus. sed si uulneratum mortifere liberum et heredem esse iusseris, deinde decesserit, heredem eius agere Aquilia non posse,

16.—Marcianus libro IV regularum. quia in eum casum res peruenit, a quo incipere non potest.

If a mortally wounded slave perished afterwards, by the fall of a house or by shipwreck, or by another blow which hastened his death, no action on account of killing a slave, but only one on account of wounding, is applicable; but if the slave died from the wound after having been manumitted or alienated, Julianus says that an action for killing would lie. These two cases are decided differently, because although the slave is assumed as having been killed by you at the moment when you have wounded him, yet this fact does not become apparent till he dies. But in the first case, the injury caused by the fall prevents it being discovered whether he has so been killed (by you). But if you have manumitted and instituted as heir the mortally-wounded slave, and he has died after having become your heir, his (i.e. the freedman's) heir cannot sue under the Aquilian law, as a state of things has been brought about from which an action could not arise.

The decision of the first case here stated entirely agrees with that given in 11. § 3 above; see the notes to this passage. A slave had been mortally wounded, but was afterwards killed by the fall of a house or by shipwreck. It is obvious that the second event has prevented the slave dying from the wound as was to be expected, and therefore the delinquent can be sued only on account of wounding, i. e. under the third chapter of the Aquilian statute. It is, of course, different if the slave has been manumitted or alienated, and has afterwards died from the wound. Here his former master will be entitled to an action under Chapter I. This seems to be clear in itself. It was, however, necessary to mention this case, because the injured person died at a time when he was no longer subject to his master's right. It might, therefore, be argued that he—the former master—would be merely entitled to sue for the wounding the slave, i. e. under Chapter III. But, as Ulpian says, we must assume that the death of the slave had been caused when the deadly wound was inflicted on him (cf. 21. § 1 below), and therefore the person who was his owner at that period will be entitled to the action on account of killing, provided death has subsequently resulted from the wound. Therefore, in case of the manumission or alienation of the slave, an action will lie under Chapter I: in case of something falling on him or of shipwreck, however, an action under Chapter III is applicable.

But it is possible that a slave may die from his wound, and still no Aquilian action would lie. Such a case is mentioned at the end of the passage: a slave who had been mortally wounded was manumitted and instituted an heir by the will of his master, and being thus a so-called 'heres necessarius,' he had acquired ipso iure the inheritance left by his master, which therefore after his own death (from the wound) was transferred to his heir. The question whether the latter, i.e. the heir of the manumitted slave, may bring the Aquilian action, is answered in the negative by the jurist (cf. 36. § 1 below), because the present condition of the matter is such that under it an Aquilian action would not arise, 'quia in eum casum res pervenit a quo incipere non potest' (cf. Savigny, System, vol. II. pp. 69 sqq. and IV. pp. 553 sqq.); in other words, if the freedman had been mortally wounded no action under the first chapter would lie, for 'liberum corpus aestimationem non recipit' (D. 9. 1. 3. and D. 9. 3. 1 § 5.; cf. the notes to 5. § 3 above). It is true that in the case we are discussing a right of action under the first chapter had been acquired for the master by the mortal wound inflicted on his slave—although it could not be exercised till death had resulted from the wound—and it is also true that this right will be transferred to the master's heir like other rights of property, unless, as stated in the fragment, the slave himself is made the heir of his master, in which case he would have to claim his own value. As this was impossible, the right of action created by the mortal wound could not be acquired by him, and accordingly could not be transferred to his heir (compare in 36. § 1, the words—'ad heredem actionem non transmitti quae defuncto competere non potuit').

Pernice, p. 180; Vangerow, vol. III. p. 586.

17.—Ulpianus libro XVIII ad edictum. Si dominus seruum suum occiderit, bonae fidei possessori uel ei qui pignori accepit in factum actione tenebitur.

If a master has killed his slave he will be liable to the possessor in good faith, or to the person who has taken the slave in pledge, by an 'actio in factum.'

Two cases are here distinguished :—

1. A master has killed his slave whilst in the possession of another, who had acquired the slave iusto titulo and bona fide from a third person (non-owner).

2. A master has killed his slave whilst in the possession of another to whom the slave was given in pledge—as a 'pignus.' Both the injured parties, the bona fide possessor and the creditor pignoris are declared to be entitled to an actio in factum (compare 11. §§ 8, 10, 12 above). Thus the passage is a new instance of the principle that other persons besides the owner may sue for unlawful damage, although the owner alone is entitled to the actio legis Aquiliae directa. At the same time this passage also shows that such persons may bring their action against the owner himself (see the notes to 12 above) if he has violated their right. There is, however, a rather important difference between the two cases we are considering. It is obvious that if the owner who damages his own property in which another person has a right in rem, e. g. a ius pignoris as supposed in the passage, he commits an unlawful act (see 30. § 1 below); but if the owner destroys or damages his own property whilst it is in the possession (though bonae fidei possessio) of another, he seems to exercise merely his own right, and thus there would be no 'iniuria' on his part. This is undoubtedly true; it seems, therefore, to be necessary to confine the assertion that

the 'bonae fidei' possessor may sue the owner, to cases where the owner knows of the possession of the other. If the owner, in spite of such knowledge, commits the damaging act, he seems to exercise his right fraudulently to the disadvantage of the other, and it is probably from this point of view that he is declared to be liable to an action by which the other can recover the expenses he had incurred for the thing in his possession (compare the notes to 11. § 8 above).

Pernice, 196 sqq.; Ihering, Abhandlungen, p. 116 sqq.; Windscheid, n. 15. 16. 18; Vangerow, vol. III. p. 580; Brinz, § 340. n. 23.

18.—Paulus libro X ad Sabinum. Sed et si is qui pignori seruum accepit occidit eum uel uulnerauit, lege Aquilia et pigneraticia conueniri potest, sed alterutra contentus esse debebit actor.

But also if he who has received a slave in pledge has wounded or killed him, he may be sued under the lex Aquilia, or by the actio pigneraticia, but the plaintiff must be satisfied with one or the other of these actions.

According to the previous passage the owner who has given a pignus may be sued under the Aquilian law; here it is said that the creditor who has taken the pignus is also liable to this action; but whilst the former is subject to an actio in factum, the latter is exposed to the actio directa. Of more importance, however, is the fact, that the creditor holds the pledge under the contractus pigneraticius in virtue of which he is bound to bestow the care of a diligens paterfamilias in keeping the pignus; a duty which is enforced by the actio pigneraticia directa. Accordingly, if he has negligently damaged the pignus, he is liable for breach of his contractual duties as well as of his general duty not to injure another's property imposed by the Aquilian statute. Therefore, both the actions are applicable, and the plaintiff may choose between them. But if he has received satisfaction by one action, the other falls to the ground, 'alterutra contentus esse debebit actor.' Only in case he had first brought the 'actio ex contractu' (by which he received compensation for the loss sustained), and something more could be claimed in virtue of the more favourable measure of damages under the Aquilian law, an (Aquilian) action for this surplus was still admitted. See D. 13. 6. 7. § 1 and D. 44. 7. 34. § 4.

Pernice, p. 142; Vangerow, vol. III. p. 588.

19.—Ulpianus libro XVIII ad edictum. Sed si communem seruum occiderit quis, Aquilia teneri eum Celsus ait: idem est et si vulnerauerit:

20.—Idem libro XLII ad Sabinum. scilicet pro ea parte, pro qua dominus est qui agat (but of course only for the share which the plaintiff has in the ownership of the slave).

But if a person has killed or wounded a slave of whom he was a co-owner, he will be liable (viz. to his co-owner or co-owners) under the Aquilian law.

The following example will illustrate the nature of the case supposed by the jurist. Three persons have together ownership of a slave, say each one-third (as, for example, if they have inherited together from the owner), and one of the co-owners kills the slave. Each of the others will have the Aquilian action for his share, i.e. each of them will be entitled to sue for one-third of the damage done.

It is clear that a co-owner must become liable for damage committed by him, for although the thing injured by him is subject to his ownership, his right is yet restricted by the right of the co-owners, to whom the thing belongs in the same way as to the delinquent. Therefore they will be entitled each for his share in the ownership to bring the Aquilian action, just as each of them might sue for his own share by rei vindicatio any one who is in possession of the thing which is the subject of the co-ownership (Arndts, § 166. n. m.).

Pernice, p. 220.

21 *pr.*—Ulpianus libro XVIII ad edictum. Ait lex: 'quanti is homo in eo anno plurimi fuisset.' quae clausula aestimationem habet damni, quod datum est.

The lex says: 'Whatever was the highest value of the slave in that year,' which clause has in view the estimation of the damage which has been committed.

With this passage commences the explanation of the last words of the first chapter commented upon by the jurists, and it is continued in the following fragments down to 27. § 3. At first sight the remark of the jurist that the clause quoted by him applies to damage done seems to be superfluous, expressing merely what is understood by itself. The jurist, however, apparently lays stress on the words 'quod datum est,' and intends to say that the object of the valuation under Chapter I. is a damage or loss which has occurred in the past, and that, accordingly, circumstances which have happened since are not to be taken into account. It might be a very important question with reference to what period compensation for damage is to be assessed. Suppose a case in which a slave was unlawfully wounded by a person, and was shortly afterwards killed by an accident, which accident would equally have happened to him if he had not been wounded. If in such a case the period of the commission of the damage is decisive, compensation can be claimed; if the time when the action was brought, nothing can be claimed, for no actual loss has resulted from the act to the plaintiff's property. Generally speaking, in Roman law the time when the demand is made is to be considered: in case of an 'actio stricti iuris' the time of the litiscontessation: in case of an 'actio bonae fidei' and an 'actio in rem,' however, the time when the judicial sentence was passed: D. 13. 6. 3. § 2. But it is different if a delict has been committed, especially if damage has been unlawfully done to the property of another, for here the period of the commission of the injury is decisive. Accordingly, if a thing unlawfully damaged by a person is afterwards destroyed by accident, this fact does not prevent the injured party from suing under the Aquilian statute, as is clearly stated in D. 6. 1. 27. § 2, where Paulus supposes the case of a slave who was claimed by rei vindicatio, and who had been intentionally wounded by the defendant, but died afterwards from an accident. It is decided in the passage that the plaintiff cannot claim compensation by the rei vindicatio for the injury done to the slave, because no loss has resulted from it to him 'quia nihil interest petitoris,' but it is certain that he may claim compensation under the Aquilian statute 'legis autem Aquiliae actio durat.'

Savigny, System, vol. V. pp. 199–214; Windscheid, n. 20.

21. § 1.—Annus autem retrorsus computatur ex quo quis occisus est: quod si mortifere fuerit uulneratus et postea post longum interuallum mortuus sit, inde annum numerabimus secundum Iulianum, ex quo uulneratus est, licet Celsus contra scribit.

The year too is reckoned backwards from the time when some one has been killed; and even if a slave has been wounded mortally, and dies after a long interval, we shall still count, according to Julian, the year from the moment he has been wounded, although Celsus gives an opinion to the contrary.

This passage gives at once an application of the principle contained in the principium of the fragment. The period which is decisive for assessing damages is the moment when the injury has been done, and from thence backwards the year, according to the first chapter—the thirty days according to the third chapter—are to be fixed. There was, however, a doubt possible in case a slave was wounded mortally, but did not die till a long time after the wound had been inflicted on him. According to the opinion of Celsus he was 'occisus' at the moment of his death, and therefore the year to be taken into account when assessing the highest value of the slave was the year reckoned backwards from that period. According to the opinion of Julian, however, which, as Ulpian states, is commonly recognised (see also 15. § 1 above), the year is to be reckoned from the moment the deadly wound has been inflicted on the slave.

Pernice, p. 239; Windscheid, n. 20; Savigny, System, vol. V. p. 214.

21. § 2.—Sed utrum corpus eius solum aestimamus, quanti fuerit cum occideretur, an potius quanti interfuit nostra non esse occisum? et hoc iure utimur ut eius quod interest fiat aestimatio.

It was, however, questioned whether we should assess only the value of the slave himself, that is, how much he was worth when he was killed, or whether we should assess the interest we have in his not being killed. And it is a recognised law with us that the interest is to be assessed.

We are told in the Institutes (h. t. § 10), that the words 'quanti ea res .... fuerit' in the lex Aquilia referred originally to the market value of the thing damaged or destroyed, but gradually they were understood by the jurists as comprehending the whole loss which the injured person had sustained by the damage to his property (the word 'property' being taken in the sense of a universitas or complex of legal relations, rights as well as duties); accordingly compensation was to be given for everything which the plaintiff had lost through the act of damage; in other words, the *difference* in the plaintiff's property, as it was after the damaging act and as it would have been if the act had not been committed; and this so-called interesse or interest became the object of the action (cf. 22, 23 pr. §§ 2, 4, 5, 6).

In the case therefore which is supposed in the fragment we are considering, when a slave has been killed, compensation is to be given not only for his mere market value, i.e. for what he was worth to everybody, but for the whole loss sustained by his master through the act of killing, or, in other words, for what the slave was worth to his master as a portion of his property, 'quanti interfuit nostra non esse occisum.' As a rule, this interest will go beyond the market value of the thing, and only such cases are contemplated by Paulus in the above passage, as well as in the passage of the Institutes which we have quoted (I. IV. 3. § 10); but it is possible that this interest may be less than the market value; for instance, if the creditor pignoris sues for compensation under the lex Aquilia, his interest in the thing damaged is naturally restricted to full satisfaction for his claim secured by the pignus given to him. (Cf. 30. § 1 below: other instances are to be found in D. 43. 17. 3. § 11; D. 43. 16. 6; D. 4. 2. 21. § 2; D. 47. 2. 46. 1.)

It is of course understood that though the jurists gradually substituted the notion of the interest for that of the ordinary or the market value of the thing, nothing was altered as to the period with reference to which compensation was to be assessed, namely, the last year (or last month) previous to the inquiry.

Pernice, p. 242; Windscheid, n. 19; Savigny, System, vol. V. p. 444; Vangerow, vol. III. p. 585.

22 *pr.*—Paulus libro XXII ad edictum. Proinde si seruum occidisti, quem sub poena tradendum promisi, utilitas uenit in hoc iudicium.

Accordingly, if you have killed a slave whom I have promised to transfer into the ownership of another under a penalty, the interest will be the object of the action.

The case underlying the decision of Paulus is the following: I have promised to somebody else to transfer to him ownership in a slave of mine (for the word 'tradere' is technically used to denote the transfer of ownership, 'traditio' being one of the acquisitiones naturales of ownership). In order to give greater security for the fulfilment of this obligation (cf. D. 45. 1. 68) I have made the promise under a penalty. It must be understood that this promise was made in the form of a stipulation, for otherwise it would have been nudum pactum, which in Roman law was not actionable, D. II. 14. 7. § 4. But before I have fulfilled my primary duty, you have killed the slave whom I had promised to transfer. Being thus unable to fulfil my promise, I must pay the penalty to the stipulator. Accordingly you are liable to indemnify me for the loss of the advantage (utilitas) of freeing myself from paying the penalty by the transfer of the slave.

It is obvious that such loss of the plaintiff is not the immediate and necessary consequence of the act of injury (like the loss of the slave), but is produced indirectly by certain other circumstances, i.e. in the above case by the fact of the stipulatio having been made. The notion of 'interest,' however, requires that not only the damage directly sustained by the plaintiff (damnum directum), but also all such damage as results through the medium of other circumstances (damnum indirectum) should be taken into account, because the plaintiff is to be put into the condition in which he would have been if the damaging act had not been committed.

The word 'utilitas' in the passage is frequently used as an equivalent to the phrase 'id quod interest,' i.e. the interest of the plaintiff. In using these expressions the Roman jurists had in view the condition of the plaintiff's property after the damaging act, and from this point of view the interest appeared to be an advantage (utilitas) which had been lost and was to be recovered. (D. II. 11. 14; D. 13. 4. 2. pr. § 8; D. 19. 1. 11. § 18; D. 43. 4. 1. § 5; D. 47. 2. 81. § 1; D. 39. 2. 4. § 7; Mommsen, Beiträge, vol. II. p. 41.)

22. § 1.—Item causae corpori cohaerentes aestimantur, si quis ex comoedis aut symphoniacis aut gemellis aut quadriga aut ex pari mularum unum uel unam occiderit: non solum enim peremti corporis aestimatio facienda est, sed et eius ratio haberi debet, quo cetera corpora depreciata sunt.

Similarly the particular circumstances attaching to the thing itself are to be taken into account as if one of a company of slave actors or orchestra players, or one of a pair of twins, or one of four chariot-horses, or of a pair of mules is killed; for not only the value of the individual thing is to be assessed, but also account is to be taken of the extent to which other things have been depreciated.

We are told in this fragment that the causae corpori cohaerentes, i. e. those peculiar circumstances which had an influence on its value for the injured person are to be taken into account. Accordingly, if one of a set of things which form together one whole is destroyed, in addition to the value of the thing destroyed it must be ascertained to what extent the other things have been depreciated. Suppose, for example, that one of four chariot-horses which are together worth £1000, whilst each of them is worth only £100, is killed. In such a case the damage directly inflicted on the owner is £100, but the indirect loss, sustained in consequence of the causa corpori cohaerens, is £600, as there are left only three single horses being worth together £300. It is obvious that these remarks apply equally to the other cases in the passage, all of which are instances where the loss sustained in consequence of the existence of particular facts, other than the act of damage itself, is to be assessed by the court. (Cf. the pr. of the above fragment, and 23 pr. § 4 below; further, D. 19. 1. 13 pr.; D. 19. 2. 19. § 1; D. 13. 6. 18 pr.

Pernice, p. 241; Windscheid, § 455. n. 19, and § 258. nn. 12 and 13.

23 *pr.*—Ulpianus libro XVIII ad edictum. Inde Neratius scribit, si seruus heres institutus occisus sit, etiam hereditatis aestimationem uenire.

Neratius writes that in case a slave has been killed who was instituted an heir, the value of the inheritance will have to be taken into account.

This passage contains another example of a case in which special damage is caused to a person, over and above the ordinary damage, by reason of a particular circumstance, viz. the fact that the slave who has been killed has been instituted an heir. It is well known that in such cases the slave could enter on the inheritance only by order of his master, who thus acquired the inheritance through the slave in the same way as he would acquire any other right. In the case we are considering, however, the slave had been killed before he had entered on the inheritance, and accordingly it could not be acquired for the master, who was thus prevented from making a gain to which he was entitled. It is consequently not only the positive loss which the plaintiff had sustained, directly or indirectly, which constitutes the interest to be recovered by the Aquilian action (the so-called damnum emergens) but also the negative loss inflicted on the plaintiff by not having made a gain which he would have made without the interference of the damaging act, i. e. the lucrum cessans. Although, on principle, the notion of interesse embraces equally positive and negative loss, it is easier to establish the evidence required in case of positive damage, for in the one only the causal connection between two facts, viz. the act of damage and the loss inflicted on the plaintiff, is to be proved, whereas in the other evidence is to be given that, if a certain act had not been performed, another fact would have been existing, evidence which, strictly speaking, it is impossible to give. For on one hand, it is in itself always doubtful whether the injured party would have availed himself of the opportunity of the acquisition offered to him, and, on the other hand, it may be doubted whether, in case the injury had not been committed, all the other requisites would have been in existence (Fr. Mommsen, Beiträge, vol. II. p. 174 sq.). It is, however, generally assumed, that any act which would have been performed by a diligens paterfamilias, would not have been omitted by the injured party. Applying this principle to the case we are discussing, we infer that an order to enter on a (solvent) inheritance would have been given by the master of the slave instituted; and as to the other requirements of the acquisition (e. g. whether the slave instituted would have been still alive, if he had not been killed), doubts are hardly admissible that they would have existed, if the slave had not been slain before he had entered on the inheritance (cf. D. h. t. 51; I. h. t. § 10; and Gaius III. 212). Accordingly it is decided by Neratius that the value of the inheritance is to be taken into account in assessing the damages.

Windscheid, § 455. n. 19, and § 258. n. 16; Friedr. Mommsen, Beiträge, vol. II. p. 179.

23. § 1.—Iulianus ait, si seruus liber et heres esse iussus occisus fuerit, neque substitutum neque legitimum actione legis Aquiliae hereditatis aestimationem consecuturum, quae seruo competere non potuit: quae sententia uera est. pretii igitur solummodo fieri aestimationem, quia hoc interesse solum substituti uideretur: ego autem puto nec pretii fieri aestimationem, quia, si heres esset, et liber esset.

Julian says, if a slave who was freed and instituted an heir has been killed, neither the heir substituted in his place nor the intestate heir of the testator will receive, by the Aquilian action, the value of the inheritance, which could not belong to the slave, and this opinion is correct. Therefore there will be only an assessment of the value, because this only seems to be the interest of the substitute. I think, however, that there will be no assessment even of the slave's value, for if he had not been killed, and had thus become the heir of the deceased, he would have been a free man.

In opposition to the principium of the fragment, the above section gives an instance in which the value of the inheritance cannot be claimed, although a slave who was instituted an heir had been killed unlawfully. The case supposed by the jurist is the following:—A slave was manumitted in the will of his master, and at the same time instituted his heir. Accordingly he was a so-called heres necessarius, i.e. an heir who necessarily by force of law acquired the inheritance of the testator as soon as it was offered to him, which happened, as a rule, when the testator died. But before the death of the testator the instituted slave had been slain, and therefore the inheritance was acquired by the person who was instituted as heir by the testator in case the slave should not become his heir, i. e. the substitute; or if the substitute did not take the inheritance, or if a substitution had not been made, by the heir-at-law (legitimus) of the testator. It is obvious that the substitute (or intestate heir) cannot claim compensation for the inheritance which could not belong to the slave as long as he was not manumitted, and which, besides, had been acquired by the substitute himself precisely in consequence of the death of the slave. Julian therefore thought that the interesse claimed by the Aquilian action would consist only in the value of the slave, clearly for the reason that the right of action was already acquired for the deceased, and accordingly transferred to his heir as a portion of the inheritance. Ulpian, however, thought that even the value of the slave could not be claimed by the injured person, for if he had not been killed, and had thus become the heir of the testator—'si heres esset'—he would also be a free man. In other words, the testator had, by the manumissio testamento, exempted the slave from becoming in future times part of his inheritance; the slave is accordingly not a possible object of value to the heir, and therefore no damage whatever is done to him by the act of killing. Without 'damnum,' however, no Aquilian action is applicable, although some corporeal thing has been unlawfully violated (see Part II. § 8).

Pernice, pp. 98 sq. and 184.

23. § 2.—Idem Iulianus scribit, si institutus fuero sub condicione 'si Stichum manumisero' et Stichus sit occisus post mortem testatoris, in aestimationem etiam hereditatis pretium me consecuturum: propter occisionem enim deficit condicio: quod si uiuo testatore occisus sit, hereditatis aestimationem cessare, quia retrorsum quanti plurimi fuit inspicitur.

The same Julian writes that in case I have been instituted an heir under the condition 'if I shall have manumitted the slave Stichus,' and Stichus has been killed after the death of the testator, I shall recover as part of the damages the value of the inheritance, for on account of the act of killing the fulfilment of the condition has been rendered impossible. But if the slave has been killed during the lifetime of the testator the value of the inheritance is not assessed, because in estimating what was the highest value in the year, you reckon backwards from the time when the act was done.

The case supposed by Julian is that I have been instituted as heir under the condition of manumitting my slave Stichus. But before I had complied with this condition Stichus was killed by a third person. I was consequently unable to fulfil the condition of the institution—defecit conditio—and thus could not acquire the inheritance left to me. The question arises whether I shall receive by the Aquilian action not only compensation for the value of the slave, but also for that of the inheritance, which clearly is a so-called lucrum cessans. This question is answered in the affirmative in case Stichus has been killed after the death of the testator, for here there was no possibility of acquiring through the medium of the slave, i.e. by manumitting him, the inheritance offered. But if Stichus had been killed in the lifetime of the testator, there was clearly not yet an inheritance to be acquired (viventis non datur hereditas, D. 29. 2. 27; D. 18. 4. 1; Arndts, § 469), and therefore the particular circumstance, that the owner of the slave had been instituted as heir under the condition of manumitting the slave, did not as yet increase his value for his master; he was not yet a medium by which the inheritance could be acquired. It is true that, if the testator died afterwards (without having altered his will), the owner of the slave was equally prevented from taking the inheritance; but the loss of this advantage, which did not exist in the lifetime of the slave, could not be taken into account, because, in assessing compensation, we have to reckon backwards from the act of damage (see the notes to 21 pr. above).

Fr. Mommsen, Beiträge, vol. II. pp. 180 and 202; Windscheid, § 258. n. 16; § 455. n. 19 and 20.

23. § 3.—Idem Iulianus scribit aestimationem hominis occisi ad id tempus referri, quo plurimi in eo anno fuit: et ideo et si pretioso pictori pollex fuerit praecisus et intra annum, quo praecideretur, fuerit occisus, posse eum Aquilia agere pretioque eo aestimandum, quanti fuit priusquam artem cum pollice amisisset.

The same Julian writes that the assessment of the value of the slave who is killed is made with reference to the period at which he had the highest value in that year, and therefore, if a slave who is valuable as a painter has had his right thumb cut off, and within a year of its being cut off he has been killed, his master can sue under the Aquilian action, and in the assessment the slave must be reckoned at the price he was worth before he had been deprived of his skill by the loss of his thumb.

The case discussed by Julian is very simple: a slave of very high value, who was a distinguished painter, had become almost valueless from having had his right thumb cut off, and consequently being disabled from exercising his profession any longer. But before one year had passed, say after eleven months, the slave was unlawfully killed by another person, who, accordingly, can be sued under the first chapter of the statute. It is decided that his master[1] will get compensation for the value which the slave had before the loss of his thumb, i. e. the highest value of the slave during the last year previous to the act of killing.

Unlike the previous passages (21. § 2–23. § 2), according to which the whole interesse, damnum directum and indirectum, damnum emergens and lucrum cessans, is the object of the action, the passage we are discussing speaks only of the value of the thing which has been destroyed. But this does not make any difference. It is, according to the interpretation of the jurists, always the interesse of the plaintiff which is to be fixed, with reference to that period of the last year which is most favourable to the plaintiff; but this interesse may consist—and will probably consist in most cases—only in the real, or market value, of the thing; and this is supposed in the above case, which does not mention any particular circumstance which would increase the value of the slave for his master.

Windscheid, n. 20.

23. § 4.—Sed et si seruus, qui magnas fraudes in meis rationibus commiserat, fuerit occisus, de quo quaestionem habere destinaueram, ut fraudium participes eruerentur, rectissime Labeo scribit tanti aestimandum, quanti mea intererat fraudes serui per eum commissas detegi, non quanti noxa eius serui ualeat.

[1] Cuiacius proposes to read 'erum' instead of 'eum;' a highly probable conjecture, although it does not affect the sense of the passage.

But if a slave of mine has been killed, who had committed extensive frauds in administering my property, and whom I intended to put to the torture in order that his accomplices in these frauds might be detected, Labeo writes very properly that the amount assessed must equal my interest in having the frauds committed by the slave discovered, not merely the value of the noxious slave.

In this passage clearly a lucrum cessans is in question. My slave, who had, together with some other persons, defrauded me in the management of my property, has been killed. If this had not been the case, I should have been in a condition to learn from him the names of his accomplices, and, accordingly, to sue them (or their masters) for compensation and penalties on account of the delict committed by them. One may object to this, that it is uncertain whether the slave would have named his accomplices. But according to common experience a bad slave always did so if put to the rack; and as in the above case the master actually intended to have a quaestio[1], i.e. an interrogation by torture, in order to learn the truth, we must assume that he really would have gained the advantage to be derived from such an inquisition. Accordingly, the master's interest in the discovery of the frauds committed, and not merely the value of the guilty slave (noxa), is the object of the action. The word 'noxa' is here used in the sense of the individual who has done the damage (so also in I. 4. 8. § 1); more commonly the word 'noxa' or 'noxia' is used to denote the act or delict by which damage was caused, D. 50. 16. 131 pr.; I. 4. 8. § 1; D. 9. 1. 1. § 1; sometimes it also signifies the damage itself caused by the act, D. 9. 1. 1. § 11, or the compensation for such damage, as in the words noxae s. ad noxam dedere, noxae deditio, noxae accipere, D. 7. 1. 17. § 2; cf. Heumann, Handlexicon zu den Quellen des römischen Rechts, 4th edit., Jena, 1869; and Dirksen, Manuale Latinitatis ——, Berolini, 1837, sub vv. noxa and noxia.

Pernice, p. 242; Windscheid, n. 19.

[1] A definition of quaestio, which was commonly employed against slaves in order to extort the truth from them, is given by Ulpian in D. 47. 10. 15. § 41: 'Quaestionem intellegere debemus tormenta et corporis dolorem ad eruendam veritatem.—Quaestionis verbo etiam ea quam malam mansionem dicunt, continebitur. cum igitur per vim et tormenta quaestio est, tunc quaestio intellegitur.' Cf. also Paul. Sent. Rec. v. 14, 16; D. 48. 1. 8: C. 9. 41; Rudorff, Römische Rechtsgeschichte, vol. ii. p. 445.

23. § 5.—Sed et si bonae frugi seruus intra annum mutatis moribus occisus sit, pretium id aestimabitur, quanto ualeret, priusquam mores mutaret.

But also if an honest slave has been killed, after he has changed his character within the year, the value which he had before the change took place is to be assessed in the Aquilian action.

The passage is a simple application of the principle that the highest value of the slave during the year previous to the act of killing is the object of the action under the first chapter (cf. § 3 above).

Windscheid, n. 20.

23. § 6.—In summa omnia commoda, quae intra annum quo interfectus est pretiosiorem seruum facerent, haec accedere ad aestimationem eius dicendum est.

In short, we must say that everything which would render the slave more valuable within the last year is to be included in the assessment of his value.

This sentence gives a short abstract of the different cases in the fragments 22 and 23 pr.–§ 5 above. The object of the action under Chapter I. of the Aquilian statute is the whole interest of the plaintiff, who at the same time can claim to have that interest assessed with reference to any period of the year previous to the act of killing (21. § 2 above). Accordingly we are told in the present passage that every circumstance which would increase the value of the slave to his master is to be taken into account in assessing the damages; e. g. the fact that the master was in a condition to avoid payment of a penalty by the transfer of the slave (22 pr.), that the individual thing killed (slave, horse, mule, etc.) belonged to a certain set of things the remainder of which were diminished in their value (22. § 1), or that something would have been gained by means of the killed slave, e. g. an inheritance, or the right of suing his accomplices (23 pr. §§ 2 and 4), or that the slave himself had had a higher value at some time within the last year (23. §§ 3 and 5).

Windscheid, n. 20; Savigny, System, vol. V. p. 444 n. c.

23. § 7.—Si infans sit occisus nondum anniculus, uerius est sufficere hanc actionem, ut aestimatio referatur ad id tempus quo intra annum uixit.

If a child not yet one year old has been killed, the better opinion is that the action can be maintained, so long as the assessment refers to that period during which the child was living within the last year.

According to this passage the question seems to have been discussed whether an action under the first chapter was applicable if a slave child less than one year old was killed. It is, however, decided that the action should lie, but the assessment under it had to be made with reference to the time during which the child was alive, for previously to its birth the child had no independent existence of its own, and therefore was not yet the object of valuation. But in all cases where reference to the whole of the last year was possible, the value might be taken at any period of the year, even although the plaintiff had not been entitled to the thing injured during the whole time; see 12 above. Windscheid, n. 20.

23. § 8.—Hanc actionem et heredi ceterisque successoribus dari constat: sed in heredem uel ceteros haec actio non dabitur, cum sit poenalis, nisi forte ex damno locupletior heres factus sit.

It is settled that this action is also given to the heir and to the other successors, but it does not lie against them, unless the heir has been made richer by the act of damage.

It is an established rule that the Aquilian action, like other actions, is transmitted to the heir of the injured person and to the other successors who may take the place of the heir, as the bonorum possessor and the universal fideicommissary, unless there are such special circumstances as are mentioned in § 15, § 1. i. f., 23. § 1 and 36. § 1. But the Aquilian action does not lie against the heir of the delinquent or against his other successors, and this is explained by the penal character of that action, 'cum sit poenalis,' a characteristic which is likewise attached to it in many other passages, D. h. t. 11. § 2, 51. §§ 1, 2; Paulus, Sent. Rec. I. 13. a. § 6; Gaius, III. 211. If, however, we remember that its object is compensation, we should be inclined to look upon it as a so-called reipersecutoria actio, or, in cases where a surplus beyond the real compensation can be claimed, an actio mixta, an assumption which is strongly supported by Justinian in I. IV. 6. § 19. But this was certainly not the view of those jurists from whose writings the fragments in the Digest are taken. They not only called the actio legis Aquiliae a penal action, but in practice they treated it also as a penal action; compensation in their idea being claimed as a penalty by that action. Accordingly, (1) the Aquilian action was available, like other penal actions, as actio noxalis, where damage was done by a slave or filius familias, Gaius, IV. 75; D. 47. 1. 1. § 2. (2) If several persons joined in the commission of unlawful damage, each was liable to pay the whole damages (11. § 2 above), whilst in reipersecutoriae actiones compensation was to be given only once (C. 4. 8. 1). (3) The Aquilian action, like other actions ex delicto, does not lie against the heir of the delinquent (Gaius, IV. 112, I. IV. 12. 1; D. 50. 17. 111. § 1), a rule which is recognised in the fragment we are considering. But the heir ought not to make any profit out of the delict of the deceased—as, for instance, he would do if he had eaten the meat of the ox slain, or had sold its skin, etc.—and therefore he is declared to be liable to an action as far as his property is increased by the damaging act. But it must be noticed that he is not liable on account of the delict of the deceased as his successor, but merely on account of the increase of his property which had taken place without a justifiable cause. The action therefore given against the heir is in its true nature a condictio ex iniusta causa (D. 47. 8. 2. § 27; D. 43. 16. 1. § 48) and not the action arising under the delict of the lex Aquilia (D. 10. 3. 10 and I. IV. 3. § 9).

Pernice, p. 126; Windscheid, n. 22 and 28; Savigny, System, vol. V. p. 50; Brinz, § 340. n. 39.

23. § 9.—Si dolo seruus occisus sit, et lege Cornelia agere dominum posse constat: et si lege Aquilia egerit, praeiudicium fieri Corneliae non debet.

If a slave has been killed maliciously, his master may also proceed against the delinquent under the lex Cornelia, and the fact of his having first sued under the Aquilian statute ought to be no prejudice to a proceeding ex lege Cornelia.

The lex Cornelia, viz. de sicariis et veneficis, provided, amongst other cases, against murder and manslaughter (see 5 pr. above) without any distinction as to the legal condition of the killed person (I. IV. 3. § 11; D. 48. 8. 1. § 2; and D. 19. 5. 14. § 1). Accordingly, if a slave has been killed intentionally, as supposed in the above passage, both the actions, the Cornelian and Aquilian, were applicable, and, as is further stated in the fragment we are considering, and also in C. 9. 31. 1, the injured person was not prevented from proceeding against the delinquent under the Aquilian statute. This statement seems to be contradicted by D. 48. 1. 4, but this passage only forbids the prosecution of the delinquent criminally whilst the Aquilian action is still pending (cf. D. 47. 8. 2. § 1); there is, however, no objection to proceeding with the criminal action when the Aquilian action had once been decided.

Pernice, pp. 103 and 131.

23. § 10.—Haec actio aduersus confitentem competit in simplum, aduersus negantem in duplum.

This action lies in simplum against a person who admits his liability, in duplum against him who denies it.

Ulpian having hitherto, in his commentary on the edict, book 18, fully interpreted the terms of the first chapter (see the fragments 3, 5, 7, 9, 11, 13, 15, 17, 19, 21, 23 pr.–§ 7, and their inscriptions), and having added some general remarks as to the transmission of the action and its concurrence with other actions (in 23. §§ 8, 9), turns, in the above passage, to the consideration of the formulae, the terms of which, however, are not handed down to us. As indicated by the words of the passage, two different actions—and, accordingly, two formulae—were given under the first chapter: an actio confessoria, if the defendant admitted his liability before the praetor, and an actio in infitiantem, in case he denied it, and thus compelled the plaintiff to prove the claim asserted by him (see notes to 2. § 2 above). The actio confessoria was the first actio dealt with in the edict, as we may gather from fr. 23. §§ 12 and 25 of Ulpian, and 24, taken from the commentaries of Paulus to the edict. No doubt, both the edict and commentaries mentioned, in the second place, the actio aduersus infitiantem, but there is no reference to it in the title of the Digest which we are explaining, these portions having been cancelled by the compilers. In its place we find two other actions, shortly discussed in 27 pr.–§ 3 below (also in D. 9. 4. 2), both arising under the first chapter: the actio in solidum aduersus dominum, si seruus sciente domino occiderit, and the actio noxalis, si seruus insciente domino occiderit.

It is hardly necessary to say that the simplum which is claimed by the actio confessoria is, according to the terms of the lex, the highest value during the last year (or during the last month, under Chapter III.), and, according to the interpretation of the jurists, the interesse of the plaintiff (21. § 2 above) is to be fixed with reference to that period. This simplum was to be doubled if the defendant denied his liability. Similarly, the interesse is to be doubled, or quadrupled, in case of an actio de seruo corrupto, actio quod metus causa, etc., D. 11. 3. 10; D. 4. 2. 14. § 7; D. 40. 12. 18. In case of an actio furti, however, the basis of the penalty to be paid is the value of the stolen thing, which is to be either duplicated or quadruplicated, D. 47. 2. 50 pr. The object of the actio vi bonorum raptorum is a quadruplum of the market value, and not of the interesse, D. 47. 8. 2. § 13.

Vangerow, vol. III. p. 579; Lenel, Das Edictum perpetuum, p. 157.

23. § 11.—Si quis hominem uiuum falso confiteatur occidisse et postea paratus sit ostendere hominem uiuum esse, Iulianus scribit cessare Aquiliam, quamuis confessus sit se occidisse: hoc enim solum remittere actori confessoriam actionem, ne necesse habeat docere eum occidisse: ceterum occisum esse hominem a quocumque oportet.

If a person has falsely admitted that he has killed a slave who is alive, and afterwards is ready to prove that the slave is living, Julian writes that the Aquilian action cannot be maintained, notwithstanding that the defendant has admitted that he killed the slave, for the actio confessoria only releases the plaintiff from the necessity of proving that the defendant has killed the slave; the slave, however, must have been killed by somebody.

It is well known that a defendant who has admitted his liability in iure was looked upon by the Roman law in the same way as if he had been condemned by a judicial sentence. Confessus pro iudicato est' is the principle expressed in several passages, D. 42. 2. 1; Paulus, Sent. Rec. V. 2. §. 2; C. 7. 59. There was, however, under the formulary procedure, this difference between confessio and iudicatum, that the latter always contained a condemnation to pay a certain sum of money. Therefore it was only in cases where an action was brought for a definite sum of money, and was admitted by the defendant, that the whole dispute w s at an end. In other cases, where the defendant admitted merely his liability, but could not be induced to assent to pay the sum of compensation claimed by the plaintiff (D. 42. 2. 6. § 1), a further proceeding was necessary, a so-called iudicium or arbitrium rei aestimandae, 25. § 2, the only object of which was to assess the damages occasioned by the injury, liability for which was admitted by the defendant. Accordingly, the confessio may be compared with a pronuntiatio in case of actiones arbitrariae, which similarly, if not complied with by the defendant, was to be completed by judicial proceedings, in order to assess compensation for the plaintiff, D. 42. 2. 6. § 2. But the confessio has the effect mentioned only if the fact which was admitted by the defendant was not impossible. 'In totum autem confessiones ita ratae sunt, si id quod in confessionem uenit et ius et naturam recipere potest,' says Javolenus in D. 11. 1. 14. § 1; cf. also D. h. t. 24 and 25 pr.; D. 42. 2. 4 and 8. Otherwise the confessio cannot take any effect. A case of this kind is supposed in the above fragment. The defendant has admitted that he had killed unlawfully the plaintiff's slave, 'seruum iniuria occisum esse a se' (cf. the words in the rubric of Coll. XII. 7, 'Si fatebitur iniuria occisum;' to which 'a se' must be added, according to the passage we are considering). But, in fact, the slave was still alive, and the defendant was afterwards ready to prove this fact. In such cases, Julian says, 'cessare Aquiliam,' in spite of the admission. It is true that, in virtue of such admission ('actione confessoria'), the plaintiff is released from the necessity of proving his assertion, viz. that the defendant has unlawfully killed the slave, but the fact which is thus established does not hold good against the evidence to the effect that the object of the confessio itself was impossible, as in the above case, where the defendant had proved that the slave was still alive, or, as supposed in 25 pr., that the slave, although he had died, had not been killed. But it would not be sufficient for the defendant to prove that the slave was killed by a third person, for in this way the assumption that the defendant had participated in some way or other in the commission of the delict would not be absolutely excluded, and this idea is clearly stated in D. 42. 2. 4, a fragment with which the final words of our passage, 'ceterum occisum esse hominem a quocunque oportet,' are entirely in accordance.

Pernice, pp. 109 sq., 112 sq.; Savigny, System, vol. VIII. pp. 7 and 18 sqq.; Keller, Civilprocess, § 63.

24.—Paulus libro XXII ad edictum. Hoc apertius est circa uulneratum hominem: nam si confessus sit uulnerasse nec sit uulneratus, aestimationem cuius uulneris faciemus? uel ad quod tempus recurramus?

This is more obvious with regard to a wounded slave; for if some one has admitted that he has wounded a slave who has not been wounded, there is clearly neither a wound to be assessed in money value, nor a period with reference to which compensation may be fixed.

This passage is fully explained by the notes to 23. § 11 above. But there is this difference between the two passages, that in case of the admission of having killed the slave the value of the slave might be assessed in a sum of money, whilst in case of the admission of having wounded a slave, the compensation naturally would depend on the nature of a particular wound inflicted, and therefore, if there is no wound, assessment is absolutely impossible.

Savigny, System, vol. VII. pp. 18 sq.

25 *pr.*—Ulpianus libro XVIII ad edictum. Proinde si occisus quidem non sit, mortuus autem sit, magis est, ut non teneatur in mortuo, licet fassus sit.

Similarly, if the slave had not been killed, but had died, according to the better opinion, the defendant is not liable in respect of the dead slave, although he has admitted that he has killed him.

The passage is clearly a continuation of 23. § 11, and presupposes, accordingly, the same case, namely, that the defendant has admitted that he has unlawfully killed a slave. In such cases, according to the above fragment, the Aquilian statute cannot take effect, if it is afterwards proved by the defendant, that although the slave had died, his death was not due to the wound inflicted on him, but to another cause, e. g. internal disease or accident. This opinion, however, seems to have been accepted only after some hesitation (—magis est, ut teneatur—), the reason clearly being that such cases were more capable of admitting a doubt, whether it was absolutely impossible that the slave had been killed. But as the counter-evidence given by the defendant might be fully sufficient to show such impossibility, e. g. if the defendant had proved that the slave had not sustained any injury, and died from an inherited internal disease, the opinion stated in the above text was commonly recognised.

See the notes to 23. § 11, and the passages quoted there.

25. § 1.—Si procurator aut tutor aut curator aut quiuis alius confiteatur *aut* absentem uulnerasse, confessoria in eos utilis actio danda est.

If a procurator or tutor or curator or any other person has admitted that the person represented by him has inflicted a wound, an actio confessoria utilis is to be given against them.

Before any explanation of the passage the text of it has to be settled, for the reading '*aut* absentem uulnerasse' is clearly wrong. We must either cancel the 'aut,' as due to an error in transcription, or suppose that some words introduced by a second aut have dropped out. Mommsen, taking the latter view, proposes to insert after 'aut absentem' the words 'aut pupillum aut adultum.' This is, however, not satisfactory, for (1) there would be no parallelism between the persons representing, four in number, and the persons represented, three in number, and (2) any such addition seems to be superfluous, for if a procurator, tutor, curator are said to have made a confessio, it is implied that they have done so only for the person represented by them. It is only with reference to the 'quiuis alius' in the passage that it was necessary to express that he had admitted the liability of the person represented by him (absentem uulnerasse), and therefore it seems to be correct to follow the edition of Kriegel in cancelling the word 'aut' before 'absentem.'

The case supposed in the decision of the jurist is very simple: A person has committed damage to property and on that account an actio utilis has been brought by the injured party against his representative: his tutor or curator—if he was under tutela (impuberum) or cura (minorum or prodigi)—or his procurator, i. e. an agent who had been ordered by the delinquent to defend his case, or somebody else who had taken his place without being ordered to do so (D. 44. 2. 11. § 7; D. 46. 3. 23; Keller, Röm. Civilprocess, n. 720). In case a representative admitted in iure the liability of the person represented by him, as supposed in the above fragment, then not the dominus or principal, but the representative himself was bound by the confessio, exactly in the same way as if he had denied the claim of the plaintiff in iure, and litiscontestatio had therefore taken place. In case of litiscontestatio with a representative, he became formally a party to the suit, whether he took the place of the plaintiff or the defendant. For although the formula contained in its intentio the disputed legal relation and the names of the original parties to it, yet the condemnatio contained always the name of the representative. If therefore an action was brought against the representative, and he denied the claim asserted by the plaintiff, he was condemned in person by the final judicial sentence, a necessity expressed in the formula by which the iudex was instructed. Accordingly, the formula, in case a definite sum of money was recovered—by condictio certi—from a representative of the real debtor, ran as follows: Si paret Publium Maevium Aulo Agerio H. S. x milia dare oportere, iudex Lucium Titium Aulo Agerio H. S. x milia condemna, si non paret absolve (Keller, Röm. Civilprocess, § 52). In the same way as the representative was to be condemned in consequence of the litiscontestatio, so he became subject to the legal consequences attached to the confessio, if he had admitted the liability of his principal; therefore the actio confessoria was to be given against him, but as an analogous action (actio utilis), for he—not being the delinquent—was not liable under the terms of the Aquilian statute itself. Thus the effect of the action formally attached to the person of the confessus; practically, however, it was secured against the person represented, and therefore the actio iudicati, in order to enforce the contents of the judicial decision, was given against him.

Keller, Röm. Civilprocess, § 64. n. 732 and § 53.

25. § 2.—Notandum, quod in hac actione, quae aduersus confitentem datur, iudex non rei iudicandae, sed aestimandae datur: nam nullae partes sunt iudicandi in confitentes.

26 *pr.*—Paulus libro XXII ad edictum. Puta enim, quod qui conuenitur fateatur se occidisse et paratus sit aestimationem soluere, et aduersarius magni litem aestimat.

It must be noticed that in this action which lies against a person who admits his liability, the judge is not appointed in order to decide the case, but to assess damages, for there are no judicial functions to be performed against persons who admit their liability. Such an assessment is necessary, for the defendant may admit that he has killed the slave and may be ready to pay compensation, but may say that his adversary assesses it too highly.

According to the previous notes a person who has admitted his liability in iure is in the same condition as a iudicatus, provided of course that the confession is valid, e.g. not impossible, as supposed in 23. § 11, 24 and 25 pr. above (see Keller, Röm. Civilprocess, § 63. n. 730–735). Accordingly, the iudex cannot inquire whether damage was really done unlawfully or not (nullae sunt partes iudicandi), but his only possible task is to assess the sum of money to be given as compensation to the plaintiff. But this is of course necessary only if the defendant, whilst admitting his liability, does not consent to pay the sum claimed by the plaintiff.

Savigny, System, vol. VII. pp. 10 and 18 sq.

27 *pr.*—Ulpianus libro XVIII ad edictum. Si seruus seruum alienum subripuerit et occiderit, et Iulianus et Celsus scribunt et furti et damni iniuriae competere actionem.

If a slave has stolen the slave of another and has killed him, Julian and Celsus write that an actio furti and an actio damni iniuriae are applicable.

In the case suggested by Julian and Celsus there are two different delicts: a furtum, because a slave had been stolen, and a damnum iniuria datum, because he had been afterwards killed by the thief. Accordingly, there are two separate claims for penalties, and therefore also two different actions available in favour of the injured person, and if one action is brought the other is not extinguished, as is expressly stated in D. 47. 1. 2. § 1; see also in the same fragment the pr. and §§ 2, 4, 5, 6 and D. h. t. 32. § 1. It is, however, different if substantially there is only one claim existing between the parties, although several actions are applicable in order to enforce it, e. g. if a res commodata, deposita, pignori data, etc., has been unlawfully damaged by the person to whom it was entrusted under the contract. In consequence of this damage a claim for compensation arises. This claim, however, may be enforced either by an action on the contract or by an action of delict for damage to property. One action excludes the other; only in case the delinquent was sued first on the contract and something more could be claimed under the peculiar provisions of the lex Aquilia, this surplus might still be obtained by bringing an Aquilian action; D. h. t. 18; D. 19. 2. 43; D. 44. 7. 34. § 2; D. 17. 2. 47. But it was a matter of great controversy among the Roman jurists whether this principle was to be applied if several *penal* actions had arisen between the same persons, e. g. if a person had been robbed, in which case an actio vi bonorum raptorum, as well as an actio furti, was applicable; D. 44. 7. 32, 34 pr., 53, 60; cf. also Savigny, System, vol. V. § 234; Vangerow, vol. III. § 572; Arndts, § 105. n. 1. i. f. In the case we are considering, it is supposed that a slave has committed the delicts and therefore noxal actions are applicable against his master (Gaius, IV. 76, and I. IV. 8. 4). It must, however, be noticed that a noxal action on account of damage done to property lies only if the act was committed *insciente* domino, for if it were done *sciente* domino, i. e. if the master knew of the commission of the delict and was at the same time in a condition to hinder the act, he is liable in the same way as if he had committed the delict himself (see D. 9. o. f. 2 pr. in comparison with D. h. t. 45 pr.). In accordance with this exposition there are, in addition to the actio confessoria and the actio aduersus infitiantem, two other actions applicable under the first chapter of the Aquilian statute: the action in solidum aduersus dominum, si seruus sciente domino occiderit, and the actio noxalis, si seruus insciente domino occiderit.

O. Lenel, Das Edictum perpetuum, p. 157; Savigny, System, vol. V. p. 236.

27. § 1.—Si seruus communis, id est meus et tuus, seruum meum occiderit, legi Aquiliae locus est aduersus te, si tua uoluntate fecit: et ita Proculum existimasse Urseius refert. Quod si non uoluntate tua fecit, cessare noxalem actionem, ne sit in potestate serui, ut *tibi*[1] soli seruiat: quod puto uerum esse.

If a slave who belongs to me and to you in common has killed my slave, the Aquilian action lies against you if he has done this with your consent, and Urseius reports that Proculus was of the same opinion. But that if he has not done this with your consent, a noxal action is not applicable, as otherwise it would be in the power of the slave to choose which of his masters he would serve ('tibi soli' equals 'utri'), and I think that this is right.

The case supposed by the jurist is of the following kind: A slave who is subject to the ownership of Titius and Seius has damaged the property of Titius. The question arises whether Titius, the injured party, is entitled to sue Seius. In answering this question the jurist distinguishes two cases. In case the delict was committed with the consent of the other co-owner, Seius (tua uoluntate), the Aquilian action will lie against him; in case it was not done with his consent a noxal action will not lie.

This distinction is substantially the same as that drawn by Ulpian in D. 9. 4. 2 pr., according to which passage in case a slave has been killed sciente domino, an actio in solidum is given against the master, just as if he had been himself the delinquent; if, however, it was done insciente domino, the latter will be liable to an actio noxalis on account of the delict of the slave. The word 'sciens' is to be understood with regard to a master who, whilst he had it in his power to hinder the act, suffered its commission (see

[1] Mommsen, in accordance with the Basiliks, proposes to read 'utri' instead of 'tibi,' and this conjecture may be safely accepted, although it is not improbable that the jurist in discussing the case has changed the persons, using the word 'tibi' instead of 'mihi.'

fr. 45 pr., scientiam hic pro patientia accipimus). In so far the delict of the slave seems to have been committed with his consent (uoluntate). The principle is equally applicable if the delinquent slave belongs to several persons in common. If these co-owners are scientes, they are liable directly to an Aquilian action ex propria culpa; if nescientes, they are liable to a noxal action on account of the delict of the slave. It is, however, different if, as supposed in the passage we are explaining, such a slave damages property which belongs to one of his co-owners. If he had done so with the consent of the other master (or masters) the latter are considered to be guilty of the delict; but if the slave had committed the delict insciente condomino no noxal action lies against the co-owner. The reason which is given for not admitting the noxal action is simply that otherwise the slave would be at liberty to serve, according to his choice, either the one or the other of the co-owners exclusively. It would have been only necessary for him to damage the property of the master to whose exclusive power he intended to become subject, and thus to expose the other co-owner to an actio noxalis, in virtue of which, if he did not prefer to pay damages, he would be compelled to surrender the slave to the injured party. Although this view might serve as an equitable ground for the decision given by the jurist, the true reason of it seems to be that in consequence of damage done by the slave, each of his co-owners is liable to a noxal action: the injured party himself, who is one of the co-owners, would be therefore a defendant in the action. It is, however, a principle of Roman law that a person who has to defend a suit cannot be plaintiff in the same action (D. 11. 3. 14. § 2; D. 9. 4. 41; see also D. 9. 4. 8. i. f., dominus enim pro parte factus non potest cum socio noxali experiri). But the fact that the noxal action does not lie does not free the co-owner from liability, for the injured party may bring an actio communi dividundo, in virtue of which the co-owner is, according to the discretion of the judge, either to be condemned to pay compensation or to transfer his share in the delinquent slave to the plaintiff, D. 9. 4. 41, and D. 47. 2. 62.

Pernice, p. 220.

27. § 2.—Item si seruus communis meus et tuus sit occisus a seruo

Titii, Celsus scribit alterum ex dominis agentem aut litis aestimationem consecuturum pro parte aut noxae dedi ei in solidum oportere, quia haec res diuisionem non recipit.

Similarly, if a slave who belongs to you and me in common has been killed by the slave of Titius, Celsus writes that either of the masters who brings an action will either receive compensation in proportion to his share in the ownership of the killed slave, or will have the slave surrendered to him alone, for the act of delivery does not admit of division.

A master, on account of the damage done by his slave, is liable either to pay full compensation according to the lex Aquilia, or to transfer the delinquent slave to the injured party by noxae deditio. If, therefore, the slave is subject to the ownership of several persons, and has committed damage to the property of other people, each of the owners is entitled to an actio noxalis, by which he can claim either compensation in proportion to his share in the ownership of the slave, or to have the slave surrendered to him alone, for, as is stated in D. 9. 4. 8, the noxae deditio, as an act of delivery, does not admit of division; it is either to be performed or not performed, it cannot be performed pro parte. In a similar way a real servitude, e. g. a ius itineris, which has been promised to several co-owners of a piece of land, can be established only so as to benefit the land itself, and accordingly all the persons who own it, D. 8. 5. 4. § 3.

27. § 3.—Serui autem occidentis nomine dominus tenetur, is uero cui bona fide seruit non tenetur. sed an is qui seruum in fuga habet teneatur nomine eius Aquiliae actione, quaeritur: et ait Iulianus teneri et est uerissimum: cum et Marcellus consentit.

The owner is liable on account of his slave who has killed the slaves or cattle of another. But he whom the slave has merely served in good faith is not liable. It is, however, questioned whether a person whose slave has run away is liable on this account under the Aquilian statute. Julian asserts his liability, and this is perfectly correct, and it is also agreed to by Marcellus.

It is quite reasonable that the owner should be declared to be liable—by noxal action—on account of his slave's delict, for he is the person who is entitled to the full enjoyment of the slave. In addition to this it must be noticed that only he, the owner, can possibly transfer by noxae deditio the noxious slave into the ownership of the injured party. A bonae fidei-possessor is incapable of doing so, and this seems to be the reason why the noxal action is not admitted against him[1]. On the other hand, a noxal action is declared to be available against the owner of a fugitive slave. It is true that he cannot at once transfer the slave into the ownership of the other party (either by mancipatio, which required the presence of the thing to be mancipated, or by traditio, which required its actual delivery), but he may cede his actions, especially the rei vindicatio, and he may give security to deliver over the slave, in case he should recover possession of him.

Brinz, Zum Rechte der bonae fidei possessio, in the Festgabe der Münchener Facultät zu Arndts' Doctorjubiläum, München, 1875, pp. 130 sqq.

27. § 4.—Huius legis secundum quidem capitulum in desuetudinem abiit.

The second chapter of the statute has fallen into disuse.

According to this passage, the second chapter of the Aquilian statute has been abrogated by so-called 'non usus' or 'desuetudo.' The same statement is made in the Inst. IV. 3. § 12: 'Caput secundum legis Aquiliae in usu non est.' But the contents of this chapter are reproduced by Gaius, III. 215, where it is said that by it an action was given against the adstipulator for the amount of which

[1] The above view is clear on principle, yet it is not unopposed. For the bonae fidei possessor may actually deliver the delinquent slave to the injured party, and the latter, if afterwards sued by the real owner, may oppose the rei vindicatio by an exceptio doli, for the owner is doubtless bound by the delict of the slave. In accordance with these views in D. 9. 4. 11 and 13 an actio noxalis is given against the bonae fidei (and even against the malae fidei) possessor in case the slave has committed a furtum, whilst according to D. 9. 4. 28 the bonae fidei possessor is declared to be subject to an actio noxalis in general, without any reference to the particular delict committed by the slave. The discrepancy between these passages on the one hand and fr. 27. § 3 above on the other has not yet been satisfactorily explained.

he had defrauded the stipulator, in case he had fraudulently discharged the promisor by acceptilation. If the defendant denied his liability, the sum sued for in the action was to be doubled, in the same way as under Chapters I. and III. Gaius (III. 216) thinks any such provision unnecessary, because the actio mandati is applicable in such cases. It must, however, be noticed that (according to the researches of Voigt, Ius naturale, vol. IV. p. 604) mandatum was not recognised as an actionable contract before the first half of the seventh century, A. U. C., and therefore a legal remedy for the protection of the stipulator was needed at the time of the passing of the Aquilian statute, 467 A. U. C.[1] That Chapter II. should have disappeared from the law of the later times is quite natural, for, first, the actio mandati became applicable in such cases, and, secondly, the institution of adstipulation gradually fell into disuse in the later times of the Roman empire (Puchta, Cursus der Institutionen, Bd. II. § 294. n. f–l).

Savigny, System, vol. I. pp. 152 and 421.

27. § 5.—Tertio autem capite ait eadem lex Aquilia: 'Ceterarum rerum praeter hominem et pecudem occisos si quis alteri damnum faxit, quod usserit fregerit ruperit inuria, quanti ea res erit in diebus triginta proximis, tantum aes domino dare damnas esto.'

In the third chapter, however, the same lex Aquilia says: 'If any one has done damage to the property of another, otherwise than by killing his slaves or his cattle, he shall be bound in respect of what he has unlawfully burned, crushed, or broken, to pay as much money to the owner as the thing shall have been worth during the last thirty days.'

Chapters I. and III. form together the basis of the Roman law of damage to property. Whilst Chapter I. provides against the killing of slaves and cattle, Chapter III. refers to every other damage done to property, either by urere or frangere or rumpere. There is no doubt that Ulpian intends to reproduce in the above passage the very words of the lex; nevertheless objections have been raised as to particular words. Thus it seems to be highly probable that instead of the word

[1] See also Pernice, Labeo, vol. i. p. 443; Ihering, Vermischte Schriften, Leipzig, 1879, p. 192; Lotmar, Kritische Studien in Sachen der Contravindication, p. 13 sq.

'domino' the archaic word 'ero' was used in the statute (see 11. § 6 above). Still more objectionable is the future in the phrase 'quanti ea res *erit*,' for the assessment of compensation is to be made with reference to the past; in other words, what has to be assessed is the value of the damaged thing during the thirty days previous to the act of injury. We should expect to find rather 'fuit,' as we read in 3 pr. above, where the words of the first chapter are reproduced. But as the lex is to be applied in the future, it is probably right to assume that the future perfect 'fuerit' was used by the lawgiver; an assumption which is confirmed by the abstract given by Gaius (III. 214 and 218) of the contents of Chapters I. and III. (cf. the notes to 2 pr. above and Part II. § 3).

Just as the terms of Chapter I. have been commented upon, so now the subsequent passages (27. §§ 7–35, 28 and 29), which with one exception (28 by Paulus), are taken from the commentaries of Ulpian, have for their object the explanation of the successive terms of Chapter III. Accordingly, the word 'usserit' is commented upon in this fragment, §§ 6–12; 'ruperit,' in §§ 13–24; 'damnum faxit,' in §§ 25–28; 'iniuria,' in §§ 29–38, fr. 28 and 29 pr.–§ 7; and lastly, the phrase 'quanti in xxx diebus proximis fuit,' in 29. § 8; although it must be noticed that the single sections cannot be ascertained with exact accuracy.

Pernice, p. 96; Savigny, System, vol. VI. p. 205; Windscheid, n. 2, 14, 20; Vangerow, vol. III. p. 579.

27. § 6.—Si quis igitur non occiderit hominem uel pecudem, sed usserit fregerit ruperit, sine dubio ex his uerbis legis agendum erit. proinde si facem seruo meo obieceris et eum adusseris, teneberis mihi.

If, therefore, a person has not killed slaves or cattle, but has done damage by burning, crushing, or breaking, without any doubt the action is to be brought under these words of the statute. Accordingly, if you have thrown a torch at my slave, and burnt him, I shall have an Aquilian action against you.

The passage shows clearly that the third chapter not only refers to things other than slaves and cattle, but to them as well, if they have not been killed, but merely wounded or otherwise damaged by one of the acts mentioned in Chapter III. Accordingly, if a person has thrown a burning torch at a slave of mine, and has thus injured him, I shall be entitled to an action under the third chapter.

27. § 7.—Item si arbustum meum uel uillam meam incenderis, Aquiliae actionem habebo.

Similarly, if you have set on fire a plantation or a country-house belonging to me, I shall have the Aquilian action.

In opposition to the last paragraph, in this passage things which are not mentioned in the first chapter, viz. trees and houses, are the object of the damaging act. They have been burned and therefore an action under Chapter III. is applicable, without any distinction whether the things were destroyed by the fire, or merely damaged by it.

27. § 8.—Si quis insulam uoluerit meam exurere et ignis etiam ad uicini insulam peruenerit, Aquilia tenebitur etiam uicino: non minus etiam inquilinis tenebitur ob res eorum exustas.

If a person has intended to burn down my detached house, and the fire has spread to my neighbour's house, he will be liable under the Aquilian statute to my neighbour also, and he will in the same way be liable to the tenants in respect of their property which is burned.

It is obvious that a person who intentionally sets a detached house on fire (the word 'insula' in the passage signifies a house or pile of houses detached from others) is liable under Chapter III. of the Aquilian statute; he is even subject to a prosecution under the lex Cornelia, Coll. XII. 7. 2. The question, however, seems to have been discussed, whether a person who sets a detached building on fire could be considered as having burned a neighbouring house to which the fire has spread, and as being therefore subject to an actio legis Aquiliae (directa), or whether he has not rather produced a condition of things from which the damage arose (causa incendii). The decision of the jurist is, as we learn from the passage under consideration, in favour of the first alternative, although in similar cases (27. § 10 and 30. § 3) the other view was taken, and an actio in factum was declared to be applicable.

The incendiary is also said to be liable to the tenants occupying the neighbour's house, not of course in so far as they are disturbed in the occupancy of their rooms (for they enjoy these under the contract of hiring, i. e. in virtue of a right in personam, the disturbance of which, as a rule, does not give rise to an Aquilian action, see the notes to 11. § 9 above), but because things which are subject to their ownership have been destroyed or damaged.

Pernice, p. 153.

27. § 9.—Si fornacarius seruus coloni ad fornacem obdormisset et uilla fuerit exusta, Neratius scribit ex locato conuentum praestare debere, si neglegens in eligendis ministeriis fuit: ceterum si alius ignem subiecerit fornaci, alius neglegenter custodierit, an tenebitur qui subiecerit? nam qui custodit, nihil fecit, qui recte ignem subiecit, non peccauit: quid ergo est? puto utilem competere actionem tam in eum qui ad fornacem obdormiuit quam in eum qui neglegenter custodit, nec quisquam dixerit in eo qui obdormiuit rem eum humanam et naturalem passum, cum deberet uel ignem extinguere uel ita munire, ne euagetur.

If the slave of a tenant being in charge of a furnace has fallen asleep and the farm-house is burnt down, Neratius writes that the colonus, when sued under the contract of hiring and letting, must pay compensation, if he has been negligent in choosing his servants for their respective functions. But if one man has lighted the fire and another has negligently attended to it, it may be asked whether he who has lighted the fire is liable under the Aquilian statute; for the person who has been watching the fire has not done any act, whilst the other who has kindled it properly is not guilty of any negligence. What then is the answer? I think that an actio utilis is applicable as well against the man who fell asleep at the furnace as against him who has attended to the fire negligently, and no one can object as to the person who went to sleep that nothing has happened to him which might not happen to any one in the ordinary course of nature, for at least he ought either to have extinguished the fire, or to have taken precautions that it did not spread.

The case which underlies the discussion and decision of the jurist is the following: A person has let on hire a farm-house (villa) in which there was a furnace. The hirer (conductor or colonus) appointed one of his slaves to take care of the furnace, but he, after having lighted the fire, fell asleep by it, and thus the house was burned down. The jurist Neratius raises the question whether the colonus is liable under the contract of hiring and letting (ex locato) to pay damages (praestare debere scil. damnum) and answers it in the affirmative, provided there is culpa on the part of the colonus, i. e. if he has been negligent in choosing his servants for their functions.

We should expect that the jurist would also discuss here the question of liability under the Aquilian statute, but before touching upon this point he complicates the case a little by supposing that one man has lighted the fire, and another has afterwards taken his place in watching it and has altogether omitted to attend to this task. It is obvious that the latter has not done anything (nihil fecit); there is therefore no urere nor any other act which could constitute liability under the terms of the Aquilian statute; the former, however, who has lighted the fire properly is not at all in culpa (non peccavit), and therefore he also cannot possibly be subject to an Aquilian action. But the one who has neglected to attend to the fire, is declared to be liable to an actio utilis. The same is said by the jurist of the slave who set light to the fire and then went to sleep whilst watching it. One may of course object to this view that a man cannot always help falling asleep, and that so far he cannot be blamed. This objection, however, does not touch the real question, for it is not the slave's falling asleep, but his act of kindling the fire, to which the conflagration is due. Lighting a fire under such circumstances as supposed in the passage is in itself a dangerous act, and must therefore be attributed to the culpa of the doer, just in the same way as it is attributed to the fault of a carrier if damage is done by stones falling from his waggon in consequence of his having loaded it improperly. It is only where the person who has lighted the fire has afterwards taken suitable precautions to prevent the fire from spreading that no culpa could be laid to his charge. Cf. § 33 in this fr. below and the notes to 8 pr. above.

It seems at first sight as if in the case where a man has taken the place of him who has lighted the fire liability were attached to a mere omission. It is obvious that a person who has in some way or other meddled with the fire, as, for example, by having used poker and shovel, can be spoken of as having caused the damage by his act. This, however, cannot be said where he has not touched the fire at all. But even here it is in reality the slave's positive act or conduct to which the damage is due, for he has approached the furnace apparently with the intention of taking care of it, and has thus induced the other who had lighted the fire to give up watching it, in consequence of which the fire has spread so as to endanger and destroy the whole house. If understood in this sense the above passage is perfectly in harmony with D. 7. 1. 13. § 2, in which the principle that an actio for damnum iniuria datum lies only if damage was caused by a positive act is clearly announced (see notes to 8 pr. above and Part II. § 5).

Pernice, p. 164 sq.; Windscheid, § 401. n. 5 and § 455. n. 9; Hasse, Culpa, p. 22; Brinz, § 340. n. 12.

27. § 10.—Si furnum secundum parietem communem haberes, an damni iniuria tenearis? et ait Proculus agi non posse, quia nec cum eo qui focum haberet: et ideo aequius puto in factum actionem dandam, scilicet si paries exustus sit: sin autem nondum mihi damnum dederis, sed ita ignem habeas, ut metuam, ne mihi damnum des, damni infecti puto sufficere cautionem.

If you have an oven placed against a wall which is the common property of you and your neighbour, it may be asked whether you will be liable to him on account of unlawful damage caused by the fire. Proculus, however, says that the action would not lie in such case, because neither is the action given against him who has a hearth which has caused similar damage, and therefore Ulpian thinks it more equitable that an actio in factum should be given against him, if the wall has been burned down. But if you have not yet caused damage to me, but have your fire in such place that I am afraid of damage arising from it to my property, according to the opinion of Ulpian, the cautio damni infecti will be sufficient.

A baker, so we may suppose according to the contents of the passage, had his oven against a wall which belonged in common to him and to his neighbour, and by the heat of the fire damage was caused to the wall. The neighbour is said to have no action under the terms of the statute itself, evidently for the reason that the act of the defendant in consequence of which damage is caused to the wall is not considered to be an urere, but merely a causam incendii praestare; but an actio in factum is given to him by which he can get compensation, provided of course he has really sustained damage by the fire.

There is, however, the peculiarity in this case that the paries is said to be communis, and this raises the question whether the same action would lie if the neighbour's building had a separate wall of its own which was damaged by the fire. It is well known that in case a building, in consequence of its defective condition, as by falling down, or otherwise, causes damage to the neighbour's property, as a rule no Aquilian action will lie (D. 39. 2. 7. §§ 2, 8); the damage thus caused being looked upon as having happened without any interference of the owner, like damage caused by an animal, D. 39. 2. 7. § 1, in the case of the actio de pauperie. Therefore special provision was made for such cases by the cautio damni infecti, by which the security was obtained of a promise to compensate for the damage, where damage was threatened by the defective condition of buildings and land to the neighbour's property. Moyle, Instit. vol. I. p. 396; Arndts, § 328; Windscheid, §§ 458–460. One might expect that in most cases of that kind an Aquilian action would be applicable, for an owner who allows his house to become so ruinous as to endanger neighbouring property, certainly seems to be in culpa, nevertheless the right to such action is denied. The idea of the Roman jurists was evidently that a person in dealing with his own property is not obliged to bestow diligentia boni patris familias in order to avoid damage to others. If therefore, under the circumstances stated, a wall belonging exclusively to the neighbour should have been damaged, an Aquilian action would not lie. But in the case supposed in the passage the baker, by keeping an oven near the wall, does not deal with his own property alone, for the wall is common to him and his neighbour, and in so far he is bound to take care that by his acts the neighbour's property is not interfered with, and therefore he is declared to be subject to an actio (in factum) ex lege Aquilia.

If, however, damage has not yet happened, but is merely expected, obviously no actio under the Aquilian statute can lie (D. 39. 2. 7. § 1). Cautio damni infecti, however, may be claimed, by which security is to be given against damage which may arise from the condition of the building in future.

Pernice, p. 153.

> 27. § 11.—Proculus ait, cum coloni serui uillam exussissent, colonum uel ex locato uel lege Aquilia teneri, ita ut colonus possit seruos noxae dedere, et si uno iudicio res esset iudicata, altero amplius non agendum. sed haec ita, si culpa colonus careret: ceterum si noxios seruos habuit, damni eum iniuria teneri, cur tales habuit. idem seruandum et circa inquilinorum insulae personas scribit: quae sententia habet rationem.

Proculus says that when the slaves of an agricultural tenant (colonus) have burned down the farm-house, the colonus will be liable, under the contract of hiring as well as under the Aquilian statute, retaining, of course, in the latter case, the power to make a noxal surrender of the slave, and that when one action has been brought to a final determination the injured party cannot proceed with the other. But this only holds good if the tenant was free from culpa, for if he has kept mischievous slaves, he is liable on account of damage unlawfully done, because he has kept slaves of that kind. And this applies, according to Proculus, to tenants of a house also: an opinion which is well founded.

Slaves have burned down a house belonging to a farm which had been hired by their master, who therefore is called in the passage colonus. It is obvious that this act was either done intentionally or negligently, therefore the lex Aquilia is applicable, although the action under this statute is given as actio noxalis against the colonus. But the owner of the house may also sue the colonus under the contract of hiring; if, however, one action has been finally decided, the plaintiff cannot sue in any other; but this decision is applicable only on the assumption that the colonus was free from any culpa, 'sed haec ita si colonus culpa careret.'

Thus it would seem that not only an actio noxalis under the lex Aquilia, but also an actio ex locato is applicable, in cases where there is no culpa on the part of the master of the slave; and so the passage seems to contradict § 9 above, where the colonus of a slave who has fallen asleep is said only to be liable if he has been negligent in appointing the slave to his functions. This raises the general question, whether a person who, like the colonus uillae, is bound in contract or quasi-contract, is liable also for dolus and culpa on the part of other persons, i. e. his agents and assistants? It is well known that, according to a view which was formerly recognised, and which possibly may prevail even now, a person is not answerable for the culpa of others, unless he is himself in culpa, as having, for example, improperly chosen his servants and assistants (cf. Windscheid, § 401, especially n. 5). This view is, however, very strongly opposed, and it is asserted that a person is sometimes considered to be answerable for the acts of other persons in contractual and quasi-contractual relations. Thus it is said by some modern jurists that the culpa of persons employed in carrying out work which was undertaken by their employer is the culpa of their employer; and he is declared to be answerable just in the same way as he is answerable for his tools. Therefore the objection that he has been as careful as possible in choosing and superintending his workmen and assistants is quite irrelevant, for it is shown ex post facto that something has been neglected, either in choosing or conducting or superintending the business. It is quite in accordance with this view that, in the Corpus Iuris, an employer is simply declared to be in culpa because he had chosen the wrong man; D. 3. 5. 21. § 3; D. 13. 6. 11; D. 19. 2. 60. § 7; and D. 17. 2. 23 pr. Similarly it is considered to be culpa if the custody of a thing is entrusted to any one and the duty thus imposed upon him is not complied with by the fault of his servants. Accordingly, the colonus who has taken a farm on hire is answerable for the servants and other people whom he admits to the farm (in inducendis, D. 19. 2. 11 pr.), and for the way in which he employs his servants, especially as watchmen, shepherds, etc., D. 19. 2. 41.

Thus we have stated the two main views on this very important topic. If we now look at the above passage, it is clear that the second view is there followed, for the colonus is declared liable for the damage done by his slaves although he is not himself in culpa.

It must be granted that other passages do not agree with this view, and this has made it possible for modern theories to differ so widely as has been stated above. In fact, the liability of the principal or employer was itself a controverted topic amongst the Roman jurists, and this is very clearly shown by Coll. XII. 7. 9, which contains the above fragment, but without certain abbreviations made by the compilers of the Digest. There it is expressly stated that Sabinus denied that an actio ex locato would lie in such a case, whereas Proculus was in favour of the admission of this action. We see accordingly that the point was controverted among these jurists; the compilers, however, have omitted all mention of the controversy, and have simply stated the liability ex locato. Therefore there can be no doubt that in cases of this kind the person bound under the contract was considered to be liable according to the law of Justinian, although he was not himself in culpa, but only his servants or assistants.

In the last sentence of the passage under consideration the above principles are said to be applicable, if a house (insula) has been let on hire; in this case the tenants are liable for their slaves, in the same way as the colonus is liable for the slaves employed by him (see Coll. XII. 7. 9, where the case is more fully stated).

Pernice, p. 225; Windscheid, § 401. n. 5, and § 455. n. 12; Hasse, Culpa, p. 14.

27. § 12.—Si cum apes meae ad tuas aduolassent, tu eas exusseris, legis Aquiliae actionem competere Celsus ait.

Celsus says that the Aquilian action is applicable if my bees have joined yours and you have burned them.

It seems to be obvious that a person who burns bees belonging to another is liable under the Aquilian statute. Nevertheless this liability was, as we gather from the above passage, and more fully from Coll. XII. 7. 10, denied by some jurists, especially by Proculus. He seems to think that, if bees have once flown away from a person's hive, they cease to be subject to his ownership, for bees belong to wild animals (apium ... natura fera est, I. II. 1. § 14), which cease to be subject to any rights of individuals as soon as they recover their natural liberty (§ 12 eod.; Arndts, § 127. n. c.). This view, however, was opposed by

Celsus, on the ground that such bees would return to their former hive and be again of use to their owner; having, therefore, not yet lost the so-called 'consuetudo revertendi,' the right of ownership in them remains unaltered (I. II. 1. 15), and may be violated by an act of damage done to the bees.

27. § 13.—Inquit lex 'ruperit.' rupisse uerbum fere omnes ueteres sic intellexerunt 'corruperit.'

The law says 'ruperit,' but nearly all the jurists before the time of Augustus have taken this verb in the sense of 'corrumpere.'

The third chapter is concerned with damage, but only damage done by certain acts—urere, frangere, or rumpere; a very old interpretation of the jurists, however, attributed to the term rumpere the sense of corrumpere. Thus in every case where a thing had been damaged by the physical action of another person upon it, or, in other words, wherever there was a damnum corpore corpori datum, an actio legis Aquiliae directa was made applicable, Gaius, III. 217; I. 4. 3. § 13; Windscheid, n. 3; Vangerow, vol. III. p. 579.

27. § 14.—Et ideo Celsus quaerit, si lolium aut auenam in segetem alienam inieceris, quo eam tu inquinares, non solum quod ui aut clam dominum posse agere uel, si locatus fundus sit, colonum, sed et in factum agendum, et si colonus eam exercuit, cauere eum debere amplius non agi, scilicet ne dominus amplius inquietet: nam alia quaedam species damni est ipsum quid corrumpere et mutare, ut lex Aquilia locum habeat, alia nulla ipsius mutatione applicare aliud cuius molesta separatio sit.

And therefore Celsus—considering the case where a person has cast weeds and tares into the crop of another, and the corn has thus become full of weeds—says that the owner, or, if the farm has been let on hire, the tenant (colonus) will not only be entitled to an interdictum quod vi aut clam, but also to an actio in factum, and if the colonus brings this action he must give security that no other action will be brought, i.e. that the owner himself will not trouble the delinquent any more, for it is one kind of damage to spoil and alter a substance of a thing so as to bring the Aquilian statute into operation, another kind to add, without altering the substance of the thing, something to it which it is difficult to separate.

A person, so we learn from the passage, has sown weeds and tares in the crop of another; Celsus has considered the merits of the case (quaerit), and states as the result of his investigation (this must be added to quaerit) that the owner of the land will be entitled to two legal remedies:—

1. To an interdictum quod vi aut clam, which is applicable if a person has made some alteration in a fundus vi aut clam, to the disadvantage of another person. The object of this action is to have the previous condition of the land restored and full compensation paid. The interdictum, however, is not applicable unless there is an opus in solo factum as supposed in the above case; it would not lie, for instance, if weeds and tares had been mixed with the corn after it had been already reaped, D. 43. 24. 7. § 5.

2. To an actio in factum on the ground of the Aquilian statute. It is obvious that under the given circumstances an actio directa is not applicable, for, strictly speaking, there is no damage done to the corn, its substance is not altered, but all that has happened is that something has been added to it which can be separated only with great trouble, and which therefore considerably lessens the value of the corn.

If, however, the land has been let on hire, these two actions are given to the colonus as well. There is nothing strange in the fact that the colonus may avail himself of the interdictum quod vi aut clam, for it is given to everybody whose legal interest in the land is injured by the opus factum. Therefore the fact that the owner is entitled to the action does not prevent the colonus from being equally entitled; the latter may bring this action even concurrently with the owner, in so far as his right to the perception of the fruits is violated; the former on the ground of other damage caused by the act, D. 43. 24. 12. But that an action (in factum) under the Aquilian statute as well should be given to the colonus seems to be remarkable, for the colonus has merely a ius in personam as to the fruits, available only against the other contracting party, i.e. the owner of the land.

It must be noticed that this is the only passage according to which a person who has merely a ius in personam is entitled to an Aquilian action, and it seems therefore correct to restrict its application to cases where a person is entitled to take the fruits instead of the owner himself (cf. the notes to 11. § 9 above). But though the colonus may thus bring the action, the owner himself is not thereby deprived of a right which, strictly speaking, belongs to him alone, and therefore the colonus in suing must give the defendant security against a second action on the part of the owner, cf. D. 23. 3. 29.

Pernice, p. 207; Windscheid, n. 3 and 17; Brinz, § 340. n. 27.

27. § 15.—Cum eo plane qui uinum spurcauit uel effudit uel acetum fecit uel alio modo uitiauit, agi posse Aquilia Celsus ait, quia etiam effusum et acetum factum corrupti appellatione continentur.

One may, however, as Celsus says, bring an Aquilian action against a person who has fouled wine, or has spilled it, or has made it sour, or has damaged it in some other way, because spilling wine and making it sour are comprehended under the notion of corrumpere.

Differing from the case in the last section, the case here under consideration comes within the terms of the statute, for acts by which wine is fouled, made sour, etc. are certainly a species of spoiling the wine (cf. § 20 below), and therefore an actio directa on account of corrumpere is applicable.

Windscheid, n. 4.

27. § 16.—Et non negat fractum et ustum contineri corrupti appellatione, sed non esse nouum ut lex specialiter quibusdam enumeratis generale subiciat uerbum, quo specialia complectatur: quae sententia uera est.

And Celsus does not deny that urere and frangere are both comprehended under the term corrumpere; but he says that it is no new thing for a law, after having enumerated several particular points, to add a general term in which those points are embraced.

According to the view of Celsus, the term rumpere was in the statute itself already used in the sense of corrumpere, and therefore the mention of urere and frangere was quite superfluous. This assertion is, however, highly improbable. For although in the time of the classical jurists it was not uncommon for the law to sum up several particular points by a general term; the language of the leges in the early times is so very scanty and precise that we cannot assume that more words were used than were necessary to express the intention of the lawgiver. Besides, it is quite in accordance with the development of law from the concrete and particular to the abstract and general, that at first only certain specific acts (rumpere rem in the XII Tables; urere, frangere, rumpere in the lex Aquilia) should be provided against, and that it should be only due to the interpretation of the jurists that rumpere was taken in the general sense of corrumpere (cf. Part II. § 2).

Lotmar, Kritische Studien in Sachen der Contravindication, München, 1878, p. 18.

27. § 17.—Rupisse eum utique accipiemus, qui uulnerauerit, uel uirgis uel loris uel pugnis cecidit, uel telo uel quo alio, ut scinderet alicui corpus, uel tumorem fecerit, sed ita demum si damnum iniuria datum est: ceterum si nullo seruum pretio uiliorem deterioremue fecerit, Aquilia cessat iniuriarumque erit agendum dumtaxat: Aquilia enim eas ruptiones quae damna dant persequitur. ergo etsi pretio quidem non sit deterior seruus factus, uerum sumptus in salutem eius et sanitatem facti sunt, in haec mihi uideri damnum datum: atque ideoque lege Aquilia agi posse.

We must understand that a person is guilty of rumpere who has wounded or has beaten a slave with a stick or a strap or with his fists, or with a weapon, or anything else, so as to lacerate his body or raise a swelling, provided however that unlawful damage to the master's property has been so caused; but if the money value or worth of the slave has not been lessened the Aquilian action does not lie, and only an actio iniuriarum is applicable. For by the lex Aquilia only such acts of rumpere are provided against as cause damage to property; therefore, although the actual money value of the slave has not been lessened, yet, if I have incurred expense upon saving his life and curing him, damage seems to have been caused to me, and accordingly I shall be able to bring the Aquilian action.

We learn from this passage that every physical act done to a slave's body by which a wound or some other injury is inflicted upon it, gives rise to an action under the third chapter on account of rumpere, and this is clearly in accordance with the wide sense in which this word was understood by the jurist (§ 13 above). This general statement is subject to an important restriction; a real damnum, i.e. a loss to the injured person's property must have resulted from the wound or the other act of damage. Therefore if the value of the slave has not been at all depreciated, no action lies, in spite of the injury inflicted on him; for instance a castration of a slave boy is not actionable, for it only increases his value (§ 28 below), although in this and similar cases an actio iniuriarum, on account of the personal insult implied by the act, will be applicable (Part II. § 8). On the other hand, it must be noticed that it is sufficient that some loss to the plaintiff's property has resulted from the act, although no trace whatever of the injury is left on the thing itself which had been damaged. Accordingly, the Aquilian action is said to be applicable if expenses for the cure of the wounded slave have been incurred, even though he has not been depreciated in value; D. h. t. 45. § 1 below; cf. D. 9. 1. 3 and D. 9. 3. 7.

Pernice, pp. 27 and 97 sq.

27. § 18.—Si quis uestimenta sciderit uel inquinauerit, Aquilia quasi ruperit tenetur.

If a person has torn or soiled clothes of another, he is liable under the Aquilian law, as if he were guilty of rumpere.

It is obvious that tearing and soiling garments is, strictly speaking, no rumpere, but such acts certainly come under the notion of corrumpere, and accordingly give rise to an action under Chapter III.

27. § 19.—Sed et si quis milium uel frumentum meum effuderit in flumen, sufficit Aquiliae actio.

But if some one has thrown millet or corn of mine into a river, the Aquilian action covers the case.

If corn or other things have been thrown into a river, one might think at first sight that although the corn has been lost for its owner there is no damnum corpori datum, and that accordingly not a direct action, but an analogous action (in factum or utilis) is applicable, and this is assumed by the glossa with the reasoning 'nec enim corpus est laesum.' Ulpian, however, seems to have held a different opinion; for the substance of the corn itself is affected by the water, and therefore he thinks that there is no need of an analogous action, but that a direct action under the terms of Chapter III. is sufficient.

Windscheid, § 455. n. 4.

27. § 20.—Item si quis frumento harenam uel aliud quid immiscuit, ut difficilis separatio sit, quasi de corrupto agi poterit.

Similarly if some one has mixed sand or something else with corn, so that the separation is difficult, he will be subject to an action on account of corrumpere.

My corn has been mixed by another person with sand or something else. Strictly speaking the substance of the corn is not affected by the sand, but the mixture may be so complete as to make a separation of the fine sand impossible, and in so far the corn must be said to be spoiled. This seems to be the reason why an action under Chapter III. on account of corrumpere is said to be applicable, whereas we might expect to find an actio in factum, as in the case reported in § 14 above, where weeds or tares having been mixed with the crop of another, an actio in factum was granted.

Windscheid, n. 3; Vangerow, vol. III. p. 583.

27. § 21.—Si quis de manu mihi nummos excusserit, Sabinus existimat damni iniuriae esse actionem, si ita perierint, ne ad aliquem peruenirent, puta si in flumen uel in mare uel in cloacam ceciderunt: quod si ad aliquem peruenerunt, ope consilio furtum factum agendum, quod et antiquis placuit. idem etiam in factum dari posse actionem ait.

If a man has knocked money out of my hand, Sabinus thinks that an actio on account of damnum iniuria datum would lie, if the coins have been lost in such a way that they have not come into the hands of another person; for instance, if they have fallen into a river, or the sea, or a sewer. But if the money has come into the hands of another, an action is to be brought on account of aiding and abetting a theft, and this view was shared by the ancient jurists. Ulpian says that an actio in factum might also be applicable in cases of such kind.

It is obvious that in case money has been knocked out of my hand and has fallen into the sea, etc., the substance of the coins remains unaltered, and therefore no Aquilian action will lie, but the money is lost for me not less than if it had been destroyed. Therefore the principles of the Aquilian statute were extended to cases of such kind, and an action on the analogy of the statute (actio in factum) was declared to be applicable. The words of the fragment, however (existimat damni iniuriae esse actionem), seem to be rather in favour of the actio legis Aquiliae directa; but as Ulpian himself, in another passage (D. 5. 14. § 2), denies the direct action (see also Inst. IV. 1. 11, and D. 41. 1. 55), and asserts that an actio in factum is applicable, his intention here seems to have been to state in general that in cases of such kind an action on the ground of the Aquilian statute is admissible without considering whether it would be a direct or an extended action. In the case, however, where the coins knocked out of my hand have come into the hands of another person, Sabinus, with the approval of Ulpian, declares an actio furti—on account of aiding and abetting a theft—to be applicable, provided, of course, we must add, that the person who has struck my hand has been acting with the intention of advancing the commission of a theft, 'si ideo fecit, ut alius tolleret isque sustulerit,' as is laid down in D. 47. 2. 52. § 13. If such an intention did not exist, for instance, if the same thing were done in jest—'per lasciviam,' an actio in factum, on the ground of the Aquilian law, would lie (see Inst. IV. 1. 11). It is also by the absence of the animus furandi that we must explain the last words of the passage, which state that an action in factum will lie in cases where the money has come into the hands of other people. It is obvious that this sentence has in view cases in which the intention of advancing a theft does not exist.

Hasse, Culpa, pp. 36 sq.; Windscheid, n. 6; Vangerow, III. p. 583.

27. § 22.—Si mulier pugno uel equa ictu a te percussa eiecerit, Brutus ait Aquilia teneri quasi rupto.

If a woman or mare, in consequence of a blow from you, has miscarried, Brutus says that you are liable for an act of rumpere.

If a blow struck by a person causes a slave woman or a mare to miscarry—'eiicere' equals 'abortum facere,' or miscarry—there is certainly as regards the owner a damnum corpore corpori datum. But the act was not rumpere in the strict sense of the word. Nevertheless, the jurist, M. Iunius Brutus (living about 620 A. U. C.; see D. I. 2. 2. § 39; Rudorff, Römische Rechtsgeschichte, I. p. 159), in accordance with the extensive interpretation given to that term by the Roman jurists, assumed that the act of inflicting the blow should give rise to an action on account of rumpere.

One might perhaps think that in the above case an action under Chapter I., on account of killing the young, would lie. But it must be remembered that fruits, so long as they are in connection with the chief thing, are legally considered merely a portion of it, and therefore not the object of any legal relations; D. 6. 1. 44; D. 7. 1. 27 pr.; Arndts, § 55. n. c.

Pernice, p. 17; Windscheid, n. 4.

27. § 23.—Et si mulum plus iusto onerauerit et aliquid membri ruperit, Aquiliae locum fore.

If a mule has been overburdened, and one of its limbs has been broken, the Aquilian action will hold.

My mule has been too heavily burdened by another, who was entitled to the use of it, as, for instance, in virtue of his having hired it, as in D. 19. 2. 30. § 2, where, in such cases, liability under the contract and under the lex Aquilia is assumed. It is obvious that the person who has thus by this act caused damage to my property is liable under Chapter III., and it does not make any difference that the damage did not happen till some time after the mule had been burdened.

Pernice, p. 80.

27. § 24.—Si nauem uenaliciarum mercium perforasset, Aquiliae actionem esse, quasi ruperit, Uiuianus scribit.

In case a person has bored holes in the hull of a merchant-vessel, Vivianus writes that an Aquilian action will lie against him, as he has done damage by rumpere.

According to the extended notion of rumpere, an act of boring holes in a ship, which sinks in consequence, is declared by Vivianus (who wrote under Tiber and his followers) to entail liability under Chapter III.

Pernice, p. 152.

27. § 25.—Si oliuam inmaturam decerpserit uel segetem desecuerit inmaturam uel uineas crudas, Aquilia tenebitur: quod si iam maturas, cessat Aquilia: nulla enim iniuria est, cum tibi etiam impensas donauerit quae in collectionem huiusmodi fructuum impenduntur: sed si collecta haec interceperit, furti tenetur. Octauenus in uuis adicit, nisi, inquit, in terram uuas proiecit, ut effunderentur.

If a person has plucked olives before they were ripe, or cut down a crop before it was ripe, or gathered grapes still sour, he is liable under the Aquilian statute; but if they are already ripe, the Aquilian action falls, for there is no damage done (nulla iniuria), since he had saved you the expenses which are incurred for gathering fruits of such kind; but if he has purloined the fruits gathered, he is liable on account of theft. Octavenus, however, adds with reference to the grapes, that this view (viz. that the gatherer is not liable under the Aquilian statute) is true only provided they are not thrown on the ground so that the juice runs out.

Fruits, so long as they are not separated from the plant which bears them, form a portion of it (note to § 22 above), and the plant seems accordingly to be damaged if they are plucked by a third person. But such act entails liability under the lex Aquilia only if the fruits are not yet ripe. It is different if ripe fruits are gathered, for though in this case there is also an act interfering, culpa and iniuria, with the crop of another, yet no damnum results from it, and therefore no liability under the Aquilian statute is possible (see § 17 above); on the contrary, a person who has gathered ripe fruits confers an advantage on the person entitled, because the latter is saved the expense of gathering the fruits. It is, however, different if the person purloins the (ripe) fruits he has gathered, for in this case he will be subject to an actio furti (which, it must be understood, will be applicable also if unripe fruits are taken away). But this statement, that the person who has gathered fruits is, according to Octavenus (a jurist who was living in the middle of the first century B.C., Rudorff, Römische Rechtsgeschichte, I. p. 185), subject to the exception that he who has picked grapes has not thrown them on the ground so that their juice runs out, an exception which is understood by itself, for in such cases damnum is caused to the owner, although not by the act of picking the grapes.

Pernice, pp. 28, 98; Hasse, Culpa, p. 35; Windscheid, n. 4.

27. § 26.—Idem et in silua caedua scribit, ut, si immatura, Aquilia teneatur, quod si matura interceperit, furti teneri eum et arborum furtim caesarum.

The same distinction is, as Octavenus writes, applicable with reference to a coppice, so that if some one has cut down the wood before it is fully grown, he is liable under the lex Aquilia; if he has, however, purloined wood which was ripe for cutting, he is subject to an actio furti and an actio arborum furtim caesarum.

The decision is exactly in accordance with the contents of the previous section. Cutting of trees and other wood, before it is fully grown, entails liability under the Aquilian statute[1], for damage is thus done to the owner of the land. Felling of trees, however, which are fit to be felled does not inflict any loss on the owner, and therefore no Aquilian action is applicable, but possibly other actions would lie, viz. in case the trees were cut secretly, the actio arborum furtim caesarum, or, in case they were taken animo lucri faciendi, the actio furti.

[1] In the same case an interdictum quod vi aut clam is applicable, if the act was done vi aut clam; but this interdictum also is excluded if the wood was not yet fit for cutting, D. 43. 24. 18 pr. For the notion of silua caedua see D. 50. 16. 30 pr.

Hasse, Culpa, p. 34; Voigt, Die XII Tafeln, Leipzig 1883, vol. II. p. 536. n. 2.

27. § 27.—Si salictum maturum ita ne stirpes laederes, tuleris, cessare Aquiliam.

If you have cut down an osier-bed which was fit for cutting without injuring the roots, the Aquilian action is not applicable.

The text of the passage admits of a double interpretation. It may be that a person has cut and carried off the osiers without injuring the roots which are left in the soil; or it may be that he has taken away the whole plants, roots and all, but without doing any damage to the roots. It is, however, obvious that the latter view cannot be maintained, for, if the whole plants have been taken away, an Aquilian action will certainly lie, because there the owner will suffer loss, since osier-beds are kept in order to be cut from time to time, when the shoots are fit for being used, e. g. for making baskets. It is different when an osier-bed is merely cut at the proper time; for in this case, provided, of course, that the stocks are not injured, the owner suffers no damage whatever, but is, on the contrary, saved the trouble of cutting the bed. Accordingly, no Aquilian action lies, but there are possibly other actions: actio furti and arborum furtim caesarum, which may be available (compare the previous section).

In perfect harmony with this explanation of the passage Mommsen proposes, in accordance with the contents of the Basiliks, to read 'secueris' instead of the word 'tuleris,' a conjecture which doubtless is to be preferred to the reading confirmed by the manuscripts of the Digest.

Pernice, p. 98.

27. § 28.—Et si puerum quis castrauerit et pretiosiorem fecerit, Uiuianus scribit cessare Aquiliam, sed iniuriarum erit agendum aut ex edicto aedilium *aut*[1] in quadruplum.

If some one has castrated a slave boy, and thus made him more valuable, the Aquilian action is not applicable; but, as Vivianus writes,

[1] 'Aut' must be omitted for the reasons stated in the explanation of the passage.

one may sue him by the actio iniuriarum, or, under the edict of the aediles, by an actio in quadruplum.

If the value of a boy has been increased by castration, his master cannot sue under the Aquilian statute, as there is no damnum iniuria which has resulted from the act (§ 17 above). But there is certainly an iniuria atrox committed against the slave, on account of which his master is entitled to an actio iniuriarum (D. 47. 10. 15. § 48; Puchta, Instit. § 212. nr. 2). In addition to this it is stated in the text that an action in quadruplum under the edict of the aediles is applicable. We do not know anything else as to this action, but, according to the passage itself, it is very probably a penal action, the object of which is payment of fourfold the value of the slave (for no other actio in quadruplum is imaginable). This assumption is quite in accordance with the later law, which made castration a special crime by subordinating it to the provisions of the lex Cornelia de sicariis, D. 48. 8. 3. § 4. i. f., 4. §§ 2, 5 and 6; see also C. 4. 42. 1 and 2.

One might object to this interpretation that the manuscripts of the Digest read 'ex edicto aedilium aut in quadruplum,' and that accordingly, in addition to an actio iniuriarum, an actio under the edict of the aediles as well as an actio in quadruplum is applicable. But this reading must certainly be rejected, for the following three reasons:

1. There would be no explanation whatever for the actio in quadruplum.

2. We should have to understand by the actio under the edict of the aediles the so-called actio redhibitoria. This actio, however, does not lie on account of a delict committed (like castration), but only if a seller in selling a thing does not communicate its defects to the purchaser (see 11. § 7 above). We should have to suppose that the master has sold the boy without disclosing the fact of his castration: but of this there is no indication in the passage; and, in the second place, supposing such an action intended, the master would be the defendant, and not the plaintiff: but this is clearly in opposition to the whole tenour of the passage, which has in view only actions available in favour of the owner or master (actio legis Aquiliae and actio iniuriarum) on account of the injury done to his slave.

3. The omission of the 'aut' is confirmed by the paraphrase of the above passage given in the Basiliks.

Pernice, p. 98; Lenel, Das Edictum perpetuum, pp. 435 and 443.

27. § 29.—Si calicem diatretum faciendum dedisti, si quidem imperitia fregit, damni iniuria tenebitur: si uero non imperitia fregit, sed rimas habebat uitiosas, potest esse excusatus: et ideo plerumque artifices conuenire solent, cum eiusmodi materiae dantur, non periculo suo se facere, quae res ex locato tollit actionem et Aquiliae.

If you have given an artificer a cup of filigree work to be repaired, and he has broken it through want of skill, he will be liable on account of damage done; if, however, he has not broken it through want of skill, but because the cup was badly cracked, he may be excused, and therefore artificers, if things of this kind are given to them to mend, usually make it a condition that they will not do it at their own risk, and this agreement supersedes the actio ex locato as well as the actio legis Aquiliae.

Some one has given an artificer a very delicate piece of work, a cup of filigree work, to mend, and thus a locatio conductio operis is entered upon by the parties. If the cup is broken by reason of the artificer's want of skill, he is liable under the Aquilian law and under the contract; if the cup is broken in consequence of any inherent defect of its own, he is not at all liable (cf. D. 19. 2. 13. § 5). The reason clearly is that the artificer has a right to deal with the cup, and that therefore there is no iniuria (cf. Part II. § 6) on his part. If, however, the artificer had tried to mend the cup without being authorized to do so by its owner, he certainly would be liable under the Aquilian statute, for through an act of his own damage would have been done unlawfully to the property of another person.

Although, on principle, there is no doubt as to the decision to be given in the case, yet the fact that the cup was broken by an act of the artificer, on the face of it, proves the plaintiff's claim, and therefore it will be incumbent on the defendant to prove that the damage complained of was due to a defect in the cup itself, and in so far the acquittal of the defendant will depend on the evidence furnished by him (potest esse excusatus). In order to avoid this danger, artificers, in undertaking such work, usually agree not to do it at their own risk, an agreement which supersedes the liability under the Aquilian law as well as that under the contract, provided, of course, that they have not been acting dolo.

Pernice, p. 79 sq.; Windscheid, § 401. n. 3; Vangerow, pp. 590 and 592.

27. § 30.—Si cum maritus uxori margaritas extricatas dedisset in usu eaque inuito uel inscio uiro perforasset, ut pertusis in linea uteretur, teneri eam lege Aquilia, siue diuertit siue nupta est adhuc.

If a husband has given to his wife loose pearls for her use, and she has pierced them, without his wish or knowledge, in order to wear them on a string, she will be liable under the Aquilian statute, whether she is still married or a divorce has taken place.

From the standpoint of the Aquilian statute the case is perfectly clear: a wife who has made holes through pearls, which were lent to her by her husband, is liable on account of damage to property. The only point to be noticed is, that it is a wife who is declared to be liable to an Aquilian action. The same is stated in D. 24. 1. 37, but this is at variance with the principle expressed in C. 5. 21. 2 (Arndts, § 393 g), that actiones poenales (and similarly actiones famosae which make the defendant infamis, if condemned), are not admissible between husband and wife. But as the action under the Aquilian statute had for its object compensation, and was gradually more and more looked upon by the jurists as an actio rei persecutoria, it is natural that it was also admitted between husband and wife, but was very probably strictly confined to compensation for the damage sustained by the plaintiff; arg. D. 11. 3. 17. It was, of course, due to the tie of marriage that husband and wife were held incapable of suing one another under certain actions; but after the dissolution of that tie sometimes actions were admissible which were excluded during the continuance of marriage, i. e. the actio rerum amotarum after divorce had taken place (D. 25. 2, and C. 5. 21; Arndts, § 415). The action, however, on account of damage to property, was admitted even during the time of marriage, though this liability was not recognised without considerable hesitation; D. 24. 1. 37.

27. § 31.—Si quis aedificii mei fores confregerit uel refregerit aut si ipsum aedificium diruit, lege Aquilia tenetur.

If a man has battered down or broken open the doors of my house, or has destroyed the house itself, he is liable under the lex Aquilia.

The passage gives some instances of damnum, by frangere, the notion of which certainly is one covered by that of corrumpere. It is understood by itself that the Aquilian action is applicable as there is a physical act on a corporeal thing, by which damage was caused to its owner.

Pernice, p. 152.

27. § 32.—Si quis aquae ductum meum diruerit, licet cementa mea sunt quae diruta sunt, tamen quia terra mea non sit qua aquam duco, melius est dicere actionem utilem dandam.

If a person has destroyed my aqueduct, although the stones, which have been pulled down, belong to me, yet, as the ground over which the aqueduct is carried does not belong to me, it is better to say that an actio utilis is applicable.

I have a right of carrying water over my neighbour's land (servitus aquaeductus), and this right is interfered with by destroying the aqueduct itself built from my stones. The question arises whether I may not bring an actio legis Aquiliae directa on account of damage done to the masonry. It is, however, decided that I must bring an actio utilis, for though the single stones themselves are subject to my ownership, the whole of the aqueduct forms merely a portion of my neighbour's land and is subject to his right in virtue of the well-known principle inaedificatum solo cedit (Moyle, Inst. vol. I. p. 199). Accordingly, my ownership in the materials is not recognised so long as they are fixed in the soil, and therefore it is not this right of ownership which is interfered with but my ius in re aliena, i. e. the servitus aquaeductus, and on that ground I am declared to be entitled to an actio utilis (cf. 11. § 10 above).

Pernice, pp. 42 and 160.

27. § 33.—Si ex plostro lapis ceciderit et quid ruperit uel fregerit, Aquiliae actione plostrarium teneri placet, si male composuit lapides et ideo lapsi sunt.

It is settled that, if a stone has fallen from a waggon and has broken or crushed something, the driver is liable to an Aquilian action, if he has piled up the stones badly and they have fallen in consequence.

In the case under consideration there is no immediate act of rumpere or frangere on the part of the waggoner, but certainly damage has been done in consequence of a physical act of his own which is due to his negligence, and accordingly liability under the Aquilian statute is recognised. The case is similar to that mentioned in § 9 above, where a person has lighted a fire but has afterwards neglected to attend to it. In both the cases it is the act which is the cause of the damage which has happened afterwards.

Windscheid, n. 12.

27. § 34.—Si quis seruum (conductum) ad mulum regendum commendauerit (ei), mulum ille ad pollicem (suum eum) alligauerit, de loro (et) mulus eruperit sic ut et pollicem auelleret seruo et se praecipitaret, Mela scribit, si pro perito imperitus locatus sit, ex conducto agendum cum domino ob mulum ruptum uel debilitatum, sed si ictu aut terrore mulus turbatus sit, tum dominum eius, id est muli, et serui cum eo qui turbauit habiturum legis Aquiliae actionem. mihi autem uidetur et eo casu, quo ex locato actio est, competere etiam Aquiliae[1].

In case a person has recommended a slave for driving a mule and he fastened the mule by the rein to his thumb and the mule has broken away with such force as to wrench off the slave's thumb and to fall down a precipice, Mela writes that, if an unskilled slave has been let as a skilled one an actio under the contract of hiring will lie against

[1] The words bracketed in the text are, according to Mommsen, due to the insertions of the copyists.

the master of the slave on account of the hurt or damage to the mule. But if the mule has been frightened by a blow or some other event, the owner of the slave will have an Aquilian action against the person who has frightened the mule. I think, however, that in the case where an actio under the contract lies, an Aquilian action will also be applicable.

The case which is considered in the above passage is the following: A master has recommended to another person one of his slaves for the purpose of driving a mule, the slave has fastened the rein to his thumb, but the mule has broken away, and in so doing has wrenched off the thumb of the slave. The mule has also fallen down and been injured. It is decided that the master of the slave will be liable for the injury to the mule under the contract if he has let out an unskilled slave as a skilled one. But if the damage complained of was due to the interference of a third person who terrified the animal, this person will be subject to an Aquilian action on the part of the owner of the damaged mule as well as on the part of the master of the slave. But in case neither the master nor a third person has been in culpa, no liability will arise, e. g. if the mule has been frightened by some sudden and unexpected accident. But it may be asked whether in every case where there has been culpa on the part of the driver, his master also is considered to be in culpa. Is it necessary to prove in the particular case that there was negligence on the part of the master, because he had carelessly let out as a mule-driver a slave who was not fit for that post, or is culpa on the part of the master to be presumed, because it is shown by the culpa of his slave that something has been overlooked by the master in choosing the employment of the slave? The latter view seems to be that which is approved by the Roman jurists, for in D. 19. 2. 60. § 7 essentially the same case is discussed. There a mule had been killed by the negligence of a slave who had been hired from his master for that object, and it is decided that the master must compensate for culpa of the slave because he has chosen a man who has caused to the plaintiff the damage complained of (quod eum elegissem qui eiusmodi damno te adficeret), see the notes to 27. § 11 above.

In addition to the liability under the contract the master may be sued by an action under the lex Aquilia, but whether on his own behalf or by an actio noxalis is not stated. Considering, however, that according to 27. § 11 in a similar case the actio under the contract of hiring is applicable concurrently with the actio noxalis, we are probably right in assuming with the glossa that the jurist in the case we are considering also has in view a noxal action.

In the case, however, where the damage was due to the interference of a third person, he is declared by Mela to be liable to an actio legis Aquiliae (directa). This is at variance with the decision of Ulpian, who in a similar case in D. 9. 1. 1. § 7 (see also I. IV. 3. § 16) expressly states that the delinquent is liable 'in factum magis quam lege Aquilia.' The latter opinion is obviously correct, for nothing is done directly to the mule; but with regard to certain cases there seems to have been a fluctuation of opinion as to which of the two actions (directa or utilis) should be applicable. But want of accuracy in the expression may be due to the fact that the jurists sometimes merely considered whether an action on account of damage to property would lie in accordance with the principles recognised by them, without thinking of the formal distinctions of the actions. Cf. 28 pr. below, 5. § 3 above, C. 5. 35. 5, as containing other instances of this rather careless use of language.

Pernice, pp. 154 and 215; Vangerow, vol. III. p. 588.

27. § 35.—Item si tectori locaueris laccum uino plenum curandum et ille eum pertudit, ut uinum sit effusum, Labeo scribit in factum agendum.

Similarly, if you have given a vessel full of wine to a worker in clay to have it repaired, and he has broken a hole in it, so that the wine has been spilled, Labeo writes that an actio in factum is applicable.

Some one has a vessel, laccus, probably of earthenware, full of wine, and has given it to a tector, i.e. a worker in clay, to repair. The latter, in the course of repairing it, has made a hole in the vessel, and thus the wine has been spilled. It is said that an actio in factum lies against him. It is hardly necessary to say that what the jurist is here thinking of is not the damage done to the vessel, but the loss of the wine. But as the wine was not directly affected by the delinquent, not an actio directa, but an actio in factum is declared applicable.

Windscheid, n. 5.

28 *pr.*—Paulus libro X ad Sabinum. Qui foueas ursorum ceruorumque capiendorum causa faciunt, si in itineribus fecerunt eoque aliquid decidit factumque deterius est, lege Aquilia obligati sunt: at si in aliis locis, ubi fieri solent, fecerunt, nihil tenentur.

Persons who dig pitfalls for catching bears and stags will be liable, under the lex Aquilia, if they have dug them in roads, and something has fallen in and has suffered damage; but if they have digged them in other places, where they are usually made, they are not liable.

According to these words a person who has made pitfalls in ground over which people are accustomed to pass is declared to be liable to the actio legis Aquiliae directa for the damage resulting in consequence to the property of another. But it is obvious that the words 'lege Aquilia obligati sunt' are not used with strict accuracy, for there is no damnum corpore—though a damnum corpori—datum, and therefore not a case of the actio legis Aquiliae directa, but of an actio in factum or utilis (cf. the note to 37. § 34).

If, however, pitfalls have been made in places which are commonly used for such purposes no liability, according to Paulus, will arise in consequence; and this view is perfectly in agreement with several other passages, such as 9. § 4 (where people were throwing javelins), and 11 pr. (where people were playing at ball). From this we may infer that there is a general tendency in Roman law not to recognise liability in case acts had been committed in places which were set aside for the commission of such acts.

Pernice, pp. 73 and 147.

28. § 1.—Haec tamen actio ex causa danda est, id est si neque denuntiatum est neque scierit aut prouidere potuerit: et multa huiusmodi deprehenduntur, quibus summouetur petitor, si euitare periculum poterit.

This action, however, only holds if there is good reason for it, i.e. if no warning has been given, or if the injured person did not know of, or could not have foreseen the danger, and many similar circumstances may be conceived of, in virtue of which the plaintiff's claim may be rebutted if the defendant could have avoided the danger[1].

This section restricts the general decision in the principium of the fragment. For though damage has been done by pitfalls which have been made in the places not destined for such purpose, yet no Aquilian action is applicable, and that for one of two reasons: Either there has been no negligence on the part of the doer, in so far as he has done everything which a diligens paterfamilias would do in such cases, e. g. by giving due notice of the danger (denuntiatum est; cf. also 31 below); or though he has been in culpa, there has yet been contributory negligence on the part of the injured person, who, while he knew or might have known of the danger (scierit aut prouidere potuerit), carelessly drove cattle over the dangerous place.

It is, however, said in the fragment, that, in virtue of circumstances of this kind, the plaintiff's claim may be rebutted, summouetur petitor; and this shows clearly that such facts were brought forward by means of the exceptions to be proved by the defendant. It is enough for the plaintiff to show that an act has been done by the defendant, which apparently has caused damage to his, i. e. the plaintiff's, property. It will be left for the defendant to prove that, in spite of such act, there is no reason for his becoming liable under the Aquilian statute, on the ground that culpa was absent on his part, or contributory negligence present on the part of the plaintiff himself. (Cf. 9. § 4 above; 30. § 4 below; Paul. Sent. Rec. 1. 15. § 3, as containing other instances of contributory negligence.)

Pernice, p. 235; Windscheid, § 258. n. 17.

29 *pr.*—Ulpianus libro XVIII ad edictum. Quemadmodum si laqueos eo loci posuisses quo ius ponendi non haberes, et pecus uicini in eos laqueos incidisset.

An Aquilian action is likewise applicable if you have set traps in a place where you have no right to set them, and a neighbour's cattle has fallen into them.

This fragment is in its sense obviously connected with the sentence, 'Haec tamen actio ex causa danda est,' in the previous section

[1] Mommsen proposes 'poterat' instead of 'poterit.'

(28. § 1), and is of course subject to the same restrictions stated therein, viz. that due notice was not given to the neighbour, etc. It is also obvious that here an actio in factum (or utilis), and not a direct action, is applicable.

> 29. § 1.—Si protectum meum, quod supra domum tuam nullo iure habebam, reccidisses, posse me tecum damni iniuria agere Proculus scribit: debuisti enim mecum ius mihi non esse protectum habere agere: nec esse aequum damnum me pati reccisis a te meis tignis. aliud est dicendum ex rescripto imperatoris Seueri, qui ei per cuius domum traiectus erat aquae ductus citra seruitutem rescripsit, iure suo posse eum intercidere, et merito: interest enim, quod hic in suo protexit, ille in alieno fecit.

If you have cut away my roof, which I had projecting over your house without any right, Proculus writes, that I am entitled to bring an actio legis Aquiliae against you, for you ought to have brought an actio negatoria against me, to prove that I had no right to have the roof, and he says, that it is not fair that I should suffer damage through your cutting away my beams. A different decision, however, is given by a rescript of the Emperor Severus, who wrote to a person, through whose house an aqueduct had been carried without a right of servitude, that he might destroy the aqueduct in virtue of his own right; and this is perfectly correct, for there is this difference, that the latter was protecting himself in his own property, the former was dealing with property of another.

Two cases are clearly distinguished: (1) a person cuts away the roof of another which projects over his ground, and (2) a person destroys the aqueduct of another which is carried over his land. In neither case does there exist any right on the part of the neighbour who has made the protectus or aqueduct. In both the cases we should therefore expect that the person who destroys the arrangements made unlawfully in or over a place which is subject to his ownership exercises merely a right of his own, and that therefore no liability can be attached to his act, according to the principle 'Qui suo jure utitur neminem laedit.' But this view is taken only in deciding the second case, where the aqueduct was carried over the neighbour's ground, while in the first case, where the roof was cut away, the doer is said to be subject to an actio legis Aquiliae, for he 'in alieno fecit,' whilst the former 'in suo protexit.' And there is really an important difference indicated by the Latin words we have quoted, for a protectus or proiectus (roof, balcony, etc.) forms only a portion of the house to which it belongs, and is accordingly subject to the ownership of the person to whom the house belongs (cf. note to 27. § 32 above), whether it reaches over the neighbour's ground or not, and therefore he who cuts down the roof interferes in so far with the right of ownership of his neighbour, and the latter is accordingly declared to be entitled to the actio legis Aquiliae (viz. directa). But an aqueduct, on the other hand, i. e. the materials forming it, is simply a portion of the soil on which it is built, and if the owner of the soil destroys such building, he cannot possibly be liable if there is no corresponding right to the servitus on the part of the plaintiff. Accordingly the difference between the two cases is that the right of the owner who complains of the unlawful arrangements is in one case counterbalanced by a right on the part of the adversary, in the other it is not. Therefore, in the first case, the injured party cannot destroy proprio motu the existing protectus without becoming liable to an actio legis Aquiliae, and must sue by an actio negatoria, an action by which the plaintiff asserts freedom of his ownership from the servitude asserted by the other (Moyle, Inst. p. 530, and Poste, Gaius, note to IV. § 3, 2nd edition, p. 487). The object of this action was, accordingly, that the freedom of the ownership of the plaintiff should be recognised by the judicial sentence, and that the lawful state of his property should be restored, and that compensation should be given, as well as, if necessary, security against further disturbances, so-called 'cautio de amplius non turbando' (Arndts, § 169).

Pernice, p. 41; Windscheid, n. 11.

29. § 2.—Si nauis tua inpacta in meam scapham damnum mihi dedit, quaesitum est, quae actio mihi competeret. et ait Proculus, si in potestate nautarum fuit, ne id accideret, et culpa eorum factum sit, lege Aquilia cum nautis agendum, quia parui refert nauem immittendo aut serraculum ad nauem

ducendo an tua manu damnum dederis, quia omnibus his modis per te damno adficior: sed si fune rupto, aut cum a nullo regeretur, nauis incurrisset, cum domino agendum non esse.

If your ship has run my boat down and so caused me damage, it has been asked which action I should make use of. And Proculus says, if it was within the power of the sailors to prevent the accident, and the collision happened by their culpa, an Aquilian action is to be brought against them, because it makes very little difference whether you have done the damage by letting the ship drive, or by turning the helm, or by your own hand, because in all these ways damage is done to me by your act. But if a ship has run foul of another, because the cable has broken or because no one could steer it, an action against the owner does not lie.

If my boat has been damaged by being run down by your ship, I shall be entitled to sue the sailors by an actio legis Aquiliae, for it does not make any difference whether the damage is done by one's own hand or mediately by misdirecting a vessel. This decision is perfectly clear. It is, however, difficult to say what is meant by the following words, that if the damage was due to the breaking of the cable or because no one was steering the ship, no action would lie against the owner. It might be asked whether in such case an action would lie against the sailors who might have been in culpa. It seems, however, more probable that the jurist is thinking of a mere accident, or, more strictly speaking, of cases where the damage was caused by the condition of the vessel itself, without any culpa on the part of a definite person. In cases of such kind the owner is declared not to be answerable for his ship, and therefore no action is available (see D. 39. 2; 7. § 1). It is understood by itself that if the seamen are slaves of the owner of the ship, the latter is liable to a noxal action, in case they have been in culpa; he may, however, also be liable himself to an Aquilian action if he has employed slaves who had shown themselves to be dangerous to the property of others (see 27. § 11 above, the words 'ceterum si noxios seruos habuit —').

Pernice, p. 77.

29. § 3.—Item Labeo scribit, si, cum ui uentorum nauis impulsa esset in funes anchorarum alterius et nautae funes praecidissent, si nullo alio modo nisi praecisis funibus explicare se potuit, nullam actionem dandam. idemque Labeo et Proculus et circa retia piscatorum, in quae nauis piscatorum inciderat, aestimarunt. plane si culpa nautarum id factum esset, lege Aquilia agendum. sed ubi damni iniuria agitur ob retia, non piscium, qui ideo capti non sunt, fieri aestimationem, cum incertum fuerit, an caperentur. idemque et in uenatoribus et in aucupibus probandum.

Similarly Labeo writes that if a vessel has been driven by force of the wind on to the cables of another, and the crew have cut the cables, no action is applicable, if they could not free themselves in any other way except by cutting the cables. The same is stated by Sabinus and Proculus with reference to fishing-nets into which the vessel has been driven. Though, of course, if the damage has been due to the culpa of the sailors an actio legis Aquiliae may be brought; but if an action is brought on account of damage done to the nets, the value of the fish which have in consequence not been caught is not to be assessed, as it is uncertain whether they would have been caught. The same is to be recognised with regard to hunters and fowlers.

It is obvious that if a ship which was driven on to the cables of another, although without any culpa on the part of the seamen, was freed by cutting through these cables, damage is done to their owner, and that this damage is to be imputed to the culpa of the doers, because the act was done intentionally. Nevertheless no liability under the Aquilian statute ensues, because the seamen could only avert damage from their own vessel by damaging property of another person; they were accordingly acting under urgent necessity, or so-called compulsion by necessity, which in several passages is recognised as a reason for not becoming liable for damage done. Having therefore, according to the view of the Roman jurists, a right to do the act, the requirement of iniuria is wanting on the part of the crew, and therefore the Aquilian action is not applicable. See D. h.

t. 49 § 1, D. 19. 5. 14 pr., and D. 47. 93. § 7, where it is said, 'nec enim iniuria hoc fecit, qui se tueri uoluit, cum alias non posset.' This view, however, is not uncontroverted, for according to the opinion cited by Ulpian (in D. 43. 24. 7. § 4) from Servius Sulpicius Rufus, that jurist does not, strictly speaking, recognise urgent necessity as a reason for not becoming liable for damage done. But there is no doubt that it is recognised as an excuse by the compilers of the Digest (see especially D. 47. 9. 3. § 7, and Part II. § 6).

The decision given in the case of the cables having been cut through is equally applicable where fishing-nets have been torn under the compulsion of necessity. If there was no such compulsion, an action on account of the tearing of the nets will be applicable; but it was questioned whether the value of the fish which had not been caught on account of the damage to the nets, was to be taken into account in assessing damages. This question, however, is decided in the negative, 'cum incertum fuerit, an caperentur.' This seems to be entirely in accordance with the manner in which the lucrum cessans is dealt with, for only such profits as may reasonably be expected as certain are to be taken into account in assessing damages.

One might, however, object that, although it is uncertain whether any fish will be caught, and, if any, what quantity; yet an average quantity may be fixed, and be the object of compensation. This view is strongly supported by D. 19. 1. 12, according to which an assessment of the draught of fish is admissible (si iactum retis emero et iactare retem piscator noluit, incertum eius rei aestimandum est). Accordingly, assessment of a draught of fish is, on account of its uncertainty, excluded in one case (where damage is done to property), and is, in spite of its uncertainty, admitted in another case (where the produce of the draught has been sold). It is very difficult to account for this difference. Probably it is explained by the wide discretion possessed by the Roman jurists. The judge in fixing compensation was not inclined to favour the defendant if there was dolus on his part; therefore where the seller refuses to fulfil his promise, the profit of which the buyer had been deprived was to be taken into account; whereas, in case of damage done to the fishing-nets through negligence, the judge would not burden the defendant too heavily.

Pernice, pp. 38 and 243; Windscheid, § 455. n. 11, and § 258. n. 16;

Vangerow, vol. III. p. 585; Mommsen, Beiträge, vol. III. p. 191 and p. 257 sq.

29. § 4.—Si nauis alteram contra se uenientem obruisset, aut in gubernatorem aut in ducatorem actionem competere damni iniuriae Alfenus ait: sed si tanta uis naui facta sit, quae temperari non potuit, nullam in dominum dandam actionem: sin autem culpa nautarum id factum sit, puto Aquiliae sufficere.

If a ship has sunk another which has come in its way, Alfenus says that an action for the damage done will lie against the steersman or against the captain; but if the ship was being driven so violently that it could not be controlled, no action is to be given against the owner of the ship: if, however, the collision was due to the culpa of the seamen an Aquilian action, according to Ulpian's opinion, is sufficient.

A ship has sunk another. Such a result is, as a rule, due to the culpa of the persons who have directed the ship, i. e. either the captain (ducator), if he has not foreseen the danger and given suitable commands to the steersman and the rest of the crew; or to the steersman (gubernator), if he has not obeyed the commands given to him or has not steered properly. It may, however, be that the sinking the ship was due to a mere accident, because the ship was beyond control on account of the heavy gale. In this case no action is available against the owner of the ship, as he is not answerable for damage done by inanimate things belonging to him. Whether he becomes liable in case the seamen were in culpa depends on the particular circumstances of the case (see the notes to the last passage); but this question is not considered in this passage; it is only said that if the damage was due to the culpa of the seamen an actio legis Aquiliae (viz. directa) is sufficient, because the damnum was considered to be corpori corpore datum, although inflicted by means of the ship. Therefore it was not necessary to provide an actio in factum for the case.

Pernice, pp. 75 and 214.

29. § 5.—Si funem quis, quo religata nauis erat, praeciderit, de naue quae periit in factum agendum.

If some one has cut a cable by which a ship has been fastened, and the ship has been lost, an actio in factum is to be brought on account of it.

In the case stated in the text there is no damnum corpore datum, for there is no physical act of the delinquent on the ship damaged, therefore an actio directa does not lie against him; but he is subject to an actio in factum, as in consequence of his act damage has resulted to the ship.

Windscheid, n. 5.

29. § 6.—Hac actione ex hoc legis capite de omnibus animalibus laesis, quae pecudes non sunt, agendum est, ut puta de cane: sed et de apro et leone ceterisque feris et auibus idem erit dicendum.

One must sue in an action under this chapter on account of every injury done to all animals which are not cattle, as, for instance, for injury done to a dog; and this holds good with regard to bears, lions, and all other wild beasts and birds.

It is clear from the terms of the third chapter that under its provisions an actio (hac actione, i. e. the actio directa under Chapter III.) can be brought in case an injury has been done to any animals whatever, unless they belonged to the class of cattle. But even in case of cattle, an actio under the third chapter was applicable if they were only wounded; see 27. §§ 5, 6, and 17 above; and I. h. t. § 13.

29. § 7.—Magistratus municipales, si damnum iniuria dederint, posse Aquilia teneri. nam et cum pecudes aliquis pignori cepisset et fame eas necauisset, dum non patitur te eis cibaria adferre, in factum actio danda est. item si dum putat se ex lege capere pignus, non ex lege ceperit et res tritas corruptasque reddat, dicitur legem Aquiliam locum habere: quod dicendum est et si ex lege pignus cepit. si quid tamen magistratus aduersus resistentem uiolentius fecerit, non tenebitur Aquilia: nam et cum pignori seruum cepisset et ille se suspenderit, nulla datur actio.

Municipal magistrates who have inflicted unlawful damage may become bound under the Aquilian statute, for in case such a magistrate had taken cattle in pledge, and had caused them to die of hunger by refusing to allow you to feed them, an actio in factum is to be given. Similarly, if whilst he thinks that he is taking a pledge lawfully, he has not done so in accordance with the law, and has returned the things taken in a spoiled or damaged condition, the lex Aquilia will be applicable; and the same applies also if he has taken a pledge lawfully. If, however, a magistrate has been acting too violently against a person who resisted his authority, he will not be liable under the lex Aquilia; for in the case where he had taken a slave as a pignus, and the slave hanged himself, no actio was applicable.

There is no doubt that a person who shuts up slaves and cattle, which are starved in consequence, is liable to an actio in factum (9. § 2 above) or an actio utilis (Gaius, III. 219; cf. also C. 3. 35. 5). The question, however, was discussed, whether such acts, if performed by competent magistrates, would entail liability. It is certain that, if they are acting in exercise of their magisterial functions, they cannot become liable, D. 47. 10. 13. § 1. Accordingly, if a municipal magistrate lawfully takes cattle or a slave in pledge, he does not become liable, although damage has resulted from the act, e. g. if the slave has committed suicide (see the last sentence of the passage). But it is different if, after the magistrate has taken the pledge, he has hindered the feeding of the cattle, and thus has caused their death; for in so far he has not acted within the limits of his functions, and therefore he is said in the above fragment to be liable under the Aquilian statute (see also D. 47. 8. 2. § 20, where a similar decision is given with reference to publicani who had impounded cattle).

It is another question, whether a magistrate, who has been acting in good faith, whilst not legally entitled to do the act, should become answerable for damage done. This question of principle, however, is not answered by Ulpian. He only says that if a magistrate has taken something in pledge, whilst thinking himself entitled to do so, he will be liable if he afterwards restores the things in a damaged condition. This decision is quite clear; for though the magistrate may be excused (cf. D. 47. 8. 2. § 20) for having taken the pledge without being entitled to do so, he certainly is not entitled to do damage to the pledged property, and therefore he is declared to be liable under the provision of the Aquilian statute. And in like manner, as it is not the act of taking the pledge, but the subsequent negligence in dealing with it, which entails liability, the magistrate must be liable, even if he has taken the pledge lawfully and has afterwards returned it in a damaged condition; and this consequence is expressly stated in the above passage. But if he, whilst intending to take a pledge, had been acting with excessive violence against a person who resisted his authority, he will not be liable; for he was exercising the functions of his office, and the excess of his powers is excused by the circumstances of the case.

It is obvious that the principle, which underlies the decision of the above cases, is that a magistrate who keeps within the limits of his functions is free from any liability for damage which has resulted from his acts; and it seems to be implied that even in cases where he has been acting merely in good faith he should be excused. If, however, magistrates are not acting in virtue of their office, they are liable for damage caused by them, and this is true without any distinction whether they belong to the higher or the lower magistrates (D. 4. 2. 3. § 1, and D. 18. 6. 14). There was only this difference, that an in ius uocatio could not take place against magistratus maiores cum imperio. Therefore they could not be sued as long as they held their office, although they might be sued afterwards (D. II. 4. 2; D. 4. 6. 26. § 2; D. 47. 10. 32; Keller, Der Römische Civilprocess, § 46. n. 526). But this was not the case if a delict was committed by a minor magistrate, as e. g. a municipal magistrate, as supposed in the above fragment, or an aedile (see D. 18. 6. 14), who could be sued even whilst in office, fr. 32 cit.

29. § 8.—Haec uerba: 'quanti in triginta diebus proximis fuit,' etsi non habent 'plurimi,' sic tamen esse accipienda constat.

The words: 'what the thing was worth during the last thirty days,' although they do not speak of the highest value, are yet to be understood in that sense.

According to the tenour of the third chapter (27. § 5 above), the object of the action was the payment of the value which the damaged thing had had during the thirty days preceding the injury. It is obvious that the plaintiff was not prevented from claiming the highest value of the thing during the previous month. But it was left to the judge to fix the compensation with reference to any period in that time. The jurists, however, following the authority of Sabinus (I. h. t. § 15), interpreted the terms of the statute so as to comprehend the word 'plurimi,' and consequently the judge was bound to condemn the defendant to pay the highest value which the damaged thing had attained at any period of the last month.

Windscheid, n. 21; Savigny, System, vol. VI. p. 205.

30 *pr.*—Paulus libro XXII ad edictum. Qui occidit adulterum deprehensum seruum alienum hac lege non tenebitur.

A husband who has killed a slave of another, whom he has seized in adultery with his wife, is not liable under the Aquilian statute.

A husband has a right to kill the adulterer whom he has seized in flagrante delicto. This right is expressly recognised by the lex Julia de adulteriis (Puchta, Cursus, vol. I. § 107), although only in certain cases, see D. 48. 5. 25 pr.; but it is expressly permitted by that statute to kill an adulterer if he is a slave. The husband, accordingly, acting in virtue of a right of his own, cannot become liable under the lex Aquilia, for the requirement of iniuria is absent (cf. Part II. § 6).

Pernice, p. 38; Windscheid, n. 11.

30. § 1.—Pignori datus seruus si occisus sit, debitori actio competit. sed an et creditori danda sit utilis, quia potest interesse eius, quod debitor soluendo non sit aut quod litem tempore amisit, quaeritur. sed hic iniquum est et domino et creditori eum teneri. nisi si quis putauerit nullam in ea re debitorem iniuriam passurum, cum prosit ei ad debiti quantitatem et quod sit amplius consecuturus sit ab eo, uel ab initio in id quod amplius sit quam in debito, debitori dandam actionem. et ideo in his casibus in quibus creditori danda est actio propter inopiam debitoris uel quod litem amisit, creditor quidem usque ad modum debiti habebit Aquiliae actionem, ut prosit hoc

debitori, ipsi autem debitori in id quod debitum excedit competit Aquiliae actio.

If a slave given in pledge has been killed, the actio belongs to the debtor. But it is questioned, whether an actio utilis is to be given to the creditor, because he may have an interest in it, if his debtor is insolvent or he himself has lost his right of action by lapse of time. Yet it is unfair that the delinquent should be liable to both the owner and the creditor, unless it should be thought that the debtor will not suffer any loss, as the satisfaction of the creditor is of advantage to him, so far as the amount of the debt is concerned, and as he will receive the surplus from the delinquent (ab eo), or it may be thought that the action should be given to the debtor from the very beginning for the excess of the sum to be claimed under the Aquilian statute over the amount of the debt. And therefore in those cases in which the creditor is to be allowed to bring the Aquilian action on account of the poverty of the debtor or because he has lost his right of action, the creditor will certainly be entitled to sue by the Aquilian action for damages up to the amount of the debt, so that this is to the interest of the debtor (who is thereby discharged from his debt). But to the debtor himself the actio legis Aquiliae will belong for the excess of the sum to be claimed over the amount of the debt.

The case supposed by Paulus is the following: A master has given a slave of his own in pledge to his creditor, and afterwards the slave has been killed by a third person. There is no doubt that the action will belong to the debtor who, being the owner of the slave, is entitled to the actio legis Aquiliae according to the terms of the statute (2 pr. and 11. § 6 above). But it was discussed among the jurists, whether an actio utilis should not lie in favour of the creditor, because he may have an interest in bringing an action. In itself the fact of damage is not sufficient to constitute such an interest. For, in spite of the fact that the slave has been killed (or wounded), the creditor may be in the condition to realise his claim by an action to be brought against his debtor. But if he is no longer able to do so, i. e. if either his debtor has become insolvent or his actio in personam (debitoris) has been lost by lapse of time, then there is a real damnum suffered on his part which could be remedied only by giving him an Aquilian action (utilis or in factum, cf. 17 above) up to the amount of his claim. This is clearly enough the opinion of the jurist. But he objects to it, that it seems to be unfair to make the delinquent liable to both the owner and the creditor (—iniquum est et domino et creditori eum teneri—), provided, so the jurist supposes, that the action of the dominus would lie for the full value of the killed slave. But this will not be the case, for what is received by the creditor, releases the owner from his debt, and he therefore will receive only the surplus, due on account of the damage done to his property, by an action which may be brought either at once or after the creditor has sued the delinquent.

The result is accordingly the following: The fact that a thing, given in pledge, has been destroyed or damaged, is not sufficient to give rise to an Aquilian action in favour of the creditor. But he must have lost the possibility of suing his debtor effectually; otherwise there would be no damnum. But there clearly is a damnum, if the creditor is barred from suing his debtor by limitation of action, 'quod litem tempore amisit.' It is true that Paulus, to whom the general prescription of actions (introduced 424 p. Chr.) was unknown, may have used the words just quoted only with regard to the peculiar prescription of a law-suit (not of a right of action not yet exercised), to which a so-called iudicium legitimum was subject, if not finished within one year and a half, Gaius, IV. 104. But since this prescription was unknown in later times, it follows that in the Digest, as a portion of the law of Justinian, the words must be understood of all cases, where an action has been lost by lapse of time, and they are so taken by the Basiliks and the Glossa.

But it is not only when the action is entirely lost, but also when it is impossible to sue the debtor with the effect of receiving satisfaction for one's claim, that the Aquilian action will be applicable, for it practically makes no difference whether a person is prevented from suing his debtor by law or by his adversary's poverty, 'nam is nullam videtur actionem habere cui propter inopiam adversarii inanis est actio' (Gaius in D. 4. 3. 6). Accordingly in case also of the insolvency of the debtor (Javolenus in D. 50. 16. 114: 'Solvendo esse nemo intellegitur, nisi qui solidum potest solvere') the creditor will be entitled to the Aquilian action against the delinquent.

From all this it follows that this action is given to the creditor merely as a substitute for the actio in personam he has lost, and therefore only up to the amount of his claim. Accordingly the debtor is entitled to sue the delinquent for the amount by which the damage done exceeds the debt due to the creditor, and at the same time is released from his debt by the payment received by the creditor in consequence of the action he has brought.

Pernice, pp. 28 and 200; Windscheid, n. 15; Vangerow, vol. III. p. 580; Stölzel, in the Archiv für die civilistische Praxis, vol. XXXIX. 2.

30. § 2.—Si quis alienum uinum uel frumentum consumpserit, non uidetur damnum iniuria dare ideoque utilis dando est actio.

If a person has consumed wine or corn of another, he does not seem to have caused damage unlawfully, and therefore an actio utilis is applicable.

The Aquilian action applies, according to the terms of the statute, to cases where the substance of a thing has been damaged in some way or other. But this is clearly not the case, if things have been used for the object which they naturally serve, for instance if eatables, as supposed in the above passage, have been eaten by other people. Although in such cases there is no corrumpere whatever, and accordingly no damnum is done to the things which would entitle the owner of the food consumed to make use of the direct action, there is yet the same result for the owner as if things have been spoiled and therefore an analogous action—actio utilis—is to be brought against the person who has consumed the food. See D. 19. 5. 14. § 3, where in a similar case the actio legis Aquiliae (directa) is excluded and an actio in factum is said to be applicable.

Pernice, pp. 156 and 160; Windscheid, n. 6; Vangerow, vol. III. p. 583.

30. § 3.—In hac quoque actione quae ex hoc capitulo oritur dolus et culpa punitur: ideoque si quis in stipulam suam uel spinam comburendae eius causa ignem immiserit, et ulterius euagatus

et progressus ignis alienam segetem uel uineam laeserit, requiramus, num imperitia eius aut neglegentia id accidit. nam si die uentoso id fecit, culpae reus est (nam et qui occasionem praestat damnum fecisse uidetur): in eodem crimine est et qui non obseruauit, ne ignis longius procederet. at si omnia quae oportuit obseruauit, uel subita uis uenti longius ignem produxit, caret culpa.

By the action also which arises under the third chapter, dolus and culpa are provided against. Therefore, if a person has set fire to his stubble or brushwood and the fire has spread and has, in advancing, damaged the crop or vineyard of another, we have to inquire whether this has happened in consequence of his want of experience or of his negligence. For if he has lit the fire on a windy day, he is guilty of culpa (for a person also who brings about a state of things from which damage arises is considered to have done the damage), and the same fault lies with him who has not taken precautions to prevent the fire spreading. But if he has done everything which he ought to have done, and a sudden gust of wind has carried the flames on to the neighbour's land, he is free from culpa.

In like manner as Chapter I, so Chapter III comes into operation only, if there was either dolus or culpa on the part of the doer. It must therefore be inquired, whether in cases where apparently damage is caused to another's property, it is to be attributed to the culpa of a certain person. Accordingly Paulus in the above passage says, in the case when a person has set on fire the stubble on his own ground and the fire has spread to the neighbour's crop or vineyard, it is to be asked, whether this damage is due to his want of experience (for 'imperitia culpae adnumeratur,' see 7. § 8 and 8. § 1 above) or his negligence. This is obviously the case if a person has made the fire on a windy day, for he either knew or must have known that the fire would spread (8. § 1 above); but it is also the case if he has lighted the fire on another day, and afterwards has not prevented it from spreading (27. § 9 above).

It must be noticed that the neighbour's property is not directly damaged by a physical act upon it. There is no urere of his property, but only a so-called occasionem or causam incendii praestare. But whether a person is guilty of urere or causam damni praestare does not affect his liability (cf. D. 19. 2. 11. § 4, and D. 48. 8. 15—nihil interest occidit quis an mortis causam praebeat), although the question was commonly discussed among the Roman jurists, whether a certain act would fall under the terms of the statute or were to be considered merely what is called causam damni praestare (see 7. § 6 above), but this was done only with reference to the formula to be applied in a certain law-suit. As the facts of the case we are considering constitute merely a causam incendii praestare, an actio in factum is thought to hold good, and this is expressly stated in Coll. XII. 7. §§ 4. 5. It seems, however, strange that in a similar case where a person has set on fire his own house and the fire has spread to the neighbour's building, an actio directa is declared to be applicable (see 27. § 8 above, and Coll. XII. 7. § 2); and this clearly shows that it was sometimes very difficult to distinguish between damage in the sense of the statute and causam damni praestare, which entitled the person thereby injured to an actio on the analogy of the statute. In both the cases, however, culpa must have existed on the part of the person who has caused the damages. If, therefore, the man who has set fire to his stubble has done everything to prevent the fire from spreading, and nevertheless, by a sudden gust of wind, the flames have been carried to the neighbour's crop or vineyard, he will not be liable, for he has done all in his power to deprive the act of kindling the fire of its dangerous character, therefore 'caret culpa.' This decision suggests the question whether a person, in order to escape liability under the Aquilian statute, is bound to be as careful and diligent as possible. It is clear from the following fr. 31, that only such diligentia is required as is peculiar to a bonus pater familias. Accordingly, if in the above case the person who has lit the fire has done what a diligens pater familias would do under the circumstances of the case, in order to prevent the fire from spreading, he will not be liable, although an extremely cautious or careful man might have avoided the damage.

Pernice, p. 66; Windscheid, n. 5 and 12; Hasse, Culpa, p. 22.

30. § 4.—Si uulneratus fuerit seruus non mortifere, neglegentia autem perierit, de uulnerato actio erit, non de occiso.

If a slave has been wounded, but not mortally, and he has died through negligence, an action will lie on account of wounding and not of killing the slave.

A wound which is not mortal has been inflicted on a slave; afterwards the slave has died, because the master has neglected to have the wound properly attended to. Here the delinquent is declared to be liable only under Chapter III, and not on account of killing the slave. It is true that without the wound the slave would not have died, but the death is equally due to contributory negligence on the part of the injured person and therefore liability on account of killing is excluded. But of course the delinquent is liable for the act of wounding, as to which there was no contributory negligence on the part of the master.

Pernice, p. 61; Windscheid, § 258. n. 17.

31 *pr.*—Idem libro X ad Sabinum. Si putator ex arbore ramum cum deiceret uel machinarius hominem praetereuntem occidit, ita tenetur si is in publicum decidat nec ille proclamauit, ut casus eius euitari possit. sed Mucius etiam dixit, si in priuato idem accidisset, posse de culpa agi: culpam autem esse, quod cum a diligente prouideri poterit, non esset prouisum aut tum denuntiatum esset, cum periculum euitari non possit. secundum quam rationem non multum refert, per publicum an per priuatum iter fieret, cum plerumque per priuata loca uolgo iter fiat. quod si nullum iter erit, dolum dumtaxat praestare debet, ne immittat in eum quem uiderit transeuntem: nam culpa ab eo exigenda non est, cum diuinare non potuerit an per eum locum aliquis transiturus sit.

If a man who is lopping branches from a tree and has flung one down—or if a workman on a scaffold—has killed a slave who was passing by, he is liable, if the branch falls into a public place and if he has not given warning by crying out, so that its fall might have been avoided. But Mucius further stated, that if the same thing has happened on private ground, an action may be brought on account of culpa, for that it is culpa when a danger might have been foreseen by a careful man, no precautions have been taken or if warning has been given only when it was impossible to avoid the danger. According to this view it does not make much difference whether the way runs over public or over private ground, for people are often accustomed to walk over private ground. But if there is no path or way across the land, the man lopping the branches will be liable only for dolus, i. e. he may not fling a branch down upon a person whom he sees passing; for it would not be fair to make him liable for culpa (viz. levis), as he could not have foreseen that any one would have been passing by that place.

According to the above passage a person who lets something fall from a tree or stage is liable for the damage if the thing has fallen into a public place. But according to the opinion of Sabinus, this is true also of the case where the same thing was done in a private ground across which it was usual to pass; for under the lex Aquilia the only question is whether there is culpa on the part of a certain person, and there is clearly culpa where precautions have not been taken, whilst the danger might have been foreseen by a careful man. The danger, however, in the above case might have been foreseen equally, whether the ground was public or private. One might think that in all cases where a man was doing something even in places where there was no way, the danger might have been foreseen and precautions taken against it. Yet such a diligentia is not required by law; for no one is bound to bestow all possible care to avoid injury to his neighbour, but he is bound only to bestow such diligence as usually is bestowed by a careful man, a diligens pater familias. (Cf. 30. § 3 above). But it must be noticed that although the conduct of a man who carefully looks after his affairs, is always to be taken into account in determining the liability under the Aquilian statute, yet a careful man will behave differently under different circumstances; e. g. he certainly will be more careful in carrying glass than in carrying stones. Accordingly in a given case it is sometimes a higher (see I. h. t. § 7; D. 1. 18. 6. § 7; D. h. t. 7. § 8, 8. § 1, 27. § 29; D. 50. 17. 132), sometimes a lower amount of diligentia the omission of which entails liability under the Aquilian statute. The circumstances of a certain case may be of such kind that only a very low degree of care can be expected; it even may be the case that culpa levis cannot come into existence. Whilst the person who is lopping trees over a way is certainly obliged to carefully avoid damage to passers-by, and whilst he will become liable also if he has not seen them approaching, yet if there is no way running by, no one can require him to take precautions, nevertheless, in order to warn people who should happen to be crossing the ground, for such an amount of care would have been taken only by an extremely cautious man; on the contrary, every one who chooses to pass over ground across which no way runs, must take care himself, and has to attribute it to his own negligence if he is damaged in consequence. In such cases the lopper can only become liable if he sees some one approaching and in spite of this fact throws down a branch. Such a fact, however, implies certainly either dolus, if he intended the damage, or, at least, culpa lata, if he thought the passer-by would not be hit by the branch. Accordingly the man lopping the branches is said to be liable for dolus, which term, as usual, comprehends the notion of lata culpa (cf. D. 11. 6. 1. § 1—'lata culpa plane dolo comparabitur'—; D. 50. 16. 226; Arndts, § 250. n. c. and d.), whereas the following word culpa is to be understood in the sense of culpa levis, 'dolum dumtaxat praestare debet, culpa ab eo exigenda non est.' We might infer from the last words quoted that, as an exception, a person is declared not to be answerable for culpa; this, however, is not the case, but the expression is inaccurate: in both the cases stated in the fragment, where there was a way and where there was none, the existence of culpa levis would be sufficient to give rise to an Aquilian action, in the latter case, however, where there was no way, the circumstances are of such kind that culpa levis is absolutely impossible (cf. I. IV. 3. §§ 4 and 5; D. h. t 9. § 4).

Pernice, pp. 51 sq., 62, 66; Hasse, Culpa, p. 68 sqq.; Windscheid, n. 9 and 12; Mommsen, Beiträge, vol. III. p. 368.

32 *pr.*—Gaius libro VII ad edictum prouinciale. Illud quaesitum est, an quod proconsul in furto obseruat quod a familia factum sit (id est ut non in singulos detur poenae persecutio, sed sufficeret id praestari quod praestandum foret si id furtum unus liber fecisset), debeat et in actione damni iniuriae obseruari. sed magis uisum est idem esse obseruandum, et merito: cum enim circa furti actionem haec ratio sit, ne ex uno delicto tota familia dominus careat eaque ratio similiter et in actionem damni iniuriae interueniat, sequitur ut idem debeat aestimari,

praesertim cum interdum leuior sit haec causa delicti, ueluti si culpa et non dolo damnum daretur.

It has been asked whether what the proconsul states with regard to a furtum committed by the set of slaves belonging to one master—namely, that no prosecution for penalty is admissible on account of the several accomplices, but that it is sufficient to pay what would have to be paid if one free man had committed the furtum—must be observed in case of an actio on account of the damage to property also. According to the prevalent opinion this question has been answered in the affirmative, and this is correct, for as there is with regard to the actio furti this reason that the master should not be deprived of all his slaves in virtue of one delict only, and as this reason equally applies to the actio for damage to property, it follows that the same view is to be taken with regard to this delict, especially as sometimes the facts of the case are here of a less serious character, for instance, if damage has been done negligently and not intentionally.

It is well known that if a delict is committed by several persons each of them is liable to its legal consequences (cf. the notes to 11. § 2 above). Accordingly if the familia of a person, i.e. the slaves belonging to him (D. 21. 1. 25. § 2) have joined in the commission of a delict, the master is subject to an actio noxalis on behalf of each of his slaves. In this way the master might easily be deprived of all his property, for he has either to pay the penalty—and compensation besides if damage has been sustained by another person—or he has to surrender by noxae datio all his slaves (D. 47. 6. 1 pr.). Naturally these consequences were very seriously felt in case of those delicts which commonly were committed by slaves. It was therefore provided by the praetor—and the same enactment was put into the edicts of the governors of the provinces (see the inscription of the fragment and the words 'proconsul —observat')—that the master should be bound to pay only so much as was to be paid, if the furtum had been committed by a single free man (see D. 9. 4. 31, where the contents of the edict are reported:— 'ait praetor, cum familia furtum faciat, ad eum modum se actionem daturum, ut tantum actor consequatur, quantum si liber fecisset consequeretur'). Accordingly the master had to pay a duplum or a quadruplum of the value of the stolen things, if he had been sued by the actio furti (noxalis), and besides he had to pay compensation if sued by the condictio furtiva (D. 47. 6. 2).

From the passage we are considering, we learn that it had been discussed amongst the jurists, whether the provision of the edict should not apply to cases of damage to property, for the actio legis Aquiliae could also be brought against several delinquents (11. § 2 above), and it has been said in favour of such extension that the ratio legis, viz. that the master may not become deprived of all his slaves (ne ex uno delicto tota familia dominus careat), applies equally to cases of damage to property. And on that account it has been decided that also in cases where unlawful damage has been done by a familia of a master, his liability should be equally restricted, i. e. he should be liable to pay only so much as was to be paid if a single free man had done the damage.

It is obvious that the reason of the praetor would justify an extension of the enactment to all possible delicts which were committed by the slaves belonging to one master. But there is no evidence whatever that the enactment has been applied to delicts other than furtum and damnum iniuria; cf. D. 2. 1. 9 and D. 47. 10. 34.

Lenel, Das Edictum perpetuum, p. 267. n. 10.

32. § 1.—Si idem eundem seruum uulnerauerit, postea deinde etiam occiderit, tenebitur et de uulnerato et de occiso: duo enim sunt delicta. aliter atque si quis uno impetu pluribus uulneribus aliquem occiderit: tunc enim una erit actio de occiso.

If one and the same person has wounded a slave and has afterwards killed the same slave, he will be liable on account of wounding and of killing the slave, for there are two separate delicts. It is different if a man has killed a slave in one attack by several wounds, for then there will be only one action as to the killed slave.

The decision of Ulpian that a person who has wounded a slave and afterwards killed him is subject to an action under Chapter III as well as under Chapter I, is entirely in accordance with the contents of fr. 27 pr. above, where a man who has killed the slave stolen by him is said to be liable to an actio furti and an actio legis Aquiliae (cf. the notes to 27 pr.). In both the passages there are two different facts, each giving rise to a particular action, but, whilst in 27 pr. the delicts are different in their nature, in the fragment under consideration both the cases concern damage to property (see also 48 below, where a similar case is stated). But as each of the acts constitutes a delict of its own, being due to a special state of mind of the doer, the injured party is not prevented from claiming the penalties forfeited by the acts which have been committed.

It is different if a person uno impetu inflicts several wounds on a slave and thus causes his death. Here the several blows are inflicted at the same time and due to the same intentions of the doer. Therefore they are considered to constitute one delict only, viz. that of killing the slave which accordingly gives rise to actio under Chapter I of the Aquilian statute.

Savigny, System, vol. V. pp. 207 and 235 sq.

33. *pr.*—Paulus libro II ad Plautium. Si seruum meum occidisti, non affectiones aestimandas esse puto, ueluti si filium tuum naturalem quis occiderit quem tu magno emptum uelles, sed quanti omnibus ualeret. Sextus quoque Pedius ait pretia rerum non ex affectione nec utiltate singulorum, sed communitur fungi: itaque eum qui filium naturalem possidet non eo locupletiorem esse quod eum plurimo, si alius possideret, redempturus fuit, nec illum qui filium alienum possideat tantum habere quanti eum patri uendere posset. In lege enim Aquilia damnum consequimur: et amisisse dicemur quod aut consequi potuimus aut erogare cogimur.

I think that in case you have killed my slave the feeling of affection is not to be taken into account in assessing damages, as, for instance, if a person has killed your natural son whom you would have bought at a high price, but it is to be ascertained what his value is to everybody. Sextus Pedius also writes that the prices of things are to be determined neither with reference to affection nor to their utility to single individuals, but that prices have a common validity. Accordingly, he who possesses a natural son of his own is by no means richer because he would have bought the son at the highest price, if another had possessed him, and he who possesses a natural son of another does not possess the value for which he might sell the slave to his father, for in suing under the Aquilian statute we receive compensation for the loss which we have sustained, and we are said to have lost what we either might have acquired or what we are compelled to spend.

The object of the Aquilian action is the interesse (21. § 2 above) i. e. the loss caused to the plaintiff's property by the act of damage. Consequently the fact that the injured person is prepossessed in favour of the thing damaged cannot be taken into account in assessing damages[1]. This interest of affection ('Affectionsinteresse') does not alter the condition of the plaintiff's property. Accordingly, it is decided in the passage under consideration that an owner is not entitled to any compensation merely on account of the fact that the killed slave was his son, whom he would have bought at a very high price, if he had been subject to the power of another person. It is due to the same principle that a master is not entitled to an Aquilian action in case his slave has been castrated, 27. § 28 above; for the same reason a free man is not thought to be entitled to any compensation on account of his disfigurement (deformitas), D. 9. 1. 3 and D. 9. 2. 7 pr.; and a testator cannot sue on account of damage done to his property if his testamentum has been destroyed, 41 pr. below, although in all these cases the feeling of affection of the injured person may be seriously interfered with.

But the fragment we have to explain does not only exclude the interest of affection, but seems to exclude also the peculiar value of the thing to the injured person, and seems to restrict the compensation to the mere market value of the slave to 'quanti omnibus valeret;' nevertheless doubts as to the intention of Paulus are admissible, for in his time it was generally recognised that the interesse was the object of the Aquilian action, as by Ulpian (in 21. § 2 above), who died under Alexander Severus before his contemporary Paulus, and even by Paulus himself in 22—utilitas venit in hoc iudicium—(see Puchta, Cursus der Institut. § 100. n. t–w). In addition to this it is expressly stated by Paulus, in several instances, that a higher value than the value of the damaged thing itself can be claimed by the Aquilian action; thus in case where a slave has been killed whose transfer has

[1] An exception to the principle stated in the text is not to be found in D. 17. 1. 54. § 1. See Vangerow, vol. III. p. 46.

been promised under penalty (22 pr. above), and, secondly, in case one of a set of four chariot-horses has been killed (22. § 1 above). Under these circumstances we must infer that it cannot have been the intention of Paulus to restrict the compensation to be paid to the ordinary value of the thing destroyed. And this view is supported by the last words of the passage, according to which the object of the action is also 'quod—consequi potuimus,' i. e. the lucrum cessans, which clearly is an addition to the value of the thing itself.

That nevertheless not only the 'affectio' but also the 'utilitas singulorum' seems to be excluded from being taken into account is probably due to the fact that Paulus did not intend to consider the notion of interesse, but only to ascertain clearly the negative principle that the value attached to things by personal affection is not to be taken into account. This is said primarily, 'non affectiones aestimandas esse,' and if he opposes the ordinary value to it, 'quanti (seruus) omnibus valeret,' it is because he is not thinking of peculiar circumstances which may increase that value. It is the same view which leads Paulus to quote words of Pedius, which very probably do not at all refer to cases where the interesse, but merely to cases where the ordinary or the so-called market value of the things is to be ascertained (cf. D. 35. 2. 63 pr.). It is true that, if we interpret the passage in this way, Paulus is charged with an inaccuracy of language, but such an assumption seems to be more correct, than to say that the passage is at variance with principles which undoubtedly were recognised by Paulus himself.

But it is possible that it is still another idea which underlies the decision of the jurist. In every case where the value of a thing (slave, horse) to the injured person exceeds the ordinary value, there is necessarily some other object of his property, the relation to which occasions the higher value of the thing destroyed. In order to illustrate this by the above instances of Paulus, it is to the fact that a penalty is promised that the higher value of the slave is due, and the same is to be said of the fact that the horse has belonged to one of four chariot-horses. We may therefore in such cases, instead of ascertaining directly the value of the thing to the injured person—look at those objects by which the higher value is occasioned. Thus in case where a slave has not been transferred, the amount of the penalty forfeited is to be taken into account instead of the value of the slave himself, and where one of four chariot-horses has been killed, in addition to the value of the killed horse, the depreciation of the others is to be assessed. It is obvious that from this point of view only the ordinary value (pretium commune) is to be taken into account, and it is obviously this view, which has found expression in D. h. t. 22. § 1; Gaius, III. 212; I. 4. 3. § 10. It is not improbable that in the above passage also Paulus has been led by the same idea, and that it is accordingly by this view that his assertion is to be explained that the ordinary value and not the utilitas singulorum is to be taken into account.

Pernice, p. 243 sq.; Mommsen, Beiträge, vol. II. pp. 214 and 122; Windscheid, § 258. n. 16, and § 455. n. 6.

33. § 1.—In damnis quae lege Aquilia non tenentur in factum datur actio.

In cases of such damage as do not fall under the Aquilian statute, an actio in factum is applicable.

According to these words we might think that in all cases which do not fall under the terms of the statute and yet damnum is done to a person's property through the culpa of another, an actio in factum is applicable, without any distinction whether a corporeal thing has been injured or not. This, however, is not correct, for if we examine all the passages in which an analogous action can be maintained, we find that most of them contain cases where a real injury was done to a corporeal thing, although not by such an act of the delinquent (occidere or corrumpere) as required by the statute, i. e. where there is a damnum corpori datum (see 7. §§ 3 and 6; 9 pr. §§ 2 and 3; 11. §§ 1 and 5; 27. §§ 10 and 35; 29. §§ 5. 7; 30. § 3 above and 53 below, and the notes to these passages). In addition to this only those cases are recognised, where, although strictly speaking, a thing has not been destroyed or damaged, yet the same result for its owner has happened; thus if a person has consumed eatables of another (30. § 2 above), if the value of things has been diminished by mixing them with others (27. § 14), or if one man deprives another of his property without having the animus lucri faciendi (27. § 21). These are the extremest limits to the application of the principles of the Aquilian statute, and it is therefore with this restriction that the general words of Paulus are to be understood. They apply only to such cases of damage as have been thought fit to be brought under the Aquilian statute (cf. about the relation of the notion of actio in factum to that of actio utilis the notes to § 11 and § 2 above).

Pernice, p. 147; Windscheid, n. 6; Vangerow, vol. III. p. 583.

34. *pr.*—Marcellus libro XXI digestorum. Titio et Seio Stichum legauit: deliberante Seio, cum Titius uindicasset legatum Stichus occisus est: deinde Seius repudiauit legatum. perinde Titus agere possit ac si soli legatus esset,

35.—Ulpianus libro XVIII ad edictum. quia retro adcreuisse dominium ei uidetur:

36.—Marcellus libro XXI digestorum. nam sicut repudiante legatario legatum heredis est actio perinde ac si legatus non esset, ita huius actio est ac si soli legatus esset.

A testator has left his slave Stichus both to Titius and Seius in the way of legacy. Whilst Seius was thinking whether he should accept the legacy, and after Titius had claimed it, Stichus has been killed by a third person; and afterwards Seius has repudiated the legatum. Titius will be entitled to sue under the Aquilian statute in the same way as if the slave had been bequeathed to him alone, because he is considered as having acquired retrospectively the ownership in the slave: for in the same way as the Aquilian action belongs to the heir in case of repudiation on the part of the legatee, as if no legatum had been made, so here the actio belongs to the collegatarius as if the slave had been left to him alone by the legatum.

If something has been left by legatum per vindicationem, as is supposed by Marcellus in the passage under consideration, the legatarius acquires according to the view of the Sabinians (Gaius, II. 195 and 200), which is recognised in the Corpus Iuris (cf. D. 8. 6. 19; Arndts, § 560. n. 2) ownership in the thing bequeathed as soon as the heir has entered on the inheritance, by force of law independently of his wish and knowledge; but if he afterwards refuses to take the legatum, in case of the so-called repudiatio legati, it was considered as if no legatum had been made, and therefore ownership in the thing had never been acquired by the legatee.

If we apply these principles to the case under discussion, it follows that ownership in the slave has been acquired for both the legatarii at the moment of the aditio hereditatis, but as Seius afterwards has refused to take the legatum, the acquisition of co-ownership on his part is considered by law as not having taken place. So it is decided that Seius does not take any share in the legatum, but as Stichus has been bequeathed not only to him, but also to Titius, it is at the same time settled that ownership in the whole slave has been acquired by Titius, and this from the moment of the aditio hereditatis, for the whole acquisition on the part of Seius is considered as having been extinguished from the very beginning, and therefore the share Seius had in the ownership of the slave is taken as having belonged retrospectively to Titius, 'quia retro dominium accrevisse videtur' (cf. Gaius, II. 199; I. II. 20. § 8; Windscheid, § 644; Arndts in Glück, Ausführliche Erläuterung der Pandekten, vol. 476 sqq.). It follows from this that if Stichus has been killed at some period after the heir had entered on the inheritance, the Aquilian action will belong exclusively to Titius, because he alone is considered to have been the owner of the slave at the time of the injury (cf. 13. § 3 above). And this is entirely in accordance with the decision of the case where something has been left to a single legatarius and has been destroyed by another person, and afterwards the legatee has refused to take the legatum, for here also the Aquilian action will belong to the heir, who is equally considered as having been the owner during the whole time; D. 34. 5. 15 pr.

Savigny, System, vol. III. p. 151: Windscheid, § 644. n. 8.

36. § 1.—Si dominius seruum, quem Titius mortifere uulnerauerat, liberum et heredem esse iusserit, eique postea Maeuius exstiterit heres, non habebit Maeuius cum Titio legis Aquiliae actionem scilicet secundum Sabini opinionem, qui putabat ad heredem actionem non transmitti, quae defuncto competere non potuit: nam sane absurdum accidet, ut heres pretium quasi occisi consequatur eius cuius heres exstitit. quod si ex parte eum dominus heredem cum libertate esse iusserit, coheres eius mortuo eo aget lege Aquilia.

If a master has manumitted and instituted as heir a slave of his own, who has been mortally wounded by Titius, and if afterwards Maevius has become the heir of the manumitted person, Maevius will have no Aquilian action against Titius, that is to say, according to the opinion of Sabinus, who thinks that an action which could not belong to the deceased cannot be transferred to his heir; for it certainly would be an absurdity that the heir should receive the value of the person to whose property he had succeeded by inheritance on account of his having been killed. If, however, the master besides manumitting his slave has instituted him an heir pro parte only, his co-heir, after his death, will be entitled to an Aquilian action.

The case which is here stated is exactly the same as the case in 15. § 1 and 16 above (see the notes): a slave, who had been mortally wounded by Titius, was manumitted and instituted an heir by the will of his master, and being a so-called heres necessarius the slave had acquired ipso iure the inheritance left by his master, which consequently after his own death (from the wound) was transferred to his heir Maevius.

In this case a right of action under the first chapter of the Aquilian statute has been acquired for the master by the mortal wound inflicted on his slave, although it cannot be exercised till death has actually resulted from the wound (15. § 1 above), and this action is strictly speaking transferred to the heir of the injured master like every other right of property. No doubt this consequence was recognised by the jurists who opposed the view of Sabinus. This distinguished jurist, however, was impressed by the fact that in the case under consideration the manumitted slave himself had become the heir of the injured person, and therefore in his own person a right was to be recognised to compensation for the value which he had formerly himself. This seemed to be at variance with the principle that there is no action in case a free man has been killed unlawfully (see the notes to 5. § 3 above and the passages quoted there; cf. also D. 9. 3. 5. § 5 i. f.), although one may maintain the view, and this was certainly done by the opponents of Sabinus, that if we would attach the right of action to the manumitted slave as the heir of the deceased master, its object would not be the value which the manumitted slave has as a free man, but that value which he had before, being still a slave.

The view of Sabinus is of course applicable only if the slave himself is an heir. It is different if the testator, in addition to the slave, had instituted some other person. Here the co-heir of the manumitted slave will be entitled to sue under the Aquilian statute as soon as the former slave has died. But it is obvious that the co-heir will have the action only in proportion to his share in the inheritance, for, according to the XII Tables, obligations, provided they are divisible in their object, as is a claim for compensation, are ipso iure divided amongst the heirs (Arndts, § 526. n. 1; Windscheid, vol. III. § 608. n. 7 and 11; Voigt, XII Tafeln, vol. I. p. 707, and vol. II. p. 396), and this legal consequence cannot be altered by the fact that one of the heirs is prevented from exercising his right by some special reason[1].

Pernice, p. 184.

37 *pr.*—Iauolenus libro XIV ex Cassio. Liber homo si iussu alterius manu iniuriam dedit, actio legis Aquiliae cum eo est qui iussit, si modo ius imperandi habuit: quod si non habuit, cum eo agendum est qui fecit.

If a free man has done unlawful damage by command of another person, the Aquilian action lies against him who has given the command, provided only that he had had the right of command; but if he had no such right, the action is to be brought against him who actually has done the damage.

It is obvious that persons who have a right of command over others, like a master over his slaves, a father over his children, a husband over his wife, a guardian over his ward, are not entitled to order the persons subject to their control to commit illegal acts. But it must be considered that the superior has a great influence over the person subject to his power, and that the latter will probably suffer severely if he attempts to disobey the commands addressed to him. For this reason, and probably also in order not to weaken the necessary discipline in those relations which are in question wherever a person has a ius imperandi, the responsibility, if a free man has committed unlawful damage ('iniuriam,' cf. 27. § 25, and 30. § 1 above), is thrown on the person who has given the command, who is declared subject to an actio

[1] Nevertheless the contrary view is taken by Pernice.

legis Aquiliae (viz. directa), whilst the doer himself is free from any liability as clearly is stated in D. 50. 17. 169 pr. 'Is damnum dat qui iubet dare: eius vero nulla culpa est cui parere necesse est.' In spite of these words the doer is rather excused by law than free from culpa, for, in the strict sense, the act is to be attributed to him (D. 50. 17. 157 pr.—ignoscitur servis;—cf. also id. 167. § 1). One might expect that this principle is equally applicable in all cases of delicts committed by command of persons with ius imperandi. We are, however, expressly told that in delicts of a more serious character, as e.g. killing of slaves and free men, theft, robbery (D. 44. 7. 20), and similarly, if a person has been ordered to insult another (D. 47. 10. 11. § 5), not only the commander, but also the doer will be liable. The principle accordingly refers only to delicts which, as D. 50. 17. 157 pr., says, 'non habent atrocitatem facinoris vel sceleris,' as are ordinary cases of damage to property, and to cases where an interdictum quod vi aut clam would be applicable, D. 43. 24. 11. § 6.

Though it is not expressed in the passage we are explaining, it is yet to be understood by itself that, if a slave has been commanded by his master to do damage to the property of another, the master will be liable directly to an Aquilian action, for such liability takes place whenever damage has been committed by a slave 'sciente domino,' 27. § 2 above; 44. § 1, 45 pr. below.

A person may, however, give a command to another over whom he has no right of command, as, for instance, if some one has hired another for the purpose of insulting other people D. 47. 10. 11. § 4). Here, according to the fragment we are considering, the doer will be liable on account of the delict committed by him, although the person who has given the command will also be subject to an action, in so far as he has aided and abetted the delict of another person (cf. D. 47. 10. 11. § 4; D. 39. 3. 5; D. 39. 2. 18. § 14; D. 47, 7. 7. § 4).

Pernice, pp. 29 and 152; Windscheid, n. 27.

37. § 1.—Si quadrupes, cuius nomine actio esset cum domino, quod pauperiem fecisset, ab alio occisa est, et cum eo lege Aquilia agitur, aestimatio non ad corpus quadrupedis, sed ad causam eius (in quo de pauperie actio est) referri debet, et tanti damnandus est is qui occidit iudicio legis Aquiliae quanti

actoris interest noxae potius deditione defungi quam litis aestimatione.

If a quadruped on account of which an actio de pauperie was brought against its owner has been killed by another person, and he is sued under the Aquilian statute, the assessment in this action is not to be made with reference to the individual of the quadruped, but to its accessories—which include the actio de pauperie—and he who has killed the animal is to be condemned in the Aquilian action to pay so much to the plaintiff as his interest consists in delivering the quadruped by noxal surrender, instead of paying compensation for the damage done by it.

A quadruped has done damage contra naturam sui generis, and in consequence a so-called actio de pauperie (Inst. IV. 9) was brought by the injured person against its owner. He was accordingly bound either to pay full compensation for the damage done or to deliver by noxal surrender the animal which had caused the damage. But whilst this action was pending, a third person killed the quadruped, and thus the owner was deprived of the possibility of delivering the animal, and was bound to pay full compensation. It is obvious that the owner is entitled to the action under the first chapter of the Aquilian statute, but its object will not be the value of the killed quadruped, but the so-called 'causa rei,' i. e. those circumstances are to be taken into account which increase the value of the thing for its owner. In the case we are explaining the owner of the quadruped has lost the advantage of delivering the animal instead of paying compensation. Suppose, for instance, the loss inflicted on the injured party by the quadruped amounted to £100, whilst the value of the quadruped was £20 only. Here the interesse which the owner of the quadruped had in its noxal surrender, instead of paying compensation in the actio de pauperie, will be £100, for if he had been able to deliver the animal, he would not have been bound to pay the sum of £100. Therefore this sum will be the object of the Aquilian action (see the notes to 23. § 6 above).

Pernice, p. 241; Windscheid, n. 19.

38.—Idem libro IX epistolarum. Si eo tempore, quo tibi meus seruus quem bona fide emisti seruiebat, ipse a seruo tuo uulneratus est, placuit omnimodo me tecum recte lege Aquilia experiri.

If my slave, whom you had bought in good faith, in the time during which he was serving you, has been wounded by your slave, it has been settled that, at any rate, I may sue you under the Aquilian statute.

My slave, whilst subject to your bonae fidei possessio, has been wounded by your slave. There is no doubt that if the bonae fidei possessor has retained the possession of the slave he could be sued by rei vindicatio, and by this action the owner might receive also compensation for the damage done to the slave (D. 6. 1. 13; Arndts, § 167. n. c.). If, however, as is supposed in the case under discussion (eo tempore quo—*serviebat*), the possession of the slave is lost, the owner will be restricted to the action under the lex Aquilia. It is to be understood that this action is to be brought as a noxal action against the master of the delinquent slave, provided the latter had not inflicted the wound 'sciente domino' (27. § 1 above; 44. § 1, and 45 pr. below). It is true nothing is said about the noxal action in the passage, but the only question the jurist is thinking of is, whether an action on account of the damage done should be applicable. This evidently was a point which was subject to a controversy amongst the jurists and was not settled till after some time (placuit). The doubt of the jurists probably was founded on the consideration that a bonae fidei possessor, whether in his own person or by means of his servants, deals with the slave in his possession as with his own property, and therefore in case of bad treatment of the slave he seems to abuse his own property. And this view has been recognised by the senatus consultum Iuventianum under the provisions of which bonae fidei possessores could not be sued by hereditatis petitio, if they had lost or destroyed or damaged the goods belonging to the inheritance in their possession, 'si quid dilapidaverunt perdiderunt, dum re sua abuti putant' (2. § 11; D. 5. 3; Arndts, § 533. n. 2). It is for the same reason that the actio servi corrupti was denied against a person who had corrupted the slave in his bonae fidei possessio. But as to the actio legis Aquiliae the jurists were quite right to set aside the doubt entertained by them. For the fact that the person possesses a thing in good faith does not affect the true requirements of that action, which is applicable if damnum has resulted from an act of a person committed by him culpa and iniuria (cf. Part II. § 9. i. f.).

Pernice, p. 194 sqq.; Brinz, Zum Rechte des bonae fidei possessio, München, 1875, p. 121 sqq.

39. *pr.*—Pomponius libro XVII ad Quintum Mucium. Quintus Mucius scribit: equa cum in alieno pasceretur, in cogendo quod praegnans erat eiecit: quaerebatur, dominus eius possetne cum eo qui coegisset lege Aquilia agere, quia equam in iciendo ruperat. si percussisset aut consulto uehementius egisset, uisum est agere posset.

Quintus Mucius writes: A man drove away another's mare which was grazing on his ground, and the mare being in foal miscarried in consequence. The question was raised, whether the owner of the mare might bring the Aquilian action against the person who had driven away the mare, because she had been damaged by the miscarriage, and it was decided that he might bring the Aquilian action, if the other had either beaten the mare or had purposely driven her too violently.

There is no doubt that an owner has a right to drive away animals grazing on his land. He exercises merely a right of his own, and 'qui iure suo utitur, nemini facit iniuriam.' Accordingly, in the above case, the mere fact of driving away the mare would not entail liability, although a damnum (miscarriage) has resulted from the act. Nevertheless the person might become liable, (1) 'si percussisset,' i. e. if he had beaten the mare, for by doing so he exceeds his right of driving the mare away, and a person who acts in excess of his right is liable in exactly the same way as if he had no right at all; (2) 'si—consulto uehementius egisset,' i. e. if he, knowing that the mare was in foal, had driven her away too violently, for here he would have purposely exercised his right to the disadvantage of her owner, whereas such exercise of a person's right is forbidden by law (see Part II. § 6).

Pernice, p. 43 sq.

39. § 1.—Pomponius. Quamuis alienum pecus in agro suo quis deprehendit, sic illud expellere debet quomodo si suum deprehendisset, quoniam si quid ex ea re damnum cepit, habet proprias actiones. itaque qui pecus alienum in agro suo deprehenderit, non iure id includit, nec agere illud aliter debet quam ut supra diximus quasi suum: sed uel abigere debet sine damno uel admonere dominum, ut suum recipiat.

Although a person has found another man's cattle on his own land, he must drive them off in the same way as if it was his own cattle which he had found, for he has special actions if he has suffered damage from their being there. Therefore, he who has seized cattle on his own ground will not be entitled to shut them up, and, as stated above, he must not drive them off in any other way than he would if they were his own; but he must either drive them away without doing damage to them, or give the owner warning to take back his property.

Pomponius says here that a person who finds cattle on his own ground must deal with them as if they were his own. This assertion seems to imply that the owner is liable only for the omission of the diligentia quam suis rebus, or so-called culpa in concreto. The idea underlying the decision of the jurist is, however, different. A person who finds cattle on his own ground may become very angry and afraid of the damage they may do to his property, and may therefore drive them away recklessly. This, however, is by no means allowed; on the contrary, he must drive the cattle very carefully, in the same way as he would do if he were the owner; in which case he would naturally take every reasonable care in order to avoid damage to himself. It is accordingly not the idea of the jurist to lessen his liability, but to state that, although we might expect that his liability would be lessened in such cases, nevertheless the same diligentia is required as usual, i. e. the diligentia boni patris familias, and it is only in order to express this idea that reference is made to the care which the owner himself would bestow if he should find his cattle grazing somewhere on his own ground. But if the owner of the land does not like to drive away the cattle, he must inform their owner that he may take away his property. It is true that by taking precautions of this kind the owner of the land might suffer damage from grazing, etc., but this disadvantage, as we are told in the above passage, is met by special actions given to him, namely, the actio de pastu pecoris (see the notes to 1 pr. above) and the actio de pauperie, Paulus, Sent. Rec. I. 15. § 1 (see also Part II. § 2; Pernice, p. 74 sq.; Voigt, Die XII. Tafeln, p. 538.

40.—Paulus libro III ad edictum. In lege Aquilia, si deletum chirographum mihi esse dicam, in quo sub condicione mihi pecunia debita fuerit, et interim testibus quoque id probare possim, qui testes possunt non esse eo tempore quo condicio extitit, et si summatim re exposita ad suspicionem iudicem adducam, debeam uincere: sed tunc condemnationis exactio competit cum debiti condicio extiterit: quod si defecerit, condemnatio nullas uires habebit.

If in an Aquilian action I assert (and prove) that a promissory note in my favour, declaring a sum of money to be due to me under a condition, has been destroyed, and if in the meantime—i. e. before the fulfilment of the condition—I am also in a position to prove the debt by witnesses, but the witnesses may not be in existence at the time, when the condition is fulfilled, and if this last fact can on a summary statement be rendered probable in the eyes of the judge, I must succeed with my action, but I shall be entitled to the execution of the judgment only at the time when the condition of the debt has been fulfilled; but if this has become impossible, the judgment will have no effect whatever.

The case underlying the decision of the jurist is of the following kind: Titius owes me a hundred solidi under a condition, e. g. 'si navis ex Asia venerit,' and has attested this claim of mine by a written record, a chirographum, given to me by means of which I could prove my right. Afterwards this promissory note is destroyed by Seius. The question whether I may sue Seius under the Aquilian statute at once, whilst the condition of the debt is still pending, is answered in the affirmative; but Seius, the defendant, is to be condemned only provided that I, the plaintiff, have proved that the note has been destroyed, and further, that I am entitled to the conditional claim attested by it, and lastly, that I have established it as probable that the witnesses could not be produced at the time when the condition should be fulfilled, because, being very old, they might die before (D. 47. 2. 32. § 1). If these requirements were fulfilled by the plaintiff, the defendant was at once condemned, although the decree could not be carried into execution until the condition of the debt had been fufilled.

This decision is remarkable in several respects. The requirements of the lex Aquilia do not seem to be present. It is true there is an act of damage—the record has been destroyed culpa and iniuria—which is in itself sufficient to bring an Aquilian action into operation, but a loss to the plaintiff's property (damnum) has not yet resulted from it. It will result only if the creditor at the time of the fulfilment of the condition is unable to prove his claim by some means of evidence other than the chirographum which has been destroyed. But although the Aquilian action would then be applicable, it would be impracticable on account of the absence of evidence. It is for this reason that the action under the lex Aquilia can be brought even whilst the condition is pending, in spite of the principle that an action can be maintained only if there is an actual claim of the plaintiff [iudicium—antequam aliquid debeatur, (accipi) non posse—D. 5. 1. 35. i. f.], and consequently also the case is decreed by the judge, although, as a rule, no condemnation under a condition can be made, D. 49. 4. 1. § 5.

The condition on which the execution of the condemnatio is dependent is the same as the condition of the debt; as long as it is not fulfilled there is no damnum to be compensated for, and on the other hand, if it has become certain that the condition will not be fulfilled, it is also certain that no damnum has resulted from the act of injury complained of. But it may be the case that the condition is fulfilled and yet an execution cannot take place, because there are still witnesses present, who can prove the claim of the plaintiff, for in this case also no damnum has resulted from the act, and therefore nothing is to be compensated for, D. 47. 2. 27. §§ 1–3, 32.

Pernice, p. 94 sq.; Mommsen, Beiträge, vol. II. p. 120.

41.—Ulpianus libro XLI ad Sabinum. Si quis testamentum deleuerit, an damni iniuriae actio competat, uideamus. et Marcellus libro quinto digestorum dubitans negat competere: quemadmodum enim, inquit, aestimatio inibitur? ego apud eum notaui in testatore quidem hoc esse uerum, quia quod interest eius aestimari non potest, uerum tamen in herede uel legatariis diuersum, quibus testamenta paene chirographa sunt. ibidem Marcellus scribit chirographo deleto competere legis Aquiliae actionem. sed et si quis tabulas testamenti apud se depositas deleuerit uel pluribus praesentibus legerit, utilius est in factum et iniuriarum agi, si iniuriae faciendae causa secreta iudiciorum publicauit.

Let us see whether an action on account of unlawful damage can be brought if a person has destroyed a will. And Marcellus in the fifth book of the Digesta, after considering the question, denies that an Aquilian action is applicable; for how, says he, will an assessment be made? I have added a note to this statement that this is indeed true of the testator, because his interesse cannot be assessed; but that it is different with the heir and legatees, to whom wills have nearly the significance of promissory notes, i. e. of bills by which existing claims can be proved, and Marcellus himself, in the book we have quoted, writes that, if the promissory note has been destroyed, an Aquilian action is applicable. But also if a person has destroyed the tablets of a will deposited with him, or if he read them in the presence of several people, it is more advantageous to bring an actio furti [probably not actio in factum] and an actio iniuriarum, the latter of course if he has published the secrets of the last disposition for the sake of insulting the testator.

We learn from the passage that it has been discussed among the jurists, whether an actio on account of damage to property should lie in case a testamentum has been destroyed. Marcellus has answered this question in the negative, and Ulpian agrees with him so far as the testator is concerned. It is of course not taken into account by the jurists that the testamentum itself might have some value of its own, for in so far as the testator should have incurred expense in making it (for wax, thread, etc.), there would be no doubt that he as the owner of the will might get compensation by an Aquilian action, cf. D. 47. 2. 27 pr. But beyond the value of the tablets themselves there is no interesse which could give rise to an action; for though the testator naturally attaches importance to the preservation of his will, this interest ('Affectionsinteresse,' as German writers call it; interest of affection?) is not sufficient, and cannot be assessed in a sum of money, 'quia quod interest eius aestimare non potest.' This is different with regard to the heir and the legatees, for their claims as to what is left to them by the testator can be proved only by the contents of the will; just as what is due to a creditor may be proved by a promissory note. But although there is possibly a real interesse, i. e. a loss to their property resulting from the act of damage, it yet may be doubted whether an Aquilian action would lie in their favour. For the heir is certainly not the owner of the document before he has entered on the inheritance. He acquires the inheritance itself and accordingly the hereditary goods, including the document, when he enters on the inheritance. It seems therefore to follow that he will be entitled to the action only after that period, and this is implicitly recognised in D. 4. 3. 35, in which fragment Ulpian, who is also the author of the passage we are explaining, gives an actio de dolo to the instituted heir if, before he has entered on the inheritance, the testamentum has been destroyed and he has thus been prevented from entering on the inheritance. As the actio doli is applicable only in cases where no other action lies (see the words of the edict in D. 4. 3. 1. § 1; Arndts, § 334; Windscheid, § 451. n. 10), in the opinion of Ulpian the instituted heir is not entitled to an Aquilian action, evidently for the reason that he has not yet acquired ownership in the will.

In the Fr. 35 which we have quoted it is also stated that the legatee may bring an actio doli, under the same circumstances as the heir; but as he never acquires ownership in the will, it would seem to follow that he will be restricted to this action, even after the heir has entered on the inheritance, although the tenour of the fragment under consideration seems to be rather in favour of the Aquilian action, for it is said that to both the heir and the legatee wills have nearly the same significance as chirographa, and it is settled that in case of a destroyed chirographum the Aquilian action is applicable (D. 47. 2. 27. § 3).

It is still more difficult to account for the last sentence in so far as it is here stated that a person, who has destroyed the will deposited with him, is liable to an actio in factum, for there seems to be no reason why in this case the actio should not be directa. It is, however, not improbable that the text is corrupt and the jurist thought of the actio furti; at any rate this would be in accordance with the continuation of the fragment in § 1. Assuming this alteration ('furti' for 'in factum'), the idea of the jurist seems to have been that, in case a person has deposited his testamentum with another who has destroyed it or has read its contents to other people, it is more advantageous to bring the penal actions arising from such acts than to avail oneself of the actio depositi. And these actions are the actio furti, provided the will has been destroyed 'animo lucri faciendi' (§ 1 of the same fragment) or the actio iniuriarum, if the contents of the will have been read with the intention of insulting the testator, e.g. to show his poverty (D. 16. 3. 1. § 38; C. 10. 35. 2. § 2; D. 48. 19. 38. § 1).

Pernice, pp. 211 sq., 244, and 156. n. 10; Mommsen, Beiträge, vol. II. p. 123.

41. § 1.—Interdum euenire Pomponius eleganter ait, ut quis tabulas delendo furti non teneatur, sed tantum damni iniuriae, ut puta si non animo furti faciendi, sed tantum damni dandi deleuit: nam furti non tenebitur: cum facto enim etiam animum furis furtum exigit.

Pomponius neatly says that sometimes a person who destroys the tablets of a will is liable, not on account of a furtum, but only on account of damage done to property; for instance, if he has destroyed the will with the intention not of committing a theft, but merely of doing damage, for he will not be liable for theft, since theft requires in addition to the act of stealing the intention of a thief.

A testamentum will usually be destroyed because the doer expects from this act some pecuniary advantage either to himself or to other persons; e.g. the intestate heir. Accordingly to such cases an actio furti will be applicable, for a furtum requires nothing but a 'contrectatio fraudulosa animo lucri faciendi' of a thing belonging to another (see D. 47. 2. 27. § 3). But if such animus does not exist, there is neither any furtum—'quia furtum sine affectu furandi non committitur' (I. IV. 1. § 7)—but merely an act of damage which may give rise to an Aquilian action, whether there is an intention to do the damage (animus damni dandi), as is supposed in the passage under consideration, or merely negligence (see 5. § 1, and 27. § 9 above), on the part of the person, to whose act the damage is due.

Pernice, p. 56; Hasse, Culpa, p. 35.

42.—Iulianus libro XLVIII digestorum. Qui tabulas testamenti depositas, aut alicuius rei instrumentum, ita deleuit ut legi non possit, depositi actione et ad exhibendum tenetur, quia corruptam rem restituerit aut exhibuerit. legis quoque Aquiliae actio ex eadem causa competit: corrupisse enim tabulas recte dicitur et qui eas interleuerit.

A person, who has disfigured the tablets of a will deposited with him or the record of some other transaction in such a way that they cannot be read, will be liable to an actio depositi and an actio ad exhibendum, because he has restored or produced the thing in a spoiled condition. An Aquilian action also can be brought on the same ground, for a person too who has obliterated tablets is correctly declared to have spoiled them.

Where a will or other document has been deposited with another, or has been in his detention without being deposited, and has been rendered illegible by his obliterating the characters, there are possibly three actions applicable.

(1.) An actio depositi (viz. directa), given to the person who has deposited the document, provided of course that the damage is due to the dolus of the depositarius—as seems supposed in the above passage—or to his lata culpa.

(2.) If no depositum has been made, an actio ad exhibendum given to the owner of the document, and therefore also to the testator as the owner of the will (see D. 43. 5. 3. § 5). Usually the object of this action will be to compel the detentor to show to the plaintiff the document detained, and thus to enable him to identify it, and, if necessary, i.e. if it is not voluntarily delivered to him, to sue the defendant by rei vindicatio. If, however, the defendant is unable to comply with this demand, because he has parted with the thing in order to avoid producing it, or he has maliciously destroyed the thing, he is to be condemned to pay to the plaintiff full compensation for his interesse; D. 10. 4. 5. § 2, 8. And this view applies to the facts of the case which we are explaining, for although the document itself is still in existence, yet the same effect has been produced as if it had been destroyed (D. 10. 4. 9. § 3; C. iii. 32. 7).

(3.) An actio legis Aquiliae, as the document is doubtless damaged by the act complained of, provided a damnum has resulted from the act.

It is clear that these actions may be brought also by the heir (after he has entered on the inheritance), for the right to bring the actio legis Aquiliae as well as the actio depositi will be transferred to him like other rights of property, and as to the actio ad exhibendum, he, as the owner of the will or other document, may, like the deceased, have a legal interest in having the document produced; D. 29. 3. 3.

It might seem that this explanation is at variance with D. 4. 3. 35, a passage which, in case a will has been deposited, recognises only an actio doli, and consequently no actio depositi. But it must be noticed that the actio doli is given to the heres scriptus, who has not entered on the inheritance, and to whom consequently no right of action belonging to the deceased has been transferred.

Pernice, pp. 153, 212 sq. n. 12; Hasse, p. 35; Vangerow, vol. III. p. 588.

43.—Pomponius libro XIX ad Sabinum. Ob id quod ante quam hereditatem adires damnum admissum in res hereditarias est, legis Aquiliae actionem habes quod post mortem eius cui heres sis acciderit: dominum enim lex Aquilia appellat non utique eum qui tunc fuerit cum damnum daretur: nam isto modo ne ab eo quidem cui heres quis erit transire ad eum ea actio poterit: neque ob id quod tum commissum fuerit cum in hostium potestate esses, agere postliminio reuersus poteris: et hoc aliter constitui sine magna captione postumorum liberorum, qui parentibus heredes erunt, non poterit. eadem dicemus et de arboribus eodem tempore furtim caesis. puto eadem dici posse etiam de hac actione quod ui aut clam, si modo quis aut prohibitus fecerit, aut apparuerit eum intellegere debuisse ab eis ad quos ea hereditas pertineret, si rescissent, prohibitum iri.

You have an Aquilian action on account of damage done to property forming part of an inheritance before you have entered on the inheritance, if it is done after the death of him whose heir you are; for the lex Aquilia regards as owner in some cases a person who was not the owner at the time when the damage was committed, for, if it did not, that action could not even pass from the deceased to his heir, nor could you bring an action in virtue of the ius postliminii on account of damage committed whilst you were a prisoner of war, nor could the rule be otherwise laid down without serious injury to posthumous children, who will become the heirs of their parents. These views are applicable to the case where trees have been secretly felled during the same period, i. e. hereditate iacente, and I think the same may also be said of the interdictum quod vi aut clam, provided only that a person has either done an act, though forbidden to do it, that it is clear that he ought to have known that those to whom the inheritance will belong would have forbidden the act had they been aware of it.

The case, supposed by the jurist, is the following: A person has been instituted by another as his heir, but before he has entered on the inheritance—i. e. hereditate iacente—a third person has damaged things belonging to the inheritance. The question accordingly arises whether the heir instituted should be entitled to the Aquilian action. Strictly speaking, this action can be brought only by him who was the owner at the time of the injury, but the words of the statute are not to be taken in this narrow sense. For otherwise serious inconvenience would follow: (1) if this were the case, an Aquilian action could not pass from a deceased person to his heir; (2) it could not be maintained by a prisoner of war after he had returned home, which would be very unfair; (3) it could not be brought by a posthumous child who only acquires the inheritance of his father upon birth. It is, however, settled that the Aquilian action is transferred to the posthumous child as well as to every other heir, and that in virtue of the postliminium the prisoner of war on his return is entitled to the Aquilian action which had accrued during his absence, just as the legatarius becomes entitled to it by means of the ius accrescendi (see 34 and 35 above).

What is stated of the Aquilian action is also applicable to the actio arborum furtim caesarum (see notes to 1. § 1 and Arndts, § 325) and the interdictum quod ui aut clam (Arndts, § 329). Accordingly if trees, whilst belonging to a hereditas iacens, have been felled secretly (furtim) by another, the actio thus acquired will pass over to the heir if he has entered on the inheritance, and similarly if the condition of a piece of hereditary land has been altered, in spite of an express prohibition, e. g. by the deceased,—ui—or whilst the doer knew or ought to have known that his act would be objected to (D. 43. 24. 4)—clam,—the heir, after the hereditatis aditio, will be entitled to the interdictum quod ui aut clam.

Pernice, p. 206 sq.; Hasse, Culpa, p. 245; Windscheid, n. 14; Brinz, § 340. n. 21; Arndts, Gesammelte Civilistische Schriften, Stuttgart, 1873, vol. II. p. 5.

44 *pr.*—Ulpianus libro XLII ad Sabinum. In lege Aquilia et leuissima culpa uenit.

Under the Aquilian statute, even the slightest neglect is to be taken into account.

The lex Aquilia does not distinguish different degrees of culpa. In order to entail liability under that statute it is sufficient if an act of damage can be imputed to a certain person, or, in other words, if it is due to his culpa in the wider sense, that is, whether there was dolus or culpa lata, or culpa levis, or culpa in concreto on his part. It is only if the damage is due to casus, i.e. a mere accident or misadventure, that liability does not arise (see I. h. t. § 3 and fr. 30. § 3. i. f.). Damage, however, is considered to be due to the culpa of a person if he has not taken such care and diligence as would have been bestowed by a diligens pater familias, in the particular case in question; but if that degree of care has been taken, no liability ensues under the Aquilian law, even though an extremely capable and foreseeing man might have avoided the damage. See 31 above, and the notes to this passage, Part II. § 7.

Pernice, p. 64; Hasse, Culpa, p. 65; Windscheid, n. 11.

44. § 1.—Quotiens sciente domino seruus uulnerat uel occidit Aquilia dominum teneri dubium non est.

Whenever a slave, with the knowledge of his master, wounds or kills another, there is no doubt that the master is liable to an Aquilian action.

We have seen above (see the notes to 27. § 1) that a master may be sued on his own account by an actio legis Aquiliae, 'si seruus sciente domino occiderit.' This action applies, according to the passage we are considering, not only to the case of killing, but also that of wounding slaves and cattle, that is to say, to cases coming under the third chapter. When it is remembered that—besides the action against a person who admits his liability—an actio adversus infitiantem was applicable under each of the chapters of the Aquilian statute (see the notes to 2. § 1. and 23. § 10 above), it follows that the same four actions were available under Chapter III as under Chapter I, viz. (1) the actio confessoria, (2) the actio adversus infitiantem, (3) the actio adversus dominum, si seruus sciente domino damnum dederit, and (4) the actio noxalis. (See Lenel, Das Edictum perpetuum, p. 160.)

Windscheid, n. 9 and 27.

45. *pr.*—Paulus libro X ad Sabinum. Scientiam hic pro patientia accipimus, ut qui prohibere potuit teneatur, si non fecerit.

Knowledge is here taken in the sense of acquiescence, so that a master who might have prevented an act, is liable, if he did not prevent it.

This fragment is intended to continue 44. § 1. Accordingly it was not sufficient that a master merely knew of an act of damage being done, he must also have been in a position to hinder the act (see the notes to 27. § 1 and C. 3. 41. 4), otherwise he would not be himself subject to an Aquilian action, but only to an actio noxalis. The fact that the master knows of the commission of the delict by the slave, does not affect the truth that the real delinquent is the slave. And if there is a delict of the slave, we should also expect an actio noxalis available against his master. In accordance with this view the interpretation of the jurists declared an actio noxalis applicable in addition to the action given against the master on his own account (see D. 9. 4. 2 and 3), although the injured party could avail himself only either of one or the other, D. 9. 4. 4. § 2. It was only in case the slave did the act in obedience to an express command of his master that the master was liable to the Aquilian in his own name alone, and there was no liability (by noxal action) on account of a delict of the slave; D. 9. 4. 2. § 1.

Pernice, p. 218; Windscheid, n. 9 and 27.

45. § 1.—Lege Aquilia agi potest et sanato uulnerato seruo.

An action may be brought under the Aquilian statute even after the wounded slave has been healed.

In order to entail liability under the Aquilian statute a person must have done damage, culpa and iniuria, to the corporeal thing of another, and from this act some loss to the property of that other must have resulted (D. h. t. 27. §§ 5 and 19; D. 8. 2. 18). Accordingly, if a slave has been wounded and the owner has suffered loss in consequence—

through the expense incurred for his cure (27. § 17) and the loss of his labour—he will be entitled to an Aquilian action, although the slave does not bear even a trace of the wound, and is therefore absolutely undiminished in value. On the other hand, if there is no loss to a person's property, though there may possibly be other actions, no Aquilian action can be maintained, in spite of an act by which a corporeal thing has been violated; D. h. t. 27. § 17; cf. §§ 25–28 eod. (Part II. § 8).

Pernice, pp. 97 and 244.

45. § 2.—Si meum seruum, cum liberum putares, occideris, lege Aquilia teneberis.

If you have killed my slave, believing him to be a free man, you will be bound under the Aquilian statute.

If a person kills a free man he does not become liable to an Aquilian action, although he will be subject to a criminal prosecution under the lex Cornelia de sicariis, if the act was done intentionally (see the notes to 23. § 9 above). The fact, however, that a person who has killed a slave thought him to be a free man cannot affect his liability according to the lex Aquilia, for, in spite of such belief, the requirements of that liability are in existence.

45. § 3.— Cum stramenta ardentia transilirent duo, concurrerunt amboque ceciderunt et alter flamma consumptus est: nihil eo nomine potest agi, si non intellegitur, uter ab utro euersus sit.

Two slaves, who were jumping over heaps of burning straw, knocked one against the other, and both fell, and one was burned to death. No action can be maintained on that account, unless it is known which of the two knocked the other over.

It was usual in Rome, at the end of the feast of the Paliliae, to jump over burning trusses of straw and hay. Two slaves, as we are told in this passage, were so jumping, when they dashed together, and in consequence one of them perished in the fire. It is clear that the other slave will only be liable under the Aquilian statute—and his master accordingly subject to a noxal action—in case the collision was due to his culpa, as, for instance, if he jumped although he saw that the other was about to jump in the same direction. But if the collision was due to the fault of the slave who was killed by the fire, whether the other was also in culpa or not, no liability will attach to the case.

This decision is perfectly clear, and it is hardly necessary to say that it is in no way at variance with the principle which we find elsewhere recognised (7. § 4 above, and 54. § 4 below), that whoever takes part in a game in which there is some risk of danger, can only blame himself for any consequences which may follow; for here the collision complained of is not the natural consequence of the customs of the Paliliae, as is an injury done to one of the players in a game at ball or a pugilistic combat.

Pernice, p. 58.

45. § 4.—Qui, cum aliter tueri se non possent, damni culpam dederint, innoxii sunt: uim enim ui defendere omnes leges omniaque iura permittunt. sed si defendendi mei causa lapidem in aduersarium misero, sed non eum sed praetereuntem percussero, tenebor lege Aquilia: illum enim solum qui uim infert ferire conceditur, et hoc, si tuendi dumtaxat, non etiam ulciscendi causa factum sit.

Persons who have done unlawful damage, when they could not protect themselves by any other means, are not liable, for all statutes and laws allow men to repel violence by violence. If, however, I have thrown a stone at an assailant and have missed him and hit a passer-by, I shall be liable under the lex Aquilia, for we are only allowed to strike a man who is attacking us, and that only if it is done to protect and not to revenge ourselves.

It is a generally recognised principle that acts which are committed in virtue of the right of self-defence do not entail any liability (4 pr. above). If I therefore kill or wound the slave of another person, who is going to attack me, I do not become liable on account of the damage done. But it must be noticed that there is still an act, which is imputed to the doer, and which is in itself fit to entail liability under the Aquilian statute. If, therefore, a third person is injured in consequence of the act, I shall be liable on account of the damage done to him, and the same must be said of the case where the aggressor has been injured, but merely for the sake of revenge, for in so far the doer has not exercised his right of self-defence.

It may be added that the use of the term culpa in the above passage is peculiar, for culpa is always used in the sense of imputability, that is, the mental condition of a person in virtue of which an act is to be attributed to him, but never in the sense of the act or damage itself. It seems, therefore, advisable to read with Mommsen, 'damni quiddam dederint,' instead of 'damni culpam dederint.'

Pernice, pp. 29 sq., 43 and 74; Windscheid, n. 11.

45. § 5.—Qui idoneum parietem sustulit, damni iniuria domino eius tenetur.

A person who has removed a wall which is still sound, is liable to its owner on account of unlawful damage to property.

The only difficulty raised by these words is that their sense seems too obvious, and therefore the statement of the jurist superfluous. It may be that the idea of the jurist was to assert that by pulling down a wall the land of which it formed an integral part has been damaged. But if we take into account the fact that the word paries is used of the wall of a house in its original sense (Dirksen, Manuale Latinitatis—sub v. paries: 'Murus quo aedificii partes continentur,') and if we also consider that the paries is said to be 'idoneus,' it seems to be more probable that the jurist was considering a case in which a wall has been used to support a building (house), and that it is therefore not the damage done to the wall, but the damage caused to the house, which he has in view. Accordingly, the question seems to have been whether the damage done to a building, by taking away a wall supporting it, would entail liablility directly under the terms of the statute itself (ch. III), or whether an extended action would not rather be applicable; a question which seems to be answered in the first alternative.

46.—Ulpianus libro L ad Sabinum. Si uulnerato seruo lege Aquilia actum sit, postea mortuo ex eo uulnere agi lege Aquilia nihilo minus potest.

If an action under the lex Aquilia has been brought in a case where a slave has been wounded, one may sue nevertheless under the lex Aquilia if the slave has afterwards died from the wound.

It might seem, at first sight, that in both the actions the same claim is involved, and that therefore the second actio is not admissible according to the principle, 'Bis de eadem re ne sit actio' (Keller, Der Römische Civilprocess, § 41. n. 464). This, however, is not correct, for what is sued for the second time is compensation on account of killing the slave, whilst in the previous suit a different claim—de seruo uulnerato, ch. III—was raised; a claim which, strictly speaking, did not exist, for the slave was killed by the wound, and therefore only an actio under the first, not under the third chapter, was applicable.

47. *pr.*—Iulianus libro LXXXVI digestorum. Sed si priore iudicio aestimatione facta, postea mortuo seruo, de occiso agere dominus instituerit, exceptione doli mali opposita compelletur, ut ex utroque iudicio nihil amplius consequatur, quam consequi deberet, si initio de occiso homine egisset.

But if, after damages have been assessed in the former suit, the master, on the subsequent death of his slave, has brought an action on account of killing, he will be met by an exceptio doli and compelled to so limit his claim that he recovers no more by both actions than he ought to have recovered if he had at once sued on account of killing his slave.

If, in the case supposed in the previous fragment, the action under the first chapter is brought whilst the action on account of wounding is not yet decided, the former alone will be the object of the judicial inquiry, for it has become certain by the subsequent death from the wound, that the slave has not been wounded (in the sense of the lex), but has been killed. If, however, the first action has already been decided, i. e. if the delinquent has been finally condemned to pay a definite sum of money as compensation on account of the wound inflicted on the slave, it would be unfair that the delinquent should be condemned to pay under the second action what would be due on account of killing the slave. Therefore an exceptio doli is given to the delinquent, by which he can coerce the owner, who is going to sue for that amount, to restrict his claim to the excess of the amount due on account of killing the slave over the amount to which the delinquent was condemned in consequence of the action on account of wounding the slave; accordingly the plaintiff does not receive more than he would have received if he had immediately brought the action under the first statute of the lex Aquiliae.

48. *pr.*—Paulus libro XXXIX ad edictum. Si seruus ante aditam hereditatem damnum in re hereditaria dederit, et liber factus in ea re damnum det, utraque actione tenebitur, quia alterius et alterius facti hae res sunt.

If a slave has damaged goods forming part of an inheritance, before the inheritance has been entered upon, and has also damaged the same goods after becoming free, he will be liable to both the actions, for the actions in question are grounded on distinct classes of facts.

A slave who has been manumitted by will of his master has, after the master's death, but before the inheritance was entered upon by the instituted heir, unlawfully damaged things belonging to the inheritance. It is obvious that the delict of the manumitted person, who only becomes free by the aditio hereditatis, is committed against the hereditas itself, which, as a juristic person (13. § 2 above), is the owner of all the things of the inheritance, and therefore also the domina of the slave. A dominus of a slave, however, has no action against his own slave, although the slave may afterwards be manumitted or alienated (Gai. iv. 78, J. 4. 8. 6). Accordingly, this difficulty was met by a special edict of the praetor with the following rubric: 'Si is qui testamento liber esse iussus erit, post mortem domini ante aditam hereditatem surripuisse aut corrupuisse quid dicetur' (D. 47. 4). This edict granted an actio in duplum in cases where hereditate iacente, hereditary property, was either stolen or damaged by a slave who has been manumitted by the will of the testator, provided that in case of damage done to the property this was due either to dolus or culpa lata of the slave (see D. 47. 4. 1 pr. §§ 1 and 2).

It follows that in the above case the delinquent will be subject to such an action, after he has become free in virtue of the will of his master. But if he afterwards again damages the same property, he will be liable in the same way as every other free man to an actio legis Aquiliae, and that action naturally lies concurrently with the action in duplum of the praetorian edict, for there are two separate delicts which have originated these actions.

Lenel, Das Edictum perpetuum, p. 266; Savigny, System, vol. V. p. 235 sq.

49. *pr.*—Ulpianus libro IX disputationum. Si quis fumo facto apes alienas fugauerit uel etiam necauerit, magis causam mortis praestitisse uidetur quam occidisse, et ideo in factum actione tenebitur.

If a person by making a smoke has driven away another's bees, or has even killed them, he seems to have created a condition of things from which their death resulted, rather than to have killed them, and therefore he is subject to an actio in factum.

The decision is perfectly clear, but it seems to be at variance with that given in 27. § 12, where in a similar case an actio directa is declared (by Celsus) to be applicable. This, however, may be explained by the assumption that in case of 27. § 12 a fire has been made under a swarm of the bees, whereas in the case we are considering the fire has been made to keep away the bees and they have flown into it.

Pernice, p. 153 sq.; Hasse, Culpa, p. 30. n. 2.

49. § 1.—Quod dicitur damnum iniuria datum Aquilia persequi, sic erit accipiendum ut uideatur damnum iniuria datum, quod cum damno iniuriam attulerit: nisi magna ui cogente fuerit factum, ut Celsus scribit circa eum qui incendii arcendi gratia uicinas aedes intercidit: nam hic scribit cessare legis Aquiliae actionem: iusto enim metu ductus, ne ad se ignis perueniret, uicinas aedes intercidit: et siue peruenit ignis siue ante extinctus est, existimat legis Aquiliae actionem cessare.

When it is said that the Aquilian action lies for damage done 'iniuria,' it will be understood that the damage is presumed to have been done iniuria, for an act of damage will naturally imply iniuria, unless it has been committed under urgent necessity, as Celsus writes of a person who pulled down a neighbour's house in order to keep off a fire from his own; for he writes that the Aquilian action does not hold, because the person has pulled down the house under a justifiable fear lest the fire should spread to his own; and he accordingly thinks that the Aquilian action does not lie, whether the fire has spread so far or has previously been extinguished.

The word 'iniuria,' in the passage we are about to explain, is evidently used of an act done by a person who has no right to do the act (as in I. h. t. § 2 as opposed to the following § 3; cf. Part II. § 6 and the notes to fr. 3 above); and it is stated that it is presumed that an act of damage has been done iniuria in this sense unless the contrary is proved, i. e. unless it is proved that the person acting had a right to do the act complained of. This, however, as we are told in the passage, will be the case if a person pulls down neighbouring buildings in case of an approaching fire, provided he had good reason for fear (cf. D. 19. 2. 27. § 1), and accordingly he will not be subject to an Aquilian action whether the fire has or has not been extinguished before reaching the site of the buildings destroyed.

But in D. 43. 24. 7. § 4 (of Ulpian also) the contrary view is taken. Here in the same case liability under the Aquilian statute is denied only in the case where the fire would have spread to the site of the building demolished, and this simply because in that case no damnum would have resulted from the act, since the house would have inevitably perished by the fire if it had not been pulled down.

Although there is thus a discrepancy between the two passages, there can be no doubt that the last fragment is merely intended as a historical notice, and the fragment we are explaining contains the real intention of the lawgiver; for (1) here Ulpian expresses his own opinion, there he merely quotes the view of the jurist Servius Sulpicius Rufus (a contemporary of Cicero); (2) in D. 47. 9. 3. § 3 Ulpian, considering the same case, blames Labeo for having taken the same view as Servius, and expressly denies that an Aquilian action will lie; (3) in several other passages (D. h. t. 29. § 3, and D. 19. 5. 14. § 1) the principle which underlies the decision in the passage under consideration is clearly expressed, namely, that a person who inflicts damage on another, whilst he could not avert damage from himself in any other way, is not liable under the Aquilian statute (cf. the notes to 29. § 3 above, and Part II. § 6).

Pernice, pp. 34 and 39; Windscheid, n. 11; Hasse, Culpa, p. 27.

50.—Ulpianus libro VI opinionum. Qui domum alienam inuito domino demolit et eo loco balneas exstruxit, praeter naturale ius, quod superficies ad dominum soli pertinet, etiam damni dati nomine actioni subicitur.

If a person has pulled down the house of another against his wish, and built a bath upon the site, apart from the rule of natural law that what is built on a soil belongs to the owner of the soil, he is also subject to an action on account of damage done.

It is obvious that a man who destroys a house commits damage to the owner of the land of which the house has formed an integral part, and therefore he is subject to an Aquilian action. If he afterwards builds a bath or something else on the ground, these buildings will form a portion of the land, being accessories to it, and accordingly ownership in them will belong to the owner of the land (Inst. II. 1. §§ 29 and 30; Arndts, § 152. n. h.).

51 *pr.*—Iulianus libro LXXXVI digestorum. Ita uulneratus est seruus ut eo ictu certum esset moriturum: medio deinde tempore heres institutus est et postea ab alio ictus decessit: quaero, an cum utroque de occiso lege Aquilia agi possit. respondit: occidisse dicitur uulgo quidem qui mortis causam quolibet modo praebuit: sed lege Aquilia is demum teneri uisus est qui adhibita ui et quasi manu causam mortis praebuisset, tracta uidelicet interpretatione uocis a caedendo et a caede. rursus Aquilia lege teneri existimati sunt non solum qui ita uulnerassent ut confestim uita priuarent, sed etiam hi quorum ex uulnere certum esset aliquem uita excessurum. igitur si quis seruo mortiferum uulnus inflixerit, eundemque alius ex interuallo ita percusserit ut maturius interficeretur quam ex priore uulnere moriturus fuerat, statuendum est utrumque eorum lege Aquilia teneri.

A slave was wounded in such a way that it was certain that he would die of the blow; after that he was instituted heir, and later still he was struck by another and died. The question is whether an Aquilian action can be brought against both the delinquents for killing. It is answered in general, a man is said to have killed another, if he has in any way occasioned his death; but liability under the lex Aquilia itself has been considered to arise only where a man has caused the death of another by actual violence, and, as it were, with his own hand, the interpretation of the word 'occidere' being of course derived from 'caedere' and 'caedes.' Again, persons are considered liable under the lex Aquilia not only when they have so wounded others as immediately to deprive them of life, but also when they have inflicted a wound from which death certainly will result. Therefore if one man has mortally wounded a slave, and another has, some time after, struck the same slave, so that he died sooner than he would have died of the previous wound, it must be held that both of them will be liable under the Aquilian statute.

The facts of the case supposed by Julian are the following: A person had mortally wounded a slave; before the slave died from the wound he was instituted an heir, and it is to be understood that the inheritance was offered to him; afterwards, but before he had entered on the inheritance, the slave, having been wounded by another person, died, but earlier than he would have died from the first wound inflicted on him (cf. the words at the end of the passage—ut maturius interficeretur, quam ex priore uulnere moriturus fuerat—). The jurist raises the question whether, on the ground of these facts, both the delinquents will be liable to an action 'de occiso' on account of killing the slave. The answer to this question, so he thinks, depends on the wider question, as to what is meant by the term 'occidere.'

It is true, says Ulpian, that a person who in any way whatever has caused the death of another is said to have killed him; but according to the terms of the statute itself, only a person who has done so by some personal act of violence is liable on account of 'occidere' in accordance with the derivation of this word from caedere and caedes (7. § 1 above); on the other hand, a person is guilty of occidere whether death is the immediate consequence of his act, or has only followed after some time (cf. 21. § 1). In accordance with this statement, the person who wounded the slave on the second occasion will be subject to an action under the first chapter, for he is guilty of an act from which apparently death has resulted, and which seems to fall under the term occidere (cf. the words: 'ab alio ictus decessit' and 'ita percusserit, ut maturius interficeretur'). On the other hand, it also follows from the statement that he who was the first to wound the slave is liable 'de occiso,' for he has inflicted a wound from which death must have necessarily followed, and from which also death has apparently resulted in the given case, although under the concurrent influence of another wound, and therefore earlier than was to be expected. In short, the death of the slave, happening when it does, seems to be due to both the wounds inflicted on the slave,—at least nothing else is in evidence—and therefore both the delinquents will be liable on account of the death of the slave, i. e. to an actio under the first chapter of the Aquilian statute. It is obvious that, understood in this sense, the above passage is not at all in contradiction with 11. § 3 and 15. § 1 above, where, though a mortal wound has been inflicted on a slave, yet his subsequent death is due to another event (see the notes to 11. § 3).

Pernice, p. 179 sqq.; Vangerow, vol. III. p. 586 sqq.; Windscheid, § 258. n. 16.

51. § 1.—Idque est consequens auctoritati ueterum, qui, cum a pluribus idem seruus ita uulneratus esset ut non appareret cuius ictu perisset, omnes lege Aquilia teneri iudicauerunt.

And this decision logically follows from the view of the ancient jurists, who held that where several persons had wounded a single slave, so that it did not appear who struck the blow which killed him, all the accomplices were liable under the first chapter of the Aquilian lex.

This statement of Julian clearly refers to 11. § 2, where it is said that if several persons have beaten a slave, who has died in consequence, he who struck the blow which actually killed the slave will be liable for his death; but if this cannot be proved, each of the accomplices will be liable as if he had killed the slave, the reason evidently being that as far as appears each of them is guilty of his death (see notes to 11. § 2).

A similar doubt as to the person who actually caused the death is admissible in the case stated in the principium of the fragment, for whether the actual cause of the death was the first or the second wound cannot be ascertained. If, therefore, both the delinquents are equally declared to be liable under Chapter I of the Aquilian statute, this is in perfect harmony with the view of the veteres, as we are told by Julianus. It may be added that this passage clearly shows that the death of the slave was not thought to be exclusively due to the second wound, as it would be in case of decapitation (11. § 3), for, if that were the case, the doubt as to the person who killed the slave would not be possible.

Vangerow, vol. III. p. 588; Savigny, System, vol. V. p. 234.

51. § 2.—Aestimatio autem perempti non eadem in utriusque persona fiet: nam qui prior uulnerauit tantum praestabit quanto in anno proximo homo plurimi fuerit repetitis ex die unlneris trecentum sexaginta quinque diebus, posterior in id tenebitur quanti homo plurimi uenire poterit in anno proximo quo uita excessit, in quo pretium quoque hereditatis erit. eiusdem ergo serui occisi nomine alius maiorem, alius minorem aestimationem praestabit, nec mirum, cum uterque eorum ex diuersa causa et diuersis temporibus occidisse hominem intellegatur. quod si quis absurde a nobis haec constitui putauerit, cogitet longe absurdius constitui neutrum lege Aquilia teneri aut alterum potius, cum neque impunita maleficia esse oporteat nec facile constitui possit, uter potius lege teneatur. multa autem iure ciuili contra rationem disputandi pro utilitate communi recepta esse innumerabilibus rebus probari potest: unum interim posuisse contentus ero. cum plures trabem alienam furandi causa sustulerint, quam singuli ferre non possent, furti actione omnes teneri existimantur, quamuis subtili ratione dici possit neminem eorum teneri, quia neminem uerum sit eam sustulisse.

The value of the slave killed will, however, be differently assessed with reference to the two delinquents, for the one who inflicted the first wound will pay a sum equal to the highest value of the slave during the last year, reckoning three hundred and sixty-five days from the day of the wound, while the one who inflicted the second wound will be liable to pay the highest price for which the slave could have been sold during the year previous to his death, which also comprehends the value of the inheritance. Thus for killing one and the same slave the one will pay a higher, the other a lower compensation, for they are considered to have killed the slave by different acts and at different periods. But if any one should think this decision of ours absurd, let him reflect that it is far more absurd to say that neither is bound by the lex Aquilia or that one is bound rather than the other;

for neither ought delicts to be left without due penalty, nor can it be ascertained which of the two should be bound rather than the other. For that many rules which cannot be logically deduced are recognised by the civil law for the sake of common utility can be proved by innumerable instances. For the present I shall be content to state one example. If several people, with the intention of stealing, have carried off a beam belonging to another, which no one of them could have carried by himself, all of them are held to be subject to an actio furti, although it may be said that according to strict logical consequence none of them can be liable, for no one of them has taken away the beam.

In the case stated in the principium of the fragment under consideration, both the delinquents are said to be liable under Chapter I. But as a person who is liable on account of killing is considered to have killed the slave at the time when the wound was inflicted (21. § 1 above), and as the assessment is to be made with reference to the year reckoned backwards from that moment (21 pr., 23. § 2), the person who has inflicted the first wound will be bound to pay the highest value (or interesse) which the injured slave has had at any time during the year previous to the injury, whilst the interesse in the action against the person who has subsequently wounded the slave will comprehend, besides the highest value of the slave during the last year, the value of the inheritance which could not be entered upon in consequence of his death. When the jurist says that this decision might be thought absurd, his reason evidently is that according to it damages are to be assessed for killing a slave, who is supposed to have been already killed by some one else. But, so adds the jurist, if we did not accept this view, the result would be still more absurd, for we should have either to say that no one was bound, which would be against the generally recognised principle that delicts are not to be left without due penalty (D. 5. 1. 18. § 1; D. 9. 4. 4. § 2; D. 46. 1. 70. § 5; D. 11. 2. 20; C. 1. 55. 6; C. 9. 47. 14), or to assume that one or other of the two killed the slave, an assumption which cannot be proved.

It is true, strictly speaking, that neither the one nor the other can be said to be liable under Chapter I, yet logical consequences are not always recognised by law; for very often rules of law, regardless of strict logical deduction, are due to convenience or common utility, as is the case in the above instance. And this is illustrated by the jurist by yet another example: if several persons have stolen a beam, too heavy to be carried by any one of them, each is declared to be liable on account of theft, although no single individual has taken away the beam and thus done such an act as would establish the delict of furtum (cf. 11. § 4 above).

Pernice, p. 121; Windscheid, § 455. n. 20, and § 285. n. 16; Vangerow, vol. III. p. 588.

52 *pr.*—Alfenus libro II digestorum. Si ex plagis seruus mortuus esset neque id medici inscientia aut domini neglegentia accidisset, recte de iniuria occiso eo agitur.

If a slave has died from the blows inflicted on him, and his death has not been due either to want of knowledge in the surgeon or neglect on the part of his master, an action on account of killing the slave can be rightly maintained.

The case underlying the decision of the jurist is certainly the following: A master has brought an action in which he has asserted that the defendant has killed his slave by blows inflicted on him. The defendant has denied the claim of the plaintiff, on the ground that the slave has died either through want of skill in the physician or through the neglect of the plaintiff himself. The jurist considering these assertions decides that if the death has actually resulted from the blows and not from something else, the defendant will be liable de occiso, i. e. under Chapter I. But as in order to cause death the wound must have been mortal, the jurist clearly means that liability under Chapter I is possible only if there was really a mortal wound. It follows from this that if the wound was not mortal 'si uulneratus fuerit seruus non mortifere' (30. § 4 above), but the slave has died for other reasons, the defendant cannot be made liable de occiso, but merely de uulnerato (cf. 8 pr. above).

It is hardly necessary to say that no case of contributory negligence is contemplated by the jurist. The question is merely whether one thing or another is the real cause of the death of the slave, and therefore it is wrong to argue from the passage that if the death was due to the blows, as well as to the negligence of the master or physician, no liability would take place. This consequence is by no means implied by the decision; it is only implied that if the death was not due to the blows of the defendant, he cannot become liable de occiso.

Pernice, p. 61; Windscheid, § 258. n. 17 and 18; Vangerow, vol. III. p. 39; Mommsen, Beiträge, vol. II. p. 160 sqq.

52. § 1.—Tabernarius in semita noctu supra lapidem lucernam posuerat: quidam praeteriens eam sustulerat: tabernarius eum consecutus lucernam reposcebat et fugientem retinebat: ille flagello, quod in manu habebat, in quo dolor inerat, uerberare tabernarium coeperat, ut se mitteret: ex eo maiore rixa facta, tabernarius ei qui lucernam sustulerat oculum effoderat: consulebat, num damnum iniuria non uidetur dedisse, quoniam prior flagello percussus esset. respondi, nisi data opera effodisset oculum, non uideri damnum iniuria fecisse, culpam enim penes eum qui prior flagello percussit, residere: sed si ab eo non prior uapulasset, sed cum ei lucernam eripere uellet, rixatus esset, tabernarii culpa factum uideri.

A shopkeeper had by night set a lamp upon a stone in a footpath; some one passing by carried it off; the shopkeeper followed him, demanded back the lamp and caught hold of him as he was running away. To make the shopkeeper leave go, the thief began to beat him with a heavy whip, which he held in his hand; then a fierce struggle began, in the course of which the shopkeeper knocked out the eye of the man who carried off the lamp. The question was asked whether the shopkeeper is to be thought to have done unlawful damage as he was first of all struck with the whip. I answered that unless he intentionally knocked out the other's eye, he is not considered to have done unlawful damage, for the fault lies with him who first struck him with the whip; but if he was not first beaten, but began the struggle in the attempt to snatch away the lamp, the damage seems to have been committed through the fault of the shopkeeper.

There is no doubt that the shopkeeper is entitled to follow the thief to seize him and to take back his own property, for in taking the lamp the thief has attempted to unlawfully infringe another's right, and such attempt may be resisted by the injured person even with violence, provided of course the degree of violence used is not greater than is necessary to meet the threatened wrong (cf. 5. 45. § 4 above; D. 43. 16. 1. §§ 27 and 28; 17; C. 8. 4. 1; Arndts, § 94. n. a–c; Windscheid, § 123. n. 1 and 2).

But though there is no fault on the part of the shopkeeper, in so far as he has claimed back the lamp and has seized the thief, it is different with the latter if he has beaten his pursuer in order to free himself and to escape with the property he has stolen. The shopkeeper is doubtless entitled to resist this unlawful opposition in order to succeed in his attempt to save his property, and if, in the course of the struggle which has followed, he has knocked out an eye of the thief, he cannot be made liable for such an act which has been done merely in the course of self-defence.

One may, however, suppose that the struggle which followed the attack of the thief continued, even after the shopkeeper had succeeded in getting back his lamp, and that in the course of this fight the thief's eye was knocked out. And if so then it would be certain that the tabernarius would be liable on account of the injury done to the thief, for the blow which had caused the loss of the eye was not given in self-defence, but in order to revenge himself, ulciscendi causa, as in 45. § 4 above[1].

Of the same nature is the case supposed at the end of the passage, namely, if the shopkeeper has not been first beaten by the thief, but has, whilst going to seize the lamp, at the same time inflicted a blow on the thief, and thus himself caused the struggle, which has resulted in the loss of the eye. It is obvious that here the blow has not been inflicted by the shopkeeper in exercising a right of his own, and therefore he is declared to be liable for the harmful consequence of his act.

Pernice, p. 63 sq.; Arndts, § 94. n. b; Windscheid, § 123. n. 2.

52. § 2.—In cliuo Capitolino duo plostra onusta mulae ducebant: prioris plostri muliones conuersum plostrum subleuabant, quo facile mulae ducerent: inter superius plostrum cessim ire coepit et cum muliones, qui inter duo plostra fuerunt, e medio exissent, posterius plostrum a priore percussum retro redierat et puerum cuiusdam obtriuerat: dominus pueri consulebat,

[1] Differing from the above explanation is that given by Pernice, p. 63 sq., who thinks that there is a case of contributory negligence (*culpa-compensation*). The rixa is caused by the thief, and in so far he has contributed to his own injury.

cum quo se agere oporteret. respondi in causa ius esse positum: nam si muliones, qui superius plostrum sustinuissent, sua sponte se subduxissent, et ideo factum esset ut mulae plostrum retinere non possint atque onere ipso retraherentur, cum domino mularum nullam esse actionem, cum hominibus qui conuersum plostrum sustinuissent lege Aquilia agi posse: nam nihilo minus eum damnum dare qui quod sustineret mitteret sua uoluntate, ut id aliquem feriret: ueluti si quis asellum cum agitasset non retinuisset, aeque si quis ex manu telum aut aliud quid immississet, damnum iniuria daret. sed si mulae, quia aliquid reformidassent et muliones timore permoti, ne opprimerentur, plostrum reliquissent, cum hominibus actionem nullam esse, cum domino mularum esse. quod si neque mulae neque homines in causa essent, sed mulae retinere onus nequissent aut cum coniterentur lapsae concidissent et ideo plostrum cessim redisset atque hi quo conuersum fuisset onus sustinere nequissent, neque cum domino mularum neque cum hominibus esse actionem. illud quidem certe, quoquo modo res se haberet, cum domino posteriorum mularum agi non posse, quoniam non sua sponte, sed percussae retro redissent.

Two heavily-laden waggons were being drawn by mules up the Capitoline hill; the first waggon had tilted over and was being held up by the muleteers to make it easier for the mules to draw; whilst this was going on, the first waggon began to slip backwards, the drivers, who were between the two waggons, got out of the way; but the second waggon, being struck by the first, ran backwards and crushed a boy belonging to a third person. The master of the boy has asked against whom he must bring an action. I have answered that the law to be applied depends on the facts of the case (in causa), for if the muleteers who were holding up the first waggon got out of the way of their own accord, and thus it came about that the mules could not hold the waggon and were themselves dragged back by the weight of it, there will be no action against the owner of the mules, but the men who were holding up the waggon may be sued under the Aquilian statute, for certainly a man commits unlawful damage if he voluntarily lets go something which he is supporting so that it hurts another; for instance, if some one, whilst driving a young ass, does not hold him in, and so too if a person has let a weapon or anything else go from his hand, he does unlawful damage. But if the mules were frightened at something and started back, and the muleteers left the waggon from fear of being crushed, there will be no action against the men, but an action will lie against the owner. If, however, neither the mules nor the drivers were to blame in the case, but the mules could not support the weight, or in their attempt to do so slipped and fell, and the waggon ran back on that account, and if at the same time the men could not hold up the waggon, tilted over as it was, no action will lie either against the owner of the mules or the drivers. Whatever might have been the facts of the case, it is certain that no action will lie against the owner of the mules of the second waggon, for they have not gone back of their own accord, but have been driven back by the others.

The question has been raised as to the person liable under the Aquilian statute, in case two waggons were being drawn up a hill and damage was done by the first waggon rolling back on the second. It is obvious that, in the first place, the drivers of the first waggon are liable, if they have left the waggon without necessity, for instance, as not liking the trouble.

If the drivers had not been in culpa it might have been the case that the requirements of the actio de pauperie were fulfilled, e. g. if the mules have been frightened by some sudden cause, and have therefore started back and thus caused the damage. If that also is not the case no action whatever can be maintained on account of the damage done; e. g. if the weight was too heavy to be drawn up the hill, and the mules have broken down and the waggon has slipped backward in consequence, and thus caused the damage complained of. It is, of course, possible that the drivers were liable, in so far as they had previously overburdened the waggon (arg. 7. § 2), or had taken the wrong way. It seems, however, certain that the jurist did not think of cases of such kind.

Pernice, p. 214.

52. § 3.—Quidam boues uendidit ea lege, uti daret experiundos: postea dedit experiundos: emptoris seruus in experiundo percussus ab altero boue cornu est: quaerebatur, num uenditor emptori damnum praestare deberet. respondi, si emptor boues

emptos haberet, non debere praestare: sed si non haberet emptos, tum, si culpa hominis factum esset, ut a boue feriretur. non debere praestari, si uitio bouis, debere.

A person sold a pair of oxen on approval; he afterwards delivered them to be tried, and the slave of the purchaser in trying the oxen was struck by the horn of one of them. The question was asked, whether the seller is bound to pay compensation to the purchaser. I answered, that if the purchaser has already made up his mind to take the oxen, compensation is not to be given; but if he has not, compensation is also not to be given, if the damage done was due to the culpa of the slave, but it is to be given if it was due to a defect of the ox.

A person sold a pair of oxen to another, and the parties agreed at the same time that the purchaser should be entitled to try the oxen to see whether they would suit his purposes. In case they should not be approved by him, 'si displicuissent,' it is implied that the oxen should not be considered to have been bought. This so-called 'pactum displicentiae' (Arndts, § 249. n. 1) makes the question whether the sale concluded by the parties should become effectual dependent on the will of the purchaser. If he afterwards disapproves of the sale, that is if the condicio resolutiva is fulfilled, the whole transaction is dissolved, and its effects are rescinded, just in the same way as if it had never taken place (Arndts, § 71. n. 5 and 6).

If accordingly, in the above case, the purchaser declares his approval of the oxen, it is at once settled that the sale, and consequently the transfer of ownership in the oxen, has become irrevocable. The purchaser, therefore, has from the moment of sale been the owner of the oxen, and being thus injured by his own property no Aquilian action is possible. If, however, the purchaser disapproves of the oxen, the whole thing is regarded as if no sale has been entered upon, and accordingly no ownership has been transferred. It is now decided that the seller has been the owner of the oxen during the whole time, and therefore he may be sued for the injury done by his property to the purchaser. But as there is no culpa on his own part, he can be liable only to an actio de pauperie if one of his oxen has done damage contra naturam sui generis; cf. I. IV. 9. This action, however, is applicable only if the damage is not due to the culpa of a certain person (D. 9. 1. 1. § 7), and, therefore, if the slave himself has caused the damage by his own negligence, no action is applicable, for a master cannot maintain an action against his own slave.

Pernice, p. 60.

52. § 4.—Cum pila complures luderent, quidam ex his seruulum, cum pilam percipere conaretur, impulit, seruus cecidit et crus fregit: quaerebatur, an dominus seruuli lege Aquilia cum eo cuius impulsu ceciderat agere potest. respondi non posse, cum casu magis quam culpa uideretur factum.

Several people were playing at ball, and one of them pushed a slave-boy, who was trying to get hold of the ball; the boy fell and broke his leg. It was asked whether the master of the boy could bring an Aquilian action against the man who pushed him over. I answered that no action can be brought, for the damage is rather due to an accident than to negligence.

Where in the course of a game one of the players is wounded by another, the injury is apparently to be attributed to the person who does the act. It is, however, decided in the passage which we are explaining, that a player is not liable under the Aquilian statute to the master of the boy whom he has wounded. And this is quite natural, for a person who joins a game, which may possibly bring him into danger, must attribute the consequences to himself. He who participates in a game enjoys all the benefits which it confers, but has also to bear the disadvantages connected with it. If liability for such injuries should be recognised, people would not readily join in the games, and thus the great advantages of such games, viz. the development of the strength and dexterity of the body, could not be attained.

The same decision is given if in a wrestling match or pugilistic combat, one of the players has been wounded, although slaves were not admitted to exercises of such kind (7. § 4 above; cf. also 45. § 3 and Part II. § 7).

Pernice, p. 54; Windscheid, n. 12.

53.—Neratius libro I membranarum. Boues alienos in angustum locum coegisti, eoque effectum est ut deicerentur: datur in te ad exemplum legis Aquiliae in factum actio.

You have driven oxen into a narrow passage, and the consequence of this is that they have fallen down a precipice; an actio in factum, on the analogy of the Aquilian statute, will be applicable against you.

It is obvious that in the case of oxen which have been driven into a narrow passage and have fallen down, there is no damnum corpore datum, and therefore an action under the terms of the Aquilian statute itself is not applicable. But as the oxen have suffered damage in consequence of an act of the driver, he is declared to be liable to an actio in factum. In other passages in the same case an actio utilis is said to hold good (D. 47. 2. 51; I. h. t. § 16; Gaius, III. 219). This difference, however, is explained by the fact that the term actio utilis is used in a wider sense, which comprehends the notion of the in factum actio, if given on the analogy of an existing action; see the notes to 27. § 34.

Pernice, p. 150; Windscheid, n. 5; Savigny, System, vol. V. p. 96; Rudorff, Römische Rechtsgeschichte, vol. II. § 51. n. 8.

54.—Papinianus libro XXXVII quaestionum. Legis Aquiliae debitori competit actio, cum reus stipulandi ante moram promissum animal uulnerauit: idem est et si occiderit animal. quod si post moram promissoris qui stipulatus fuerat occidit, debitor quidem liberatur, lege autem Aquilia hoc casu non recte experietur: nam creditor ipse sibi potius quam alii iniuriam fecisse uidetur.

The debtor is entitled to the Aquilian action if, before there has been any delay in the delivery of the animal which has been promised by him, it has been wounded by the stipulator, and the same is the case if the stipulator has killed the animal. But if the stipulator has killed the animal after the delay of the promisor, the promisor, it is true, will be discharged from his debt, but in this case no action under the Aquilian statute will be rightly maintained, for the creditor seems to have done rather damage to himself than to another.

A person has promised by stipulatio the transfer of an animal to another person (reus stipulandi = stipulator). Afterwards the latter himself has wounded or killed the animal. It is decided that the promisor will be entitled to sue the delinquent by an actio legis Aquiliae, clearly for the reason that the promisor is still (before the traditio) the owner of the animal, and therefore the creditor has no right whatever to interfere with his property. But on the other side it is to be noticed that the creditor, by killing the animal, renders the fulfilment of the obligation impossible, and on that account the debtor is released from his duty (I. 3. 14. 2; D. 44. 7. 1. §§ 4–6; D. 45. 1. 33 and 37; Arndts, § 274. n. d.). We should therefore expect that he would be prevented from bringing an Aquilian action, as there does not seem to be any loss suffered by him through the act of injury. But it must be remembered that the interesse to be assessed under the first chapter of the statute may far exceed the actual value of the killed animal, from the transfer of which the debtor has been released by the act of the creditor, and in so far (viz. for this surplus) the Aquilian action is applicable in the case. This, however, is true only if the debtor has not yet become guilty of any delay with regard to the transfer of the animal—so-called mora soluendi (cf. Moyle, Inst. I. p. 409 sq.). Under this supposition, i. e. if the debtor, though admonished by the creditor (Arndts, § 251. n. i and k), has not complied with his duty, he cannot complain of the damage done, for if he had transferred the animal, as he ought to have done, ownership in it would vest with the creditor, and he accordingly would be entitled to deal with his property as he pleased. And it is for this reason that the creditor is declared at the end of the passage rather to have done damage ('iniuriam'; for the same use of this word see D. 43. 8. 2. § 10; D. h. t. 27. § 25; 30. § 1; 37 pr.) to himself than to the promisor.

Pernice, pp. 28 and 209; Brinz, § 340. n. 27, 34 and 35.

55.—Paulus libro XXII quaestionum. Stichum aut Pamphilum promisi Titio, cum Stichus esset decem milium, Pamphilus uiginti: stipulator Stichum ante moram occidit: quaesitum est de actione legis Aquiliae. respondi: cum uiliorem occidisse proponitur, in hunc tractatum nihilum differt ab extraneo creditor. quanti igitur fiet aestimatio, utrum decem milium, quanti fuit occisus, an quanti est quem necesse habeo dare, id est quanti mea interest? et quid dicemus, si et Pamphilus decesserit sine mora? iam pretium Stichi minuetur, quoniam liberatus est promissor? et sufficiet fuisse pluris cum occideretur uel intra annum. hac quidem ratione etiam si post mortem Pamphili intra annum occidatur, pluris uidebitur fuisse.

I promised Stichus or Pamphilus to Titius, whilst Stichus was worth ten thousand, and Pamphilus twenty; the stipulator killed Stichus before any delay in the delivery was made; the question as to what could be claimed in the Aquilian action was raised. I answered that, as the creditor killed the cheaper slave, his condition did not at all differ from that of any other person who killed the slave. What is accordingly the measure of damages in the Aquilian action, whether ten thousand, that is the value of the killed slave or the value of the other slave, whom I am bound to transfer to the stipulator, that is, how much my interesse has been? And how is the case to be decided, if Pamphilus has died without mora on the part of the promisor? Is it not that what is to be paid for Stichus will be diminished, because the promisor had been released from his duty? But it will be sufficient that Stichus had a higher value when he was killed, or within the previous year. And for the same reason, Stichus will be considered as having had a higher value than that of himself, also if Pamphilus died first and Stichus had been killed before one year had passed over.

The case under discussion is the following:—

I have promised in the alternative either Stichus or Pamphilus to Titius, Stichus being worth ten and Pamphilus twenty; and it is supposed—this is the first point to be decided—that Titius, i. e. the stipulator himself, has killed Stichus before he had come into mora.

There is no doubt that in this case the Aquilian action will be applicable, according to the contents of the last passage (54); but the question has been raised as to whether the sum to be recovered in this action will be ten, i. e. the value of the killed slave, or twenty, i. e. the value of the slave, who is now—after the death of Stichus—in obligatione, and it is decided in the passage that twenty can be claimed by the Aquilian action. And this is perfectly correct, for by the act of killing the transfer of the killed slave became impossible, and consequently the debtor became bound to deliver the only object which had been left; in other words, the alternative obligation has been changed into an obligatio of a species[1] (D. 13. 4. 2. § 3; D. 18. 1. 34. § 6; D. 23. 3. 10. § 6; D. 23. 5. 9. § 2; D. 45. 1. 16 pr.). The debtor accordingly has lost the advantage of freeing himself by the transfer of Stichus, and is bound to transfer the more valuable Pamphilus; it is therefore the loss of Pamphilus for which he is to be compensated. It is obvious that under this assumption the debtor will be brought by the Aquilian action into the same pecuniary condition in which he had been before the act of damage: he has lost Stichus, whom he intended to transfer to the stipulator, and he is in possession of twenty thousand, i. e. an amount equal to the value of Pamphilus whom he intended to retain.

A second question which is raised by the jurist is whether the object of the action will be altered if, after Stichus had been killed, Pamphilus has died, whilst there was no mora on the part of the debtor, for here the debtor is discharged by the extinction of the only object which is still due. We should therefore expect that the compensation to be given on account of killing the slave Stichus would be restricted to the value which he actually had. But as the assessment under the Aquilian statute is to be made with reference to the past, the amount of compensation once forfeited under the statute cannot be altered by a subsequent fact.

The third question decided by the jurist arises by assuming that Pamphilus has died first, and afterwards, before one year has passed over, Stichus has been killed by Titius. By this act the debtor will be freed from his obligation, because the only object yet due in virtue of the obligation has been destroyed (see the notes to 54 above). In so far we might think no Aquilian action can be brought against the

[1] The above principle is generally recognised. It, however, is asserted by several authorities on the topic (Mommsen, Beiträge, vol. i. p. 310 sqq.; Vangerow, vol. iii. pp. 21 and 23), that the debtor, provided he has the right of choosing the object to be delivered, can free himself by paying the value of the thing which has been destroyed. But such an inference is in our opinion not to be drawn from the passages (D. 30. 47. § 3; D. 46. 3. 95. § 1) quoted in favour of this view (see Puchta, § 203. n. d.), for first it seems to be at variance with the nature of the alternative obligation, according to which either one thing or the other, and not something else, is to be given; and secondly, it is, strictly speaking, at variance with the passage which chiefly is declared to support this view (D. 30. 47. § 3), for here it is said that the heir who owes either Stichus or Pamphilus as a legatum is at any rate bound to deliver the surviving slave, but perhaps he also may pay the value of the deceased slave, 'fortassis uel mortui pretium.' These words seem most naturally to admit of the explanation that under certain circumstances, namely, if this appears to be the intention of the testator, the heir may free himself by paying compensation for the thing which is destroyed.

creditor, but it may be the case that the amount due under the Aquilian statute exceeds the amount from the payment of which the debtor has been released. And this is really true according to the facts stated in the above passage, for in reckoning backwards we come to a period when, besides Stichus, Pamphilus was alive, and on that account Stichus would have been to be assessed at a sum of twenty if he had been killed at that period. And as a full year has not passed since the act of damage, the same sum will be due under the Aquilian action; but as the debtor is released from a debt amounting to ten, he will be entitled to sue only for the surplus due in virtue of the Aquilian statute, that is, the remaining ten.

Windscheid, n. 19 and 20; Brinz, § 340. n. 34 and 35; Arndts, § 274. n. 2 c; Vangerow, § 569. n. 2 (vol. III. p. 23 sqq.); Mommsen, Beiträge, vol. I. p. 312 sq.

56.—Idem libro II sententiarum. Mulier si in rem uiri damnum dederit, pro tenore legis Aquiliae conuenitur.

If a wife has done damage to the property of her husband, she can be sued under the terms of the Aquilian statute.

It has been doubted amongst the jurists whether the Aquilian action as an actio poenalis was to be admitted between husband and wife; but as gradually the Aquilian action was more and more looked upon as an actio by which compensation was attained—actio reipersecutoria—the question has been answered in the affirmative; see the notes to 27. § 30 above.

57.—Iauolenus libro VI ex posterioribus Labeonis. Equum tibi commodaui: in eo tu cum equitares et una complures equitarent, unus ex his irruit in equum teque deiecit et eo casu crura equi fracta sunt. Labeo negat tecum ullam actionem esse, sed si equitis culpa factum esset, cum equite: sane non cum equi domino agi posse. uerum puto.

I have lent you a horse; whilst you were riding on it and at the same time several other people were also riding, one of the other riders knocked against the horse, whereby its legs were broken. Labeo denies that there is any action against you, but an action against the other rider, if it was done by his culpa, but he says that there is certainly no action against the owner of the horse. And I think that this decision is right.

A person who has borrowed a horse is doubtless liable for every culpa under the contract of commodatum. But as there is, according to the facts of the case, absolutely no culpa on the part of the commodatarius, neither an actio commodati nor an Aquilian action can be brought against him. But an Aquilian action can be maintained against the rider whose horse knocked against the borrowed horse, provided the collision was due to the rider's culpa. If this was the case —and this is supposed in the fragment we are considering—an actio de pauperie against the owner of the horse, which has caused the damage, is excluded; but it must be understood that such an action would be applicable, if its requirements were present (I. IV. 9), as if the horse without his rider's culpa (D. 9. 1. 1. §§ 3–7) had caused the damage by an unusual fit of savageness (contra naturam sui generis).

PART II.

SYSTEMATIC EXPOSITION

OF THE

ROMAN LAW

OF

DAMAGE TO PROPERTY.

THE ROMAN LAW OF DAMAGE TO PROPERTY.

§ 1. *The date of the lex Aquilia*[1].

In modern Roman law it is a general rule that a person who by his act unlawfully damages another man's property, is liable to pay compensation for the loss thus sustained, and it is well known that the lex Aquilia is the basis on which this rule is founded. This enactment, however, did not contain the general rule mentioned, but only provided for particular cases of damage done to property. We may safely assume that the earlier law on the same topic was of a yet more special character, but as our sources of information with regard to this question are very insufficient, a careful examination and consideration of the passages concerned are required. Before entering on this inquiry, which will be the object of § 2, it seems desirable, first of all, to consider separately a single point connected with the historical development of the law of damage to property, namely, the question as to the date of the issue of the Aquilian statute, which is itself a matter of some controversy.

Upon this question we feel inclined to follow those authors who assign this lex to the year 467 A. U. C., for, although there is no direct testimony in our sources to prove this assertion, there are a good many circumstances which in their connection direct the investigator to that year[2].

Ulpian in D. h. t. 1 pr. reports that the lex Aquilia has displaced (derogavit) all the previous laws relating to damage to property: the XII Tables as well as the later laws on the topic. Accordingly the lex was issued at any rate some time after the Decemviral legislation (302–304 A. U. C.). Of course we cannot exactly say how much later it was published, but considering the fact that legislation was not

[1] Pernice, Zur Lehre von den Sachbeschädigungen nach römischem Rechte; Weimar, 1867, pp. 15–20.

[2] Cf. Pernice, p. 15 sqq.

frequent in those ancient days, a century or a century and a half is probably not too short a period to assume. These considerations direct us to the middle of the fifth century after the foundation of the city. Before that time the lex could not very well have been issued.

On the other hand, we know that the lex was already at the commencement of the seventh century A. U. C. subject-matter of a rather detailed interpretation on the part of the jurists. In D. h. t. 27. § 22 a passage of Brutus, commenting on the words of the lex, is quoted, and this jurist, one of the three so-called fundatores iuris ciuilis (cf. Pomponius in D. 2. 1. 2. § 39), was living about 620 A. U. C. It follows as a matter of course that the lex Aquilia had then been long in existence.

To these facts it must be added that all writers are unanimous in calling the lex Aquilia a plebiscitum, and therefore it must have been made in the time when the force of law was accorded to this kind of enactments. It is true there are different laws which are declared by Livy to have given to plebiscits the force of law, i. e. the lex Valeria Horatia, 305, the lex Publilia, 415, and the lex Hortensia, 467 A. U. C., and it is also true that the relation of these three leges to each other is not quite clear, but *without any doubt* plebiscits take the place of real leges from the date of the issue of the last lex mentioned.

Thus we are led to the year 467 A. U. C. But there is a circumstance which especially indicates this year as the date of the lex. Theophilus in commenting on the Inst. (IV. 3. § 15) expressly states that this lex was made in a time of discord between Patricians and Plebeians. This statement apparently points to one of the three secessions of the Plebs. It is quite clear that this secession can be only the last one—in montem Ianiculum—467 A. U. C., for the first secession—in montem sacrum—260, was made some time before, and the second one—in montem Auentinum—was made immediately after the issue of the XII Tables. It is also impossible to refer the statement of Theophilus to any other 'discord' of the two classes, for from the time of the lex Hortensia up to the disturbances of the Gracchi (620–633), when the lex Aquilia had been a long time in force, there was no other internal struggle of importance. It is true some authors have attempted to weaken the evidence afforded by the passage of Theophilus, by saying that it is either a mere invention or else a hasty inference from other passages (D. h. t. 1. § 1, and D. 2. 1. 2. § 8); but his statement is too definite to be got rid of by such an assertion.

In such circumstances it is but natural that the year 467 should be recognised by most of the authors [1] who have written on this topic, as the date of the issue of the lex Aquilia.

§ 2. *The relation of the lex Aquilia to the former law as to damage to property* [2].

The opinion is frequently expressed [3], that lex Aquilia abolished all previous laws dealing with the subject of damage unlawfully done to property, damnum iniuria datum, and it must be admitted that this opinion is clearly and unambiguously expressed in the passage of Ulpian, already quoted in the beginning of the first section (D. h. t. 1 pr.).

> Ulpianus libro octavo decimo ad ędictum. Lex Aquilia omnibus legibus quae ante se de damno iniuria locutae sunt, derogavit: siue duodecim tabulis siue alia quae fuit: quas leges nunc referre non est necesse.

In spite of this very definite testimony we may entertain doubts whether it is quite correct, not so much on the general ground that Roman jurists were not specially well acquainted with legal history, and that therefore their historical notices are to be accepted with great caution [4], as for the more definite reason that the lex Aquilia does not give a definition of damage to property, damnum iniuria datum, but only attaches liability to particular cases of such damage. These cases are, according to the first chapter, the killing of slaves or quadrupeds —occidere seruum alienum quadrupedemue pecudem alienam; according to the second chapter the discharge of a debtor by the

[1] Compare, in addition to Pernice, C. Sell, Die actio de rupitiis sarciendis, p. 14. n. 1; M. Voigt, Die XII Tafeln, vol. ii. § 131. n. 1. p. 526; Baron, Pandekten, § 313. I.; Schrader, Institutionum libri IV, Berolini 1832, note to I. IV. 3. § 15. Pighius, without any foundation, in his Annales Romanorum, Antwerpiae, 1665, mentions the year 573 (cf. Pernice, p. 18; Rudorff, Römische Rechtsgeschichte, vol. i. § 41. n. 3). Windscheid, Pandekten, § 455. n. 1, is uncertain as to the date, and only puts it before the seventh century.

[2] Pernice, pp. 1–10 and 21–25.

[3] Thus by Hasse, Culpa, p. 17, and with a few restrictions by Glück, vol. x. p. 308.

[4] Cf. Lotmar, Kritische Studien in Sachen der Contravindication. München 1878, ch. i. pp. 1–57.

adstipulator so as to defraud the stipulator—pecuniam in fraudem stipulatoris acceptam facere; and according to the third chapter the urere, frangere, rumpere rem.

These, which are the undoubted contents of the lex Aquilia, we have to compare with what we believe to have been contained in the XII Tables on the same subject. Laws issued in the later times, which, according to Ulpian, also were abolished by the lex Aquilia, are absolutely unknown to us, and nothing therefore can be said about them. But we have still sufficient materials to reconstruct the law of the XII Tables on this topic, and thus to settle the relations of the Decemviral legislation to the Aquilian enactment. In this way it will be possible to decide whether the general assertion of Ulpian in the passage so often quoted is or is not correct [1].

Tracing the law backwards, we find that in the earlier times the unlawful damage which since the lex Aquilia is called 'damnum iniuria datum' was signified by the expressions noxia nocita, noxiam nocere, or simply nocere. But a definition of noxia is no more given by the XII Tables than is the notion of the damnum under the lex Aquilia defined by that enactment. The XII Tables classify simply the single cases which are comprehended by the notion of noxia. This notion comprises, in opposition to the notion of damnum iniuria datum, not only the violation of another's property, by destroying or damaging a thing which is owned by him, but also the violation of his own body by wounding his person. The latter injury consists in one of two acts, either 'membrum rumpere,' or 'os frangere,' and these have now to be considered. The foundation of the distinction made between these two kinds of injuries rests on the notion of dividing the human body into head, trunk, and limbs (membra); thus the breaking of the latter is considered to be membri ruptio, whilst breaking a bone in the head or trunk is conceived of as ossis fractio [2].

1. In the first case, by the action which is given, the so-called actio de membris ruptis, the injured person can claim Talio according to the words of the XII Tables (Tab. VII. 14): 'Si membrum rupit, ni cum eo pacit, talio esto.' Such retaliation was to be decreed by the

[1] Cf. for the following, especially Voigt, Die XII Tafeln, vol. ii. §§ 131–134. All the following quotations of passages of the XII Tables are taken out of this work, vol. i. p. 691 sqq.

[2] Voigt, XII Tafeln, vol. ii. § 132.

judge and afterwards executed by the plaintiff. But the parties were directed by the lex itself to substitute a pecuniary composition in lieu of the retaliation (pactum de redimenda talione). But even in cases where such a composition had not been agreed on, and the judge had decided that retaliation should take place, its execution by legis actio per manus iniectionem could be avoided if the defendant asked for an arbiter (arbitrium de membro aestimando), who had to estimate the Talio in a fixed sum of money, the payment of which absolved the defendant.

2. The principle of composition was absolutely established in case of the ossis fractio, when, instead of retaliation, a fixed sum of money was to be paid in virtue of the law[1], for by the action given in this case, de ossibus fractis, 300 asses were claimed if a free man had sustained an ossis fractio, and 150 asses if such an injury was done to a slave [cf. Tab. VII. 15: 'Manu fusti si os fregit homini libero CCC, seruo CL poenas[2] sunto '].

It may be urged against our classification of the membri ruptio and ossis fractio, under the head of noxia, that in the time of the Emperors these delicts were considered to be insults of a personal character, i.e. iniuriae in the narrower sense, and were accordingly enumerated amongst them (Gaius, II. 223, Paulus, Sent. Rec. V. 4. 6; Coll. II. 5. 5, Gellius, XX. 1. 32) and not under the heading of noxia or damnum iniuria datum. But this classification is wrong in point of system, and is to be explained by circumstances of a merely external character[3]. An iniuria in the narrower sense must be in its nature committed intentionally (dolo), whilst the membri ruptio (Gellius, XX. 1. §§ 16–34), and certainly also the ossis fractio, can be committed by mere negligence (culpa). Further, in case of iniuria, the object of the law is to punish the guilty intent of a person who insults another, whilst the lawgiver in the cases in question is apparently looking at the result of the unlawful act, the fact of the ossis fractio and membri ruptio, and for this damage compensation is to be given. Besides, the ossis fractio is to be punished by a sum of 150 asses in case of

[1] Cf. R. von Ihering, Geist des römischen Rechts, vol. i. 3rd ed., Leipzig 1873, p. 138.

[2] The word 'poenas' is here equivalent to asses. Cf. Festus sub h. v. '*Viginti quinque poenas*' in XII significat viginti quinque asses (ed. of Müller, p. 371).

[3] Cf. Voigt, XII Tafeln, vol. ii. p. 521.

wounding a slave of another person. This is far too high a sum to be conceived of as a mere penalty for the insult (iniuria) to the master, which might possibly be implied by the act done to the slave.

3. In opposition to the membri ruptio and ossis fractio all the following cases which we are now going to consider are instances of damage done to property.

While for the damage done to the body of a person it was originally the leading principle that like should be returned by like, the principle of noxiam sarcire prevailed in case of damage to property, i.e. the damage done is to be compensated in natura whether by repairing the thing injured or by giving another of the same quality[1].

This principle of noxiam sarcire came into operation in case a person had killed a slave or a quadruped of another man. It is true there is no direct testimony which would prove the existence of an action provided for in such a case, the so-called actio de seruo quadrupedeue occelso (= occiso), nevertheless it must be accepted, for there was not only the practical necessity for such an action, but also the fact that the os serui frangere was punished by the XII Tables, which in comparison with killing a slave or a quadruped is certainly a matter of less importance.

4. In the same way a person is bound to make good the damage he had done by setting on fire a building or a stack of corn near a dwelling-place, urere aedes aceruumue frumenti iuxta tugurium positum. In case such an act was done intentionally, the offender was subject to a criminal prosecution [cf. Tab. VII. 14: 'Qui aedes aceruumue frumenti iuxta tugurium positum combusserit, uinctus, uerberatus igni necator, si sciens dolo malo incensit; ast casu, noxiam sarcito aut si minus idoneus sit uerberator']. The action to get compensation by noxiam sarcire is the actio de aedibus incensis (D. II. 14. 7. § 13).

[1] Sarcire is expressly declared to be an 'in integrum facere' by Charisius in his Institutiones Grammaticae (Grammatici Latini ex recensione Henr. Keilii, vol. i. p. 220); compare also Salemonis ecclesiae Constantiniensis episcopi glossa. *Sarcit:* redintegrat, renovat, reemendat, reconsuit, iungit. That the word sarcire was really used in the XII Tables in its original sense, follows from the fact that in those days Romans still provided for their necessities chiefly by self-production (cf. Voigt, XII Tafeln, vol. i. p. 16 sqq.). In the time of the emperors, the original meaning of the word is quite unknown, and therefore it is simply used in the general sense of paying compensation.

If the defendant was condemned and did not obey the judgment, then execution was to be claimed, as in all other cases, by actio judicati. But the usual consequences of early execution followed only in case the defendant was solvent; if he was insolvent (minus idoneus), he was to be whipped on account of his insolvency. The reason for this distinction clearly is that the insolvency of the defendant should not occasion his capitis deminutio maxima, which was the ordinary result of execution under the XII Tables[1].

5. If the owner of *pecora*, i.e. such animals as are kept on a farm (not only of quadrupedes pecudes, i.e. quadruped animals which usually are kept in flocks or herds), allows them to enter a field on which the crop had already come up (so-called *laeta seges*) and to graze there, he is liable to make good in natura the damage done in this way by ceding the crop standing on his own soil. In order to enforce this duty the actio de pastu pecoris is given to the person injured. [Cf. in Tab. VII. 10: 'Si impauit in laetam segetem alterius noxiam sarcito[2].']

6. The fact of arborem succidere, i.e. if a person has unlawfully[3] felled a tree of another one, makes him liable to an actio de arboribus succisis, the object of which is the payment of twenty-five asses [cf. Tab. VII. 12: 'Si alienam arborem succidit XXV poenas esto'], and not 'noxiam sarcire,' which in this case was impossible, as the defendant could not exactly substitute another tree in the place of that which he had cut.

It is common to all the actions arising out of the violation of another's property, which we have hitherto considered (nr. 3–6), that the liability is determined by the nature of the thing damaged. In other words, there are only particular things (slaves, quadrupeds, houses, crops, trees) the violation of which is brought within the operation of the law, and so the actions for compensation are of a limited character. But the XII Tables recognise also one action by which a person was

[1] Cf. Poste, Gaius, pp. 344 and 345; Moyle, Justinian, p. 640; Voigt, Die XII Tafeln, vol. i. p. 626 sq.

[2] According to the continuation of this passage, the delict mentioned therein is to be criminally prosecuted, if it was committed during the night and intentionally.

[3] The requisite of unlawfulness is expressed by Plinius, Hist. Nat. 17. 1. 7 (iniuria occidisset alienas arbores), but it does not imply that the act was done secretly as it is required by the (praetorian) actio arborum furtim caesarum, which must be clearly distinguished from the above mentioned actio de arboribus succisis. Cf. Voigt, XII Tafeln, § 133. n. 1 and 2.

made liable on account of damage without any distinction of the thing which was injured. It is true the act of damage must be of a certain kind, i. e. there must be a 'rumpere rem,' which in its original meaning is equivalent to sever, tear, or break a thing; nevertheless the action given in such a case is of a general character, because the rumpere of all possible things made a person liable.

We must admit that there is no quite unambiguous testimony which would prove the existence of this action, the so-called actio de rupitiis sarciendis[1] or simply actio de rupitiis[2], but there are two passages of Festus, from which this inference is to be drawn:—

1. *Rupitias* (in) XII significat *damnum dederit.* According to this the word rupitiae is equivalent to damage done to property. But without any doubt the expression meant only damage done by rumpere in the original sense of this word, for if the lex Aquilia, issued more than one century and a half after the XII Tables, distinguished in its third chapter between urere, frangere, rumpere rem, then it follows that these expressions were used in order to denote different kinds of actions; if rumpere were equal to doing damage in general, the mention of the two other words, frangere and urere, was quite superfluous[3]. There can be hardly any doubt that Festus, in explaining the word rupitiae, was misled by the interpretation of the jurists which took the word rumpere in the general sense of corrumpere, i. e. to spoil or to corrupt a thing (D. h. t. 27. § 13).

2. *Sarcito* in XII Seruius Sulpicius ait significare *damnum soluito, praestato.* According to these words sarcito signifies to pay for the damage done, to make it good. In this case also the commentator seems to have in view the more general meaning of the word sarcire, i. e. to pay compensation instead of the original one: to restore a thing to its former state (in integrum facere) by repairing it or by giving a new thing of the same quality.

On the basis of these two passages the following sentence was accepted as the probable contents of the XII Tables: 'Rupitias qui iniuria faxit . . . sarcito[4],' or 'Si rupitias faxit . . . noxiam sarcito[5].'

[1] C. Sell, Die actio de rupitiis sarciendis der XII Tafeln und ihre Aufhebung durch die lex Aquilia, Bonn, 1877.

[2] This expression is preferred to the former by Voigt, XII Tafeln, § 133. VII.

[3] Cf. Lotmar, Kritische Studien, p. 20.

[4] Huschke, Gaius, Leipzig, 1855, p. 106.

[5] Voigt, Tab. VII. 13.

Several authors have greatly objected to this combination of the two passages of Festus, but their doubts are without foundation, for, according to the first passage we have quoted, it is certain that the XII Tables contained the word rupitiae[1]; accordingly some legal consequences must have been attached to 'rupitiae' by that law. The only question is as to their nature. Considering the fact, that it was a general principle in those ancient days that damage done should be made good in natura (by noxiam sarcire as in case of the actions de seruo quadrupede occelso de aedibus incensis and de pastu pecoris), the word 'rupitiae' must be taken as being necessarily connected with the word 'sarcire,' as no other legal consequence could have attached to it[2].

But though we thus accept the former existence of the actio de rupitiis, a doubt occurs to us on the subject which appears to have more weight than any of the objections which we have just referred to.

It seems to be absolutely true that there was no general action to get compensation for damage done in early times, but there were only special actions recognised by law given in cases in which special objects as slaves, cattle, houses, crops, were injured. Things of such a kind were protected by law against violation of other persons, but no protection was given against damage to *property* simply, although done by a certain kind of action like rumpere. Thus I am informed, by one of the greatest authorities on Scandinavian law, that there is not a single instance in the earlier sources of this law which would recognise a general action for compensation of damage done to property[3]. But we must return for answer that, although this may be quite true, some time or other a general action must have come into existence. Undoubtedly the lex Aquilia grants such an action in so far

[1] Even this word and its explanation by Festus were matters of controversy. Comp. especially Th. Mommsen in the Rheinische Museum für Philologie, Neue Folge, vol. xv. (1860), p. 464 sq. But the objections made are rightly rejected, especially by Voigt, XII Tafeln, vol. i. p. 721, note 17 (to be compared with vol. ii. § 133. n. 16). Cf. also C. Sell, Actio de rupitiis, p. 4 sq.

[2] This opinion must be maintained, although the signification of the word sarcito allows also references to other passages, for instance to D. 47. 9. 9.

[3] With the above assertion the very thorough researches of Professor v. Amira into the old Swedish law are entirely in accordance. See in Nordgermanisches Obligationenrecht von Karl von Amira, vol. i. Leipzig, 1882, the chapter on torts (pp. 368–406), and especially the instances of damage to property given pp. 384–391.

as it determines in its third chapter the urere, frangere, rumpere rem; consequently, if every damage done is not included it still to a great extent comprehends such damage. But that such an enactment should have been made without having a precedent is hardly to be assumed as everywhere the development starts from the concrete and individual and ascends to the abstract and general[1]. It is then from this view quite credible, that already in the earlier times damage done to property in a more limited way gave rise to an action, as we stated above in proving the connection between the two terms of the XII Tables, 'rupitias' and 'sarcito.' Thus the development was probably the following: the enactment of the XII Tables relating to 'rupitiae' was probably the germ out of which the further-reaching provisions of the lex Aquilia (Chapter III) were developed, and these again were the basis for that general duty of paying compensation, which, in modern Roman law, takes place in all cases where a person by his unlawful act has caused damage to the property of another.

According to the exposition we have given hitherto, there are seven kinds of acts which are comprehended in the notion of noxia in the XII Tables:—

1. Rumpere membrum ciui,
2. Frangere os ciui seruoue,
3. Occidere seruum quadrupedemue pecudem,
4. Urere aedes aceruumue frumenti iuxta tugurium positum,
5. Impescere in laetam segetem,
6. Succidere arborem, and
7. Rumpere rem.

If we now look at the provisions of the lex Aquilia [1 occidere seruum . . . 2 pecuniam in fraudem stipulatoris acceptam facere, 3–5 urere, frangere, rumpere rem] we see that the fraudulent acceptilation by the adstipulator is not mentioned in the XII Tables; it is ruled for the first time by the lex Aquilia. On the other hand, the first and second of the acts mentioned in the XII Tables are not affected by the lex Aquilia, as this law concerns only damage done to property and not injury done to

[1] Cf. Ihering in the treatise 'Das Schuldmoment im römischen Privatrecht' (Vermischte Schriften, Leipzig, 1879, p. 192 sqq.), who, by explaining different instances (actio mandati actio legis Aquiliae, actio doli), shows how special actions preceded a general one.

the body of a person (only in so far as the frangere os seruo contains a damage done to his master's property, it falls under the provision of the third chapter of the lex Aquilia). In a similar way the special facts mentioned in 4, 5, and 6 are not immediately affected by the lex Aquilia [1], whilst 3 expresses exactly the same injury which is provided against in Chapter I of the Aquilian law, and 7 represents one of the three acts which are regulated by the third chapter of the lex (urere, frangere, rumpere rem). Accordingly the two actions which are attached to these injuries, the actio de seruo quadrupedeue occelso and the actio de rupitiis, are abolished by the lex Aquilia, but not the actions arising out of the other facts mentioned (actio de aedibus incensis, de pastu pecoris and de arboribus succisis).

The statement of Ulpian therefore, that the lex Aquilia has repealed (derogavit) all the previous laws on damage to property, especially the XII Tables, is not quite true, being too general. It is not the lex Aquilia alone, but this lex in connection with the different enactments of the XII Tables which forms the law on the topic of damage to property as it was in force in the period subsequent to the lex Aquilia.

It will be seen that this view of the subject is right if we look at the corpus iuris ciuilis, where the different special delicts of damage to property, which in our opinion are not affected by the lex Aquilia, are still mentioned.

Thus Gaius in D. 47. 9. 9 reproduces the sentence of the XII Tables, according to which a person who intentionally sets on fire a house or a stack of corn is to be burned; but a person who has done so negligently is liable to make good the damage in kind (by 'noxiam sarcire'), provided he is not insolvent, in which case he is to be whipped for his negligence. Accordingly this enactment was still formally in force in the time of the classical jurists; and it even still possessed practical importance in its criminal portion [2], but it is not less certain that the passage, in so far as it provides compensation for the

[1] It is true one may object to this assertion, that setting on fire of houses, etc. is nevertheless an urere rem regulated by the third chapter of the lex Aquilia; but it is a special fact, and the enactment which concerns it, a lex specialis, which, as a rule, is not superseded by a following lex generalis. Lex generalis non derogat priori speciali.

[2] Cf. D. 48. 19. 28. § 12; Paulus, Sent. Rec. v. 3. § 6 to be compared with id. v. 17. § 3.

damage done, fell into disuse in consequence of the lex Aquilia; for not only was the 'sarcire' in its original meaning unknown to later times, but the cases provided against by the enactment of the XII Tables came also under the provisions of Chapter III of the lex Aquilia, since setting on fire houses and stacks of corn is certainly a 'urere res;' and in addition to this an action on the basis of the lex Aquilia was more advantageous to the plaintiff, for it permitted him to claim the highest value which the thing injured possessed during the month previous to the injury done. It is therefore quite natural that in all cases, where such things were set on fire as are mentioned in the enactment of the XII Tables, the actio legis Aquiliae is granted to the injured person[1], and not the actio de aedibus incensis of the XII Tables.

The same is the case with the actio de pastu pecoris. Its validity a long time after the issue of the lex Aquilia is also in evidence[2]. But in consequence of the comprehensive interpretation of the word 'rumpere' in the third chapter, which was considered to be equal in meaning to 'corrumpere,' the lex Aquilia became applicable in this case also[3]; and it is only natural that the lex Aquilia should be made use of, since the mode of assessing damages under it was more favourable to the plaintiff than in the actio de pastu pecoris. This is undoubtedly the reason that the latter action has practically disappeared in course of time.

Special consideration must be given to the action respecting unlawful felling of trees. It is certain that the action provided for this case by the XII Tables, the object of which was the payment of twenty-five asses, disappeared from the later law. It is, however, mentioned in our sources of Roman law (thus in Gaius, IV. 11; D. 47. 7. 3. § 3; D. 12. 2. 28. § 6; D. 43. 24. 19) as if it were still in force. This fact is to be explained by the circumstance that in

[1] D. h. t. 27. §§ 7 and 8; C. h. t. 2; D. 47. 9. 3. § 7.

[2] By Aristo in D. 19. 5. 14. § 3, also in D. h. t. 39. § 1, in so far as the words 'habet proprias actiones' undoubtedly allude to this action. Arndts, § 327, does not think that it requires the culpa of a person. This opinion is rightly rejected by Voigt, XII Tafeln, vol. ii. p. 537. Cf. especially Paulus Diaconus: Impescere in laetam segetem: pascendi causa *immittere*.

[3] C. 3. 35. 6 (Diocletianus et Maximianus): De his quae per iniuriam depasta contendis, ex sententia legis Aquiliae agere minime prohiberis. Cf. Unterholzner, Schuldverhältnisse, § 683, who believes the actio de pastu pecoris to be abolished in the later times.

the pretorian edict there was a second action on the basis of the former, i. e. resting upon the same enactment of the XII Tables; but this action had the special requisite that the unlawful cutting down of trees had to be done secretly, furtim, wherefore the action is called actio arborum furtim caesarum. Both actions being in this sense based on the XII Tables, it is natural that they should be sometimes confounded with one another (for instance in D. 47. 7. 7 pr. and 8. § 1), although the requirements of the second action were increased and its legal consequences different, having for its object payment of the double value of the damage done. It is clear that, as a rule, in such cases as those in which the actio arborum furtim caesarum is applicable, there will be also a damnum iniuria datum which would justify the injured person in bringing the actio legis Aquiliae. But this does not necessarily follow, for if trees, which were already fit for being felled, were secretly cut down, then the actio arborum furtim caesarum will hold good, but not the actio legis Aquiliae, for in such a case no real damage has resulted from the act (D. h. t. 27. § 26).

According to this exposition the three special actions of the XII Tables (actio de aedibus incensis, de pastu pecoris, de arboribus succisis), although they were not formally repealed by the lex Aquilia, fell practically into disuse, and their place was taken by actions given either by the lex Aquilia itself, or by the extension of that statute to other cases. It is true that the actio arborum furtim caesarum remained in force in later times in addition to the actio legis Aquiliae; but it has its own special use on account of the penalty which it inflicts on the defendant: in this way protection is given against acts of secret cutting of trees, whether such cutting had caused actual damage to the plaintiff or not.

These considerations enable us to understand the sentence of Ulpian (D. h. t. 1 pr.) which is in question. Although the repealing effect of the lex Aquilia itself was limited to the two delicts which were ingrafted into it (the occidere . . . and the rumpere rem), the three other delicts fall, if not within the original contents of the lex, still within the sphere which interpretation assigned to it. On that account the actions based on the lex Aquilia were applicable to these cases, and naturally superseded the actions of the XII Tables, although the latter were never formally abolished. In consequence of this development, the lex Aquilia, not by the effect of its actual terms, but as it was interpreted by the later jurists, is really the only source of the law of damage to property. There is no exception to this rule, although some scholars have asserted that one is to be found in D. 9. 4. 2. § 1 ; D. 44. 7. 32, but against these opinions see Hasse, Culpa, pp. 17–20. Considering this fact, Ulpian was entitled to say, as he actually did, that the lex has repealed all previous law on the topic, although such an assertion is not literally true, as we have seen in the foregoing explanation.

§ 3. *The fundamental provisions of the lex Aquilia*[1].

It is mentioned above, that the first and the third chapters form the basis upon which the law of damage to property was further developed by the Roman jurisprudence and the pretorian edict. We have, therefore, to deal with these fundamental provisions more in detail, whilst with the second chapter we have nothing to do, as it does not at all concern damage done to corporeal things.

The text of the first chapter is delivered to us by Gaius (libro VII ad edictum provinciale) in D. h. t. 2 pr. in the following words :—

> Lege Aquilia capite primo cauetur: 'ut qui seruum seruamue alienum alienamue quadrupedem uel pecudem iniuria occiderit, quanti id in eo anno plurimi fuit, tantum aes dare domino damnas esto.'

The text of the third chapter is given by Ulpian (libro XVIII ad edictum) in D. h. t. 27. § 5 :—

> Tertio autem capite ait eadem lex Aquilia. 'Ceterarum rerum praeter hominem et pecudem occisos si quis alteri damnum faxit, quod usserit, fregerit, ruperit iniuria, quanti ea res erit in diebus triginta proximis, tantum aes domino dare damnas esto.'

There can be hardly any doubt that it is intended to reproduce in these passages the very words of the lex. Not only is the use of the

[1] Pernice, pp. 11–15.

imperative mood in both these passages in favour of this assertion, but also the manner of quoting the provisions, especially in the second passage ('ait eadem lex Aquilia'). Besides, it is to be observed that Gaius in his Institutes (III. §§ 210–219), although he does not there give the contents of the lex Aquilia verbatim, nevertheless uses the same characteristic words and modes of expression.

But though these passages give us on the whole the express terms of the lex, there are particular points in which they fail to do so.

1. It is quite clear that in the first passage the 'ut' is to be struck out, because it makes the sentence, i. e. the enactment of the XII Tables, dependent on the word 'cauetur,' and is therefore so far not a direct reproduction of the law; besides the '*ut*' would require the conjunctive mood and not the imperative 'esto,' which is used in the passage and which certainly stood in the lex itself. The most simple thing would be to cancel the 'ut,' which would be quite satisfactory. It is, however, preferable to read, instead of 'ut qui,' 'si quis.' This conjecture is supported not only by the terms of the third chapter (si quis alteri damnum faxit), but also by Dorotheus, who in the Basiliks (60. 3. 1), where he is apparently reproducing the terms of the lex, translates the commencing words of the first chapter with ἐάν τις οἰκέτην . . . . In accord with this reading is Gaius also, who, in his account of the same chapter says (III. 210), '*si quis* hominem alienum . . . .'

2. *Quadrupedem uel pecudem.* There is no doubt that the two words 'quadrupedem' and 'pecudem' are not to be separated by the particle 'uel;' for the passage cannot mean that a person is to be liable for killing both a quadrupes and a pecus; since it is clear that the word 'pecus' merely determines more closely the word 'quadrupes,' which in this passage is used as a substantive as in the corresponding passage of Gaius (III. 210—quadrupedem quae pecudum numero est). Consequently a person who has killed a four-footed animal (quadrupes) belonging to the kind of cattle which are usually kept in flocks or herds (pecus), becomes liable, in virtue of the first chapter of the lex Aquilia. If this view be right, the use of the expression 'uel' following the word 'quadrupedem' seems to be suspicious, as it is hardly allowable, in writing prose, to put this conjunctive particle 'uel' after the word (adjective or substantive) which is intended to be separated from the preceding word. It seems therefore necessary

to write quadrupedemue pecudem, an alteration which is approved of by most of the writers on the topic of the lex Aquilia[1].

3. Objections have been raised as to the use of the word 'id.' Although it is not very uncommon to use the neuter pronoun with reference to previous masculine and feminine words, there is yet a certain negligence in the expression which is not in accordance with the well-known accuracy of the language of the ancient laws and edicts (cf. for instance D. 4. 5. 1 pr.). If we look at Gaius (III. 214) we find instead of the 'id' the words 'ea res,' which without doubt are more satisfactory. Besides, they deserve the preference, as Gaius quotes the portion of the law which is here in question apparently in its original words (' Quod autem adiectum est in hac lege: Quanti in eo anno plurimi *ea res* fuerit'). This testimony is not contradicted by Ulpian (libro XVIII ad edictum) in D. h. t. 21 pr., where he says: Ait lex: 'Quanti *is homo* in eo anno plurimi fuisset,' for the phrase 'is homo' is simply explained by the reference made by the jurist to the formula of the action, which was of course different according to the difference of the object killed, whether it were a slave or a quadruped.

4. *Domino dare.* Instead of these words is to be read ero dare; for Ulpian, in D. h. t. 11. § 6, where he is doubtless commenting on the words of the lex, expressly says: 'Legis autem Aquiliae actio *ero* competit, id est domino.' And this antiquarian expression, which is quite in accordance with the antiquity of the lex Aquilia, must be retained, although Pomponius, in D. h. t. 43, remarks: 'dominum enim lex Aquilia appellat non utique eum . . . .'

5. The use of the future tense 'erit' in the quotation of the third chapter is rather singular, as the estimation of the damage relates to the time previous to the injury, and therefore we should expect 'fuit,' which is also to be found in the reproduction of the first chapter. And, indeed, Ulpian (in D. h. t. 29. § 8), whilst quoting the corresponding words of the third chapter, likewise uses the form 'fuit,' and with this tense the paraphrase of the passage in the Basiliks is in accordance. In so far we are entitled to accept without hesitation the reading 'fuit' instead of 'erit.' On the other hand, a law determines something for the future; the judge has to decide future cases as they

[1] Cf. Pernice, p. 12, and especially Vangerow, § 681 (iii. p. 577), who is himself of a different opinion.

arise in accordance with its provisions; therefore if a damnum iniuria has been committed, he has to condemn the guilty defendant to pay the highest value which the thing injured had had at one period of the last year or month; in other words, the defendant is to be condemned to pay the highest value which the thing in question shall have attained within the time mentioned. Accordingly, we should expect the reference to the future—in which the law is to be applied as well as to the past, i. e. the time before the injury in question. This certainly points to the future perfect 'fuerit,' and as this tense is actually used by Gaius (III. 214 and 218), in reproducing the corresponding portions of the first and the third chapter, it should, we venture to say, be preferred to the other readings.

Considering the previous remarks, the tenor of the two chapters was probably the following:—

Chapter I. Si quis seruum seruamue alienum alienamue quadrupedemue pecudem iniuria occiderit, quanti ea res in eo anno plurimi fuerit, tantum aes ero dare damnas esto.

Chapter III. Ceterarum rerum praeter hominem et pecudem occisos[1] si quis alteri damnum faxit, quod usserit fregerit ruperit iniuria, quanti ea res fuerit in diebus triginta proximis, tantum aes domino dare damnas esto.

§ 4. *The extension of the lex Aquilia by actiones utiles and in factum*[2].

According to the previous explanation, it is clear that the lex originally embraced only a few definite cases. But in course of time its provisions were extended to many other cases. This was done by the praetors granting, in circumstances where they thought it fair, an action, either an actio utilis or in factum, based on the actio given by the law itself, the actio legis Aquiliae directa, which doubtless had a formula in ius concepta[3]. But the relations of these different actions

[1] Pernice doubts whether the lex contained the words 'praeter hominem et pecudem occisos,' and considers them to be an insertion of Ulpian. But they are clearly a necessary part of the lex itself, for without them Chapter III would include only things other than slaves and quadrupeds, whereas it comprehends these classes also if they are only injured without being killed.

[2] Pernice, pp. 144–166.

[3] This follows clearly from the fact that fiction was to be inserted into the formula, if the action was to be brought

to one another raise many doubts on account of the uncertain character of our information on the subject. It is true that Justinian expressly deals with this question in his Institutes (IV. 3. § 16), but it is certain that his statement is inaccurate. According to this statement, the actio legis Aquiliae (viz. directa) will lie 'si quis praecipue corpore suo damnum dederit,' i. e. chiefly in such cases where a person had caused by some physical act of his own—*corpore* (sc. suo)—an actual damage to the corporeal thing of another—*corpori*; for instance, Titius strangles the slave of Sempronius. On the other hand, according to the same statement, the actio utilis can be brought, if the damage is caused by a person in any other way than corpore suo; in other words, if there is only a damage done to a thing, but not done by the physical act of the delinquent which is damnum *corpori*, but not corpore datum; for instance, Titius shuts up the slave of Sempronius and leaves him to die of hunger. Lastly, the actio in factum is said to be restricted to cases where a damage was done neither corpore nor corpori, i. e. to cases where there is neither a physical act of the delinquent nor actual damage done to a thing; for instance, Titius throws the golden ring of Sempronius into the sea (where it is lost without being damaged).

However probable this account of Justinian may appear at first sight, it cannot be supported, because in most of the cases where according to the passage quoted actiones utiles are given, according to other passages in the Corpus Iuris actiones in factum are applicable[1].

That which deserves more attention is the passage of Gaius (III. 219) on which the above passage in the Institutes is mainly founded. Gaius there expressly says that the Aquilian action is applicable only 'si quis corpore suo damnum dederit,' and that, if damage was done in any other way, 'alio modo,' actiones utiles should be employed. Accordingly Gaius gives us only two divisions instead of three, not mentioning actiones in factum.

There is no doubt that the expression 'actio utilis' is used in the

by an alien or against an alien (Gaius, IV. 37). Nothing else is known as to the conception of the formula, and therefore the attempts at reconstructing it differ considerably from one another. See Lenel, Das Edictum perpetuum, p. 157 sqq., and the authors quoted there.

[1] D. h. t. 9. §§ 2, 53.

Corpus Iuris in the sense of every action which is given on the analogy of an existing action (actio directa, uulgaris) for cases previously not actionable[1]. In order to attain this object, the usual formula actionis was altered in some way or other, as for instance by adding, omitting, or altering single words, by inserting a fiction (actio ficticia)[2], by transposition of the subjects of the action[3], and even by substituting in the place of the intentio a statement of the facts of the case, on the truth of which the condemnation was thus made dependent (actio in factum)[4]. Accordingly the term actio utilis comprehends the notion of actio in factum; in other words, actiones in factum, if granted on the analogy of an existing action, are a species of the actiones utiles.

It is true that, according to several passages[5], the use of the term 'actio utilis' seems to be restricted to cases where an existing action has been extended by way of fiction to a new case, and therefore actiones utiles were considered originally to have been identical with actiones ficticiae[6]; but whether this view is right or wrong, it is quite certain that the term is not used by Gaius in this sense, but in the wider sense we have stated above, for so it covers also the notion of actio in factum, and we know from many passages that actiones in factum are declared to be applicable in most of the cases in which the Aquilian statute has been extended beyond its original orbit.

Differing from the passage of Gaius, fragments of the Digest (D. h. t. 33. § 1; D. 19. 5. 11; D. 9. 1. 1. § 7; cf. also Collatio XII. 7. § 5) distinguish merely between actio legis Aquiliae and actio in factum. These passages clearly say that in case of damage which does not fall under the Aquilian statute, an actio in factum is applicable. (Paulus, in 33. § 1: 'In damnis quae lege Aquilia non tenentur, in factum datur actio.') And it seems quite probable that, as a rule, in those cases in which there was no occidere, urere, etc., as required by the statute, a description of the facts of the case was desirable and usual. But it must be understood that the fact that an actio in

[1] D. 19. 5. 21; D. 24. 3. 64. § 9; Rudorff, Römische Rechtsgeschichte, vol. ii. § 51; Keller, Der römische Civilprocess, § 89. ii. (sixth ed., Leipzig 1883, p. 467).

[2] Keller, § 31.

[3] As e.g. in case of the actio exercitoria and the other actiones adiecticiae qualitatis; Keller, § 32.

[4] Keller, § 33.

[5] Gaius, IV. 34 and 38.

[6] Savigny, System, vol. v. p. 71 sq.

factum was applicable in all cases where a direct action did not lie, did not prevent the praetor from granting in some cases also an actio ficticia, although such action was possible only where the ordinary formula might have been adapted to the case to be decided by means of a fiction [1].

These remarks will be fully confirmed when we consider the gradual way in which the lex Aquilia was extended.

1. In the interpretation of the first chapter 'occidere' and 'mortis causam praestare' are distinguished, and in the first case the actio legis Aquiliae, in the second an actio in factum is declared to be applicable. This distinction, which is illustrated in various ways in other passages by Ulpian (D. h. t. 9 pr., 11. § 1. 49 pr.), is clearly expressed by the same jurist (libro XVIII ad edictum) in D. h. t. 7. § 6.

> Celsus autem multum interesse dicit, occiderit an mortis causam praestiterit, ut qui mortis causam praestiterit, non Aquilia, sed in factum actione teneatur.

The expression 'occidere,' in accordance with its derivation from 'caedere,' was originally understood to mean beating to death, in the strictest sense of the word, by one's hand or by a cudgel or other weapon (D. h. t. 7. § 1). But soon afterwards an action under Chapter I was admitted, where there was a blow or push which had the result of killing a slave only mediately by intervention of other circumstances; thus if a person pushed a slave from a bridge and he was drowned in the river (Gaius, III. 219; I. h. t. § 16; D. h. t. 7. § 7), or again if some one threw a child against a rock by which it was killed, etc. (D. h. t. 7. § 7; cf. 7. § 2; 11. § 4). These cases resemble those of 'occidere' in the original sense of the word, in so far that the death complained of has been caused by a physical act of a person (corpore suo) on the body of the slave (corpori) who has been killed.

[1] According to Lenel (Das Edictum perpetuum, p. 154 sq.) it is, with regard to the conception of the formula, quite irrelevant whether an action is called 'utilis' or 'in factum.' For whilst he agrees with the above definition of the actio utilis, the actio in factum is with him merely an action which, whatever might be its form, has been established in opposition to the actio directa, in order to meet the particulars of a case to be decided. It is obvious that this view perfectly accounts for the different terms which are used in the Corpus Iuris, but it is by no means proved that the Romans have used the word actio in factum not only in the well-known sense of an actio in factum concepta (Gaius, IV. 46, 47), but also in the general sense attached to that term by Professor Lenel.

Gradually the jurists went beyond this original notion of occidere; thus Labeo grants the actio directa in case of poisoning a person, provided only the poison was administered by the guilty person himself, i. e. by his corporeal act (D. h. t. 9 pr.). Strictly speaking in this case there was no damnum corpore corpori datum as there was in the cases mentioned before, for the death was not caused by the act of the poisoner, but by the effect of the poison; nevertheless an action under the first chapter was admitted in this case also.

Different from these cases are those in which a person only 'causam mortis praestat.' Thus if some one puts poison instead of medicine near a sick slave and the slave takes it and dies in consequence (7. § 6 and 9 pr.), or if a person gives a madman a sword and he kills himself with it (7. § 6), or if somebody frightens a horse and the horse throws its rider into a river and he is drowned (9. § 3), or if a person shuts up cattle he has seized and they die of hunger (27. § 7), or drives cattle into a narrow way from which they fall down a precipice (D. h. t. 53), or if a person strips a slave of his clothing in winter time, who in consequence is frozen to death (D. 19. 5. 14. § 1). In all these cases there is a greater or less possibility of death not ensuing. The person who is guilty of the death does not really perform an act which causes it; there is accordingly no damnum corpore datum; he only brings about a condition or a state of things from which, with the concurrence of other circumstances, death results (damnum corpori datum).

2. The interpretation of the third chapter proceeded in a way analogous to that of the first chapter. In this third chapter there were certain concrete cases which form the basis of the interpretation, i. e. urere, frangere, rumpere rem. The meaning of 'urere' is in itself clear, but the relation between 'frangere' and 'rumpere rem' is not without difficulties. As we have seen, 'rumpere' has originally the same meaning as 'to sever,' 'tear,' 'break,' whilst 'frangere' is rather equivalent to our 'crushing.' Accordingly the latter verb would denote the annihilation of a thing, the former only the extinction of its integrity, and in so far the difference between them would be only a question of degree. But this dispute is of no importance, for a very old interpretation took the 'rumpere' in the sense of 'corrumpere,' and therefore every act of a person by which a corporeal thing of

another had been injured came within the operation of the law, and thus gave rise to an action under the third chapter of the statute itself. This, however, was subject to one important restriction. For in the same way as the conceptions of urere, frangere, rumpere rem implied an immediate dealing with the thing which had been damaged, so the act of corrumpere was required to be a physical act of the delinquent on a corporeal thing itself; in short, a damnum corpore corpori datum was considered to be necessary in order to give rise to an actio legis Aquiliae directa.

In accordance with these conditions an action under the terms of the third chapter was given (1) against a person who threw a torch at a slave and thus burnt him, on account of urere (27. § 6; see also 27. §§ 7 and 8); (2) against a person who sank a ship by boring a hole into it, on account of rumpere (27. § 24); (3) against a person who battered down the door of a house or destroyed the house itself, on account of frangere (27. § 31; cf. 27. § 29).

But an action on account of rumpere or frangere was also given if an ass was burdened too heavily and thus broke down (27. § 23), or a ship sailed into fishing-nets which thus were torn, or into another ship which was capsized in consequence (29. § 3 and § 2), or if a mare in foal was overdriven and so miscarried (39 pr.), although in all these cases the damage was not so immediately done by the delinquent's own hands as in the cases we have mentioned before.

There are also cases in our sources illustrating the meaning of 'corrumpere.' Thus, if a person mixes together corn and sand (27. § 20), or throws corn into the water (27. § 9), or if a person pours out wine and lets it become flat and sour, etc. (27. § 15; cf. also 42).

Differing from the cases hitherto considered are those in which a person creates a situation from which, in conjunction with other circumstances, damage results, 'causam damni praestat,' e.g. a hole is made in a cask and the wine therein leaks out, and nothing is done to stop the leakage. In this case, where, of course, the loss of the wine and not that of the cask is in question, an actio in factum lies (27. § 35), as it does also in the following cases: Water-pipes are laid by the side of a house, which is damaged by the dampness they cause (D. 8. 2. 18); weeds are sown in another's field, and spoil the corn growing there (27. § 14); or the cable of a ship is cut off and the vessel is in consequence lost. Similarly there is a causa incendii if a person keeps a stove against his neighbour's wall, and the wall is damaged by the fire (27. § 8), or if a person sets fire to the stubble on his own field, and the fire spreads to his neighbour's field (30. § 3); but in case a person sets his own house on fire, and the neighbouring building, or the property of his lodger, is burned, then, though the act of burning is not direct, yet it is an urere in the view of the jurists, and so the actio legis Aquiliae directa is applicable (27. § 8).

This last instance shows clearly that it was sometimes difficult to distinguish between the damnum required by the lex Aquilia, which gave rise to the actio legis Aquiliae and the 'causam damni praestare,' which led to an actio in factum. It is therefore easy to understand that sometimes in cases of the same kind one jurist thinks an actio directa to be applicable, whilst the other is in favour of an actio in factum. So Celsus declares an actio directa to be maintainable in cases where bees have been destroyed by fire (27. § 12), whilst Ulpian decides himself for an actio in factum (49). Similarly in the case where a dog, irritated by one person, has bitten another, Julianus, in opposition to Proculus, defends the application of an actio in factum, and the same difference may be found between Mela (37. § 4) and Ulpian (D. 9. 1. 1. § 7), who are both dealing with cases in which an irritated mule or horse has damaged another person under similar circumstances.

It is common to all the cases hitherto considered that there is a real damage done to a thing, damnum corpori datum, if not also corpore datum. It is true that some thing has been killed or burned or broken or otherwise spoiled through the guilt (dolus or culpa) of a certain person, and in so far the above cases are still in accordance with the contents of the lex Aquilia.

But there are cases in which there is no damage done to a thing, neither a damnum corpore nor corpori, and yet an actio in factum is said to be applicable.

1. Thus a person may deprive another of his property, without having the animus lucri faciendi; for instance, a person throws a ring or coins of mine into the river, where they are lost, although they are not damaged (D. h. t. 27. § 21; D. 19. 5. 14. § 2, 23; D. 41. 1. 55; D. 47. 2. 50. § 4; I. h. t. § 16).

2. A person, without spoiling the substance of a corporeal thing of another, as is supposed in 27. § 20, may mix something else with it, and the difficulty of separation may diminish its value; for instance, weeds and tares may be sown in the crops of another, 27. § 14.

3. A person may use up the consumable things belonging to another. Here the eatables are evidently used as they ought to be, and cannot be said to be damaged either by rumpere or corrumpere (D. 19. 5. 14. § 3).

It is obvious that in all these cases some corporeal thing is lost for its owner in quite the same way as if it had been destroyed, and it is also certain that in every instance this loss has been caused by an improper dealing of another with the thing itself. In this respect the cases resemble those in which actual damage has been done to a thing, and therefore they have been brought under the operation of the lex Aquilia. At the same time these cases determine the limits beyond which no liability under the principles of the Aquilian statute is recognised within the sources of Roman law.

According to this explanation an actio in factum is applicable within the whole sphere to which the lex Aquilia was extended by interpretation. The same must be said of the actio utilis, for such an actio is granted in the following cases: (1) if animals are driven into a narrow way and fall down a precipice (D. 47. 2. 51); (2) if a person persuades a slave to climb a tree and to descend a well, and he falls and is killed or wounded (Gaius, III. 219; D. 11. 3. 3. §§ 1, 4); (3) if animals are impounded and die of hunger (Gaius, l. c.; D. 47. 8. 2. § 20); (4) if a person drives animals so violently that they break down (Gaius, l. c.); (5) if a slave falls asleep whilst he is taking care of a fire on a hearth and thus a conflagration arises (D. h. t. 27. § 9; cf. also Coll. XII. 7. § 7); (6) if wine or corn belonging to another person is consumed (D. h. t. 30. § 2)[1].

These cases not only cover the whole ground of the extension of the lex Aquilia, but in some of them (1. 3. 6), according to other passages (D. h. t. 53 and 9. § 2 and D. 19. 5. 14. § 3), an actio in

[1] A very peculiar extension of the Aquilian statute was recognised in case a free man (pater or filius familias) had been wounded. Here an actio utilis was declared to be applicable by which the outlay incurred for the cure and compensation for the loss of the injured person's labour might be recovered: see D. h. t. 5. § 3 ad f., 6. 7 pr., 13 pr. and the notes on pp. 16–18 and 46 above.

factum is expressly granted. It is therefore quite clear that no principle can be established, according to which the cases of actio in factum and actio utilis are to be distinguished from one another. And this is quite natural if we remember that the expression actio utilis in its wide sense covers the notion of actio in factum, which is given on the analogy of an existing action, although it may be true that the jurists, in using the words actio utilis, have rather in view an action which is made more closely in imitation of the direct action, than in using the other expression actio in factum.

The Aquilian law, however, has been extended not only with reference to the act of damage, but also with reference to the persons to be entitled or bound under its provisions. It is with regard to this point only that an actio utilis in the special sense of an actio ficticia is expressly declared to be applicable; for we are told by Gaius, IV. 37, that if an Aquilian action (which originally lay merely between Roman citizens) was to be brought by an alien, or against an alien, a fiction was inserted into the usual formula in virtue of which his qualification of a Roman citizen was to be assumed by the judge, who had to decide the case. But whether there are any other cases of such an action is quite uncertain. We may assume that a formula ficticia was used wherever there was any reason for granting an action to or against some other person than the one who according to law is entitled to bring the action, or who is to be sued by it—the legitimate plaintiff or defendant,—e. g. if a guardian is sued on account of the injury done by his ward (25. § 1), or if an action is granted to a filius familias in the absence of his father; ne impunita sint maleficia (D. 5. 1. 18. § 1). But it is also possible that in such cases the actio directa was given only with a transposition of the persons in the formula[1].

It is likewise uncertain whether an actio ficticia was granted to persons who had a mere ius in re aliena. It is true, in D. h. t. 11. § 10; 27. § 32; D. 43. 24. 13 pr., a utilis actio is given to the usufructuary and usuary, but whether this expression is used in the special sense of the actio ficticia is hardly to be ascertained.

The whole division into actio directa on one side, and actio utilis and in factum on the other, was important, not as regards substantive law,

[1] Keller, Der römische Civilprocess, § 32. n. 351.

but only in respect of procedure. The praetor had of course to decide whether a case was within the terms of the lex itself, for, as we have seen, no actio legis Aquiliae directa could be brought, unless there was a damnum corpore corpori datum, whilst in all other cases of damage actio utilis or in factum was the proper remedy. But when an extended action had to be applied, the praetor was at liberty to follow more or less closely the formula of the actio directa. He could, however, only give an actio ficticia, where the case was of such a kind, that the formula of the directa actio could be applied by the insertion of a fiction, whereas the actio in factum was applicable in every possible case[1].

Our exposition clearly shows that the passage of the Institutes (IV. 3. § 16), which introduced the present discussion, is wrong; at the same time it is easy to see how the mistake in question originated. In composing the Institutes of Justinian the compilers chiefly followed the Institutes of Gaius. Accordingly they reproduced the passage so far as it expressed, that in case of damnum corpore corpori datum[2], the actio legis Aquiliae was applicable, and actio utilis in case of damnum corpori datum. But remembering very well that there was in existence also an actio in factum given on the basis of the lex Aquilia, they superficially assigned to it those cases in which damage had not been done either corpore or corpori, but in some other way[3].

§ 5. *The nature of the act, which entails liability under the Aquilian law.*

Having hitherto explained the principal provisions of the Aquilian statute, and the relation in which they stand to the earlier law on the topic of damage to property, as well as the method of the extension of these provisions to other cases, we now proceed to give a dogmatic exposition of the law of damage to property itself.

It is obvious that the conduct of a person to which liability under the terms of the statute itself attaches must consist in an act of a positive nature, that is, must be a commission; a mere omission cannot

[1] Vangerow, vol. iii. p. 584.

[2] But Justinian added 'praecipue' to these words, probably because he knew of passages where, without a damnum corpore corpori datum, nevertheless the direct action is given (C. h. t. 5; D. h. t. 28 pr.).

[3] See Lenel, Das Edictum perpetuum, p. 160 sq.

possibly give rise to an action under Chapter I or III, which require 'occidere seruum quadrupedemue' and 'urere, frangere, rumpere rem,' facts which, even according to the extensive interpretation of the Roman jurists, imply in every case a 'damnum corpore corpori datum.' But the same must be asserted of the whole field over which the original provisions have been extended; accordingly an actio utilis or in factum can be maintained only if damage has been caused by a positive act or conduct of a person[1].

This view is in perfect harmony with the leading principles which have found expression in the Roman and in modern law. Nobody, as a rule, is bound by law to do any act in the interest of another; thus I am by no means obliged to close my neighbour's shutters, although I see the storm approaching which will break the windows, and although I may prevent the damage without the slightest inconvenience to myself.

There is only the general negative duty recognised by law, that no person should interfere with the sphere of rights of his fellow-creatures[2], unless he is acting in virtue of a right of his own[3]. Therefore no person is allowed to injure another in his property, and, more especially, no person is allowed to destroy or damage things belonging to him.

That which in this way follows from the leading principles of law in general will be confirmed by a superficial survey of the different cases of actiones utiles and in factum mentioned in the last section. They apparently presuppose without any exception a commission on which the liability is based.

There are, however, a few passages from which the inference has been drawn that a liability under the Aquilian law has been recognised to a greater or less extent even on account of an omission. The question, it must be noticed, is one of the highest practical importance, for if liability should attach to an omission, every person

[1] Nearly all authorities on the topic agree with the above view; cf. Hasse, Culpa, p. 21 sq.; Unterholzner, Schuldverhältnisse, vol. ii. § 674; Arndts, § 324. n. 3; Windscheid, § 455. n. 9; J. A. Seuffert, Praktisches Pandektenrecht (4 ed. Würzburg, 1860–1872), § 400. n. 6–8. Differing but, in my opinion, not convincing: Busch in the Archiv für die civilistische Praxis, vol. xlv. p. 139 sqq., and Pernice, p. 164 sqq.

[2] 'Neminem laedere' is one of the 'praecepta iuris' in I. 1. 1. § 3.

[3] 'Qui iure suo utitur, neminem laedit, nemini facit iniuriam' (cf. D. 50. 17. 55, 151, 155. § 1).

who should not comply with a legal duty would be subject to an Aquilian action on account of the damage caused in consequence of the omission, e.g. a tenant of a house who did not strew cinders in the time of frost, as was prescribed by law or by order of the competent magistrate. It is therefore necessary to examine carefully the passages in question.

1. In 8 pr. (cf. 7. § 8)[1] it is stated that a surgeon who has operated on a slave successfully, but afterwards has neglected to attend to his cure, is liable on account of the death of the slave. It has been said that in this case the damage complained of is due to a mere omission, viz. to the fact that the surgeon has omitted to attend to the cure of the slave.

But this omission is doubtless preceded by a commission, i.e. the act of incision, which is closely connected with it. We even say: Incision and the following non-attendance form together only one whole, namely, the operation upon the slave, and this operation has not been performed as it ought to have been performed. Accordingly it is the improper performance of an act to which the death of the slave is due.

This answer, I think, true as it is, will satisfy common sense, but it may perhaps not satisfy the jurist. For he may object to it that there are two events distinctly to be separated from one another:—

(1) *The incision*, which has been made quite correctly by the surgeon, and therefore no culpa can be laid to his charge with regard to it, and

(2) The following omission, i.e. the *non-attendance* to the cure, which, being due to the negligence of the surgeon, has caused the death of the slave.

This objection, however, cannot be maintained, for the real cause of the death is not the non-attendance to the incision, but the incision itself. From the incision as it has been made death has resulted as the necessary consequence; it is therefore a positive act and not an omission to which the damage complained of is due. And it is also not admissible to say that the incision has not been made culpa, for this dangerous act has been made knowingly and intentionally by the

[1] For the full interpretation of these passages and all other passages subsequently quoted from the title of the Digest 'Ad legem Aquiliam' the notes in Part I are to be compared.

surgeon, and in so far he is in culpa. Only in case he had done everything he could do in order to deprive the incision of its dangerous effect, there would be no culpa on his part. It seems to be obvious that there is no difference between the case where the surgeon has operated unskilfully on a slave and the other where he has done so skilfully, but without dressing the wound inflicted on the slave; in both cases the death of the slave is equally due to an act to be attributed to the surgeon who has performed it.

2. Of a more complicated character are the facts dealt with in 27. § 9. In this passage there are two cases which are to be distinguished. A person had hired a farm-house (villa) in which there was a furnace, and had appointed one of his slaves to take care of the furnace, but he, after having lighted the fire, fell asleep by it, and thus the house was burned down. The question of course arises, whether the tenant (colonus) is liable to his landlord under the contract of hiring and letting, and further—and this is the point we have to deal with—whether a liability under the Aquilian law comes into existence. The same question may be asked if we suppose—and this is the second case mentioned in the passage—that one man has lighted the fire, and another has afterwards taken his place in watching it, and has altogether omitted to attend to this task.

In both these cases, it has been said, it is an omission to which the damage is due, namely, the fact that the slave, who has taken charge of the furnace, has not attended to his task.

But in the first case there is certainly a positive act, viz. that of kindling the fire to which the damage seems to be due. From the fire, as lighted by the slave and kept by him in a certain state, the conflagration has arisen. The slave has evidently put into motion a cause, for which he must be answerable, unless he has done his best to avoid its pernicious effect, either by extinguishing the fire or by so protecting it that it cannot spread.

Even in the second case, where another man has taken the place of the one who has lighted the fire, but has altogether neglected to attend to it, there is a positive act of his, to which the damage is due and for which he is answerable. For he has approached the furnace, apparently with the intention of taking care of it, and thus has induced the slave who has been watching the fire to leave his place. So it is due to his act that the fire has assumed such dimensions as to destroy the whole house.

In accordance with these views, in both the cases an actio on account of the damage done is declared to be applicable, although not an actio directa, but an actio utilis, clearly for the reason that the acts mentioned in the passage are not thought to constitute a 'urere' properly so-called, but merely a 'causam incendii praestare.'

3. Of the same nature as the two cases we were considering just now is the case dealt with in 30. § 3, where a person has set fire to the stubble on his own ground and the fire has spread to the neighbour's field. It is obvious that it is the negligence in lighting or guarding the fire which has caused the damage to the neighbour.

4. Also the case discussed in D. h. t. 31 and I. h. t. § 5, has been made use of in order to maintain the view that an omission may entail liability under the Aquilian law. According to these passages a person who, in lopping a tree in a place where people are accustomed to walk, lets fall a branch, without having given warning to a passer-by by crying out, is liable to an Aquilian action on account of the damage done by the fall of the branch. It is, however, evident that the damage is not due to the omission of the warning, but to the subsequent act of throwing down a branch. Even if the warning had been given, the damage might have happened, e. g. if the passer-by was deaf, or if he, in spite of the cry, did not choose to get out of the way. But in such cases no liability would attach to the act of throwing down the branch, for the man who threw it down would have done what a careful man—a 'diligens pater familias'—would do under the circumstances of the case. For such an act as throwing down branches or anything else in a place of public resort requires that precautionary measures be previously taken in order to avoid damage to others; otherwise such acts are not performed as they ought to be, and therefore the doer is in culpa. Accordingly in all the cases which we have considered—and there are no others which could alter the result—there is always the performance of a positive act; but, in order to perform an act properly, measures of precaution are often necessary, which must be taken either simultaneously with (30. § 3), or subsequently (8 pr.), or previously to the act itself (31 and § 5 cit.).

The result thus arrived at by an examination of the cases concerned has also found expression as a principle in D. 7. 1. 13. § 2.

> Ulpianus libro XVIII ad Sabinum. De praeteritis autem damnis fructuarius etiam lege Aquilia tenetur et interdicto quod ui aut clam, ut Iulianus ait: nam fructuarium teneri his actionibus nec non furti certum est, sicut quemlibet alium qui in aliena re tale quid commiserit. denique consultus quo bonum fuit actionem polliceri praetorem, cum competat legis Aquiliae actio, respondit, quia sunt casus, quibus cessat legis Aquiliae actio, idem iudicem dari ut eius arbitratu utatur: nam qui agrum non proscindit, qui uites non subserit, item aquarum ductus corrumpi patitur, lege Aquilia non tenetur. eadem et in usuario dicenda sunt.

According to this passage a usufructuary who has done damage to the thing subject to his usufruct is liable to the actions arising from his act, viz. an actio legis Aquiliae or an interdictum quod ui aut clam (Arndts, § 329). For the usufructuary is subject to these actions, and likewise to an actio furti in the same way as any other person who has committed such delict with regard to the thing of another. But if the usufructuary is so liable under the Aquilian statute, what is the use of the praetor granting to the owner a special action against the usufructuary? The reason simply is, so says the jurist, that there may be cases in which the Aquilian action would not lie, and nevertheless a remedy be required. For a person who does not cultivate a field, or who does not plant new vines where the old have died down, or who lets the aqueducts fall into decay, is not liable under the Aquilian law.

In this last sentence it is indicated how a usufructuary is bound by law to act; for, although he may make every use of the thing which is subject to his right, he is not permitted to alter its substance. 'Usus fructus est ius alienis rebus utendi fruendi salua rerum substantia;' I. II. 4 pr. Therefore the usufructuary is under an obligation, (1) to preserve the thing in a good condition (he must accordingly cultivate the field); (2) to supply the place of the necessary outgoings (he must plant the new vines); (3) to provide the repairs wanted (he must mend the aqueducts). If he does not fulfil these duties, that is, if he, in the above case, lets the field lie fallow, if he does not plant the vines, if he allows the aqueducts to be filled with mud and sand, the land doubtless will be damaged, and yet an action on account of this damage is expressly said not to be applicable, evidently for the reason that this statute does not recognise any liability merely on account of an omission, even if the acts which have been omitted are enjoined by law.

It is hardly necessary to add that 44. §§ 1 and 45 do not support the view, which is opposed to that we have stated here. It is said in these passages that a master is directly liable to an Aquilian action if a slave of his own has done unlawful damage to the property of another, whilst the master has known of the act and has been in the position to hinder it. But here the master is not declared to be liable for a delict of his own, i.e. the omission of interference, but—for obvious reasons of public expediency—for a delict of another person, which of course must answer the requirements of law, like every other act to which legal consequences are attached[1].

§ 6. *The requirement of iniuria.*

The act which causes damage must be committed unlawfully, iniuria, as the lex says, i.e. there must be an occidere iniuria according to the first chapter, and urere, frangere, rumpere iniuria according to the third chapter (cf. D. h. t. 2 pr. and 27. § 5). But

[1] O. W. Holmes, in his very attractive description of the development of the action of assumpsit (Common Law, p. 274 ff.), expressly states that in cases similar to those explained in this section an action of trespass on the case was given (analogous to the actio in factum legis Aquiliae). Although he says that it is the omission which occasions the damage complained of, yet he seems rather to agree with the views stated above, for he asserts that if you connect the omission with the previous acts as you ought to do, 'you have a course of action and conduct which, taken as a whole, has caused or occasioned the harm.' Besides, his manner of expression leads to the supposition that he is substantially of the same opinion. 'The immediate occasion of the damage complained of,' so he says on p. 279, 'may have been a *mere omission letting* in the operation of natural forces.' But, strictly speaking, in the cases mentioned by Mr. Holmes, it is not the omission but the preceding commission which lets in the operation of natural forces. If a carpenter, in undertaking to cover the roof of another's house, leaves a hole in it through which the rain comes in and damages the house, this damage is clearly due to the imperfect work which was done (cf. p. 277). It is very interesting to see that the law in times of Henry IV, as stated there by Holmes, is in remarkable accordance with the Roman law of damage to property under the Aquilian statute and its interpretation by the Roman jurists.

nothing is said as to what is meant by that term. The decision of the question therefore in what cases any one of the acts mentioned in Chs. I and III was done iniuria, was left entirely to jurisprudence. The jurists[1], however, considered a person to be liable only for an act apparently comprehended under the terms occidere, urere, etc., when such act could be attributed to his culpa in the wider sense of the word, that is, if the person either intended to do the act (dolus), or was not careful enough in avoiding it; in the latter case the act being due to his negligence or culpa in the narrower sense of the word. In accordance with this interpretation, any damaging act, which was done dolo or culpa, was considered to have been committed iniuria in the sense of the lex Aquilia. Thus by Gaius, III. 211:—

> *Iniuria* autem *occidere* intellegitur *cuius dolo* aut *culpa* id acciderit, nec ulla alia lege damnum quod sine iniuria datur, reprehenditur; itaque impunitus est qui sine culpa et dolo malo casu quodam damnum committit.

According to this and some other passages we might think that iniuria consists simply in the culpa of the person acting. But this is not true. For there are cases in which without doubt damage was done, and is to be attributed to the will of a certain person, and yet no iniuria is assumed. This is very clearly expressed in I. h. t. §§ 2 and 3:—

> *Iniuria* autem occidere intellegitur, qui *nullo iure* occidit, itaque qui latronem occidit, non tenebitur, utique si aliter periculum effugere non potest.
>
> Ac ne is quidem hac lege tenetur, qui *casu* occidit, si modo *culpa eius nulla* inuenitur; nam alioquin non minus ex dolo quam ex culpa hac lege tenetur.

In these passages two distinct reasons are given which prevent the Aquilian statute from coming into operation: first, the absence of iniuria, and secondly, the absence of culpa on the part of the person who was acting. It is clear that the word iniuria is used here in another sense than culpa. But, according to the passage of Gaius, quoted above, the notion of iniuria doubtless comprises that of culpa. From this it clearly follows that the term iniuria is used in a double sense:

[1] Cf. O. W. Holmes, Common Law, p. 81 sqq.

(1) in a wider sense, in which it comprehends the dolo et culpa occidere, urere, etc. as well as occidere urere . . . iniuria, i.e. without having a right to do so; (2) in a narrower sense, in which it is restricted to cases of damage done by a person without being entitled to do the act. A person who is entitled to perform a certain act does not become liable, although damage is caused by the act to another person. 'Qui suo iure utitur nemini facit iniuriam[1]' is the principle which is applicable also to cases which otherwise would fall under the lex Aquilia. This will be made clear by the following instances:—

1. Acts which are performed in virtue of a magisterial right do not entail liability under the Aquilian statute. This rule follows from D. h. t. 29. § 7[2], in which Ulpian asserts that municipal magistrates are liable for damage to property if they do not keep within the limits of their functions. If they do so no liability under the Aquilian statute arises; thus in case a magistrate had taken a slave as a pledge who then, while in the magistrate's hands, committed suicide by hanging himself. Liability, moreover, is excluded—according to the passage quoted—in a case where a magistrate acted with excessive violence against a person who illegally resisted his interference.

Another instance may be taken from the functions of the aediles. It is well known that these magistrates had to take care of the public ways, and were therefore obliged to remove everything which obstructed free passage. But they were naturally bound to keep within the limits of their rights. In accordance with these principles it was discussed by the jurists whether an aedile should be liable, if he had hacked into pieces beds which, having been sold, were put into the street by the seller, and it is decided by the jurists (Paulus and Julianus in D. 18. 6. 13 and 14) that the loss would lie on the purchaser, provided that the aedilis had acted within his rights; but if he had not done so, 'si non iure fecisset,' he was liable to an actio legis Aquiliae.

2. There is no liability under the Aquilian statute if a person is acting in self-defence[3], i.e. if he is defending himself against an un-

[1] D. 50. 17. 55. 151. 155. § 1.

[2] See the notes to this passage in Part I.

[3] Cf. Prof. Geyer's article on 'Nothwehr' in the Rechtslexicon (Part II. of the Encyclopädie der Rechtswissenschaften) of Prof. von Holtzendorff; Berner, Lehrbuch des deutschen Strafrechts, 6 ed., Leipzig, 1872, §§ 86–88.

lawful attack, whatever might be the object (life, honour, property) of the attack. For to repel violence by violence is, as we are told by the Roman jurists, the natural right of men: 'Uim ui repellere licere Cassius scribit idque ius natura comparatur,' D. 43. 16. 1. § 27; see also D. 1. 1. 3, D. h. t. 4 pr. and 45. § 4. The notion of defence, however, implies necessarily that of an attack; an attack therefore must be present whether it is made or merely imminent; and secondly, the nature of the defence is dependent on the nature of his attack, for only such degree of violence is permitted as is required to repel the unlawful attack. If these two requirements are not complied with there is, strictly speaking, an excess of self-defence which entails liability on the doer, unless he has been convinced that the acts were necessary for the sake of defence.

In accordance with these principles no Aquilian action lies, if a person has killed a slave who was waylaying him (D. h. t. 4 pr., Coll. VII. 3. 4); further, if a person kills another who is going to attack him with a drawn sword (5 pr.). But also a person, who, in fear of his life, kills a thief is free from any liability according to 5 pr., although he might have done the act without having been actually attacked by the thief. In so far there would be, as a matter of fact, an excess of self-defence; but as the person was acting in fear of his life, he certainly thought himself to be in such a condition as would justify the act of defence, and therefore he does not become liable. But a person does become liable, if he, whilst he might seize the thief and recover his property, prefers to kill him (5 pr. i. f.—maluit occidere—), for this is an act of vengeance done in excess of his right of defence.

In strict accordance with this view a person who has thrown a stone at his assailant is considered (in 45. § 4) not to be liable under the Aquilian statute, 'si tuendi dumtaxat, non etiam ulciscendi causa factum sit.'

An instructive illustration of the principles of self-defence is also furnished by D. h. t. 52. § 1. Here if the shopkeeper follows and seizes the thief, who carries off his lamp, in order to get it back, he cannot be blamed, for he merely defends his right of property against the unlawful attack made upon it. But if the thief, in order to get away with the lamp, strikes the shopkeeper, he is in the wrong, for there is no right of defence against the lawful exercise of the pursuer's right. And if, finally, the latter, in order to succeed in his endeavours, attempts to overcome this resistance, and inflicts, in the course of the struggle which has thus arisen, a wound on the thief, he will not be liable under the Aquilian statute. But the shopkeeper would be liable if he had commenced the struggle by beating the thief as soon as he caught hold of him, for so far there would be no act of defence, but merely an act of vengeance on his part.

In D. h. t. 4. § 1, a provision of the XII Tables is quoted according to which a person is permitted to kill the fur nocturnus, without distinguishing whether the person was acting in self-defence or not. This enactment has doubtless disappeared from later law (D. 48. 8. 9). But the right of the husband to kill the adulterer whom he has seized in flagranti delicto is—although subject to certain restrictions—still recognised by the modern Roman law [1]. Therefore if the adulterer was the slave of another, the Aquilian statute did not come into operation; D. h. t. 30 pr.

3. There is also no liability under the Aquilian statute, in case a person was acting under urgent necessity, when he could only avert damage from himself by damaging another person [2].

Thus it is recognised in D. h. t. 29. § 3, that if a ship was brought by the force of wind, without any negligence on the part of the crew, between the cables of another, or into fishing-nets, which were thrown out for the purpose of fishing, and the crew cut through the cables or the nets, the Aquilian action will not be applicable, provided that the ship could not be freed in another way.

D. 19. 5. 14. § 1, like the foregoing passage taken from the writings of Ulpian, says, that a person who at sea has thrown out the goods belonging to another person, in order to save his own property

[1] D. 48. 5. 24; Rudorff, Römische Rechtsgeschichte, vol. ii. p. 380.

[2] This is different from our modern conceptions. With us—though there is much controversy on the topic—urgent necessity, or, as it is called by Mr. Justice Stephen in his history of the Criminal law, 'compulsion by necessity' is to some extent recognised as a reason for not being made responsible under the Criminal law (cf. Herbert Stephen, in the Law Quarterly Review, vol. i. p. 51 ff.; Prof. Geyer's article on 'Nothstand,' in the Rechtslexicon of Prof. von Holtzendorff; A. F. Berner, Lehrbuch des deutschen Strafrechts, § 85), but the civil duty of paying compensation for damage done is by no means affected by the fact that the doer was acting under urgent necessities. Pernice p. 38.

in the vessel, is not liable; but if he had done so without any justification, an actio in factum will lie against him.

Similarly in D. h. t. 49. § 1, the following case is dealt with: a person pulls down neighbouring buildings during a fire, in order to protect his own house. If this were done under urgent necessity—magna ui cogente—which would justify serious fear, the Aquilian action will not be applicable, whether the fire had actually reached the side of the house which had been pulled down, or had been previously extinguished.

This decision, however, has not passed unchallenged. In D. 43. 24. 7. § 4, the question is raised, whether a person who was sued by the interdictum quod ui aut clam, or by an Aquilian action, would have a good plea if the act of demolishing the house was done by the defendant merely to protect himself in case of a fire which had arisen. The jurist Servius answers, that it is understood that if such an act was performed by a competent magistrate as a measure of precaution, he would have a good defence to the Aquilian action. If, however, a private person had acted in this way, then the decision would depend on the circumstance whether the fire would have extended to the building which was demolished. In this case the defendant would be protected by a good plea, and would escape condemnation, for there is in reality no damage whatever, since the house would inevitably have perished if it had not been pulled down. But if this would not have been the case, then the defendant was liable to pay compensation for the damage he had caused by his act.

It is clear that in this decision there is no urgent necessity recognised which would free a person from the Aquilian action, for, if this action is excluded, it is not on account of urgency, but simply because there is no damnum for which compensation might be claimed.

Thus the decisions given in the two passages (D. h. t. 49. § 1, and D. 43. 24. 7. § 4) are in conflict with one another. But there can be hardly any doubt that preference is to be given to the fragment we have considered first. Both the passages are taken from writings of Ulpian, yet in the former he states his own opinion, whilst in the latter he quotes merely the view of the jurist Servius. Besides there is still another passage of Ulpian (D. 47. 9. 3. § 7) in which he repeats his own opinion. Here Ulpian blames Labeo for having taken a different view of this question, and expressly denies, in the case considered—where houses were pulled down by people who were afraid of the fire—the applicability of the Aquilian action, with this reasoning: nec enim iniuria hac fecit, qui se tueri voluit cum alias non posset. It therefore cannot be questioned that this opinion was really approved by Justinian, and that the mention of the opposite view is to be regarded as a historical notice reminding the reader of the controversy which had been once raised among the Roman jurists.

4. No Aquilian action can be brought wherever the damaging act was performed in virtue of a private right.

(*a*) It is in accordance with this view that no action can be maintained by a master who had permitted a person to kill his slave, for in this case the act of killing would rest upon the permission granted (D. h. t. 7. § 4).

(*b*) A master who, in virtue of an existing contract, exercises his right of castigating his apprentice will not be liable under the Aquilian law, unless he exceeds his right (D. h. t. 5. § 3, to be compared with D. 48. 19. 16. § 2).

(*c*) In the same way the decision of Ulpian in D. h. t. 27. § 29, is to be explained. Here a case is mentioned where some one had given an artificer a very delicate piece of work, a cup of filigree work, to mend. The artificer is declared to be liable to an Aquilian action and an action under the contract, if the cup was broken by reason of the artificer's want of skill; but if it was broken in consequence of any inherent defect of its own he is not at all liable, although he would be liable if he had attempted to mend the cup without being ordered to do so, for the mere fact of meddling with the cup implies culpa. But if he has been ordered to mend the cup, he is naturally entitled to deal with it, and in so far there is no culpa, and therefore he cannot be liable on that account.

(*d*) The decision which is given in D. h. t. 29. § 1, does not seem to be quite in accordance with the leading principle we have stated. In this passage it is said, that if a person makes, without any right of his own, a roof projecting over his neighbour's ground, the latter is not entitled to destroy the roof proprio motu, otherwise the Aquilian action can be brought against him. On the other hand, if, without a corresponding right, an aqueduct was made over the neighbour's soil, an arbitrary demolition on the part of the neighbour is said to be permitted. It is quite clear that the second decision is the more rational one, for the owner is, as a rule, at liberty to exclude the interference of every other person with his property. But there is this important difference between the two cases, that the person whose roof reaches over his neighbour's ground is, though he has no right to the protectus, yet the owner of the roof which forms a portion of his house, whilst the aqueduct merely forms a portion of the soil on which it is built. Thus the right of the person who destroys the roof is counterbalanced by the right of its owner, whilst in the case of the aqueduct there is no right at all which is interfered with. So it is the regard due to a neighbour's property which forbids us to destroy his roof proprio motu, and this is entirely in accordance with the Roman law relating to landed property, by which the relations of neighbours are in many respects recognised. Thus a landed proprietor is bound to suffer the overhanging of the branches of trees fifteen feet above the soil (D. 43. 27, cf. C. 8. 1. 1), and must allow his neighbour's wall to slope as much as half a foot over his soil (D. 8. 5. 17 pr.; cf. Arndts, § 131, An. 1).

By the examples already given it is clearly shown that, wherever the damaging person has a right to act, he does not become liable under the Aquilian statute for so acting[1]. But this rule is to be restricted in a twofold way, for on one side he who acts in excess of his right becomes liable just as if he had no right at all, and secondly, rights are not to be exercised merely for the purpose of injuring another person. These two cases are distinguished very briefly in D. h. t. 39 pr. According to this passage a mare in foal, having grazed on another's ground, had been driven away by the owner and miscarried in consequence. There is no doubt the owner is entitled to drive away animals from his ground, and in so far he will not be liable. But if he had transgressed his right, having, for instance, beaten the mare, 'si percussisset,' or if he had purposely exercised his right to the disadvantage of her owner, having intentionally driven away the mare too violently, 'aut si consulto uehementius egisset,' then he will be liable to an Aquilian action.

[1] See also Pernice, pp. 90–101.

In accordance with this decision are the contents of D. h. t. 45. § 4. There it is said that a person in order to defend himself may make use of missiles, but only if it is done for his own protection, and not for the sake of vengeance; for a person who pelts another with stones to revenge himself evidently transgresses the right of self-defence which he has against a present and unlawful attack made upon him.

According to D. 47. 8. 2. § 20, publicani have by law a private right to distrain goods for the taxes due (pignoris capio). But if they avail themselves of their right in order to impound the cattle and to let them die of hunger, they will be liable to an Aquilian action, for they have intentionally exercised their right to the disadvantage of another, and have besides been acting in excess of their right, in so far as they prevented the feeding of the cattle impounded.

In the same way magistrates will be liable if they either exceed the limits of their power, or exercise it purposely to the disadvantage of other people, D. h. t. 29. § 7.

The question whether a person's right has been exercised in such a way is also dealt with in D. 20. 1. 27. A master had, on account of a trifling delict, severely punished his own slave whom he had pledged to his creditor. In consequence of this ill treatment the latter, in exercising his right of sale, sold the slave at a very low price. The question arises whether the Aquilian action is to be granted to the creditor pignoris in so far as he has been damaged by the castigation of the slave. And Ulpian answers very correctly that he will have the action only in case the master had castigated his slave with the intention of injuring his creditor[1], otherwise not, as he was merely exercising his legal right.

§ 7. *The requirement of culpa*[2].

The Aquilian law does not distinguish different degrees of culpa[3].

[1] The principle that rights are not to be exercised merely for the purpose of injuring other persons, was of an applicability going far beyond the limits of the Aquilian law; Arndts, § 92. n. *d*, § 168. n. *b*; Windscheid, § 121. n. 3; Pernice, pp. 44 and 45.

[2] Pernice, pp. 46–93.

[3] It is well known that in contractual and quasicontractual relations a party is sometimes liable only for dolus and culpa lata (e.g. the depositarius), sometimes for omnis culpa or culpa leuis (e.g. the mandatarius, commodatarius), sometimes for the so-called culpa in concreto, i.e. the omission of the diligence which the party is in the habit of taking in his own affairs—diligentia quam suis rebus adhibere solet—(e.g. the socius). Cf. Arndts, § 250; Windscheid, § 265; Moyle, Inst. vol. i. p. 469 sq.

In order to entail liability on account of damage to property, it is sufficient that a person's will is to be considered the moral cause of the damage complained of; in other words, that the damage can be imputed to him, or that he is in culpa with reference to the damage. In short, nothing but imputability or culpa in general is required, wherever damage was caused by the act of one person to the property of another[1]. This is clearly expressed in D. h. t. 44 pr.: 'In lege Aquilia et leuissima culpa uenit.' Accordingly every, even the slightest, neglect entails liability under the Aquilian statute, provided, of course, the damaging act was not done by a person who had a right to do it[2]. In a different way the same principle is expressed in I. h. t. § 3, where it is said that a person is not liable under the Aquilian statute who has killed 'casu,' provided only that there is no culpa on his part. Thus accident and misadventure alone exclude liability for damage done; but where, in some way or other, damage is due to the culpa of a person, the lex Aquilia comes into operation.

But we have not yet defined where imputability commences, and therefore mere chance is excluded; a question which is of importance not only in case of damage to property, but in every case where a person is declared to be liable for culpa (i. e. omnis culpa) or, what is the same, for culpa leuis[3]. According to the decisions of the Roman jurists a person is considered to be in culpa if he has not observed the conduct which, under the particular circumstances, would have been observed by a diligens pater familias[4]. A diligens pater familias, however, is with the Romans, as a good housekeeper is with us, a person who is possessed of the qualities (skill, knowledge, experience) required for his work, and who also makes the efforts necessary to attain his object, and takes within the whole province of his action due care and foresight. Whatever such a man *is accustomed to do or to forbear from doing* is to be observed in order to avoid the objection of culpa (or culpa leuis). But the conduct of the diligens pater familias implies only an average standard. No one can reasonably expect from a man that he should be possessed of qualities which are rarely to be

[1] Cf. chiefly Mommsen, Beiträge, vol. iii. pp. 360–371; Hasse, Culpa, pp. 62–72.

[2] Cf. § 6, p. 216 above.

[3] Brinz, § 266. p. 249.

[4] D. h. t. 31; D. 19. 2. 25. § 7; D. 19. 1. 54 pr.

found amongst men, or that he should use the utmost strength of which he is capable, or that he should be as cautious and careful as a man possibly can be. The standard is, however, an objective one. It is true the conduct of a diligens pater familias will vary, but it will vary only in accordance with the circumstances of the case: the amount of the skill, strength, foresight will always be determined by the nature of the business or work to be done, and in so far the standard is one and the same for everybody under the same circumstances.

In accordance with these views a diligens pater familias will not undertake any work which he is not capable to do, and he will sometimes bestow a higher and sometimes a lower degree of effort and care. Consequently sometimes a comparatively high degree of diligence is required in order to avoid damage to one's fellow-creatures, whilst in other cases very little diligence is sufficient to avoid liability on account of damage to property.

A higher degree of diligence is required wherever a person undertakes to do some work which cannot be done without a particular skill or some gifts which are not commonly to be found. On that account liability under the Aquilian law is assumed in the following cases:—

1. If a surgeon has badly operated on a slave, or a physician has given to a slave a bad medicine, both being deficient in the skill and knowledge required for their profession [1].

2. If a driver was unable to restrain the horses, or a muleteer the mules, driven by them, because they were not skilful or not strong enough [2].

3. If an artificer undertakes to manufacture or to mend something, and by his want of skill the materials given to him are spoiled [3].

From these instances it follows that in all cases where a person was not possessed of the capacity required for the performance of a work he has undertaken, he became liable for the damage caused thereby to another. The reason of this liability simply is that a person who undertakes something must also have the necessary skill, otherwise he is no diligens pater familias, for he either knew or ought to have

[1] I. h. t. § 7; D. h. t. 7. § 8 and 8 pr.; D. 1. 18. 6. § 7.

[2] D. h. t. 8. § 1; I. h. t. § 8; D. 9. 1. 1. § 5; Mommsen, Beiträge, vol. iii. p. 361, n. 3.

[3] D. h. t. 27. § 29; D. 19. 2. 9. § 5.

known that his incapacity might be dangerous to other people[1], and therefore the want of the necessary qualifications, so-called imperitia, is considered to be culpa. 'Imperitia culpae adnumeratur[2].' Similarly sometimes a very high degree of effort and care is to be exerted. Thus a coachman is certainly bound to use his utmost strength in restraining his horses, in order to avoid injuring another who is crossing the road, and a person who carries a heavy burden must certainly take far more care in crossing a slippery place than in walking over other ground[3].

On the other hand, the circumstances of a case may be of such kind as to require only a very low degree of care and effort; it even may be that culpa leuis cannot come into existence, because no diligence, the omission of which would imply culpa leuis, can be required according to the facts of the case.

This is illustrated by the contents of fr. 31. Here it is said that a person who is lopping branches off a tree on a way is bound to give warning to passers-by; if he omits to do so, he becomes liable, though he has not seen them. But if he was lopping branches in a place where there was no way, he is liable only if he sees a person passing the spot, and nevertheless flings down a branch. Accordingly he is liable only for dolus, if he intended to injure the passer-by, or for lata culpa, if he was acting without such intention. With reference to this case it is said, 'dolum dumtaxat praestare debet, culpa ab eo exigenda non est,' i.e. he is liable only for dolus (which includes lata culpa), but not for culpa (scil. leuis). This sentence, however, does not intend to say that culpa leuis would not be sufficient to entail liability under the Aquilian statute, but merely that it is impossible in the given circumstances; for a diligens pater familias, although he would look round in order to avoid injury to people passing by, if he were lopping trees in places where people are accustomed to walk, certainly would not take such care in a place where there is absolutely no way, and therefore a passer-by cannot be expected. Accordingly a person who has injured another by the fall of a branch in such a place will not be liable, although he might have avoided the damage by extreme care and foresight. This shows clearly that not absolutely the

[1] D. h. t. 8. § 1.
[2] D. 50. 17. 132; D. 19. 2. 9. § 5; I. h. t. § 7; cf. D. h. t. 8. § 1.
[3] D. h. t. 7. § 2.

omission of every conceivable care, but only of such care as reasonably might have been taken under the given circumstances, is to be taken into account, and in this sense the sentence in D. h. t. 44 pr. 'In lege Aquilia et leuissima culpa uenit,' is to be understood. If only the slightest thing should be neglected, which would have been observed by a diligens pater familias in the particular case, liability under the Aquilian statute would follow.

There are, however, exceptional cases in which such a degree of diligence is not required.

I. It is said in D. 41. 1. 54. § 2 that a free person who serves another bona fide as a slave may become bound to him not only by contract, but also by damage done to his property, 'ut tamen culpam in damno dando exigere debemus graviorem nec tam leuem quam in extraneo.' Although as a principle the liability of a free person under the Aquilian statute could not be controverted, it was yet to be taken into account, that he, as a matter of fact, was in the condition of a slave to the person who was injured, and so was obliged to be constantly handling his property. It would therefore be very hard to make him liable even for the slightest degree of negligence.

II. Soldiers are, in a certain degree, still more privileged by law. According to I. h. t. § 4 it is not considered as culpa if a soldier, in throwing javelins, wounds a passer-by, provided only that he is practising in the place which is set aside for such exercises. Private persons, however, are liable in such cases.

III. An injury is not imputed to the doer, in case several persons join in a game, the object of which is to develop the strength and activity of the body, and in the course of the game one of the players is hurt by another. Thus D. h. t. 7. § 4 says that the lex Aquilia does not come into operation, if in a public pugilistic combat or wrestling-match (in colluctatione uel in pancratio uel pugiles dum inter se exercentur) some one has been wounded. This rule, however, does not apply to slaves, since free-born men only are accustomed to fight with one another. But it is applicable if a filius familias has been wounded, and the actio of his father by which he could claim compensation for the loss of the son's labour and the expenses of his care could not be maintained (7 pr.). This decision is quite natural, for the nature of a fight, and also of such games as are a species of fight, makes it necessary that the requirement of diligence should be excluded; every fellow player having to do his utmost in order to become the victor. Otherwise such games cannot attain their object to develop strength and activity as far as possible. Therefore also awkwardness in the attack or defence cannot be avoided, and must not be attributed to the culpa of the doer. That this rule did not apply to slaves is also natural, because they had no share in such games, which, according to usage, were confined to free-born persons. If, therefore, a person had with his knowledge entered into such a contest with a slave, and the latter was killed or wounded, then there was guilt on the part of the doer, and consequently he was answerable for the damage, unless the slave's master himself had permitted the match to take place, in which case his right would clearly not be violated.

The decision given in the case of a game at ball differs somewhat from the foregoing. In D. h. t. 52. § 4 it is said that if a slave, while catching a ball in a game, was pushed by a fellow player (who was trying to prevent him from catching the ball)[1], and in consequence of the push broke one of his legs, his master is not entitled to bring the Aquilian action, 'cum casu magis quam culpa uideretur factum.'

The difference of this passage from the foregoing consists only in the circumstance that in case of a game at ball the Aquilian action was not applicable whether a slave or a free man was injured, whereas in the case of a pugilistic combat, etc., the action was only denied if a free man, but not if a slave was hurt. This difference is probably to be explained by the less aristocratic character of the game at ball, in which even slaves could take part. Besides, it was probably not considered to be advisable to exercise slaves in more warlike games. In other respects the leading idea of the two passages is the same. Whoever takes part in a game which possibly may bring him into danger has to attribute to himself the consequences which may ensue. Such games were generally recognised in ancient Rome, as they are with us, for the sake of their utility. He who participates in them enjoys all the benefits they confer, but has also to bear the possible disadvantages connected with them. If liability for injuries should be admitted by law, people would not readily join in such games[2].

[1] Cf. Pernice, p. 55. n. 29.

[2] D. h. t. 45. § 3, is not opposed to the contents of the passage we have considered above. Cf. p. 157.

IV. There are principles of a similar kind to the above which prevent liability from arising where a person has contributed by his own negligence to the damage—so-called contributory negligence[1]. If the person who is injured by the act of another is himself also in culpa in respect to the injury done to him, then the culpa on one side compensates for the culpa on the other—this is the so-called principle of culpa-compensation—and the Aquilian law does not come into operation. The reason for admitting culpa-compensation is certainly that the causal connection between act and damage is interrupted by the culpa of the injured party. Without his own culpa the injurious effect might perhaps not have taken place; at any rate, the fact of the damage was rendered possible to some extent by the act of the damaged person himself. Accordingly the principle of culpa-compensation is based on the maxim that a person who by his own fault suffered a damage had not been damaged in the eye of the law. 'Quod quis ex culpa sua damnum sentit non intellegitur damnum sentire,' says Pomponius, in D. 50. 17. 203.

1. In strict accordance with this principle is the decision of Paulus (Sent. Rec. I. 15. § 3), that a person who irritates an animal, which injures him in consequence, would have no action either against its owner or against its keeper:—

> Ei, qui irritatu suo feram bestiam uel quamcumque aliam quadrupedem in se proritauerit, itaque damnum ceperit, neque in eius dominum neque in custodem actio datur.

The actio in dominum clearly is the actio de pauperie (D. 9. 1; I. 4. 9; Arndts, § 327; Windscheid, § 457, nr. 3), which is applicable if an animal has done damage to another 'contra naturam sui generis,' provided the damage is not due to the culpa of another person (D. 9. 1. 1. §§ 5 and 6), as is supposed in the fragment we are considering. The actio in custodem, however, can be only an Aquilian action which, although its requirements may be in existence, is excluded on account of the (contributory) negligence on the part of the injured person himself.

[1] The fact, however, that not the injured party but somebody else has contributed to the damage done by another does not affect the liability of the latter; Windscheid, § 258. n. 18.

2. In D. h. t. 9. § 4 the case is supposed that whilst several people were throwing javelins in the place devoted to such exercises (campus iaculatorius), a slave crossed that ground and was wounded by a spear thrown by one of the players. Although negligence or want of skill on the part of the latter cannot be denied, the damage would have been avoided if the injured slave had taken due care. Thus he has contributed by his own culpa to the injury complained of, and therefore his culpa is set off against that of the injurer[1].

3. Another curious case of contributory negligence is mentioned in D. h. t. 11 pr. In the course of a game at ball one of the players threw his ball, striking it too violently, against the hand of a barber who in the neighbourhood was just shaving a slave, and thus the throat of the latter was cut. The Aquilian action at first sight seems to be applicable against the person who has thrown the ball; but if the barber had shaved the slave in a place in which it was usual to play, or which was a frequented one, the fault lies with the barber, who accordingly is to be sued, unless there is at the same time culpa on the part of the slave, who allowed himself to be shaved in a place which he knew to be a dangerous one. A fact of this kind would of course not affect the existence of culpa on the part of the barber, but it would bring the principle of culpa-compensation into operation, and on that account the Aquilian action would be excluded.

4. According to D. h. t. 28 pr. persons who dig pitfalls for catching bears and stags will be liable under the lex Aquilia if they have dug them in roads, and something has fallen in and has suffered damage. But though a person has digged pitfalls in places where men and cattle are accustomed to walk, yet no liability may attach to his act (28. § 1), either because he has done everything which a bonus pater familias would do in such cases, e.g. by giving due notice of the danger, or because the injured person himself knew of or might have foreseen the danger, and nevertheless did not take care to avoid it, e.g. has carelessly driven cattle over the dangerous place. It is obvious that in the latter cases culpa is to be objected to the digger, but in spite of it he does

[1] It may be added that fr. 9. § 4 cit. does not seem to be at variance with the Inst. h. t. § 4 (as is frequently assumed, see p. 32), for in the latter passage no case of contributory negligence seems to be contemplated, it not being expressed that the injured people were crossing, but merely that they were passing the training-field.

not become liable, because there is contributory negligence on the part of the injured person.

5. In D. h. t. 30. § 4, in the case of a slave who has been wounded, but not mortally, and has died afterwards, his master having omitted to attend properly to the wound, the delinquent is declared to be liable only under Chapter III, and not on account of killing the slave. It is obvious that the death of the slave was not merely due to the wound, but also to the negligence on the part of his master. Nevertheless, strictly speaking, an actio de occiso seruo seems to be excluded, not because there is contributory negligence of the injured party[1], but because the act of damage itself does not constitute an 'occidere' in the eye of the law, for this notion implies that death necessarily results from a certain act, whether at once or not till after some time; it is accordingly only a mortal wound which can entail liability under the first chapter of the lex Aquilia[2].

In opposition to these cases the Aquilian action does lie, if the delinquent has done the injurious act purposely, although there was culpa on the part of the injured person. Here the principle of culpa-compensation does not come into operation, for mere negligence and malicious intention are incommensurable one with another, and therefore there can be no set-off. An instance is given by fr. 9. § 4. Doubtless a slave who walks over ground where he sees people practising in throwing javelins, has to attribute it to his own culpa if he is hurt by one of the spears; nevertheless if it was thrown by one of the players at him purposely—data opera—the thrower will be liable under the Aquilian statute.

There is much controversy whether the principles we have laid down with regard to the requirement of culpa are not modified, by the nature of the obligation, if the delinquent was in a contractual or quasi-contractual relation in respect to the thing damaged. There is no doubt that if a commodatarius, depositarius, creditor pignoris, hirer, etc. had destroyed or damaged the thing which was entrusted to their custody, the person injured by the act may avail himself

[1] Cf. Pernice, p. 61, who thinks (pp. 60–64) that also in D. h. t. 52 pr. §§ 1 and 3, cases of contributory negligence are concerned; but see the interpretation of these passages in Part I.

[2] D. h. t. 21. § 1, and 51 pr.

either of the action on the contract, or that arising from the lex Aquilia. But if the plaintiff had been satisfied by one action, the other falls to the ground[1]. Only if he had brought first the contractual action, he may still bring the Aquilian action, if something more can be claimed by this action in virtue of the more favourable estimation under the Aquilian statute[2].

This concurrence of actions raises the question whether the extent of the liability under the contract or quasi-contract has not an effect on the liability ex delicto under the Aquilian law. This question is naturally without any importance in cases where a person, in virtue of the obligatory tie, is answerable for omnis culpa; but it is important in obligations which, requiring from the party obliged merely the diligence which he would bestow on his own affairs, make him liable for culpa in concreto only, as for instance the contract of partnership, and further in such relations as those in which a party is liable for dolus and lata culpa only, e. g. the depositum. Here the question to be decided is whether the party bound may be sued by the Aquilian action if he had caused damage to property merely by slight negligence (culpa leuis), for which he could not be made responsible under the contract. Thus we may ask, whether a partner (socius) will be entitled to plead the limited extent of his liability under the contract of partnership, if he is sued under the Aquilian statute on account of damage done to a thing belonging to the socii in common? further, whether a depositarius who, culpa leui, had destroyed or damaged the thing deposited with him may be sued effectually by the actio legis Aquiliae? On general principles there is no doubt as to the decision which is to be given. By the action under the contract the party entitled can claim only fulfilment of the contract; accordingly the party bound will be answerable for the degree of diligence required by it. By the Aquilian statute, however, a duty is established which exists quite independently of the contractual relations; that duty, namely, not to injure another's property by unlawful physical acts. It seems clear that this duty, which is incumbent on everybody against everybody, cannot be affected by an existing obligation. If therefore

[1] D. 13. 6. 18. § 1; cf. also D. h. t. 7. § 8, 18, 27. § 11, 34, 35, 42; D. 17. 2. 47. §§ 1–50; D. 19. 2. 25. § 5, 30. § 2, 43; D. 10. 2. 16. § 5.

[2] D. 44. 7. 34. § 2; D. 13. 6. 7. § 1.

the depositarius (bailee) damages things deposited with him merely by slight negligence (culpa leui), he will be subject to the Aquilian action, although under the contract he is answerable only for dolus and culpa lata. To this view it cannot be objected that it practically extinguishes the limited liability which legally belongs to the contract in question[1]. This limited liability will be of importance wherever the party who is bound *omits* to comply with his contractual duties; e.g. if the depositary does not return the things deposited with him when they are reclaimed; this would render him liable only if really dolus or culpa lata could be objected to him.

Wha may be thus deduced as a natural consequence from undoubted rules of law, was in all probability recognised in Roman law; for since in numerous passages the admission of the Aquilian action beside the contractual action is recognised, absolutely nothing being said of any special requisites of the Aquilian action, we must therefore assume that this action, like every other action, is applicable if its ordinary requirements exist; that is to say, whenever by a negligent act damage was done to property of another. That this was really the view of the Roman jurists is seen by the fact that whenever a concurrence of actions was in question, they examined whether the peculiar conditions required for each action were to be found, and accordingly allowed an action or rejected it. This is clearly shown by the treatment of the case in D. h. t. 5. § 3. Here a master castigates his apprentice, so that the latter suffers some bodily damage. In this case, we are told, the father of the boy might sue the master either ex locato or ex lege Aquilia; but—thus the passage continues—'an ex locato, dubitat [Iulianus sc.], quia leuis dumtaxat castigatio concessa est docenti: sed lege Aquilia agi posse non dubito.' Whatever sense one may give to these words[2], it is quite certain that the jurist is taking into consideration whether, according to the circumstances of the case, the contractual action is admissible, and that this is done with the idea that it might possibly not be the case; but, on the other hand, he unconditionally declares that the Aquilian action is applicable.

We have thus arrived at the result that the Aquilian action may be brought, wherever its requisites exist in the particular case, even if the delinquent is under an obligation which does not make him liable for

[1] Cf. Pernice, p. 79.

[2] Cf. Pernice, p. 91.

omnis culpa. This result is, however, subject to the following restriction. It is possible that the act of damage may not be attributable to the doer, because he had, in virtue of the contract, *a right* to do the act; in such a case there is of course no 'iniuria' on his part, and so the Aquilian law cannot come into operation. Thus, if a person hires an animal for carrying goods, and he burdens it in accordance with the terms of the contract, he will be free from any liability if the animal breaks down[1], although without such a contract he would have been answerable for the damage[2]. A similar case is mentioned in 27. § 29. A very fragile piece of work is given to an artificer to have it repaired, and it is broken by him, but without any unskilfulness on his part, merely in consequence of the fragile character of the materials. It is decided that the Aquilian action is not applicable, although it would be applicable in the absence of contract[3].

§ 8. *The requirement of damnum*[4].

It is not sufficient that a corporeal thing should be damaged or destroyed or otherwise lost to its owner in the way we have above explained, but it is also necessary that there should be a '*damnum*,' i. e. some loss to the property of the person who had been injured arising from the injurious act. It is in this sense that the expression 'damnum' is used in Roman law, and not in the sense of damage to the thing itself. This is clear from the words of the third chapter of the lex Aquilia (D. h. t. 27. § 5):—

> Ceterarum rerum praeter hominem et pecudem occisos si quis *alteri* damnum faxit, quod usserit fregerit ruperit iniuria, quanti ea res erit . . . dare damnas esto.

That is, if a person inflicts damage *on another* in respect to his things, he must make good what he has burned, crushed, broken, in doing so. Accordingly, it is *the owner* who sustains the damage, but not the thing. In accordance with these terms of the law itself

[1] Arg. D. 19. 2. 30. § 2.

[2] D. h. t. 27. § 23.

[3] With the view given in the text Vangerow (vol. iii. § 681. n. 3) is essentially in accordance, as also is Windscheid, § 455. n. 12. Differing, but in my opinion not convincing, is Pernice, p. 78 sqq.

[4] Pernice, pp. 93–101.

Pomponius says in D. 8. 2. 18: 'Si fistulae aedibus meis applicatae *damnum mihi* dent,' and Ulpian observes in D. h. t. 27. § 17: 'Aquilia *eas ruptiones quae damna dant* persequitur.'

It follows from the requirement of damnum in this sense that the Aquilian action lies where loss had resulted to the owner from an injury, although there is not even a trace left on the thing which had been damaged. 'Lege Aquilia agi potest et sanato uulnerato seruo,' says Paulus in D. h. t. 45. § 1. Accordingly, though the injury done to the slave is extinguished by his recovery, there is still the pecuniary loss to the master that he was deprived of the slave's services for some time, and had to pay expenses incurred for his cure.

On the other hand, it must follow that where there is a corporeal violation of a thing, but no loss of property resulting from it, the Aquilian action will not be applicable. This consequence is clearly expressed in D. h. t. 27. § 17: 'Rupisse eum utique accipiemus, qui uulnerauerit, .. sed ita demum, si damnum iniuria datum est: ceterum si nullo seruum pretio uiliorem deterioremue fecerit, Aquilia cessat iniuriarumque erit agendum dumtaxat: Aquilia enim eas ruptiones quae damna dant persequitur.' Accordingly there is a 'ruptio' in this sense if the act in question has caused a damnum. Therefore, if a wounded slave was not depreciated in value, the Aquilian action is excluded and only an actio iniuriarum is applicable. For the same reason the gathering of ripe fruits (27. § 25), the felling of trees fit for felling (27. §§ 26, 27), the castration of a slave who thereby becomes more valuable (27. § 28), do not fall under the Aquilian law. From this point of view also the decision of Ulpian in D. h. t. 23. § 1 is explained. Without doubt the master of a slave, who being instituted an heir had been killed by a third person before he had entered on the inheritance offered to him will have the Aquilian action in order to get compensation, not only for the value of the slave, but also for the value of the inheritance of which he had thus been deprived (23 pr.). If however—so continues § 1 of the same fragment—in the will of his master a slave had been instituted and manumitted at once, and had then been slain before he had acquired the inheritance, then the heir substituted in his place can neither claim the value of the inheritance nor that of the slave by the Aquilian action: not the value of the inheritance, because he has already received it, and that too in consequence of the killing of the heir instituted; not the value of the slave, because if he had not been killed, he—the slave—would have been the heir, and therefore would have excluded the substitute. Accordingly the substituted heir, having suffered no loss from the injurious act of killing, cannot be entitled to the actio legis Aquiliae.

§ 9. *The Plaintiff:* 1. *Owner and Bonae fidei possessor*[1].

The right to bring the Aquilian action is given by terms of the statute only to the owner of the thing damaged (D. h. t. 2 pr.; 27. § 5; 11. § 6: 'Legis autem Aquiliae actio ero competit, hoc est domino'). On this account if the owner of a thing is under an obligation to transfer ownership in it to another person, and the thing is injured by someone else, the owner will be bound to transfer the actio legis Aquiliae to the person entitled to the acquisition of ownership. This consequence is expressly recognised in case a thing bought by a person was damaged by another, whilst the buyer was in the condition to return it to the seller by means of actio redhibitoria. Here the Aquilian action is given to the purchaser, and not to the seller; but the former is obliged to transfer the action to the latter, if he uses his right of redhibition (D. h. t. 11. § 7).

The right of action once acquired by a person is transferred by inheritance (D. h. t. 23. § 8, D. 47. 1. 1. § 1). Accordingly, in case a thing had been damaged in the lifetime of its owner, his heir will be entitled to bring the Aquilian action. But if the damage was committed after the death of the owner, and before the heir had entered upon the inheritance, then the Aquilian action is acquired for the inheritance, 13. § 2, 43; but at the moment of the aditio hereditatis, it passes over to the heir, who thus becomes entitled to sue the delinquent in virtue of his own right (D. 5. 3. 36. § 2)[2].

[1] Pernice, pp. 183–198.

[2] In the same way a universal fideicommissary will be entitled to an actio legis Aquiliae (utilis), which was acquired by the testator or the inheritance, as soon as the inheritance is restored to him by the heres fiduciarius. But if an Aquilian action has accrued after the latter had entered upon the inheritance, and before he had restored it, this right of action belongs to the fiduciary, but is to be transferred by a special cession to the fideicommissarius. Cf. D. 36. 1. 73 pr., and 68. § 1; Vering, Römisches Erbrecht, Heidelberg, 1861, p. 797 sq.; Pernice, p. 188 sq.

In opposition to the heir, the legatarius, not being a universal successor, was not entitled to the Aquilian action acquired by the deceased person. But the legatee might become entitled to bring the action if ownership in a thing was left to him by the testator. This was done in the earlier times in the form of the so-called *legatum uindicationis*. In virtue of such a bequest ownership in the thing bequeathed passed over—according to the opinion of the Sabinians—to the legatarius as soon as the heir entered upon the inheritance, whether or no the legatee was either aware of the legacy or willing to accept it. In opposition to this view, according to the Proculians, the legatee acquired ownership only if he had declared his wish to take the legatum (G. II. 195). But in the Corpus Iuris Ciuilis the former opinion is recognised[1], consequently with the aditio hereditatis the ownership in the thing bequeathed is acquired by the legatee, and thus it never becomes subject to the ownership of the heir, D. 31. 80.

If a thing bequeathed in this way is, during the lifetime of the testator, unlawfully destroyed by another, it is quite clear that the legatum becomes void.

But also in case the thing was destroyed after the death of the testator, but before the aditio hereditatis, the legatee will have no actio legis Aquiliae, for he had not yet ownership in the thing, and was therefore not entitled to it. If the thing was merely damaged (without being destroyed) within the time mentioned—for instance, if the slave was wounded—ownership passed over to the legatee the moment the heir had entered upon the inheritance, and therefore the actio legis Aquiliae, to which the heir had no just claim, had to be transferred to the legatee; 15 pr.

It seems to be strange that in case the thing was merely damaged the Aquilian action was granted to the legatee, whilst, if it was entirely destroyed, it should remain with the inheritance, and consequently augment the heir's property. But this difference is explained by the peculiar nature of the early law of legacies. If a thing was granted by a legatum uindicationis, the only remedy for the legatee was an actio in rem (rei uindicatio), which might be brought against every person who happened to possess the thing. But if it was destroyed by

[1] Cf. Windscheid, § 643. n. 1 and 2; Arndts, § 555, note; Unger, Österreich. Privatrecht, vol. vi. § 62, note 2.

another person there was, of course, no possibility of bringing such an action, and a personal action, by which one might get compensation from the heir, did not yet exist. Under the law of Justinian, however, a legatee to whom property of the testator was left, not only acquired an actio in rem (rei uindicatio), but had besides an actio in personam against the person who was burdened with the bequest[1]. Being thus a creditor, the legatee could, like every other creditor, in case of its having become impossible to give the thing due to him, claim the cession of those actions which were created by the event (e.g. furtum, damnum iniuria datum), from which the impossibility arose[2]. Accordingly, if the res legata was destroyed by delict of a third person, the actio legis Aquiliae thus acquired, first for the inheritance and then for the heir, had to be transferred to the legatee in lieu of the thing destroyed.

It is quite clear that if a thing was destroyed or damaged after the heir had entered on the inheritance, the actio legis Aquiliae could only belong to the legatee, as he was the owner of the thing at the time the damage was done. D. h. t. 13. § 3, however, does not seem to be in accordance with this principle. Here it is said that in case a slave is killed after the aditio hereditatis, the Aquilian action belongs to the legatarius 'si non post mortem serui agnouit legatum,' i. e. only if he had not declared his wish to take the legatum *after* the death of the slave. This is clearly at variance with the principle of the law of Justinian, that ownership devolved on the legatee as soon as the inheritance is entered upon by the heir. For this and some other reason the conjecture proposed by Th. Mommsen, namely, to substitute for 'si non' the words 'si uel' is highly probable[3]. Accordingly the sense of the passage is that the Aquilian action is given to the legatee *even* in case he had declared his wish to take the legacy after the death of the slave, in opposition to the opinion of the Proculians, who would not have admitted the action in such a case.

But the acquisition on the part of the legatee might be rescinded, if he afterwards refused to take the legatum (repudiatio legati). Here the legatum was considered to be void, and ownership in the res

[1] Windscheid, §§ 646, 647; Arndts, §§ 558–560.

[2] Arg. D. 18. 1. 35. § 4; D. 19. 1. 13. § 12; D. 43. 24. 11. §§ 8–10; D. 47. 2. 14 pr.; Arndts, § 253, n. e.

[3] Cf. the interpretation of this passage in Part I.

legata as having belonged to the heir from the moment he had entered on the inheritance. Accordingly the heir, having been the owner at the time of the injury, was also entitled to the Aquilian action thereby created. It was, however, different if something was left to several legatees (collegatarii), for if one of them refused the legacy, ownership was considered as having been vested (since the aditio hereditatis) only in the other (or others), who accordingly was entitled to the Aquilian action acquired before his collegatee has expressed his refusal (D. h. t. 34, 35, 36 pr.).

In the course of time an action on account of damage to property, although not an actio legis Aquiliae (directa), but an actio utilis or in factum, was granted to other persons than the real owner, namely, to the bonae fidei possessor and such persons as had a ius in re aliena as to the thing damaged. Let us first consider the condition of the bonae fidei possessor, who, according to D. h. t. 11. § 8, 17, is entitled to an actio in factum on the basis of the lex Aquilia. It is clear that the position of the bonae fidei possessor has the appearance of ownership as a matter of fact. As a rule the bonae fidei possessor thinks himself to be the owner, and uses and enjoys the thing in his possession in exactly the same way as the owner would do. But we must add that his right is restricted by the rights of the owner, since it remains in operation only as long as the latter does not exercise his own better right. Thus the bonae fidei possessio has been aptly described as a *relative ownership*, being dependent on the real or absolute ownership. If the owner succeeds with his rei uindicatio, then the bonae fidei possessor is obliged to deliver over to the plaintiff the thing itself, with all the existing fruits and other accessories, and he can only claim by exceptio doli compensation for the expenses he had incurred for the thing: impensae necessariae as well as utiles. But in case of such an eviction, as it is called, he will, as a rule [1], be entitled to have recourse to his remedy against the person from whom he had acquired possession (auctor), and to claim from him compensation for the damage he had sustained, because he would not have been deprived of possession and the other advantages which would have accrued to him, if his auctor (commonly the seller) had been the owner of the

[1] Provided his acquisition was not founded on a so-called lucrative cause. Baron, Pandekten, §§ 288 and 239.

thing delivered to him. Thus we see bonae fidei possessio is as good as ownership, so long as the latter is not brought into operation; but on the owner asserting his right, bonae fidei possessio loses its value, except that the possessor is entitled to be indemnified for the expenses he has incurred in respect to the thing.

If we apply these principles to the question we are considering, then we must say: The bonae fidei possessor, as long as the owner does not sue for the damage, will have the right of the Aquilian action to exactly the same extent as the owner himself. And this is quite natural, for he is practically the person who suffers the loss by the damage done[1].

Of course the owner is always entitled to make use of his own right, and sue by rei uindicatio the bonae fidei possessor, who had brought the Aquilian action. Then the defendant will be bound to restore everything which he had recovered by that action. This is expressly declared in case the hereditatis petitio was brought against the bonae fidei possessor in D. 5. 3. 55; but it is equally applicable if he is sued by rei uindicatio, for this action has for its object not only the delivery of the thing itself, but also the restoration of its accessories (omnis causa), which the owner would have if his property should not have been unlawfully withheld from him[2].

> Iulianus libro LX digestorum. Euicta hereditate bonae fidei possessor quod lege Aquilia exegisset non simplum sed duplum restituit lucrum enim ex eo, quod propter hereditatem acceperit, facere non debet.

According to this fragment, the bonae fidei possessor is bound to restore to the heir and owner what he had acquired in virtue of the lex Aquilia, also double damages if he had brought his action adversus infitiantem, for a possessor in good faith ought not to make profits out of something he had received on account of the inheritance[3].

If the possessor is sued by the owner before he has brought the

[1] The same view is taken by Pernice (p. 191), Mommsen, Beiträge (vol. ii. p. 242 sqq.); differing: Ihering, Abhandlungen (p. 112 sq.); Glück (vol. x. p. 372); see also Windscheid, n. 9.

[2] Arndts, § 167, n. e.

[3] This passage is clearly at variance with the opinion that the only object of the bonae fidei possessor is recovery of the impensae incurred by him, for under this supposition there would be no 'lucrum' to be restored to the owner.

Aquilian action we might think a transfer of this action to the plaintiff would have to be made, but as the plaintiff, being the owner of the thing, is himself entitled to the actio legis Aquiliae, it will only be necessary if the possessor had acquired by usucapion ownership in the thing after the commencement of the suit (post litem contestatam) and after this period the damage complained of was committed. In such a case the defendant was condemned to transfer the Aquilian action, together with the ownership in the thing, to the vindicant[1]. This is expressly declared in D. 6. 1. 17. § 1, i. f. (Ulpianus libro XVI ad edictum): Sed quod dicit (scil. Iulianus) de actione legis Aquiliae (viz. bonae fidei possessorem actionem legis Aquiliae restituere cogendum esse), procedit, si post litem contestatam usucepit possessor, quia plenum ius incipit habere.

But, if in virtue of the rei uindicatio of the owner the bonae fidei possessor had either lost the proceeds of the Aquilian action, or was prevented from suing the delinquent by that action, he was entitled to sue his auctor (usually the seller) for the loss which he had sustained

[1] The usucapio of the ancient law was not interrupted by the rei uindicatio brought against the possessor. This is quite in accordance with the requisites of usucapio, i. e. possession founded on a iustus titulus and bona fides, during one or two years in a thing which was not exempt from usucapion. For these requirements on the part of the possessor were clearly not affected by the action of the owner. But though usucapion might be continued and completed during the suit, such completion did not help the defendant, who had to be condemned to transfer the ownership which he had acquired in the thing after the litis contestatio. 'Usucapio *frustra complebitur* anticipata lite' (fr. Vat. § 12; cf. also D. 6. 1. 17 i. f. and 18, D. 41. 4. 2. § 21 and D. 41. 6. 2). It was different with the longi temporis praescriptio in the earlier law. If here the possessor was sued by rei uindicatio before the longum tempus (ten or twenty years) was over, the possessor naturally could not exclude the action by the plea that he had possessed during the time prescribed, and in so far the longi temporis prescriptio was interrupted by the litis contestatio (C. 7. 33. 10, C. 3. 32. 26). It is, however, a question whether this rule, which evidently is based on the extinctive nature of the longi temporis prescriptio, is still in force in the time of Justinian. In the law of Justinian longi temporis prescriptio has assumed the nature of acquisitive prescription giving to the possessor ownership like the old usucapio (see Justinian in his constitutio of the year 528 in C. 7. 39. 8 pr.), and by the lex unica C. de usucapione transformanda (7. 31) Justinian has transformed the two institutions into one: namely, the ordinary usucapion of the law of Justinian which entirely shares the nature of the ancient usucapion. For this and some other reasons we must assume that the new usucapion is also not interrupted by the action of the owner, although the acquisition of ownership does not help the defendant as is expressed in the passages of the Digest quoted above. Cf. E. Grueber, Über den Einfluss der Eigenthums Klage auf die Ersitzung nach römischem Rechte (München, 1875). So also Arndts, § 163. n. 2; Brinz, Pandekten, 2 Aufl. vol. i. p. 638; Vangerow, vol. i. § 160. II; Savigny, System, vol. vi. pp 55–61. Differing: Windscheid, vol. i. § 180. n. 7. Cf. also Poste, Gaius, second edition, p. 449 b).

in his property (interesse); because he was not put into such a condition as enabled him to retain the possession of the thing (habere licere) and to enjoy the other advantages (e. g. actio legis Aquiliae) he would have had in case he had been made the owner of the thing. This follows from D. 18. 1. 35. § 4.

> Gaius libro X ad edictum prouinciale. Si res uendita per furtum perierit, prius animaduertendum erit, quid inter eos de custodia rei conuenerat: si nihil appareat conuenisse, talis custodia desideranda est a uenditore, qualem bonus pater familias suis rebus adhibet: quam si praestiterit et tamen rem perdidit, securus esse debet, ut tamen scilicet uindicationem rei et condictionem exhibeat emtori. unde uidebimus in personam eius qui alienam rem uendiderit: cum si nullam uindicationem aut condictionem habere possit, ob id ipsum damnandus est, quia si suam rem uendidisset, potuisset eas actiones ad emtorem transferre.

The case is the following. A thing sold was stolen from the seller, who had not yet delivered it to the buyer. The question of course arises whether the seller is liable to the buyer. In this respect, in the first place, the terms of the agreement made between the parties as to the custody will be decisive. But if no agreement was made then the decision depends on the fact whether such care was bestowed in keeping the thing as is usually taken by a good pater familias in his own affairs (diligentia diligentis patris familias). This is quite in accordance with the general principles of culpa, for a contract of sale being made to the advantage of both the parties imposes upon each of them liability for omnis culpa. If, notwithstanding such care being taken, the thing was lost, the seller would not be liable provided only he transferred to the buyer the uindicatio and the condictio furti, for these actions belonged here to the seller, since, according to Roman law, ownership remained in him until delivery. But if the seller had sold a thing belonging to another, then he was of course not in a condition to transfer the above actions, and on this account it was necessary that he should be condemned to pay compensation to the purchaser instead of ceding the actions.

It is quite clear that these remarks are equally applicable to other actions. The passage mentions only actions arising from a furtum, because—as a matter of fact—only such a delict was in question. If, instead of furtum, a damnum iniuria was committed, the seller was liable in the same way to transfer the actions arising from this delict, and if he was not in a condition to do so, because he was not owner, he had to give compensation.

So far it is made clear that the bonae fidei possessor can sue under the Aquilian statute, provided the owner does not exercise his right. But it may possibly happen that the possessor may maintain an action, notwithstanding that the owner exercises his right of suing; for such a possessor has a right to claim compensation for his impensae from the owner, and to the extent of this claim he is injured by any damage done to the thing: consequently with this limitation he is entitled to the Aquilian action although the owner likewise brings the action on his account.

From D. h. t. 17 we learn that the bonae fidei possessor of the thing may sue by an actio in factum even the owner who had damaged his own thing. It is quite clear that in such a case the object of the action must also be restricted to the outlay incurred by the bonae fidei possessor, as subject to this exception the thing belongs absolutely to its owner. Besides, the rule seems to require another restriction. An owner who does not know that his thing is possessed by another is certainly entitled to do with it what he likes, for in doing so he is exercising his right. Therefore the application of fr. 17 is rightly restricted to those cases where the owner had the knowledge of the possession of the other. But if, having such knowledge, he damages or destroys the thing unlawfully (iniuria), then he is guilty of an intentional abuse of his right to the disadvantage of another. But if an action of the possessor in good faith is available against the owner, it may be asked whether an Aquilian action may be brought vice versa by the owner against the bonae fidei possessor. This has been sometimes denied, as the latter, thinking himself to be the owner, has treated the thing as his own [1]. But in our opinion there is no reason to refuse the action in this case, for all the requirements for the application of the lex Aquilia are fulfilled: there is a damage

[1] Windscheid, § 455. n. 13; Pernice, p. 194 ff.

caused by a positive act which is to be attributed to the negligence (culpa) of a person who certainly had not a right to do so. In accordance with this view D. 5. 3. 36. § 2 grants to the heir (concurrently with the hereditatis petitio) the Aquilian action against the possessor without distinguishing whether he is a bonae or a malae fidei possessor. And D. h. t. 38 says expressly that a person may sue under the lex Aquilia the bonae fidei possessor of his slave, if the latter was wounded by a slave of the possessor [1].

§ 10. *The Plaintiff (continued)*: (2) *Persons entitled to a ius in re aliena* [2].

In several instances persons who have merely a right over a thing which is subject to the ownership of another (ius in re aliena) are declared to be entitled to an action on account of the damage unlawfully done to such thing. Thus an actio utilis (ex lege Aquilia) is said to be applicable in favour of the usufructuary and usuary [3]; similarly an actio utilis is given to a person who is entitled to a servitus aquaeductus [4], and, subject to certain restrictions, the creditor pignoris may avail himself of an analogous action, which in one passage is called actio in factum and in the other actio utilis [5]. Accordingly an actio on account of damage to property is declared to be available not only in case of personal and real servitudes, but also in case of a ius pignoris. This leads to the assumption that, according to the view of the Roman jurists, an Aquilian action was thought to be applicable wherever one of the iura in re aliena was infringed by the act of damage of another person and that it is merely due to an accident, if superficies and emphyteusis are not mentioned in the Corpus Iuris as giving rise to such an action.

Unlike the bonae fidei possessio, every ius in re aliena is an absolute right available against all the world, even against the owner; for in so far as a thing is subject to the right of another person, it is withdrawn from the owner's control, and therefore it may be violated

[1] Pernice (p. 195. sq.) attempts to get rid of the evidence supplied by these passages by reading into them distinctions which are in no way indicated by their contents.

[2] Pernice, pp. 198–213.

[3] D. h. t. 11. § 9, 12; D. 7. 1. 17. § 3; D. 4. 3. 7. § 4 and 18. § 2; D. 43. 24. 13 pr.

[4] D. h. t. 27. § 32.

[5] D. h. t. 17 and 30. § 1.

by him. In accordance with this statement an Aquilian action (utilis or in factum) is given to the usufructuary[1] and the creditor pignoris[2] against the owner who had damaged the thing which is subject to their right, and the same is undoubtedly true of every other person who has a ius in re aliena which is interfered with by an act of damage on the part of its owner.

In addition to this the ius in re aliena forms a definite restriction of the right of ownership in the thing. There is, however, this important difference between the several iura in re aliena, that a ius pignoris exists merely for the sake of the security given to another's right—an obligation—and is therefore dependent on it, whilst all other rights over a thing of another exist for their own sake, i.e. for the sake of the advantage granted by them. Servitudes, emphyteusis, and superficies equally imply a right of using the thing of another in some way or other; a right which is of some pecuniary value of its own, and which therefore may be assessed in a certain sum of money[3]. Accordingly the person entitled to a servitus, the emphyteuta, and the superficiarius will sue by the Aquilian action for compensation for the value of the right which has been lost by the act of damage, that is, the value which it had as a portion of their property. On the other hand the right of the owner, after deducting the value of the ius in re aliena, had also a value of its own, and therefore the owner will be equally entitled to sue by the Aquilian action the delinquent for his interesse, i. e. the value of the right of ownership as a portion of his property. Thus a division of the Aquilian action takes place in case the damaged thing is subject to the right of another person, for whilst the latter will be compensated for the value of his ius in re aliena, the owner will be compensated for the value of the ownership after deducting this right.

This view is recognised with regard to all iura in re aliena. It is only with reference to the usufructus—and the same applies to the usus[4]—that different views have been entertained as to the object of the action of the usufructuary: views which are explained by the peculiar nature of this right.

The usufructuary—it is well known—has a right to make every use,

[1] D. h. t. 12; D. 4. 3. 7. § 4 and 18. § 2.

[2] D. h. t. 17.

[3] Cf. Mommsen, Beiträge, p. 240 sq.

[4] Arndts, § 182.

and to take all the fruits of the thing which is subject to his right without impairing the substance of the thing[1]. If therefore this right is lost because its object has been destroyed[2] by a third person, we should expect that the usufructuary was to be compensated by securing him an annual income equal in value to the value of the annual use and profits derived from the usufruct.

But it is obvious that the usufruct has also a value of its own, which may be assessed by taking into account on one side the value of the annual use and proceeds of the usufruct, and on the other the probable duration of the lifetime of the usufructuary, to be determined by the calculation of experts. If this were to be the object of the Aquilian action of the usufructuary, he would receive compensation for what he had actually lost, i. e. his right of usufruct[3], and the owner would be entitled to sue on his own account for what he had lost, i. e. the value of the so-called 'nuda proprietas,' in other words the ownership after deducting the right of usufruct[4]. This way of assessing damages however seems to be objectionable, for the usufructuary may complain that he had a right to be provided for his lifetime[5], and he may live much longer than is expected according to the rules of probabilities; and the proprietarius may complain that he had a right to have the thing subject to the usufruct restored to him at the moment the usufructuary dies, and the usufructuary may live for a far shorter time than is expected according to these rules.

The difficulty thus arising seems to be met by the third way which is still conceivable in assessing damages. The usufructuary, who enjoys the whole advantage which the thing may confer to an owner, may be thought to bring the action in the place of the owner himself. Thus he would receive compensation for the full value of the thing subject to his right. This seems to be quite satisfactory, inasmuch as the usufructuary would receive instead of the usufruct in the specific thing, a quasi usufruct in the money he had received by the Aquilian action,

[1] I. 2. 4 pr.

[2] It is understood by itself that if the thing was only damaged, without being destroyed, compensation is to be given in proportion to the loss thus inflicted on the plaintiff.

[3] The right of usufruct is wholly lost if the res serviens is destroyed; it is partly lost if it is merely damaged.

[4] I. 2. 4. 1; Arndts, § 178. n. d.

[5] The usufruct is given for the lifetime of the usufructuary, I. 2. 4. 3, provided it is not restricted to a shorter period by the grantor. D. 7. 4. 15; C. 3. 33. 5; Arndts, § 194. n. g.

and the rights of the proprietarius would be secured by the cautio usufructuaria, in virtue of which the thing subject to his claim—or the money equivalent[1]—is to be restored to him at the end of the usufruct.

In order to decide which of the three possibilities we have stated is to be preferred, we must refer to our sources, which on this point are unfortunately very meagre. The only help to decide the question seems to be given by D. h. t. 12. Here the case is supposed that the owner himself, the 'dominus proprietatis[2],' has killed his slave, who was subject to my usufruct, 'in quo usufructus meus est,' and I am said to have an actio legis Aquiliae utilis against him, '*pro portione usufructus*, ut etiam ea pars anni in aestimationem ueniat, qua nondum usus fructus meus fuit.' It is, according to these words, quite certain that in assessing damages for the usufructuary, reference could be made to the whole of the last year, even if the usufruct has not yet existed during so long a time. In addition to this we must say that the words have certainly not in view the first of the above-mentioned alternatives, namely, the securing of an annual income. But whether the second or third way was actually followed by the Roman jurists is difficult to ascertain. The words 'pro portione usus fructus' may signify that the usufructuary brings his action for that aliquot part of the value of the whole slave which is formed by his right of usufruct, or, in other words, he has a claim for compensation in proportion to his usufruct, or, still more plainly, for the value of his usufruct; but this claim is to be assessed by taking into account the value of the ownership in the thing, and considering the usufruct as representing an aliquot part of it[3]. If, for example, we suppose that the highest value of the killed slave during the last year was 30, whilst the usufruct would represent one third of the value of the full ownership in the slave, then the usufructuary would receive 10 as compensation for the right which he had lost by the act of damage, whilst the proprietarius would bring an action for the remaining 20.

But the words we have quoted may also refer to a case where the usufruct is divided between several persons, and therefore simply mean

[1] Cf. D. 7. 9. 1. § 7; Arndts, § 180. n. i.

[2] Cf. I. 2. 4. § 3; Arndts, § 178. n. d.

[3] The same view is taken by the Glossa in the interpretation of fr. 12 cit.

that each usufructuary may bring his action for his share in the usufruct[1]. If this view were to be recognised, then nothing whatever is asserted as to the object of the action of the usufructuary, whether it is compensation for the value of the whole thing, or merely for that of the usufruct. But this view is hardly maintainable[2], for in the beginning of the passage which relates the facts of the case to be decided upon, nothing is mentioned about a division of the usufruct amongst several persons, and it would be very strange if, nevertheless, afterwards the words 'pro portione' were used with reference to a case where the usufruct belonged to several persons. In addition to this the words 'in quo usus fructus meus est' in the beginning, and the words 'qua nondum usus fructus meus fuit' at the end of the passage not only do speak of one usufructuary, but seem directly to exclude the supposition that there were several usufructuaries. And lastly, the use of the 'ut' (consecutivum) can only be properly explained if we assume that the action is brought *in proportion to the usufruct*, i. e. with reference to the value of the killed slave, for it is really in consequence of this fact that the whole of the year previous to the act of killing is to be taken into account in assessing damages; whilst such a mode of assessment is by no means occasioned by the fact that the usufruct was common to several people.

Thus a careful examination of fr. 12 shows that, according to the Roman view, the action was given to the usufructuary to sue for his own interest[3], and it was left to the owner to bring an action on his own account for the loss he sustained by the act of damage. But there is also a reason of a more general nature why this result must be accepted. It may be true that the usufructuary, who receives instead of the usufruct in the specific thing a quasi-usufruct in an equivalent sum of money, would have no reason to complain; but this is by no means necessary, for the interesse of the proprietarius and that of the usufructuarius are in themselves distinct from one another. Suppose a case where a person had a poor cottage in a very frequented part of a large town, and intended to pull it down, and to build in its place

[1] This view is supported by the explanation of the words given by the Scholiast in the Basiliks (Schol. Bas. 60. 3. 12; edition of Heimbach, vol. v. p. 276).

[2] It must be noticed that the above interpretation of fr. 12 is at variance with that given in Part I.

[3] Pernice on p. 199 seems to differ from, but on p. 245 to agree with the above view.

a large hotel, but the cottage was subject to the usufruct of another who not only had a suitable residence there, but was also enabled to carry on there a very lucrative trade, in virtue of which his own necessaries and those of his family were well provided for. If in such case the cottage were burned by the negligence of a third person, the proprietarius would hardly have any interest to be compensated by the Aquilian action, whilst the usufructuary would suffer severe loss and could not be at all satisfied by exercising the owner's right of action.

But there is against assessing the value of the mere usufruct still one objection which is not removed[1]. It is clear that the usufructuary need not be satisfied with a compensation which is fixed by taking into account the probable duration of his life. But this objection will be met by a security to be given for an additional compensation by the defendant in case the usufructuary should live longer than is expected according to the rule of probabilities, whilst the owner might ask for security in case the usufructuary should die earlier than is assumed in the calculation of experts[2].

From all this it clearly follows that the object of the action of the usufructuary was exactly the same as in all other cases, namely, compensation for the value of the right which the plaintiff has lost by the act of damage[3]. The same view applies, strictly speaking, also in case a ius pignoris has perished by the act of a third person. But a ius pignoris has no value of its own, and is of value only in so far as it gives security for an existing obligation. If, therefore, a thing has been destroyed, the creditor pignoris will not suffer loss by the act of damage if under the given circumstances security for his claim is not required, i. e. if he is in a condition to enforce the fulfilment of

[1] The words of D. h. t. 11. § 10 do not contradict the view stated in the text, although the interpretation in Part I. is slightly to be altered. The doubt of Julian whether the usufructuary should have the actio legis Aquiliae (directa) is explained by the assumption that he thought the usufructuary might avail himself of the action of the owner (so the notes to fr. 11. § 10); whereas Ulpian probably thought that the usufructuary had the action on his own account, and therefore declared an actio utilis to be applicable.

[2] In a similar way security might have been required if a legacy of an annual income, a so-called legatum annuum, was assessed in a fixed sum of money in order to determine the amount of the Quarta Falcidia to be left to the heir. Cf. Arndts, Civilistische Schriften, vol. ii. pp. 472 and 473. n. 431; Arndts, Pandekten, § 572. n. h; Windscheid, § 652. n. 33–35; Lenel, Das Edictum perpetuum, p. 419.

[3] In accordance with this view the words 'pro portione usus fructus' in D. h. t. 12 are to be translated by '*in proportion to the usufruct*,' and not by 'for his portion of the usufruct' (p. 43).

his claim by a personal action against his debtor. It is otherwise if the possibility of suing the debtor effectually is lost. This is the case, if the creditor is barred from suing his debtor by limitation of time and has thus lost his action entirely[1], but it is equally the case when his debtor has become insolvent[2], and it is therefore impossible to sue him with the effect of receiving satisfaction for his claim, for it practically makes no difference, whether a person is prevented from suing his debtor by law, or by his adversary's poverty[3]. Accordingly the Aquilian action is given to the creditor merely as a substitute for his actio in personam. Consequently the creditor can sue only by the Aquilian action (actio in factum or utilis) if he has lost, at least practically, his actio in personam, and further he can recover by the Aquilian action only what he would have recovered by his action in personam, i.e. satisfaction for his claim. In accordance with these views the creditor pignoris is declared in D. h. t. 30. § 1 to have an Aquilian action, utilis or in factum[4], up to the amount of his claim, whilst the debtor, who had given a thing of his own in pledge, will sue by the actio legis Aquiliae (directa) for the amount, if any, which is due on account of the damage done in excess of his debt. But the debtor is at the same time released from his debt, as far as the creditor has been satisfied by the action he has brought against the delinquent.

The result of the previous investigation is, accordingly, that a person may bring an Aquilian action in virtue of every ius in re aliena, seruitus, emphyteusis, superficies and ius pignoris, provided only some loss to his property has resulted from the act of damage to his property, and that it is always the value of the right infringed which will be the object of the action. It is, however, yet to be considered whether a person who merely has a ius in personam with reference to a thing may not bring the Aquilian action. This is stated to be so only in the case where a person is entitled to take the fruits of a thing instead of its owner[5]. In D. h. t. 27. § 14 a tenant (colonus) is said to have an actio in factum for compensation, if the crop which he is permitted to

[1] In this case according to the true opinion an obligatio naturalis of the debtor is still recognised. Arndts, § 277. n. 1.

[2] D. 50. 16. 114.

[3] D. 4. 3. 6.

[4] D. h. t. 17.

[5] Nevertheless it is sometimes asserted that an Aquilian action may be available in other cases of a ius in personam. Glück, vol. x. p. 374; Pernice, pp. 206–213.

reap under the contract of hiring and letting had been damaged by another person; but if he brings the action, then he must give security that the owner will not himself sue the delinquent. From this restriction we must infer that it is, strictly speaking, the owner who is considered to be entitled to the Aquilian action. Only because the tenant is permitted by the owner to take the fruits in his place, the tenant is also presumed to be permitted to bring the Aquilian action for the damage done to these fruits. It is therefore in truth the owner's right on which the tenant's action is based, and from this point of view the passage does not make any exception from the principle that it is only a right over a thing, whether ownership or one of the iura in re aliena, which, if interfered with by an act of damage, may give rise to an Aquilian action. Besides, it must be noticed that fr. 27. § 14 is the only passage in which such an action is given to a person with a ius in personam. In all other cases in which a person has a ius in personam with regard to the thing, as e.g. the stipulator [1], the seller [2], the commodatarius [3], not he, but the owner is declared to be entitled under the Aquilian action.

---

§ 11. *The Defendant.*

The Aquilian action can be brought only against a person who by his culpa had caused the damage complained of [4]. Clear as this assertion seems to be, it will be worth while to illustrate it by a few instances, taken from our sources, as the consequences which follow from the principle expressed are undoubtedly very important.

In D. h. t. 52. § 2 the following case is reported by the jurist Alfenus. Two heavily laden waggons, following one another, were being drawn up a steep hill by mules. The first one, being tilted over, was supported by the drivers to help the mules in bringing the burden up to the top of the hill. But suddenly this waggon gives way, the drivers get out of the way, and in rolling back it comes into collision with the second waggon, which being thereby driven backwards crushes a young slave. The question accordingly arises as to the action given to the master. The answer is, that he may bring an Aquilian action against the muleteers of the first waggon if they had left the waggon without

[1] D. h. t. 54. 55; D. 4. 3. 18. § 5.
[2] D. 19. 1. 13. § 12; I. 3. 21. § 3. i. f.
[3] D. h. t. 11. § 9.
[4] Pernice, pp. 213–228.

necessity, and had thus caused the mules to be drawn backwards by its weight. But no action is given against the owner of the mules unless the special requirements of the actio de pauperie were fulfilled, by which he might be sued for compensation: for instance, if the mules, frightened by some sudden cause, had gone backwards and had thus caused the damage. But if neither the requirements of this action against the owner of the mules nor those of the Aquilian action against the muleteers exist, then there is no remedy by which the master of the slave who was killed can get compensation.

The same view is expressed in D. 19. 2. 30. § 2.

> Alfenus libro III digestorum a Paulo epistomatorum. Qui mulas ad certum pondus locaret, cum maiore onere eas conductor rupisset, consulebat de actione. respondit uel lege Aquilia uel ex locato recte eum agere, sed *lege Aquilia tantum cum eo agi posse qui tum mulas agitasset*, ex locato etiam si alius eas rupisset, cum conductore recte agi.

If a mule was hired to be laden up to a certain weight, and afterwards was more heavily burdened than had been agreed on, and so broke down, an actio ex locato as well as an actio legis Aquiliae is applicable. But whilst the former can be brought against the other contracting party—the hirer, by the Aquilian action only the person can be sued who at the time of damage was driving the mules.

Accordingly this decision agrees entirely with that previously mentioned, in so far as the Aquilian action can be brought only against the muleteer, as he is the only person who is in culpa. The conductor, however, who has employed the muleteer is not subject to an Aquilian action, although he is liable on the contract for the damage done to the mule hired by him. It follows from this clearly that an employer, although he may be liable under the particular contract agreed on [1], is not thought to be directly liable for the delicts of the persons employed by him, not being subject to an actio ex delicto. He will be subject only to such an action if he has been himself in culpa with regard to the delict committed. This is clearly shown by the contents of D. h. t. 27. § 11. Here a case is supposed that slaves have burned down a house belonging to a farm hired by their master,

[1] P. 91 above, and, as the chief exponent of the second view there, see Brinz, § 270.

and it has been decided that the master, provided he has not been himself in culpa, will be subject to an action on the contract and an actio legis Aquiliae noxalis. But if he has kept in the farm-house mischievous slaves of whom he either knew or should have known that they were careless in dealing with others' property, he will be liable by direct action on the ground of the lex Aquilia[1]. It is true the fragment has in view only the relation of master and slave, but there can be no doubt that the principle therein stated is applicable also where the damage was done by free servants. Therefore in every case a master or employer will be liable for the damage caused by his servants or other persons employed by him, if he knew either their unfitness to perform their duties or might have known if he had been sufficiently careful.

From the principle that only a person who is really guilty of culpa can be sued by the Aquilian action, it follows as a necessary consequence that, if several persons are concerned in the commission of a damage unlawfully done to property, each of them is liable only in so far as he is himself in culpa. Therefore if a slave beaten by several persons had died in consequence, only the person by whose blow the slave was killed will be liable under the first chapter of the Aquilian law, although in case this cannot be proved all the accomplices will be equally liable, for the death of the slave is apparently due to their co-operation[2]. Of a similar nature is the case mentioned in D. h. t. 11. § 4[3], namely, if several persons carrying a beam let it fall and thus cause damage. They are all liable in the same degree, for by their act they have all caused the fall of the beam; it is indifferent whether the one or the other of them was more or less guilty, for culpa leuissima is sufficient to entail liability under the Aquilian law.

Whilst according to the previous remarks culpa of a person is required, culpa is, on the other hand, also sufficient, to make him liable under the Aquilian law, either to an actio legis Aquiliae directa or to an actio utilis or in factum. It follows that in a case where a damnum iniuria is committed by several persons, it is quite irrelevant in what way they have taken a share in the commission of the delict. They are

[1] Cf. the words: 'Sed haec ita, si culpa colonus careret: ceterum si noxios seruos habuit, damni cum iniuria teneri cur tales habuit.'

[2] D. h. t. 11. § 2, 51. § 1.

[3] Cf. D. 47. 2. 21. § 9.

equally liable whether they have committed the damage in common—as accomplices—or whether one has merely aided and abetted the other, or has instigated him to do the damage. These distinctions, so important in criminal law, are quite indifferent as regards liability under the Aquilian law, provided only the persons concerned are in some way or other guilty of culpa. This is clearly expressed in various passages of the Corpus Iuris:—

1. There is no doubt that if several people commit a delict in common, each of the accomplices is liable to the same action on account of the damage caused[1].

2. In cases where one person was merely aiding and abetting another in the commission of damage, Roman jurists speak of 'causam damni (sc. mortis, etc.) praestare[2]' in exactly the same way as in those cases where the damage was due to the act of one person only[3]. Accordingly a person who holds a slave whilst he is killed by another, is declared in 11. § 1 to be subject to an actio in factum, as having brought about a causa mortis 'quasi mortis causam praebuit.' And similarly an actio in factum is said[4] to be applicable against a person who has enticed a slave into an ambush, where he is killed by another. It is understood by itself, that in both these cases he who has actually killed the slave is subject to an actio directa under Chapter I of the Aquilian statute.

3. There is no doubt that a person who, without participating in the actual commission of the delict, has caused another, by his command, advice, or other undue influence, to commit unlawful damage is liable to an Aquilian action on his own account[5]. And, generally speaking, the same is true of the person who has been induced to do the act[6], but this is subject to an important restriction.

There are persons who have a right of command over others, a so-called ius imperandi, as e.g. a father over the children in his power, a husband over his wife, a guardian over his ward, a magistrate over the persons subject to his magisterial control. It is true, the ius imperandi does not entitle anybody to enjoin the commission of

[1] See D. h. t. 11. §§ 2. 4.
[2] D. h. t. 11. § 1.
[3] See e. g. D. h. t. 9 pr. and § 3.
[4] D. h. t. 9. § 3. i. f.
[5] D. h. t. 37 pr; D. 50. 17. 169 pr.; cf. also D. 47. 10. §§ 4. 5; D. 39. 2. 18. § 4; D. 39. 3. 5; D. 43. 2. 4. 5. § 11; D. 47. 7. 7. § 4.
[6] D. h. t. 37 pr. i. f.; cf. D. 47. 10. §§ 4. 5; D. 39. 3. 5.

illegal acts, and it is equally true that nobody is bound to obey such commands; yet it is to be taken into account, that the superior has a great influence over the persons subject to his power, and that they probably will suffer very severely in case of disobedience. For this reason as well as the other, not to weaken the discipline in the relations which are in question whenever a ius imperandi exists, the principle has been recognised that only the person who has given the command, but not he who has obeyed it, is liable for the delict committed [1]. We might expect that this principle is equally applicable in all cases where a delict is committed by command of a person with ius imperandi. We are, however, expressly told that in delicts of a more serious character, as killing of slaves and free men, theft, robbery, not only the commander, but also the doer himself will be liable [2]. The principle accordingly refers to delicts which, as is said in D. 50. 17. 157 pr., 'non habent atrocitatem facinoris uel sceleris,' but these words comprehend all the ordinary cases of damage to property, and therefore in several passages only the person who has commanded a damnum iniuria, not he who actually committed it, is said to be liable under the Aquilian law [3]. It is otherwise if a person without the ius imperandi has induced another by his command to commit unlawful damage. Here the doer is declared to be subject to an actio legis Aquiliae [4], although the person who has induced him to do the illegal act will equally be liable [5].

Whilst according to the previous explanation there may be persons who have actually committed damage to property who are yet free from any liability, so there are, on the other hand, cases in which persons who have not at all been concerned in the commission of damage, are yet declared subject to an Aquilian action. It is well known that according to Roman law a pater familias might be sued on account of damage done by his slaves and the children in his power by an actio noxalis [6], in virtue of which he had either to pay the penalty and compensation forfeited under the delict, or to surrender, by noxae deditio, the slave or the child who has done the damage to the plaintiff. This noxal

[1] D. 50. 17. 169 pr.: Is damnum dat, qui iubet dare: eius vero nulla culpa est cui parere necesse est.

[2] D. 44. 7. 20; see also D. 47. 10. 11. § 5.

[3] D. 50. 17. 169 pr. and D. h. t. 37 pr.

[4] D. h. t. 37 pr.

[5] Arg. D. 47. 10. 11. § 4; D. 39. 3. 5; D. 39. 2. 18. § 14; D. 47. 7. 7. § 4.

[6] Gaius IV. 75–79; Inst. IV. 8; D. 9. 4; Puchta, Cursus der Institutionem, § 277. n. vv–eee; Voigt, XII Tafeln, vol. ii. § 142. p. 583 sqq.

liability is still recognised under the law of Justinian with regard to delicts of slaves, but it is abolished with regard to delicts of filii familias: a father accordingly is liable for a delict of his son only if he has been himself in culpa with reference to it[1].

We know that already under the law of the XII Tables, not only the actio furti was applicable as an actio noxalis, but also the actions given in case a noxia nocita[2] was committed, provided only the slave or child had not done the delict by command of their superior, but without any distinction whether it was committed with or without his knowledge[3]. This distinction, however, was drawn by the Aquilian statute. If damage was committed 'sciente domino,' the dominus of the delinquent slave[4] was considered to be himself guilty of the delict, and therefore declared to be subject to an actio legis Aquiliae on his own behalf ('directa' as opposed to the actio legis Aquiliae 'noxalis'), provided he not only knew of the act of damage being done by his slave, but was at the same time in a condition to hinder its commission[5]; but if the damage was committed 'insciente domino' a noxal action was to be brought on account of the slave's delict[6]. The jurists, however, did not approve of the exclusion of the noxal action in cases where damage was done sciente domino; they considered it should only be so, if the delict was committed by the command of the master, 'iussu domini;' for the fact that the master had not prevented his slave from doing the injury did not affect the truth that the real delinquent was the slave, and therefore they asserted that, in the cases we are considering, in addition to the actio directa (on account of the master's scientia and patientia) a noxal action on account of the guilt of the slave (serui nomine) should be applicable against his master in accordance with the provision of the XII Tables, which recognised a noxal liability wherever damage was done by a slave 'iniussu

[1] I. 4. 8. § 7; Puchta, Cursus der Institutionem, § 278. n. ccc.

[2] Cf. § 2 above, p. 186.

[3] Cf. D. 9. 4. 2; Tabula XII. 1: Si familiaris iniussu patris familias furtum faxit noxiamue noxit quadrupedesue pecus pauperiem faxit, aut noxae dedito aut litis aestimationem sufferto.

[4] This case only is mentioned in the Corpus Iuris, although the provisions of the Aquilian statute doubtless referred also to the case where damage was committed by a filius familias.

[5] D. h. t. 45 pr.; D. 50. 17. 50: Culpa caret, qui scit, sed prohibere non potest.

[6] D. 9. 4. 2 pr.: Si servus sciente domino occidit, in solidum dominum obligat, ipse enim uidetur dominus occidisse: si autem insciente, noxalis est, nec enim debuit ex maleficio serui in plus teneri, quam ut noxae dedat.

domini.' And this view being strongly supported by Julian was at last generally recognised[1]. This double liability of the dominus does not mean that he could be sued by both the actions, but only that he might be sued either by one action or the other, i. e. with or without noxae datio[2]. But it was important in so far as the conditions of the two actions were different, for in virtue of the actio directa the dominus was personally liable; a liability which was extinguished only by his own death: his heir[3], however, was not subject to the action, whilst his noxal liability was dependent on the continuance of his potestas over the slave. Accordingly, it was absolutely extinguished if the slave died, but if the slave was alienated, it attached by force of law to his new master, and if he was manumitted, the action was applicable against the slave himself, although as an actio directa[4].

Accordingly, there is a threefold liability of the dominus which possibly may take place if a damnum iniuria datum has been committed by his slave:—

1. The dominus is exclusively subject to an Aquilian action, if the damage was done by his command (iussu domini).

2. The dominus is subject to an actio legis Aquiliae directa as well as to an actio noxalis, if the damage was done 'sciente domino,' although without his command (iniussu domini).

3. The dominus is only subject to an actio noxalis, if the damage was done 'insciente domino.'

The consequences of the noxal liability were very seriously felt in case the slaves belonging to a master, his so-called familia, had joined in the commission of damage to the property of another person. As here each of his slaves was a delinquent, a noxal action in respect of each of them was applicable[5]. Accordingly, he had either to pay the litis aestimatio in each case or to surrender by noxae datio all his slaves to the plaintiff. In order to avoid the danger that a master in consequence of one delict only might become deprived of all his slaves, it was finally, though not without some hesitation, settled that the principle of the edict of the praetor providing for cases where the familia of a master had jointly committed a furtum, should also apply if damage

[1] D. 9. 4. 2. § 1.

[2] D. 9. 4. 4. § 2.

[3] D. h. t. 23. § 8: In heredem—haec actio non dabitur cum sit poenalis. Cf. § 14 below.

[4] Gai. IV. 77; Inst. IV. 8. 5.

[5] Cf. D. h. t. 11. § 2; and § 14 below.

to property had been committed by the set of slaves belonging to one master. In accordance with this view the master had to pay only the litis aestimatio once, just as if a single free man had committed the damage, provided he did not prefer the noxal surrender of all his slaves to the plaintiff[1].

§ 12. *The Principles of Evidence*[2].

Having explained the different requisites to constitute liability under the Aquilian enactment, we are enabled to lay down the principles of evidence applicable to cases respecting damage to property. As might be expected, these principles are only an application of the general maxims of the law of evidence to the special conditions of the lex Aquilia.

It is well known that the leading principle of evidence is that a person who asserts something in his favour, has to prove the facts supporting his assertion, provided these facts are neither notorious nor admitted by his adversary: 'Ei incumbit probatio qui dicit, non qui negat.' Accordingly, the plaintiff has to prove those facts on which the existence of his right of action is dependent: 'Actori incumbit probatio.' But he has to prove only such facts as in their regular course will bring into existence the right asserted by him. He is not bound to prove the absence of facts which would extinguish the right once created, for instance, that a debt has not been discharged by payment. Nor, again, is he bound to prove that there were no impediments which would prevent the facts proved by him from having their ordinary legal consequences; for instance, that the defendant was not insane (furiosus), or not deprived of the right of administering his property, being a prodigal. If there were such circumstances, they are to be proved by the defendant who brings them forward on his side.

Similarly the burden of proof falls on the defendant if he puts in an 'exceptio' of the strict kind by which the right of the plaintiff, although not denied, is rendered ineffectual; for instance, an exceptio compensationis or exceptio quod metus causa. For the defendant has

[1] D. h. t. 32 pr.

[2] Pernice, pp. 228–238.

to prove the facts which support his right of exception just as the plaintiff has to prove the facts on which his right of action is founded. 'Reus in exceptione actor est,' i. e. the defendant is in bringing forward an exception in the position of a plaintiff.

In accordance with these leading principles, in case of an Aquilian action the plaintiff will be bound to prove that the requirements of this action exist. These requirements are, as we have seen in the previous sections (§§ 5–11): (1) that a thing was damaged by a positive act of the defendant; (2) that the act was done without a right which would entitle the defendant to such an interference with another's property; (3) that there was culpa on the part of the defendant; (4) that the injury actually caused a loss to the plaintiff's property; and (5) that the plaintiff had ownership in the thing or a ius in re aliena, or at least a contractual right which entitled him to take its fruits instead of the owner. Although as a principle the plaintiff was bound to prove all these points, it was in most cases not so difficult for the plaintiff to prove his claim as might be expected.

Originally the action under the Aquilian law was restricted to the cases of killing slaves and quadrupeds, and of burning, crushing, and breaking things. If then the plaintiff was suing under the first chapter his assertion was probably to this effect, that the defendant had killed unlawfully—iniuria—a slave belonging to him, the plaintiff. In this assertion he comprehended all the requirements mentioned above.

As we have seen, the word iniuria contained two elements: that the act was done by the defendant without having a right, and that it was due to his culpa. It is clear that the plaintiff had to prove the existence of culpa where it was denied by the defendant, since culpa is an essential ground of the action. Culpa, however, as a condition of a person's mind cannot be proved directly; it is only possible to prove facts from which the judge may draw the inference that a certain act was done, whilst the doer was in a condition of mind which is described by the term 'culpa.' But this evidence is not very difficult to establish in case damage has been done immediately to a thing. If, for instance, an animal was beaten by a man, and was found wounded by the blow, special evidence of culpa in this case would not be necessary; for although, strictly speaking, the culpa lies not so much in the act of beating as in intending an injury or in disregarding the consequences of the act, still such a condition of mind is apparent from the nature of the act committed. It will, therefore, be sufficient for the plaintiff to prove that an act was done by the defendant, and that it was the cause out of which the damage had arisen. But it is of course essential that act and damage should be connected as cause and effect. In most of the cases of actio directa there will be no doubt as to whether damage is the result of a certain act; thus, if a slave was pushed into the river and drowned[1], or if a mule was burdened too heavily and broke down[2]. It is true it might be denied that the damage had actually resulted from a certain act, but we must not suppose that the Roman jurists were very particular as to the evidence in such cases. They seem to assume that damage to a thing which happened after a corporeal act upon it had its cause in this operation, provided, of course, that, according to common experience, the damage might result from such an act. So Ulpian in D. h. t. 7. § 5: 'si quis seruum—percusserit et is obierit,' and in D. 19. 2. 13. § 2: 'Si magister navis sine gubernatore in flumen navem immiserit et tempestate orta temperare non potuerit et navem perdiderit.' But in case something had happened by which the connection between the act and the damage was interrupted, it was incumbent on the defendant to prove the existence of this interruption: as, for example, if the slave who was wounded by him had died in consequence of the unskilfulness of the surgeon who attended to his case[3]. In accordance with this view is the decision that in case several persons had beaten a slave who died afterwards, all these persons would be liable under the Aquilian law, provided it is not in evidence that the death was due to the blow of a certain person[4]. This decision is justified, as the death, having followed the joint act of the several persons, is apparently due to their co-operation, and this must be considered to be the case unless it be proved that the death was caused by the act of some one of them.

Another question is whether the plaintiff is also bound to prove that the defendant was sound in his mind (sanae mentis) and capable of committing an injury (culpae or inuriae capax[5]). We should think

[1] D. h. t. 7. § 7.
[2] D. h. t. 27. § 23.
[3] D. h. t. 30. § 4.
[4] D. h. t. 11. § 2.
[5] Cf. D. 50. 17. 111 pr.; I. IV. I. 20; D. h. t. 5. § 2, and the notes to this passage in Part I.

that in such a case the burden of proof would be on the plaintiff, as culpa on the part of the defendant is impossible, unless he is fully capable of understanding the nature of his acts. Nevertheless it is the defendant who will be bound to prove this want of capacity, as a special circumstance is thus brought into the case which prevents the facts supporting the plaintiff's claim from having their ordinary legal consequences; such impediments, however, are in accordance with the leading maxims of evidence to be proved by the defendant who asserts their existence in his favour.

Similarly as is the case with regard to culpa, so, in an actio directa, no special evidence will be required to show that the defendant has been acting 'iniuria,' i.e. without having a right to do the injurious act. For acts such as killing slaves and cattle, burning, etc., clearly imply an interference with another's property which, as a rule, will be done without any right on the part of the defendant. If the defendant asserts such a right, having, for instance, acted in exercising his right of self-defence, then such an assertion forms an exception which, like every other exception, is to be proved by the defendant; for the latter, strictly speaking, does not deny the injury he has done, he only says that he had a right to do the act complained of, and is therefore to be excused from any liability[1].

It is otherwise if it is notorious that the defendant was entitled to do the act in question, being, for instance, a master who had exercised his right of castigation over his apprentice, etc. In such cases the plaintiff is bound to prove that, notwithstanding this right of the defendant, there is iniuria on his part, because he had either exceeded his right or had exercised his right merely for the purpose of injuring the plaintiff.

Also the requisite that the injury should have resulted in actual loss to the plaintiff's property will commonly impose no special burden of evidence on him, for such loss will, as a rule, exist wherever a damage is done. If, however, the value of the property of the plaintiff was

[1] That an act of damage, although committed in virtue of a right of the doer, is in itself fit to bring the Aquilian law into operation is clearly shown by D. h. t. 45. § 4, where it is stated that a person who in defending himself wounds another will be liable to an action on the part of the latter, although he is not liable if by the same blow his assailant is hurt.

not diminished by the injurious act, which is of course a very exceptional case, as, for example, if the fruits gathered were ripe, or the trees felled were fit for being felled, or the slave castrated had become in consequence even more valuable by this act[1], such an exception had to be proved by the defendant.

The foregoing remarks are also applicable to many cases where an actio utilis or in factum is given. Thus, if cattle were driven violently along a narrow way, and fell down a precipice[2], or if a slave was shut up and died of hunger[3], it will be sufficient, if the plaintiff proves that in consequence of the act of the defendant the damage complained of was done to his property. But he will not be bound to bring forward special evidence of culpa, since its existence is implied by the facts already proved. This is also true of cases like the following: A person is sawing off branches of a tree by which a passer-by is hurt[4]; it will be sufficient if the latter proves that he was injured by a branch falling down upon him, and it will be incumbent on the defendant to give evidence to the effect that the usual measures of precaution had been taken by him, and that therefore no culpa can be attributed to him. That the burden of proof is to be distributed in this way is apparent from D. h. t. 28. In this fragment the case is supposed that a person has digged pits for catching bears or deer, and that cattle have fallen into them and were thus damaged. Here the owner of the cattle might sue the digger in virtue of the Aquilian law, if the pits were made in places where cattle might probably pass. But the defendant is only to be condemned in case he fails to prove that the danger had been announced to the plaintiff, or that the latter was himself in a condition to avoid the danger, because he had known the fact, or at least might have known it, if he had not been negligent[5]. It is quite clear, that in case the plaintiff was in a condition to avoid the danger, the burden of proof must fall on the defendant, for in bringing forward such a fact the defendant does not deny his own culpa, but asserts merely that there is a contributory negligence on the part of the plaintiff. But also in the other case, where it is in question whether the necessary measures of precaution had been taken, 'an denuntiatum sit,' the

[1] Cf. D. h. t. 27. §§ 25–28.

[2] D. h. t. 53.

[3] D. h. t. 9. § 2.

[4] D. h. t. 31; cf. also id. 30. § 3.

[5] Cf. also Bas. 60. 3. 28 (Heimbach, v. p. 301).

burden of proof lies on the defendant, and this is in strict accordance with the general principles we have laid down.

But although, as a rule, no special evidence is required to prove culpa on the part of the defendant, it is otherwise where a certain act has been followed by damage which might, according to common experience, equally be attributed to extraneous causes. Where this is the case it is incumbent on the plaintiff to prove by special evidence that the damage complained of was due to the culpa of the defendant. Thus it would not be sufficient to prove that a physician had attended to a sick slave who had died afterwards, for the death of a person may happen without any negligence on the part of the medical man attending him. It will be necessary to prove special facts from which either his unskilfulness or his negligence is evident[1]. In a similar way the mere fact that a pilot was directing a ship which foundered would not be sufficient evidence by itself.

From what we have said it is clear that—probably in the majority of cases falling under the Aquilian law (i. e. the lex itself as well as its extensions)—it is enough that the plaintiff prove that a corporeal thing of his own has been damaged by the act of the defendant, since this fact is also, as a general rule, evidence of the other requisites of the Aquilian action, i. e. of culpa and of iniuria, in the narrower sense of the word, as also of actual loss resulting to the plaintiff. But where the evidence of these requisites is not implied, the plaintiff will be bound to prove further facts from which the existence of the requisites is apparent.

There is, however, one point which we have not yet explained. The actio legis Aquiliae is given by law to the owner. Therefore ownership is to be proved by the plaintiff if it is denied by the defendant. In case a person had acquired ownership for himself, independently of another owner, i. e. by an original title, as by accession, specification, usucapion, it will be sufficient to prove the fact which constitutes such an original title. But when ownership was acquired in a derivative way, by succession, as, for instance, if the plaintiff has received the thing from another by tradition—in con-

[1] Cf. in D. h. t. 7. § 8. the words 'si medicus seruum *imperite* secuerit,' and in 8. pr. 'si medicamento *perperam* usus fuerit,' and 'qui bene secuerit et *dereliquit* curationem.'

sequence of a preceding sale—the proof of the act of succession is not sufficient; but the plaintiff is also bound to prove that the person from whom he had received the thing, that is, his auctor, was the owner; and if his auctor had derived ownership from another, then he had to prove the ownership of the auctor of his auctor, and so on, till he came to an auctor who could be proved to have acquired ownership in an original way; for instance, by specification, or till he was able to show that he and his auctors together had possessed the thing during the time prescribed for usucapion, and thus acquired ownership. It is quite clear that it was often extremely difficult to establish such evidence. It might therefore happen that a person, though he was the owner, could not prove his right in the thing, because he had acquired it by succession and was unable to prove the dominium auctoris.

But on that account the owner was not left without legal protection. If he had lost the possession of his thing, he might recover it from the present possessor by means of the actio Publiciana, available in favour of a person who was the bonae fidei possessor of a thing: an action which required only the proof that the plaintiff had received iusto titulo, i. e. on the ground of a title (e. g. sale), in virtue of which he would have acquired ownership, if his auctor had been the owner[1]. Thus the owner escaped the difficulty of proving his right of ownership.

But if the owner was protected in case another person had acquired possession of his thing, although he could not prove his right of ownership, but merely a iustus titulus, there seems to have been an equal necessity for protecting him in case another person had destroyed or damaged a thing belonging to him. It seems to be senseless that the damage done to his property should remain without its legal consequences and the delinquent should be acquitted from the action, simply on account of the difficulty of the proof of ownership.

It is most probably this difficulty of proof to which the extension of the Aquilian action to the bonae fidei possessor is due; and the same

[1] The plaintiff was not bound to prove bona fides on his part, since the law presumes the existence of good faith until the contrary is shown. Arndts, § 114. n. n.

reason supports the view that the Aquilian action was given to the bonae fidei possessor, as a rule, to the same extent as the owner[1]. It is true, that if the delinquent was condemned in an action in which the plaintiff had proved merely a iustus titulus, he might possibly be sued afterwards on account of the same damage by a person who succeeded in proving ownership in the thing damaged, but against this danger security was to be given by the plaintiff in the first action[2].

In the same way as the owner and the possessor in good faith have to prove the facts supporting their right to the thing, so a person who had a mere ius in re aliena (ususfructus, usus) or an obligatory right, in virtue of which he is entitled to sue under the Aquilian enactment, is bound to prove the facts on which such a right is usually founded.

---

§ 13. *The object of the Aquilian action*[3].

According to the first chapter of the Aquilian statute, the defendant was to be condemned to pay to the plaintiff the highest value within the previous year of the slave or quadruped killed: 'quanti id in eo anno plurimi fuit[4].'

According to the third chapter the value of the thing destroyed or damaged, during the last thirty days, had to be paid by the defendant: 'quanti ea res erit in diebus triginta proximis[5].'

These provisions are peculiar in several respects. In the first place there is a distinction drawn between slaves and cattle on one side and all other things on the other; this is to be explained by the fact that slaves and cattle were considered to be far more important than other things in those ancient days in which agriculture was the chief occupation of Roman citizens. The very high estimate of a thing to be made under Chapter I is to be accounted for in the same way, although this was probably also intended to compensate the owner for the loss which he might have suffered

[1] See § 10, p. 239 above.

[2] Arg. D. h. t. 27. § 14. Cf. Mommsen, Beiträge, vol. ii. p. 245.

[3] Pernice, pp. 238–247.

[4] D. h. t. 2. pr.

[5] D. h. t. 27. § 5.

by being deprived of the usual help rendered by the slave or animal killed, and by being compelled to acquire substitutes in their place at a time when their market-value might be far higher than at the time the damage was done. The words of the statute, however, were open to doubts with regard to the period in reference to which the assessment was to be made in cases where a slave or animal was mortally wounded, but did not die till some time after. Strictly speaking, a slave or animal was not killed till death had actually resulted from the act, nevertheless it was assumed by the jurists, on the authority of Julian, that the year should be reckoned backwards from the time when the wound had been inflicted, and not from the moment the death had ensued, D. h. t. 21 § 1.

Under the third chapter also a higher value than that which the damaged thing had at the time of the injury could be assessed; but this was entirely left to the judge, who, under the terms of the statute, could assess compensation with reference to any period of the thirty days previous to the act of damage. This discretionary power of the judge was, however, taken away in later times, since, on the authority of Sabinus, the word 'plurimi' was considered to be understood of the third chapter also, and thus the judge was simply obliged to condemn the defendant to pay the highest value of the things during the last thirty days[1].

The way of assessing damages under the terms of the Aquilian statute shows clearly its archaic character, and could not satisfy the wants of a progressive state of civilisation. This applies especially to the third chapter, in so far as under its provisions the value of the thing was to be paid, without any distinction whether it was destroyed or merely damaged by burning, crushing, breaking.

By the interpretation of the jurists, however, compensation for the value of the thing itself was gradually changed into compensation for the entire loss a person had sustained in his property by the damaging act; in other words, according to the interpretation of the jurists,

[1] Gaius, III. 218: Hoc tamen capite non quanti in eo anno, sed quanti in diebus XXX proximis ea res fuerit, damnatur is qui damnum dederit; ac ne PLVRIMI quidem uerbum adicitur: et ideo quidam putaverunt liberum esse iudici ad id tempus ex diebus XXX aestimationem redigere, quo plurimi res fuerit, uel ad id quo minoris fuerit: sed Sabino placuit proinde habendum ac si etiam hac parte PLVRIMI uerbum adiectum esset; nam legis latorem contentum fuisse quod prima parte eo uerbo usus esset.

the so-called 'interesse,' i.e. the difference between the present value of the whole property of the plaintiff and the value which his property would have had if the damaging act had not been committed, 'id quod interest actoris,' became the object of the action. That this change was really due to the interpretation of the jurists is clearly stated by Justinian in I. h. t. § 10:—

> Illud non ex uerbis legis, sed ex interpretatione placuit non solum peremti corporis aestimationem habendam esse secundum ea quae diximus, sed eo amplius quidquid praeterea peremto eo corpore damni uobis adlatum fuerit, ueluti si seruum tuum heredem ab aliquo institutum ante quis occiderit, quam is iussu tuo adiret: nam hereditatis quoque amissae rationem esse habendam constat.

This interpretation of the Aquilian statute is quite in accordance with the general development which took place in Roman law. For the expression 'quanti ea res est' (or 'fuit') in the formula, which originally denoted the verum rei pretium, or the market-value of the thing, has commonly the meaning of 'interesse' with the later jurists. Yet the original meaning of the words can be recognised in many passages; thus a person is said to be bound to restore the 'res cum sua causa' or the 'res et omnis causa[1].' These expressions indicate the way in which the change was effected in course of time. In case there were peculiar circumstances which increased the value of a thing for its owner, 'causae corpori cohaerentes,' the jurists considered it to be fair to take into account not only the loss directly sustained by the damage done to the corporeal thing belonging to him (the so-called 'damnum directum'), but also the loss which the owner had suffered indirectly through the medium of the peculiar circumstances in question (the so-called 'damnum indirectum'). Accordingly it is decided in D. h. t. 22. § 1, that if one of a set of things which form together one whole is destroyed, e.g. if one of four chariot horses or one of a company of slave actors or orchestra players is killed, in addition to the value of the thing destroyed, it must be ascertained to what extent the other things have

[1] D. 16. 3. 1. § 24; D. 50. 16. 35; D. 10. 2. 44. pr.; D. 12. 1. 31; D. 6. 1. 20.

been depreciated. Similarly if a document, for instance a promissory note or a will, has been destroyed, the owner is entitled to claim compensation not only for the value of the document[1], but also for the loss which he has suffered by being prevented from proving the claim stated in the document[2]. But probably in most cases the document itself would be of hardly any value, and so the owner would merely sue for the damnum indirectum he had sustained.

There are still other cases in which, not the value of the damaged thing, but something else is to be taken into account in assessing damages. This is, generally speaking, the case wherever the injured person was under an obligation to transfer to a third person either the thing which had been damaged, or some other more valuable object. This is illustrated by the following cases taken from the title of the Digest we are explaining:—

(*a*) A person has promised to transfer a slave to another, and in case he should not fulfil his promise, has promised to pay a penalty; if, in this case, the slave is killed by a third person, the latter will be bound to compensate the promisor for the loss, which he will suffer by being bound to pay the penalty, 22 pr.

(*b*) An owner of a quadruped was sued in an actio de pauperie; during the lawsuit the animal was killed by a third person, and thus its owner was bound to pay full compensation for the damage done by it, instead of freeing himself from this duty by noxal surrender; but he would be entitled to recover the loss thus sustained by the Aquilian action to be brought against the person who has killed the quadruped, 37 pr.

(*c*) A person promised to transfer to another either Stichus, who was worth 10, or Pamphilus, who was worth 20; afterwards Stichus was killed by somebody else, and therefore the promisor was bound to deliver to the stipulator the more valuable Pamphilus. Accordingly, the object of the Aquilian action in this case would not be ten, i.e. the value of Stichus who is killed, but twenty, that is the actual loss suffered by the plaintiff; cf. 55.

But the Roman jurists did not confine themselves to taking account

[1] D. 47. 2. 27 pr.

[2] D. h. t. 40–42.

of the actual loss caused to the plaintiff, but included in the estimation of damage also gains which he was prevented from making in consequence of the damaging act. In other words, not only the positive loss, directly or indirectly sustained by the plaintiff, the so-called 'damnum emergens,' but the negative loss, the so-called 'lucrum cessans,' became the object of the Aquilian action. In accordance with this view, it is said in D. h. t. 23 pr. and in I. h. t. § 10, that if a slave is killed who was instituted an heir, not only the value of the slave is to be assessed in the Aquilian action, but also the value of the inheritance, which thus could not be acquired for his master. And in a similar way a master who has been instituted under the condition of manumitting his slave would be entitled, if the slave has been killed after the death of the testator, to claim compensation for the inheritance which he had failed to acquire in consequence of the death of the slave to be manumitted by him; 23. § 2. A very peculiar case of the same nature is mentioned in 23, § 4: A slave, so the jurist supposes, has, in conspiracy with some other persons, committed extensive frauds in administering his master's property. The master therefore intended to examine the slave by torture, in order to find out the names of his accomplices; but before this was done the slave was killed by a third person. It is said that in the Aquilian action compensation is to be given not only for the value of the slave killed, but also for the loss which the plaintiff has suffered by being unable to sue the accomplices of his slave (or their masters) on account of the delict committed by them.

Although there is no doubt that on principle the Aquilian action comprehends equally compensation for the positive and the negative loss, yet the proof of the latter kind of loss is more difficult to establish. With regard to the positive loss sustained by the plaintiff, nothing is to be proved but the causal connection between two facts, namely, the act of damage, and the loss inflicted on the plaintiff; but in case of the lucrum cessans evidence must be given that if a certain fact (the act of damage) had not been existing, another fact would have come into existence, viz. the gain would have been realised by the plaintiff: a proof which, strictly speaking, it is impossible to establish. Nevertheless it is assumed by the jurists that a gain which may be expected as certain in the regular course of events is to be included in the assessment of the damages[1]. It is otherwise if evidence to this effect cannot be established; therefore in the case of nets being torn no compensation could be claimed for the value of the fish, deer, or birds which might have been caught by means of them, for the prospect of such gain is altogether uncertain[2].

The result which we have arrived at is that under the Aquilian statute the plaintiff can claim compensation not only for the positive loss which he has suffered directly or indirectly by the act of damage, but also for the negative loss, i.e. the gain which he has failed to realise in consequence. Accordingly, it is the whole loss which the plaintiff has sustained in his property (the word 'property' being taken in the sense of a universitas or complex of legal relations, rights as well as duties), or, in other words, the *difference* of plaintiff's property, as it was after the act of damage and as it would have been if the act had not been committed, this so-called *interesse*, 'quanti interfuit nostra non esse occisum (scil. servum[3]),' which has become the object of the Aquilian action in the course of time.

From this notion of interesse two important inferences are to be drawn:—

1. As the interesse is a loss caused to a person's property, the fact that a person has a special attachment for the thing damaged cannot be taken into account in assessing damages, for this interest of affection, as we may call it[4], does not alter the condition of the plaintiff's property. It is accordingly decided in D. h. t. 33 pr. that an owner is not entitled to any compensation merely on account of the fact that the killed slave was his son whom he would have bought at a very high price if he had been subject to the power of another person, and the same principle is applied in several other passages[5].

2. The notion of interesse is in its nature quite different from the value of the thing which has been damaged and need not have any reference to it. Usually, it is true, the interesse will comprehend the ordinary value of the thing, and often it will go beyond it, but it also may be less than this value. Thus, if a master has brought an actio

[1] See the notes to fr. 23. pr. in Part I.

[2] D. h. t. 29. § 3, but compare with reference to the particular difficulty of this passage the notes to it in Part I.

[3] D. h. t. 21. § 2.

[4] German writers use the expression, 'Affectionsinteresse.'

[5] E. g. D. h. t. 27. § 28, 41; see also p. 134 above.

legis Aquiliae (viz. directa) on account of a wound inflicted on his slave, who had been healed in the mean time[1], the master will merely receive compensation for the expenses he had incurred for the care of his slave and for the loss of his labour, the value of the slave himself is not at all concerned. And exactly the same is true of cases where a pater familias has brought an actio utilis if his filius familias has been wounded by a third person[2]. An illustration of a far more general nature is furnished by those cases in which a ius in re aliena is interfered with by the act of damage, for here compensation will be claimed for the extinguished right which, as a rule, will be less than the value of the thing itself, i.e. ownership in it; thus we are told in 30. § 1 that if a slave given in pledge has been killed, the creditor pignoris will be entitled to the Aquilian action up to the amount of his claim, whilst the same action for the surplus due on the act of the damage will be reserved for the owner[3].

Although the object of the Aquilian action has been changed in the way we have described, yet the whole change consists merely in the fact that a new sense was attached to the words of the statute referring to the assessment of damages: the 'quanti ea res fuit' is to be understood in the sense of interesse; the validity of the statute itself is not affected by the change. The interesse, therefore, is to be determined in accordance with the terms of the statute with reference either to the last year or the last month previous to the act of injury. Consequently events which have taken place afterwards cannot be taken into account in assessing damages in the Aquilian statute, although it might have become apparent from them that no loss has actually resulted from the act complained of, or, on the contrary, that in addition to the original loss some other loss has been inflicted to the plaintiff's property in consequence of the act of damage. This will be illustrated by the following two cases mentioned in the Digest:—

1. In D. 6. 1. 27. § 2[4] the case is supposed that the possessor of a slave sued by rei vindicatio had intentionally wounded the slave in his

[1] D. h. t. 45. § 1.

[2] D. h. t. 7. pr.

[3] Cf. § 10, p. 244 sqq. above.

[4] Si homo petitus dolo possessoris deterior factus sit, deinde sine culpa eius ex alia causa mortuus sit, aestimatio non fiet eius, quod deteriorem eum fecerat, quia nihil interest petitoris: sed haec quantum ad in rem actionem: legis autem Aquiliae actio durat. Cf. D. 43. 24. 7. § 4. i. f.; Mommsen, Beiträge, vol. ii. p. 202, and the notes to fr. 21 pr. in Part I.

possession, but that the slave died afterwards from another cause for which the defendant was not answerable. It is decided by the jurist (Paulus) that the plaintiff cannot claim compensation for the injury done to his slave by the rei vindicatio, for there is no loss resulting from the act of damage at the time when the case is to be decreed by the judge; there was, however, such loss at the time when the injury was committed, and therefore an Aquilian action is declared to be applicable.

2. According to D. h. t. 23. § 2, a master was instituted as heir upon condition of his manumitting his slave. There is no doubt that if the slave was killed by a third person after the death of the testator, i.e. after the inheritance had been offered to the master, the latter would be entitled to claim by the Aquilian action not only compensation for the value of the slave, but also for the inheritance which he was prevented from acquiring by being unable to fulfil the condition of his institution. But this was otherwise if the slave was killed in the lifetime of the testator, for here the slave was not yet a medium by means of which the inheritance could be acquired, there not yet being an inheritance to be entered upon; accordingly the testamentary disposition had not yet increased the value of the slave to his master, and was therefore not to be taken into account in assessing damages under the Aquilian law, although if afterwards the testator died without having altered his will, the inheritance would be lost for the master, just as if the slave had been killed in the lifetime of the testator.

---

§ 14. *The nature of the Aquilian action*[1].

There were two distinct kinds of remedies provided by the lex Aquilia: a multae petitio and the actio legis Aquiliae, of which the former was to be brought into recognition by way of criminal procedure, whilst the latter was dealt with in the forms of civil procedure.

With regard to the multae petitio our only authority is one passage of Cicero[2]. The object of this remedy was a fine, probably paid to

[1] Pernice, pp. 102–144.

[2] Brutus, § 131: atque eodem tempore accusator de plebe L. Caesulaenus fuit, quem ego audiui iam senem cum ab L. Sabellio multam lege Aquilia damni iniuria petiuisset.

the State, which, in addition to what was due under the Aquilian action, was forfeited in the more serious cases of damage to property, very likely only if slaves or quadrupeds were intentionally killed[1]. But the multa disappeared in the later times[2], since by the lex Cornelia de sicariis (of Sulla, 83–80 B.C.) intentional killing of slaves of another was punishable as homicide[3], whilst on the other side the special appreciation attached to the possession of cattle had disappeared with advancing civilisation during the later centuries of the republic.

Differing from the multae petitio, the actio legis Aquiliae, or, more strictly speaking, the different actions which are available under this name in virtue of the different chapters of the lex, were, at least as far as Chapters I and III are concerned[4], subject-matter of a very extensive and detailed interpretation on the part of the jurists; nevertheless hardly anything is reported which would throw light on the conception of the formulae of these actions, and therefore the attempts which have been made in reconstructing their tenour are open to many doubts[5]. We are, however, told that under each of the chapters of the Aquilian law the actio went in duplum, if the defendant denied in court—in iure—his liability, whilst in case he admitted it, the object of the action was merely a simplum, i.e. compensation to be fixed in accordance with the peculiar provisions of the Aquilian statute[6]. It is equally certain that this difference was expressed in the formula actionis, and therefore two formulae were provided by the praetorian edict: one for the actio confessoria[7], the other for the 'actio adversus infitiantem.' If an Aquilian action was to be brought against the master of a delinquent slave, there was an equal necessity for expressing the reason of the liability of the master, who, in case his slave had committed damage to property of another, was subject either to an action on his own account,

[1] So Huschke, Gaius, p. 103, and Rudorff, Römische Rechtsgeschichte, vol. i. p. 99. Differing: Pernice, p. 103.

[2] Rudorff, Römische Rechtsgeschichte, vol. i. p. 100.

[3] Accordingly, if a slave was killed intentionally, the delinquent was not only subject to the Aquilian action, but also to a public prosecution under the lex Cornelia; I. h. t. § 11; D. h. t. 5 pr. 23. § 9; D. 19. 5. 14. § 1; D. 48. 15. 3. § 1; Gaius, III. 213.

[4] Chapter II. fell comparatively early into disuse; see Gaius, III. 216; D. h. t. 27. § 4; p. 82 sq. above.

[5] See § 4. p. 201.

[6] See D. h. t. 2. § 1, 23. § 10, and the notes on p. 3 sq. and p. 71 sq. above.

[7] See D. h. t. 23. § 11–26; p. 72 sqq.

the so-called 'actio si seruus sciente domino damnum dederit,' or an actio noxalis serui nomine, the 'actio si seruus insciente domino damnum dederit[1].'

If it is very little which can be ascertained with regard to the *form* of the Aquilian action; there are numerous statements in our sources referring to the *nature* of that action, and which allow definite conclusions to be drawn, but the whole question wants to be carefully examined, as the passages concerned partly seem to contradict one another.

It is well known that there are actions which have for their object to make over to the plaintiff what is withheld from his property. They prevent an unlawful alteration in the proprietary rights of men from continuing. Thus, by means of the remedies we are referring to, the condition of property as it should be according to law is maintained, and therefore these actions are called by the Romans actiones rei persequendae causa comparatae, or, with modern writers, actiones reipersecutoriae (persecutory actions). The rei vindicatio and the actio ex mutuo are instances which clearly illustrate the nature of these actions.

On the other hand, there are actions by which the property of the plaintiff is altered; something is added to it, merely in order to punish by the loss the defendant for his conduct, and on that account the remedies are called in our sources of Roman law actiones poenales, or actiones poenae persequendae causa comparatae, as, for instance, the actio furti and the actio iniuriarum.

Sometimes one and the same action combines both the objects mentioned: payment of a penalty as well as recovery of compensation, in which case the actio is called mixta, tam rei quam poenae persequendae causa comparata, e. g. the actio vi bonorum raptorum[2].

If we apply these distinctions to the Aquilian action, it might seem at first sight that this action, having for its object compensation for the loss which the plaintiff had sustained, would fall under the first class mentioned above, and so would be merely a persecutory action. Considering, besides, that sometimes more than the compensation for the actual loss might be obtained by the action, in case the value of the thing was at one moment during the last year or month higher

[1] See the notes to D. h. t. 27 pr. and § 1, p. 78 sq.; see also § 13, p. 199 sq. n. 3 above.

[2] Cf. Gai. IV. 6–9, and Inst. IV. 6. §§. 16–19; Arndts, § 98; Savigny, System, v. § 210.

than at the time the injury was done, we should be inclined to think that in so far the actio is mixta by which compensation as well as penalty is attained. And, indeed, this view is strongly supported by a passage in the Institutes (IV. 6. § 19), in which Justinian says: 'sed et legis Aquiliae actio de damno mixta est—ueluti si quis hominem claudum aut luscum occiderit, qui in eo anno integer aut magni pretii fuit.' But it is certain that no practical consequences whatever are attached to this distinction between the objects of the Aquilian action, being sometimes compensation only, and sometimes compensation with an additional penalty. Moreover, the distinction made by Justinian is entirely unknown to the classical jurists [1]. But if we look at the passages which deal with the nature of the Aquilian law, its object does not seem to be so much compensation (although it is practically obtained by the plaintiff) as penalty for the unlawful act committed by the defendant. Evidently the idea pervading the decisions of the Roman jurists is that compensation can be claimed as a penalty in the Aquilian action.

In D. 5. 1. 18. § 1 the question is discussed whether a filius familias who, for the sake of his studies or for some other reasons, is absent from home, is entitled to the Aquilian action if property in his possession was damaged, and a utilis actio is granted to him, the jurist reasoning: 'ne dum pater expectatur *impunita* sint *maleficia*.'

If several persons have caused by their blows the death of a slave, they are, according to D. h. t. 11. § 2, liable under the first chapter, 'etsi cum uno agatur ceteri non liberantur: cum ex lege Aquilia quod alius praestitit, alium non releuat, *cum sit poena*.'

In D. h. t. 51. §§ 1, 2 it is considered to be a consequence of the views held by the ancient jurists that if a slave had been wounded by several persons, and it cannot be ascertained by whose blow the slave was killed, they are all liable under the first chapter, for crimes committed shall not remain without due penalty; neque *impunita maleficia* esse oporteat [2].

This view, according to which the actio legis Aquiliae is looked

[1] Cf. as to the relation of the passage of Justinian in I. IV. 6. § 19 to its original in G. IV. 9, Pernice, p. 119 sq.

[2] Cf. also Paulus, Sent. Rec. I. 13 a. § 6: Qui ancillam alienam virginem immauram corruperit, *poena legis Aquiliae* tenebitur. Gai. III. 211: itaque *impunitus* est qui sine culpa et dolo malo casu quodam damnum committit.

upon as a penal action, is by no means confined to that action; other actions also arising out of delict are said to be penal[1], although their object is merely compensation for the loss sustained by the plaintiff.

One might, however, say that it is entirely irrelevant, whether the Romans called the actio legis Aquiliae a penal action or not, if compensation could be claimed for the loss sustained by the plaintiff, just as if an action of a purely persecutory character was brought, like the actio ex mutuo or the rei vindicatio. It must, however, be observed that the consequences are not the same, but that the actio legis Aquiliae is treated in exactly the same way as penal actions are in Roman law. Three characteristics are commonly ascribed to this kind of actions[2]: (1) Penal actions can be brought as actiones noxales against the master and father if the delict was committed by his slave or filius familias; (2) if the delict was committed by several persons, each of them is liable to pay the full penalty; and (3) penal actions are not transmitted against the heir of the delinquent, for 'heres in poenam non succedit' is the principle.

The manner in which the jurists have dealt with the Aquilian action is entirely in accordance with these principles:—

1. There is no doubt that on account of damage to property done by a slave or filius familias the Aquilian action may be brought against his master or father[3]. But other actions for compensation arising out of a delict are in the same way available as noxales actiones against the superior of the delinquent. This is asserted as a principle by Ulpian, as also by Gaius[4], who says that on account of every delict committed by a son and slave a noxal action may be framed, without any distinction whether penalty or compensation is claimed by the action.

> Gaius IV. 75. Ex maleficiis filiorum familias seruorumque, ueluti si furtum fecerint aut iniuriam commiserint, noxales actiones proditae sunt.

A special application of this principle is made by Ulpianus in the following passage:—

> D. 4. 3. 9. § 4. Haec de dolo actio noxalis erit: ideo Labeo

[1] Cf. D. 4. 7. 4. § 6, 6 and 7; D. 25. 2. 21. § 5.
[2] Savigny, System, vol. v. p. 44 sq.
[3] Cf. § 11, p. 254 sqq. above.
[4] D. 47. 1. 1. § 2.

—scribit de dolo actionem serui nomine interdum de peculio, interdum noxalem dari nam si ea res est, in quam dolus commissus est, ex qua de peculio daretur actio, et nunc in peculio dandam: si vero ea sit, ex qua noxalis, hoc quoque noxale futurum.

According to this passage, the *actio de dolo* or *actio doli*[1], which is applicable as a merely subsidiary remedy, i. e. in absence of any other legal remedy, in case a person had sustained loss by fraudulent or malicious acts of another, is also available as actio noxalis. Labeo therefore says, that on account of the dolus (de dolo) of a slave one of two actions may be brought against his master: either an actio de peculio, if circumstances (ea res) existed which give rise to such an action[2], i. e. if there was a juristic act of the slave (a contract or quasi-contract), and with regard to it dolus was committed by the slave; or an actio noxalis, if the facts were such as to produce this action, i. e. if there was a maleficium of the slave.

In short the principle is the following: In case the basis of the liability of the slave[3] is a legal transaction, as contract or quasi-contract, the nature of the actio (ex contractu, etc.) is not altered by a subsequent dolus of the slave, and therefore the action is to be brought as an actio adiecticiae qualitatis (actio de peculio, etc.[4]) against his master. But when the basis of the liability is a dolus—or, in case of the Aquilian action, also a culpa—independently of an existing contract or other legal transaction, then the actio is ex delicto, and therefore available against the master as an actio noxalis.

2. In case several persons have joined in committing unlawful damage to property, each of them is liable to pay full damages in accordance with the Aquilian statute. This is clearly stated in D. h. t. 11. § 2, where several persons who have beaten a slave, who died in consequence, are all declared to be liable under the first chapter, i.e. on account of killing the slave[5], and if one had paid the full compensation required by the law, the others are not released: 'nam ex lege Aquilia quod alius praestitit alium non releuat cum sit poena[6].'

[1] Cf. Arndts, § 334.

[2] Cf. Arndts, § 247. n. h–m.

[3] The same holds good of a filius familias in the earlier law.

[4] Gaius, IV. §§ 69–74; Inst. IV. 7.

[5] Cf. also D. h. t. 51. § 1.

[6] The very artificial way in which Savigny, System, vol. v. p. 234 sq.

This rule is clearly in accordance with the principle that penalty is to be paid by every accomplice[1], but it is contrary to the rule prevailing in persecutory actions that compensation is to be given only once[2]. It is true that in case of other actions by which compensation is claimed ex delicto, e. g. actio quod metus causa, de dolo, condictio furtiua, the other accomplices are freed as soon as one has paid compensation, but none of these actions originated in the ancient civil law, like the Aquilian action, but they were introduced by the praetor's edict, the enactments of which were of a more equitable character.

3. In several passages it is clearly stated that no action arising out of a delict is transmitted against the heir of the delinquent without any distinction whether its object is merely penalty (as in case of an actio furti and iniuriarum), or penalty and compensation (e. g. in the actio vi bonorum raptorum), or only compensation (as in the case of an actio doli or actio legis Aquiliae). The general terms in which this rule is laid down in D. 47. 1. 1 pr.; D. 50. 17. 111. § 1; I. IV. 12. 1, and Gaius, IV. 112, do not admit any restrictions[3] which in no way are indicated by the contents. Compare especially the passage of Gaius, which runs as follows:—

> Est enim *certissima iuris regula* ex maleficiis poenales actiones in heredem non transire nec dari solere ueluti furti, ui bonorum raptorum, iniuriarum, damni iniuriae.

The Roman idea clearly was that a delict could only make the person who had committed it liable[4]. It was only in case an action had already been brought against the delinquent which had reached the stage of litis contestatio that it was transmitted against his heir. But

attempts to unite this passage with his opinion that the object of the Aquilian action was partly compensation, partly penalty is entirely unsatisfactory. The fiction assumed by him (p. 235) does not alter the fact that the object of the action could be claimed several times from each of the accomplices concerned, and it is, besides, contrary to the view of the Roman jurists, who simply declared in fr. 51. § 1 the liability of all the delinquents to be 'consequens auctoritati veterum.'

[1] D. h. t. 51 i. f.; D. 26. 7. 55. § 1 and C. 4. 8. 1.

[2] C. 4. 8. 1.

[3] Such as are inferred by Savigny, vol. v. p. 57. n. g.

[4] D. 48. 19. 20. See also D. 27. 3. 1. § 23; D. 11. 3. 13 pr. and D. 11. 6. 3. § 5.

though—with this restriction—the heir is not liable under the delict of the deceased person, he ought not to make any profit out of it. Therefore an action can be brought against him as far as he is enriched by the delict[1]. It must, however, be understood that the heir is not liable as the successor of the delinquent, but merely on account of the increase of his property, which had taken place without a justifiable cause. Therefore, in the strict sense, the actions given against the heir are all condictiones ex iniusta causa[2]. Accordingly, it is not a previously existing liability—ex delicto—which falls on the heir, but a liability of his own, which, if not recognised by the law apart from all question of delict, would not exist[3]. It is in exactly the same way that the actio legis Aquiliae is dealt with by the classical jurists; they deny, on one hand, as a principle, that this action is transmitted against the heir of the delinquent[4], while they allow, on the other hand, a claim for increase to his property[5].

In opposition to this characteristic, the object of the Aquilian action under the later law is the interesse, i. e. compensation for the whole loss which the plaintiff has sustained in his property, and this fact has been recognised[6]. It is accordingly decided that if the injured party had once received full compensation in an action on the contract, he could not sue the delinquent by the Aquilian action[7]. For the same reason a husband is said to be entitled to sue his wife on account of the damage done to his property[8], although on principle penal actions are not admissible between husband and wife. And thus it seems only natural that, lastly, Justinian, having chiefly in view the compensation attained by the action, declared it to be an actio mixta[9]. Nevertheless all the essential features of a penal action are still preserved in the Corpus Iuris, and therefore it seems correct to say that the Aquilian action, even in the latest stage of its development, was still thought to be an actio poenalis. Compensation is sued for as a penalty for the delinquent. This view, strange as it may

[1] D. 50. 17. 38; D. 44. 7. 35 pr.; D. 4. 2. 16. § 2 and 19; D. 3. 6. 5 pr.

[2] Cf. D. 47. 8. 2. § 27 and D. 43. 16. 1. § 48.

[3] Cf. D. 2. 10. 1. § 6. In the sense of the text also other passages (D. 47. 9. 4. § 2 and D. 50. 17. 44) are to be understood.

[4] D. 10. . 10; cf. I. 4. 3. § 9.

[5] D. h. t. 23. § 8.

[6] D. h. t. 21. § 2; see also p. 265 sq. above.

[7] See p. 231, n. 1 and 2 above.

[8] D. h. t9. § 30, 56.

[9] I. 4. 6. 19; Pernice, p. 119 sq.

seem to us, is historically explained by the fact that delicts originally gave rise to private vengeance, which gradually was replaced either by a fixed composition or compensation to be assessed by the court[1].

[1] See our remarks on the topics of ossis fractio and membri ruptio, p. 187 above, and cf. also § 13, p. 270 sq. In a similar way, according to O. W. Holmes, Common Law, p. 3, the law of trespass had been developed in England. Compare besides Ihering, Geist des römischen Rechts, vol. i. § 11 a. i. f. (p. 139 in the third edition); and Fr. Mommsen, Beiträge, vol. ii. p. 19, where he says that an exact distinction of 'private penalty' and 'interesse,' even in cases where the interesse might be claimed on account of a delict, is but the work of a more developed jurisprudence, and was by no means fully realised in Roman law.

SUMMARY

OF THE CONTENTS OF PART II

WITH REFERENCE TO THE MAIN PASSAGES QUOTED THEREIN.

---

§ 1. Date of the lex Aquilia (pp. 183–185).

The lex Aquilia, issued according to D. 9. 2. 1 pr. a considerable time after the XII Tables (p. 183 sq.), and having been in existence long before the seventh century A. U. C., D. h. t. 27. § 22 (p. 184), was very probably published, as must be inferred from Theophilus ad I. 4. 3. § 3, in the year of the third secession of the Plebs, i.e. 467 A. U. C. (p. 184 sq.).

§ 2. The relation of the lex Aquilia to the former law as to damage to property (pp. 185–196).

According to Ulpian, D. h. t. 1 pr., the lex Aquilia has repealed all former law of damage to property (p. 185). A comparison of the contents of the Aquilian statute (p. 185 sq.) with the law of the XII Tables on the same topics (pp. 186–192), however, shows that the repealing effect was restricted to the delicts especially ingrafted in the lex, namely, 'occidere seruum quadrupedemue pecudem' and 'rumpere rem,' but the actions provided for other cases, viz. the actio de aedibus incensis, D. 47. 9. 9 (p. 193 sq.), de pastu pecoris, D. 19. 5. 14. § 3, D. h. t. 39. § 1 (p. 194), and de arboribus succisis, G. IV. 11, D. 47. 7. 3. § 3 ; D. 12. 2. 28. § 6 ; D. 43. 24. 19—the latter action being different from the praetorian actio arborum furtim caesarum, D. h. t. 27. § 26 (p. 194 sq.)—were not superseded by the statute, although, in virtue of its operation, they fell gradually into disuse, D. h. t. 27. §§ 7, 8 ; C. 3. 35. 2 ; D. 47. 9. 3. § 7 ; C. 3. 35. 6 (p. 194 sq.), and, considering this fact, the above statement of Ulpian is true, for in his time the lex Aquilia was really the only source of the law of damage to property, D. 9. 4. 2. § 1 ; D. 44. 7. 56 (p. 195 sq.).

§ 3. The fundamental provisions of the lex Aquilia (pp. 196–199).

The fundamental provisions of the statute referring to damage to property were contained in Chapters I and III, the text of which is reproduced in D. h. t. 2 pr. and 27. § 5, apparently without serious deviations from the original tenour, G. III. 210–219 (p. 196 sq.); some alterations, however, seem to be necessitated by other passages, G. III. 210, 214; D. h. t. 21 pr.; D. h. t. 11. § 6, 29. § 8; G. III. 214, 218 (pp. 197–199).

§ 4. The extension of the lex Aquilia by actiones utiles and in factum (pp. 199–208).

The provisions of the Aquilian statute were extended to other cases by means of actio utilis and in factum, based on the actio legis Aquiliae directa (p. 199, n. 3). The statement of Justinian, in I. 4. 3. 16, that a direct action was applicable in case of damnum corpore corpori, an actio utilis in case of damnum corpori datum, and an actio in factum where damage was done neither corpore nor corpori, seems objectionable (p. 200); it is clearly differing from its original in Gaius, III. 219, where there is merely a distinction between actio directa and utilis, the latter term being evidently used in the wide sense of an action given on the analogy of an existing action and in so far covering the notion of actio in factum, D. 19. 5. 21; D. 24. 3. 64. § 9 (p. 200 sq.), Gaius, IV. 34 and 38 (p. 201). Consequently, the statement of Gaius is not at variance with those passages which declare either an actio directa or in factum to be applicable, D. 19. 5. 11; D. h. t. 33. § 1; D. 9. 1. 1. § 7 (p. 201 sq.), and this is clearly shown by the gradual extension of the Aquilian statute.

1. By means of 'actio in factum,' so we are told, Chapter I was extended to cases where there was not an 'occidere,' as in D. h. t. 7. § 1; and also in G. III. 219; I. h. t. 16; D. h. t. 7. § 7, and 7. § 2, 11. § 4, 9 pr. (p. 202 sq.), but a 'causam mortis praestare,' D. h. t. 7. § 6, 9 pr., § 3, 27. § 7, 53; D. 19. 5. 14. § 1 (p. 203). Chapter III also, which, according to the extensive interpretation of the jurists, was applicable wherever there were was a damnum corpore corpori datum (p. 203 sq.), whether done by 'urere,' D. h. t. 27. §§ 6, 7, 8, or 'rumpere,' 27. § 24, or 'frangere,' 27. § 31, cf. 27. § 29; D. h. t. 27. § 23, 29. §§ 2, 3, 39 pr., or 'corrumpere,' 27. § 20, 27. §§ 9, 15, cf. 42 (p. 204), was extended by means of actio in factum to cases where there was a 'causam damni praestare,' and therefore merely a damnum corpori datum, D. h. t. 27. § 35; D. 8. 2. 18; D. h. t. 27. §§ 10, 14; 30. § 3; cf. 27. § 8, but whether there was such a case, or, rather an act of damage, falling under the terms of the statute, was sometimes doubtful, D. h. t. 27. §§ 12, 49; D. 9. 1. 1. § 7, and D. h. t. 37. § 4 (p. 204 sq.). An actio in factum was admitted even in cases where there was neither damnum corpore nor corpori datum: (1) D. h. t. 27. § 21; D. 19. 5. 14. § 2, 23; D. 41. 1. 55; D. 47. 2. 50. § 4; I. h. t. § 16; (2) D. h. t. 24. § 14; (3)

D. 19. 5. 14. § 3, because a thing is lost for its owner in the same way as if it had been destroyed (p. 205 sq.).

2. The cases in which 'actio utilis' is said to be applicable are not of the same kind, but cover also the same ground as those of the actio in factum, G. III. 219; D. 47. 2. 51; D. 11. 3. 3. §§ 1, 4; D. 47. 8. 2. § 20; D. h. t. 27. § 9, 30. § 2 (p. 206 sq.); 5. § 3 i. f., 6, 7 pr., 13 pr. (p. 206, n. 19). No principle, therefore, can be established according to which the cases of the actio in factum and those of the actio utilis are to be distinguished, and this is simply explained by the wide sense in which the latter term is used (p. 207). An actio utilis in the sense of actio ficticia is expressly mentioned only once in the case where an Aquilian action was extended to and against an alien, Gaius, IV. 37; but it is hardly ascertainable if this action was thus used in similar cases also, D. h. t. 25. § 1; D. 5. 1. 18. § 1; D. h. t. 11. § 10, 27. § 32; D. 43. 24. 13 pr. (p. 207).

It is thus shown that Justinian is mistaken with reference to the different Aquilian actions, a difference which was of importance only with regard to procedure, and it is at the same time indicated how his mistake probably has originated (p. 207 sq.).

§ 5. The nature of the act which entails liability under the Aquilian law (pp. 208–214).

This act is in every case a commission (p. 208). This assertion is in harmony with the principles of law in general (p. 208 sq.), and is proved, even by those passages which are quoted in favour of the view that a mere omission is sufficient: D. h. t. 8 pr. 27. § 9, 30. § 3, 31 and I. h. t. § 5 (pp. 210–216), and is expressed as a principle in D. 7. 1. 13. § 2 (p. 213 sq.), and certainly not at variance with D. h. t. 44. § 1, and 45 pr. (p. 214).

§ 6. The requirement of iniuria (pp. 214–222).

Iniuria is used of an act done culpa, Gaius, III. 211, and an act done by a person without having a right to do so, I. h. t. §§ 2, 3 (p. 214 sq.). Therefore, there is no iniuria in the latter, the narrower (p. 216) sense, if the act was done in virtue of a right (p. 215 sq.): (1) a magisterial right, D. h. t. 29. § 7; D. 18. 6. 13 and 14 (p. 216); (2) in self-defence, D. 43. 16. 1. § 27; D. h. t. 4 pr. 5; Coll. VII. 3. 4; D. h. t. 45. § 4, 52. § 1, 4. § 1, cf. D. 48. 8. 9; D. h. t. 30 pr. (pp. 216–218); (3) under urgent necessity, D. h. t. 29. § 3; D. 19. 5. 14. § 1; D. h. t. 49. § 1; opposed to D. 43. 24. 7. § 4; D. 47. 9. 3. § 7 (pp. 218–220); (4) a private right (*a*) D. h. t. 7. § 4; (*b*) D. h. t. 5. § 3; cf. D. 48. 19. 16. § 2; (*c*) D. h. t. 27. § 29; (*d*) D. h. t. 29. § 1; its difficulties explained (p. 220 sq.). A person, however, who acts in excess of his right, or exercises it merely for the purpose of injuring another person, is liable, D. h. t. 39 pr. (p. 221), 45. § 4; D. 47. 8. 2. § 20; D. h. t. 29. § 7; D. 20. 1. 27 (p. 222).

§ 7. The requirement of culpa (pp. 222–233).

A person is liable for damage if it is due to his culpa (imputability), and he is in culpa if he has not observed the conduct which, under the particular circumstances, would have been observed by a diligent pater familias (p. 222 sq.). This is an average and objective standard, and requires sometimes a higher, sometimes a lower, degree of care and effort (p. 223 sq.).

A higher degree is required if a person, e.g. a surgeon, I. h. t. § 7; D. h. t. 7. § 8, and 8 pr.; D. 1. 18. 6. § 7; a driver, D. h. t. 8. § 1; I. h. t. § 8; D. 9. 1. 1. § 5; an artificer, D. h. t. 27. § 29; D. 19. 2. 9. § 5 (p. 224), undertakes to do some professional work, for 'imperitia culpae adnumeratur,' D. h. t. 8. § 1; D. 50. 17. 132; D. 19. 2. 9. § 5; D. h. t. § 7 (p. 224 sq.). A comparatively low degree is required in case where a person is lopping branches in a place where there is no way (p. 225 sq.). The diligence of a diligent pater familias is, however, not required: (I) if a free person serves another in good faith, D. 44. 1. 54. § 2 (p. 226); (II) if soldiers are practising in the usual place, I. h. t. § 4 (p. 226); (III) if several persons join a game, D. h. t. 7. § 4, and 52. § 4, 45. § 3 (p. 226 sq.); (IV) Contributory negligence of the injured party causes a 'culpa-compensation,' and prevents, on account of the interruption of the causal connection of act and damage, D. 50. 17. 203, liability under the Aquilian statute from arising (p. 228): (1) Paulus, Sent. Rec. I. 15. § 3 (p. 228); (2) D. h. t. 9. § 4; I. h. t. § 4 (p. 229); (3) D. h. t. 11 pr. (p. 229); (4) D. h. t. 28 (p. 229 sq.); (5) D. h. t. 30. § 4; D. h. t. 52 pr. §§ 1, 3 (p. 230). But culpa-compensation is excluded if there was dolus on the part of the injurer, D. h. t. 9. § 4 (p. 230).

In case of concurrence of the Aquilian action with an action on contract, the plaintiff may sue by either of the actions, but can receive satisfaction only once, D. 13. 6. 18. § 1; D. 44. 7. 34. § 2; D. 13. 6. 7. § 1 (p. 230 sq.). Here the liability of the defendant under the Aquilian law is not affected by the contract, D. h. t. 5. § 3, unless the defendant had, in virtue of the contract, a right to do the act (pp. 231–233).

§ 8. The requirement of damnum (pp. 233–235).

It is also necessary that there is a 'damnum,' i.e. some loss to the property of the injured person arising from the injurious act, D. h. t. 27. § 5; D. 8. 2. 18; D. 27. § 17 (p. 233 sq.). Therefore the Aquilian is applicable if there is such loss, e.g. expenses incurred for a cure, although there is not even a trace left from the act of damage, D. h. t. 45. § 1, and on the other hand the action does not lie if there is no such loss, although there is a corporeal violation of a thing, D. h. t. 27. § 17, 27. §§ 25, 26, 27, 28. From this view also the decision in D. h. t. 23. § 1 is explained (p. 234 sq.).

§ 9. The Plaintiff: 1. Owner and bonae fidei possessor (pp. 235–243 .

The right to bring the Aquilian action is given by the statute to the owner, D. h. t. 2 pr., 27. § 5, 11. § 6. Therefore, in case he is bound to transfer ownership in a thing, and it is damaged by a third person, he is also bound to transfer the actio legis Aquiliae, D. h. t. 11. § 7 (p. 235). The right of action once acquired by a person passes over to his heir, D. h. t. 23. § 8, D. 47. 1. § 1, even if it accrued hereditate iacente, D. h. t. 13. § 2. 43; D. 5. 3. 36. § 2. It passes also to his universal fideicommissary, cf. D. 36. 1. 73 pr., 68. § 1 (p. 235); but not to the legatee, who acquires ownership in the thing left to him at the moment of the aditio hereditatis, Gaius, I. 195, D. 31. 80, and therefore he is entitled to an Aquilian action which has accrued afterwards (p. 36); see, however, D. h. t. 15 pr., and 13. § 3, and the consequences peculiar to the repudiatio legati; D. h. t. 34, 35, 36 pr. (pp. 236–238).

The bonae fidei possessor, according to D. h. t. 11. § 8, 17, is entitled to an extended action, actio utilis, or in factum ex lege Aquilia. In accordance with the nature of the bonae fidei possessio (p. 238 sq.), the object of his action was the same as that of the Aquilian action of the owner, provided the owner did not assert his own right (p. 239). But if afterwards the bonae fidei possessor was sued by rei vindicatio, he had to restore everything recovered by the Aquilian action, arg. D. 5. 3. 55 (p. 239), and if he had acquired ownership by usucapion whilst the rei vindicatio was pending, he was bound to transfer to the plaintiff the Aquilian action which afterwards accrued (p. 239 sq.). But in both these cases the bonae fidei possessor was entitled to sue his auctor for his interesse, arg. 18. 1. 35. § 4 (pp. 240–242). If, however, the bonae fidei possessor maintained the Aquilian action in concurrence with the owner, or if he sued the owner himself, D. h. t. 17, he would merely recover his impensae utiles and necessariae (p. 242). An Aquilian action of the owner against the bonae fidei possessor is admissible; D. 5. 36. § 2; D. h. t. 38 (p. 243).

§ 10. The Plaintiff (continued): 2. Persons entitled to a ius in re aliena (pp. 243–250).

An Aquilian action utilis or in factum was extended also to all persons who had a ius in re aliena, D. h. t. 11. § 9, 12; D. 7. 1. 17. § 3, D. 4. 3. 7. § 4, and 18. § 2; D. 43. 24. 13 pr.; D. h. t. 27. § 32; D. h. t. 17 and 30 (p. 243), and was available even against the owner of the thing, D. h. t. 12; D. 43. 7. § 4, 18. § 2; D. h. t. 17 (p. 243 sq.). Its object was compensation for the value of the ius in re aliena, infringed by the act of damage; whilst the owner was to be compensated for the value which his ownership had after deducting the value of this right (p. 244). This is also true of the usufructuary, although it has been asserted that he merely exercised the right of action of the owner, D. h. t. 12. 11. § 10 (pp. 244–248). If, however, a thing had been destroyed which was subject to a ius pignoris, the creditor pignoris did not suffer any loss whatever, unless he had lost his actio in personam, by extinctive prescription or by insolvency of his debtor; D. 50. 16. 114; D. 4. 3. 6; and therefore only in these two cases he was entitled to an action up to the amount of his claim, whilst the debtor might sue for the surplus due under the Aquilian law; D. h. t. 30. § 1, 17 (p. 248 sq.). Of the persons who have merely a ius in personam, only the colonus, D. h. t. 27. § 14, not other persons, D. h. t. 54, 55; D. 4. 3. 18. § 5; D. 19. 1. 13. § 12; I. 3. 21. § 3 i. f.; D. h. t. 11. § 9, are said to be entitled to an Aquilian action (p. 249 sq.).

§ 11. The Defendant (pp. 250–257).

The Aquilian action can be brought only against a person who by his culpa has caused damage; therefore not against his employer; D. h. t. 52. § 2; D. 19. 2. 30. § 2 (p. 250 sq.), unless he is himself in culpa; D. h. t. 27. § 11 (p. 251 sq.); and, if several persons are concerned in the commission of a damage, only against those who really are in culpa; D. h. t. 11. § 2, 51. § 1; 11. § 4; cf. D. 47. 2. 21. § 9 (p. 252); but without any distinction whether they committed the delict in common, as accomplices, D. 11. §§ 2, 4, or one merely aided and abetted the other; D. h. t. 9 pr. and § 3; 11. § 1; or one instigated by his command or advice the other who did the damage, D. h. t. 37 pr.; D. 50. 17. 169 pr. (p. 252 sq.). But if in the last case the damage was done in obedience to a command of a person with ius imperandi, as a rule D. 44. 7. 20, D. 50. 17. 157 pr., only the commander and not the doer was liable, D. 50. 17. 169 pr.; D. 37 pr. (p. 253 sq.).

Noxal liability of a person for the damage done by his slave (or child) was already recognised by Tab. XII. 1, D. 9. 4. 2 (p. 254 sq.). Under the lex Aquilia, a direct action was applicable wherever damage was done 'sciente domino,' D. h. t. 45 pr., D. 50. 17. 50, and so a noxal action was restricted to cases where the damage was done 'insciente domino,' D. 9. 4. 2 pr. The jurists, however, admitted a noxal action also in the case of 'scientia domini,' provided damage was not done 'iussu domini,' where the owner was exclusively liable to a direct action, D. 9. 4. 2. § 1—§ 2 (p. 255 sq.). In case the familia of a master had committed damage in common, he had to pay the litis aestimatio only once; 32 pr. (p. 256 sq.).

§ 12. The Principles of Evidence (pp. 257–264).

According to the leading principles of evidence (p. 257 sq.), the plaintiff is bound to prove that the requirements of his action exist (p. 258). But in case of an actio legis Aquiliae (directa) it will, as a rule, be sufficient if he proves merely the causal connection between the act and the damage complained of, D. h. t. 7. § 5; D. 19. 2. 13. § 21, which will imply the existence of the requirements of 'iniuria,' 'culpa,' and 'damnum' (pp. 258–261). The same applies to many cases of the actio utilis and in factum, e. g. D. h. t. 53, 9. § 2, 31, and therefore if the defendant denies in a given case the existence of culpa, etc., he has to prove this assertion, D. h. t. 28 (p. 261 sq.), although in cases where the existence of these requirements is not implied, the plaintiff will be bound to give further evidence, D. h. t. 7. § 8 and 8 pr. (p. 262). The plaintiff had also to prove ownership in the thing damaged, and probably on account of the difficulty of this proof the action was also extended to the bonae fidei possessor, who had to prove merely acquisition on the ground of a iustus titulus (pp. 262–264).

§ 13. The object of the Aquilian action (pp. 264–271).

The way of assessing damages under Chapters I and III, D. h. t. 2 pr. and 27. § 5, in its peculiar and archaic character, D. h. t. 21. § 1; Gaius, III. 218, could not satisfy an advancing civilisation (p. 264 sq.). Accordingly, by the interpretation of the jurists, compensation for the value of the thing was gradually changed into compensation for the whole loss of the plaintiff, his 'interesse,' I. h. t. § 10 (p. 265 sq.), which comprehended the 'damnum directum,' and 'indirectum,' D. h. t. 22. § 1; D. 47. 2. 27 pr.; D. h. t. 40–42 (p. 266 sq.); D. h. t. 22 pr., 37 pr., 55 (p. 267), the 'damnum emergens' and 'lucrum cessans,' D. h. t. 23 pr.; I. h. t. § 10; D. h. t. 23. § 2, 23. § 4 (p. 267 sq.), provided only the latter was to be expected as certain in the regular course of events, D. h. t. 23 pr., 29. § 3 (p. 268 sq.). But the interesse excludes an assessment of the 'interest of affection,' 33 pr., and is different in its nature from the value of the damaged thing, D. h. t. 45. § 1. 7 pr., 30. § 1 (p. 269 sq.), although it is also to be determined with reference to the last year or month: (1) D. h. t. 6. 1. 27. § 2; cf. D. 43. 24. 7. § 4, (2) D. h. t. 23. § 2 (p. 270 sq.).

§ 14. The nature of the Aquilian action (pp. 271–279).

The 'multa petitio' in Cic. Brutus, § 131, is unknown to later times, the lex Cornelia de sic. having taken its place, I. h. t. 11, D. h. t. 5 pr., 23. § 9, D. 19. 5. 14. § 1, D. 48. 15. 3. § 1; Gaius, III. 213 (p. 271 sq.). The Aquilian action, although subject-matter of a detailed interpretation by the jurists, and available in a fourfold form, is yet not known as to its formula. With regard to its operation, it often is declared to be an actio reipersecutoria or mixta, I. 4. 6. 19; cf. Gaius, IV. 9 (p. 273 sq.), but it is called by the Roman jurists an actio poenalis; D. 5. 1. 18. § 1; D. h. t. 11. § 2, 51. §§ 1, 2; Paul. Sent. Rec. I. 13[a], § 6; Gaius, III. 211 (p. 274), and it really shares the nature of these actions, for (1) it is admissible as actio noxalis, Gaius, IV. 75; D. 4. 3. 9. § 4 (p. 275 sq.); (2) if the damage was committed by several persons, each of them is liable to pay full compensation, D. h. t. 11. § 2; cf. 51. § 1; 51. § 2 i. f.; D. 26. 7. 55. § 1; C. 4. 8. 1 (p. 276 sq.);

(3) in accordance with generally recognised principles, D. 47. 1. 1 pr., D. 50. 17. 111. § 1; I. 4. 12. 1; Gaius, IV. 112; D. 48. 19. 20, the Aquilian action is not transmitted against the heir of the delinquent, who can be sued only in so far as he is enriched by the delict, D. 10. 3. 10; cf. I. 4. 3. 9, D. h. t. 23. § 8 (p. 277 sq.). Thus, in spite of the interesse, D. h. t. 21. § 2—29. § 30, 56; I. 4. 6. 19, the essential features of a penal action are still preserved in the Corpus, a peculiarity which is to be explained by the historical development (pp. 278, 279).

THE END.

www.ingramcontent.com/pod-product-compliance
Lightning Source LLC
LaVergne TN
LVHW101458200926
848483LV00001B/159
* 9 7 8 1 5 8 4 7 7 4 4 7 1 *